Artisans of Glory

Charles Bernard
(Courtesy Bibliothèque Nationale)

Charles Sorel
(Courtesy Bibliothèque Nationale)

François Eudes de Mézerai
(Courtesy Bibliothèque Nationale)

Paul Pellisson
(Courtesy Bibliothèque Nationale)

Orest Ranum

Artisans of
Glory

Writers and
Historical Thought
in Seventeenth-
Century France

The University of North Carolina Press

Chapel Hill

© 1980 The University of North Carolina Press
All rights reserved
Manufactured in the United States of America
ISBN 0–8078–1413–X
Library of Congress Catalog Card Number 79–19248

Library of Congress Cataloging in Publication Data

Ranum, Orest A
  Artisans of glory.

  Includes index.
  1. France—History—17th century—Historiography.
2. Historians—France—Biography. I. Title.
DC120.8.R36 944'.03'072024 79–19248
ISBN 0–8078–1413–X

❀ *For John B. Wolf*

Contents

Preface

IN 1965 the annual meeting of the American Historical Association was held in San Francisco. Having decided to attend, I left New York by train. For my reading as I traveled across the country I took along Arthur Schlesinger, Jr.'s *A Thousand Days.* The book and the hours of reflection upon it afforded by train travel inspired what follows.

The interest expressed in my work by colleagues and friends over the years has been very important to me. Richard Hofstadter was among the first to express curiosity about the roles writers and history played in seventeenth-century France. My colleagues in the Johns Hopkins History Seminar, David Donald, Jack P. Greene, Kenneth S. Lynn, J. G. A. Pocock, and Nancy Struever, have been particularly helpful. Felix Gilbert, Clifford Geertz, John Elliott, a fellowship at the Institute for Advanced Study at Princeton, and a leave from Hopkins were indispensable in the middle years of the project. I also benefited from the many helpful criticisms given by William F. Church, Richard Golden, Herbert Rowen, and Gabrielle Spiegel. An earlier fellowship from the John Simon Guggenheim Foundation and a leave from Columbia University permitted me to do much of the basic research. Philippe Ariès, first as author of *Le temps de l'histoire* and then as critic and friend, has encouraged me by continually asking when the manuscript would be finished. Over the whole work looms Donald Kelley's scholarship; its importance cannot be sufficiently acknowledged by the frequent citations to his works. Paul Saenger, Mrs. Morton L. Deitch, Georges Dethan, and Le Comte d'Adhémar de Panat continued, as always, to offer answers to my questions. Patricia M. Ranum became a collaborator many years ago: her understanding, common sense, and help have been unstinting all along. My editor, Lewis Bateman, expressed interest in the manuscript almost from the beginning and has been helpful to the end. Trudie Calvert remained courteous and helpful throughout what the French call the *toilette du manuscrit.* The give and take in the discussion over the merits and weaknesses in the rules for citation developed by The University of Chicago Press prompted compromises without changing convictions.

1 June 1979   O.R.
Baltimore

Artisans of Glory

Introduction

*T*HREE of the themes in this book are explored in this introduction. The first is how the familial character of monarchical history came to determine the ways in which writers could construct the history of the realm. Their choice of subjects was reduced to two: they either wrote the entire history of the three races of French kings, or else the history of the reigning king. As Capetian dynastic history became French history in the late Middle Ages, writers found it difficult to include any other subjects in that history without emphasizing personal service to the dynasty. Late-medieval French history thus became a history of services rendered to the ruling dynasty.

The second theme is how the learning of the sixteenth century enriched the primordial tendencies of writers to immortalize the dead and to perceive this as the primary function of history in the realm. The rhetorical heritage from Antiquity—the *ars historica*—reinforced this tendency to define history as primarily an edifying dialogue with the dead.

The third theme introduces the principal subject of the book, namely, the writers themselves and the political, social, religious, and literary influences at work in the lives of *gens de lettres* as they attempted to assure their own self-esteem, even *gloire*, while writing to perpetuate the memory of French kings.

Dynastic History and Service

From the beginning French history has been family history. Through oral transmission and verse, on stone, ivory, parchment, paper, and glass, medieval aristocratic families took care to remember the names, marriage alliances, lands, and *haults faits* of their ancestors. The Capetians were no exception, and as their control extended over other lords and lands, their family history became French history. As in other families, their ancestors, *gestes*, and marriages would be recalled by descendants, vassals, and friends. Without history there could be no *lignage*.

Beginning in the twelfth century the fabric of aristocratic family history becomes more visible thanks to the initiative of heads of houses who either encouraged or permitted clerics to put their family histories in writing.[1] Thus began the overlaying of aristocratic family histories with ecclesiastical presuppositions.[2] The model for the synthesis of ecclesiastical and family history had already been provided by the works of clerics in Carolingian service during the ninth century. However, the arms, often crudely carved, on keystones in tower doorways and chapel vaults confirm that it was not the clerics who had established the function of family history in medieval society but the aristocratic families themselves. Indeed, as a man defended his house and kin, married, and had sons, he may have felt justified in using the family history as the last word in any discussion, the ultimate authority of the head of a noble household.

Within the house itself, the family history would be brought to bear in marriage negotiations to assess advantages and liabilities for the *lignage*. A comparative perspective over time was not only necessary but almost natural. Through the family history the dead could continue to give counsel to their descendants, perhaps satisfying what was already a personal need to be remembered as a head of the household and to be praised after death. Recollecting the *gestes* of the dead and educating the younger generations of the family were constituent parts of the same psycho-social mechanism.

The need to be remembered after death is perhaps the most pervasive theme in secular historical thought down to the eighteenth century; the recognition that history is an indispensable tool in the education of the young appears almost as frequently. For us in the twentieth century it is a temptation to break these two functions of history apart, if for no other reason than to study them separately. But for the aristocratic family, and later for commoner families,[3] these two functions were not separated. So constituted, history provided the mechanism for tying generations together and for transmitting a sense of house and later of nation in the languages and recollections of *gestes* peculiar to them. Family histories not only incorporate within them discourse peculiar to each family; they also personalize and familiarize prevailing

1. Georges Duby, *Hommes et structures du moyen âge* (The Hague, 1973), p. 149: "D'une façon plus générale, que tout noble se disait d'abord *de nobilibus ortus* ou 'gentilhomme,' c'est à dire qu'il ne se référait pas, en premier lieu, à sa puissance, ou à sa richesse, mais à ses aïeux."

2. See Chapter 3 of Georges Duby's *Medieval Marriage: Two Models from Twelfth-Century France*, trans. Elborg Forster (Baltimore, 1978); and Michel Sot, "Historiographie épiscopale et modèle familial en occident au IXe siècle," *Annales, économies, sociétés, civilisations* 33 (May–June, 1978): 433–449.

3. See Natalie Z. Davis, "Ghosts, Kin, and Progeny: Some Features of Family Life in Early Modern France," *Daedalus* 106 (1977): 87–114.

ideologies. A son is raised with the indelible memory of the story of his grandfather's death in a crusade or local battle. His pride in the name he bears is enhanced through the very repetition of the family name, until in aristocratic and royal households the names are reified into superbeings resembling the heroes of chivalric epics.

Philippe Ariès remarked long ago that family history always contains mythical elements.[4] Stories about ancestors, their noble origins, birthplaces, acts of courage, height, hair color, piety, and so forth, are repeated generation after generation. Some family members may suspect that these stories are not quite true, or a member of another house may specifically allege them to be false, but they are repeated nonetheless as part of the collective family memory. The deletion of a story may result in the loss of an entire generation or an illustrious marriage alliance—as well as the cessation of dialogue with the more remote members of the family. The question of whether or not all the elements in a family history are true is, to use Lucien Febvre's phrase, a "question mal posée." If no family history is entirely true, it behooves historians not only to attempt to sort out the myths from the facts, but also to sort out the more general, even structural, patterns and relationships of both. In medieval family histories the integration of what would become aristocratic ideology into family history led to an emphasis upon *lignage*.[5] Myths about illustrious ancestors are an obvious consequence of the impact of aristocratic ideology upon family history; the unconscious forgetting of some ignominious act committed by an ancestor may be another. In the first, the myth confirmed *exempla* that would inspire younger members of the family to great deeds; in the latter, the fear that a family shame might be repeated in succeeding generations remained very great. The histories of the Capetian family conform to all these characteristics; they are organized primarily by dynastic time rather than by annalistic or some other calendar time, and the illustrious ancestors receive far more extensive treatment than those who merely serve to perpetuate the *lignage*.

The implications of ancient political notions that were recovered by learned clerics and incorporated into Capetian family histories were mainly intellectual props for the already established functions of family history.[6] These were included in order to legitimate patterns of thought, not to create them. Indeed, like so many branches on a tree,

4. *Le temps de l'histoire* (Monaco, 1954), p. 106.

5. Georges Duby, "Lignage, noblesse, et chevalerie au XIIᵉ siècle dans la région mâconnaise," *Annales, économies, sociétés, civilisations* 17 (1972): 803–823.

6. See the evidence provided by Walter Ullmann, *The Carolingian Renaissance and the Idea of Kingship* (London, 1969), *passim*.

ideas of divine right—indeed, all theocratic kingship,[7] law-centered kingship, polity-centered kingship, and Burgundian aristocratic theory[8]—would grow upon the trunk of Capetian family history. Scarcely a legal or philosophical movement failed to leave its trace on the writing of what would only very slowly become known as the history of France.

We who study historical thought are more prone to discern change than continuity, so the trunk of marriage alliances, *haults faits*, births, and deaths of king after king has tended to be ignored in favor of the study of the changes in the branches. Yet these changes were a superstructure overlying dynastic history. As Marc Bloch observed: "Les idées qu'exposent couramment les publicistes royalistes du XVIᵉ et du XVIIᵉ siècles paraissent souvent banales à quiconque a feuilleté la littérature des périodes précédentes. Elles n'étonnent que si l'on ne sent pas en elles le long héritage médiéval; pas plus en histoire des doctrines politiques qu'en toutes autres sortes d'histoires."[9] What the clerics incorporated into Capetian family history, particularly beginning with Suger in the early twelfth century, is a subject too vast to be summarized here, but it is significant to observe a prescription for synthesizing the outlook of the specific writers of family history with the family itself. Suger and his successors not only integrated their monastery and their ideology into Capetian family history, they also contributed to the dynastic history of the family itself by forging the links between the Capetians, the Merovingians, and the Carolingians.[10] The three-part dynastic family history produced at Saint-Denis in the early twelfth century brought together all the mythical and true elements tying the Capetians to their ancestors and to kingship itself in the *Grandes chroniques de France*. The Dionysian synthesis did not fundamentally differ from that made for other families, except in scope and royalist ideology. It included statements of preeminence over other families, lands, and nations through the imperial heritage; but the primary feature remained the three races of French kings, dynasty after dynasty, reign after reign, that distinguished this family from other families. Henceforth the Capetian family history and French history would be inseparable by reason of the synthesis of *lignage* and royal titles. The dynastic structure of French history with its stress on mar-

7. Ernst Kantorowicz, *The King's Two Bodies: A Study in Medieval Political Theology* (Princeton, 1957); and *Laudes regiae: A Study in Liturgical Acclamations and Medieval Ruler Worship* (Berkeley, 1946).

8. Paul Saenger, "The Education of Burgundian Princes, 1435–1490," Ph.D. dissertation, University of Chicago, 1972, pp. 53 ff.

9. *Les rois thaumaturges* (Strasbourg, 1924), p. 347.

10. Ariès, pp. 142 ff.

riages, lands acquired, *gestes*, and so forth, would remain as the immutable past of the French down into the nineteenth century.

Of equal significance had been Suger's biographies of two individual kings, Louis VI and Louis VII, for this genre would also actively be carried on reign after reign. Einhard's nonhagiographical biography of Charlemagne had been an early but fleeting attempt to establish the genre,[11] but the hiatus between the ninth and the twelfth centuries suggests that this biography was more significant to *Imperium* than to family history. After Suger the two genres of dynastic history and royal biography would be maintained by the monks of Saint-Denis, officially charged by the Capetians to compile their history.

These same monks were also charged with protecting the bodies of the deceased members of the Capetian family in the abbey church of Saint-Denis and saying prayers for the living and the dead.[12] The linking of Capetian family history with the Merovingians and Carolingians had occurred in historical thought almost simultaneously with the construction of a series of monumental tombs to celebrate the dead members of the Carolingian and Capetian *lignages* within the abbey church of Saint-Denis. That the effigies on the tombs were completely fabricated and that these tombs did not contain bodies testifies to the compelling influence of mythical elements in family histories. The clerical stratum overlying French dynastic history grew deeper and more com-

11. *Ibid.*, p. 147.

12. See Erwin Panofsky, *Abbot Suger on the Abbey Church of Saint-Denis, and Its Treasures* (Princeton, 1946); and Gabrielle M. Spiegel, "The Cult of Saint-Denis and Capetian Kingship," *Journal of Medieval History* 1 (1975): 43–69. See also Robert Branner, *Saint Louis and the Court Style* (London, 1965); and Alain Erlande-Brandenberg, *Le roi est mort: Etude sur les funérailles, les sépultures et les tombeaux des rois de France jusqu'à la fin du XIIIᵉ siècle* (Geneva, 1975). Louis IX intended Saint-Denis as a royal necropolis, rather than a Capetian one, according to Erlande-Brandenberg (p. 25), because he planned that only kings were to be buried there and that the royal sons who had never reigned would be buried elsewhere. His plan was not adhered to, but even if it had been, the cleavage in the aristocratic family separating the head and his heir-apparent from brothers and other sons may have complemented the royalist ideology about the divinity of kings and the care of their relics and certainly preceded it in the family history. See Georges Duby, "Dans la France du nord-ouest au XIIᵉ siècle: Les 'jeunes' dans la société aristocratique," *Annales, économies, sociétés, civilisations* 9 (1964): 845. The biological continuity of the dynasty was reinforced by Jean Fouquet's illustrations for the *Grandes chroniques*, in which he painted the portraits of Dagobert, Childebert, et al. to make them resemble Charles VII (Paul Wechser, *Jean Fouquet et son temps* [Basel, 1947], p. 43).

plex over the centuries, but the celebration of the dead and the education of the living continued to be primary reasons for compiling the *Grandes chroniques*.

Gabrielle Spiegel has discovered ideological resonances in the biographies of later Capetians in the *Grandes chroniques* that reflect conflicts with the Papacy and with other European ruling families; and, as had been the case since at least Gregory VII's quarrel with the French house, these conflicts often had as a focal point marriages, annulments, and issues related to inheritance and legitimacy.[13] Needless to say, the emphasis on *lignage* did not diminish in the quarrels over the Burgundian inheritance, nor did the emphasis upon divine support, military victory, justice, love for the Church, and clean living. The clerical lens through which the family's history was viewed filtered out many, if not all, of the violations of the divine law established in the world for all Christians.

From the twelfth century on, the Capetian family history was also becoming integrated with that of increasing numbers of aristocratic families, monasteries, bishoprics, and urban and university elites. *Haults faits* were performed by common ancestors: crusades and battles against the English, Germans, and Albigensians became *gestae* in innumerable family histories. The need to be remembered in families slowly became linked to actions accomplished with and for the king. Royal courage, justice, illustrious marriages, and pious acts served an exemplary function in royal family histories, and others basked in the idealized accomplishments of the Capetians.[14] The integration of the royal house into the nation deepened as nonroyal family histories recorded all the honors, titles, and other dignities bestowed on their members by the Crown. Lesser noblemen and commoners, wherever evidence concerning them may be found, eagerly mentioned royal service when describing themselves and their families in wills, epitaphs, and charters of donation. Initially the monks of Saint-Denis tended to exclude non-Capetians from the Capetian history—the great exception being the monks of Saint-Denis themselves—but inclusion of non-Capetians occurred with

13. One might think that thaumaturgy would also be included as part of Capetian family history, but Spiegel has found very few allusions to it in the *Grandes chroniques*. See her "Studies in the Chronicle Tradition of Saint-Denis," Ph.D. dissertation, The Johns Hopkins University, 1974, *passim*; and "Political Utility in Medieval Historiography," *History and Theory* 14 (1975): 315–325.

14. See especially Bernard Guenée, "Etat et nation en France au moyen âge," *Revue Historique* 237 (1967): 17–30; and "Les généalogies entre l'histoire et la politique: La fierté d'être Capétien en France au moyen âge," *Annales, économies, sociétés, civilisations* 33 (1978): 461.

increasing frequency as the *Grandes chroniques* became longer and more detailed. Family history slowly became history *tout court*.[15] At the same time, in the remnants of surviving family histories—and they are very few—the names of kings often appeared whenever it was possible to link an ancestor with a royal name.[16]

A Capetian is often the central figure in fourteenth- and fifteenth-

15. On how family matters might pervade society in general, and justice, war, and religion, let us recall William M. Newman's trenchant prose: "Le fil conducteur de l'histoire, vue génération par génération (et non faussée par une grande vue d'ensemble dictée par l'idée de développement), était l'esprit de famille. . . . Il suffit de rappeler qu'une grande partie des guerres de l'époque furent déclenchées pour des raisons de famille, souvent à cause d'un mariage, d'un divorce, ou d'un héritage. . . . Quelle différence y a-t-il pour la société si le roi ou un grand noble prend une autre femme? Mais dans l'opinion de ceux qui gouvernaient, ce fut précisément ce qui comptait, car leurs intérêts étaient en jeu. . . . La famille se rangeait contre la famille pour des raisons de famille" (*Les seigneurs de Nesle en Picardie* . . . [Philadelphia, 1971], p. 8).

16. Suffice it to recall Charles Petit-Dutaillis's observation: "Nous n'avons pas de livres de raison qui nous fassent connaître, pour ce temps [fifteenth century], la vie, les idées et les moeurs de la haute Noblesse rurale. Il ne songeait pas à tenir de livres de raison, ce Raymond-Bernard II, huitième baron de Montpezat et de Madaillan, qui passa son existence à faire la guerre à ses voisins" (*Histoire de France*, ed. Ernest Lavisse [Paris, 1902], vol. 4, pt. 2, p. 168). Newman's work, cited in footnote 15, allows us to speculate about why family histories could remain oral. The lineaments of family histories, veritable footnotes, were found everywhere in *chartiers* and cartularies of religious and royal courts.

Claude Longeon describes how provincial and family history were integrated, and why: "A l'instar des historiens nationaux et des grands annalistes de la province, les Foréziens cultivés du XVIe siècle tentèrent une reconstruction de leur pays. Leur intention était de doter le Forez d'une vision avantageuse de lui-même, de restaurer, au prix d'une idéalisation fabuleuse, une gloire perdue et la prolonger dans le présent en soulignant la permanence des noms. Pour la réaliser, il leur fallait confondre le Forez historique avec le Forez des grandes familles. . . . L'art de la généalogie devenait ainsi un moyen de récupérer le passé en faisant un agrégat de destins individuels capable de concourir à la gloire collective et permanente de la province. . . . Surtout on triche avec l'histoire pour forger de ses ancêtres une filiation grandiose" (*Une province à la renaissance: La vie intellectuelle en Forez au XVIe siècle* [Saint-Etienne, 1975], p. 563).

The "golden age" of written aristocratic family histories would come in the seventeenth century, when the *érudits*—all of the Sainte-Marthes, the Duchesnes, the Godefroys, the Dupuy brothers, and Baluze, among others —published thousands of pages as *histoire de la maison de*. . . .

century memoirs, whose authors bask in the light of Valois and Burgundian favor. These memoir writers rarely emphasize the origins of
their own families, though noble status is asserted whenever possible.

The accretions to Capetian family history brought by these memoirs
had the effect of enriching the whole and supplementing political discourse that was not strictly familial. Dependencies are the fabric of
these memoirs, a social bond barely outside that of the family. After
the aristocratic roots of dynastic history and the clerical trunk provided
by Saint-Denis, the huge branches of the tree were provided by these
would-be *preux*. Only the smaller branches and leaves would be left
to be added by writers in the sixteenth and seventeenth centuries. The
organic metaphor seems appropriate, since genealogy remained the
dynamic principle of Capetian history. And for all the writers of
Capetian history—clerics, *fidèles*, and *gens de lettres*—the periods of
their greatest influence upon that history followed upon one another
in succession—first estate, second, and third—with learning and eloquence, not godliness or martial spirit or wisdom as councillors, being
the virtues of the last.

When service to a prince or a great nobleman, rather than simply
marriages and military action, was the principal claim to *gloire*, the
record apparently had to be written down. The links of protection
and service between Capetian history and the history of a particular
lay individual had to be established, not simply related orally to an
heir—perhaps a first step in recording lay political discourse in the
realm.

The men of letters in the sixteenth and seventeenth centuries could
not record services of a degree equal to those military and councilling
services performed by the *preux*; but service nonetheless became their
principal claim to remembrance after death. And family histories, those
of the Capetian family in particular, rarely stressed the *belles actions*
of councillors, generals, and clients. Indeed, the ambitious layman in
princely service during the fourteenth and fifteenth centuries had not
been able to rely upon the monks of Saint-Denis or other more or less
official historiographers to record their claims to *gloire*. Family histories distorted by inflating the accomplishments of their members, and
Capetian history particularly distorted by excluding anything that indicated Capetian dependency upon others. The memoirs of individuals
in their service tended to inflate their author's role as a political and military actor and occasionally his dependency. Courtly culture infuses
the historical prose of the great memoir writers of the late Middle
Ages; and although there is plenty of evidence indicating an unwillingness on their part to become servants and to abandon criticism in favor

of eulogy, these nonetheless were relationships between superior and inferior, relationships of dependency.

The dynastic wars of the late Middle Ages tested and retested the mechanisms of integration and exclusion in family histories; the Burgundian princely ideology and wars with the English necessitated refinements in the foundation of royal *lignage*, and therefore of family histories.[17] Simultaneously attempts were made—through meetings of estates, religious ceremonies, and royal entrées—to familiarize increasingly large numbers of the population with the names, arms, and *haults faits* of the rival houses.[18] Paul Saenger has noted how these dynastic wars stimulated a revisionist view of ancient Roman history, for if the Burgundian princes were to have power in the royal council, it would be convenient to find precedents in Antiquity. The Roman *Imperium* thus became more of an oligarchic structure than the royalist optic had hitherto stimulated, and the Roman Senate easily became paralleled to the king's court and Parlement.[19] It was not revisionism in Roman history that had prompted the debate over membership in the royal council, but rather the other way around.

In the meantime, the Burgundian princes had protected and caused to flourish an extraordinarily intelligent and creative group of writers and artists to establish their family history and educate their children. With few exceptions these writers neither held university degrees nor were in holy orders. As the Burgundian lands were divided and subsequently integrated into the two houses that dominated Europe, these writers switched their allegiances to those houses and received their protection. This shifting of allegiances seems to have been less painful than in later centuries, when national sentiments had grown more intense—no more painful, perhaps, than Machiavelli's shifts from repub-

17. On the meaning of ideologies and their relationship to social history, see Georges Duby, "Histoire sociale et idéologies des sociétés," *Faire de l'histoire*, Jacques Le Goff and Pierre Nora, eds. (Paris, 1974), vol. 1, pp. 147–168.

18. *Ibid.*, p. 156. Visual representations of the past were "chargées d'un sens plus lourd et de plus immédiate portée que l'écriture." See also Bernard Guenée and Françoise Lehoux, eds., *Les entrées royales françaises de 1328 à 1515* (Paris, 1968); and Jean Jacquot, ed., *Les fêtes de la Renaissance* (Paris, 1956), p. 11: "L'ordonnance de l'entrée et son contenu ne changent guère à la Renaissance."

19. Saenger, pp. 288 ff. For Burgundian historiography, see also Charles Samaran, *Histoire de Louis XI* (Paris, 1963), p. xii; and Richard J. Walsh, "Charles the Bold and the Crusade: Politics and Propaganda," *Journal of Medieval History* 3 (1977): 64 ff.

lican spokesman and citizen to someone seeking to render service to the Medici. But the long-range result was a further enrichment and sophistication of Capetian family history—often complementing and perhaps implicitly contradicting the history compiled by the monks of Saint-Denis.

Also writers in royal service, these historians continued to focus on marriages, battles, births, and other *haults faits*, but their perspectives were nonetheless more diverse and, if not more secular, at least more individualistic. To mention only a few key examples, Thomas Basin's *Histoire de Louis XI*[20] has distinctly pro-Burgundian resonances, yet its fabric is the discussion of *fidélités* to the Capetians. It is also something more than biography and family history, as are Jean D'Auton's *Chroniques de Louis XII* and, of course, Philippe de Commynes's *Mémoires*.[21] Intellectual antecedents may be found for all the political and even journalistic elements in these works, for example, in the historical writings compiled by the circle of scholars protected by Charles the Wise; but together they mark a burgeoning of historical consciousness that would powerfully affect the writing of biographies and family histories during the next century. An additional example is Robert Gaguin's *Compendium* and his *De Rebus Gestis*.[22] Burgeoning of historical consciousness? This seems to overstate the case, especially when we recall Bloch's emphasis upon the continuities of thought among royalist publicists. And so, we reach the point of departure for this book.

Beginning in the late fifteenth century, writers of histories included more information about themselves and their craft. The self-effacement, affected or otherwise, of the clerical writer may have persisted at Saint-Denis; but elsewhere writers, including clerics, busily promoted themselves as writers of histories, corresponded among themselves, and wrote prospectuses for compiling better histories than had ever been written. They submitted these outlines to the royal chancellor and the heads of aristocratic households in the hope of preferment. As we shall see, an entrepreneurial spirit about writing history infuses Guillaume Budé's

20. See René de Maulde la Clavière's introduction to the *Chroniques de Louis XII*, Mémoires de la société de l'histoire de France (Paris, 1889), vol. 1, p. xvi. D'Auton went on campaigns with Louis XII, specifically to record *haults faits*.

21. On Commynes, and after all the recent research, I still prefer the common-sense yet subtle approach found in William Bouwsma, "The Politics of Commynes," *Journal of Modern History* 23 (1951): 315–328. See also Paul Kendall, *Louis XI* (New York, 1971), Appendix I.

22. See below, p. 65.

writings, and with it came a greater self-awareness of the roles writers could play in society.

The market for histories was expanding rapidly as a result of printing. As Françoise Joukovsky observes: "Une invention technique, l'imprimerie, a inspiré aux hommes de la Renaissance une foi tenace dans le pouvoir de survie de la gloire à travers les siècles. Elle met les textes anciens ou médiévaux à la portée de tous: elle est la preuve que l'écrit est impérissable."[23] As the printed word reached greater and greater numbers of readers, the desire to be remembered after death in printed prose, and to celebrate the dead of one's own family and of the Capetian dynasty as an expression of national solidarity, became increasingly overt and extensive in the population. What may previously have been expressed only orally was now commissioned from a writer.

As family and sacred history, history had preceded the rise of national consciousness, but the latter could build upon these and be integrated into family history.[24] That by 1500 the Capetian family history bore within it something more than aristocratic and royalist ideologies goes without saying, but the celebration of the dead king's *gestes*, royalist rituals, and national accomplishments had become fused with the old genealogy of the three races of kings. The recounting of a royal coronation or death ritual by the historiographers royal may have represented an attempt to capture in words the miraculous and magical sensibilities that they had witnessed, in order that those who personally could not attend might bask in the royal presence through verbally inspired images.[25]

Curiosity about their kings appears to have been almost insatiable among early-modern Frenchmen—and one recalls the audiences for the history plays performed in London's Globe Theatre.[26] No aspect of the royal life escaped scrutiny, and when a king died, subjects needed

23. *La gloire dans la poésie française et néolatine du XVIe siècle* (Geneva, 1969), p. 13.

24. See my introduction to *National Consciousness, History, and Political Culture in Early Modern Europe* (Baltimore, 1975), pp. 2 ff.

25. On the study of funeral ceremonies, politics, and culture, see Clifford Geertz, *The Interpretation of Cultures* (New York, 1973), pp. 142 ff. On historicized royal ancestor worship, see André Coupez and Théodore Kamanzi, *La littérature de cour au Rwanda* (Oxford, 1970), pp. 23 ff.; and Arthur M. Hocart, *Kingship* (Oxford, 1927), pp. 70 ff.

26. I particularly like the evidence presented in Peter Saccio, *Shakespeare's English Kings* (New York, 1977); and, more generally, on public displays of English dynasties, in David M. Bergeron, *English Civic Pageantry 1558–1642* (Columbia, S.C., 1971).

the aid of persons skilled in writing and speaking to sum up the late monarch's life and deeds—perhaps even to assuage their guilt at having resented the late ruler's authority, resentment scarcely worth perpetuating toward the dead. The royal eulogies satisfied the same psychological needs that were manifested when a member of one's own family died. These feelings of remorse and guilt are neither quite private nor entirely public in monarchical political cultures. The orator's skills, like the historian's, were built upon his ability to synthesize society's feelings about death with the sanctity and dignity of royal persons, princes, nobles, bourgeois, and so on down the social hierarchy.[27]

The writer's art, monarchical-national ideologies, and, of course, the unique sensibilities, interests, and talents of individual writers thus combined to give form and content to historical thought. All appear as coded and recoded messages in Capetian family history as it becomes French history. To stress one without the others immediately distorts our view of the whole. Each also moves at a fundamentally different rate of change: the first being the recovery and adaptation of the *ars historica* as practiced in Antiquity;[28] the second being the *longue durée* of princely virtues shifting ever so slowly from Christian-theocratic kingship to ancient-heroic kingship; and the third being a constant change of writers as a result of shifts of patrons, religious beliefs, civil war, and princely inclination to take history seriously. Change in the usual sense is most rapid in the third, whereas continuity is much stronger in the first and second. This book has been constructed with the lives and works of officially designated historiographers as the principal focus—change being most apparent here.

Some statistical evidence for the continuity of the second—the remembering of dead French kings—is provided by combining figures

27. The parody of eulogy may serve as evidence for the pervasive need to be remembered after death. One that is especially funny, and significantly, it is about a peasant of limited intelligence, is the "Éloge funèbre de Michel Morin," Robert Mandrou, ed., *De la culture populaire au 17ᵉ et 18ᵉ siècles* (Paris, 1964), pp. 201–205.

28. The fundamental work on Renaissance language, rhetoric, and historical thought is Nancy Struever, *The Language of History in the Renaissance* (Princeton, 1970), *passim*. See also François de Dainville, "L'évolution de l'enseignement de la rhétorique au XVIIᵉ siècle," *XVIIᵉ siècle* 80–81 (1968): 19–43; Hannah Gray, "Renaissance Humanism: The Pursuit of Eloquence," *Journal of the History of Ideas* 24 (1963): 497–514; J.-Th. Welter, *L'exemplum dans la littérature religieuse et didactique au moyen âge* (Paris, 1927); and Bernard Guenée, "Histoires, annales, chroniques: Essai sur les genres historiques au moyen âge," *Annales, économies, sociétés, civilisations* 17 (1973): 1012 f.

from Henri-Jean Martin's general work on book publication[29] and Michel Tyvaert's analysis of the virtues attributed to various French kings by both learned and popular histories published in the seventeenth century.[30] According to Martin, works of history (and he separates these from belles lettres) never dropped below 20 percent of the total number of books published annually, although at times this frequency reached as high as 30 percent.[31] Among the 20 to 30 percent of history books published in any single year, the highest single proportion dealt with French kings. These were the best-sellers, reedited, augmented, abridged, and frequently embellished with portraits. Throughout the *Ancien Régime* writers would be tempted to write a book on this ever-marketable subject.

Tyvaert's statistical studies show that a remarkable uniformity and continuity in the treatment of French history prevailed throughout the seventeenth century. The large in-folio histories all conform to a structure of interpretations, and we find the same allocation of numbers of words and pages for each subject. Justice, courage, piety, and love of literature represented the hierarchy of virtues attributed to French kings; their vices were skimmed over, though love of women and of pleasure, cruelty, and weakness were sometimes mentioned. What is revealed is an almost immutable structure of moral-political principles that had been developed and attributed permanently to various French kings. Only very rarely would a remark by earlier writers be added or an attribute deleted. The same allocation of words per royal biography or number of words in long and short histories, completes the impression that French dynastic history had indeed become a series of almost immutable portraits. Regardless of which history a seventeenth-century Frenchman bought, he was certain to learn the same things about France's former rulers. Moreover, if he wanted a work of history, his only choice was either a work including all three races of kings or the

29. *Livre, pouvoirs, et société à Paris au XVIIe siècle* (Geneva, 1969), p. 1065.

30. "L'image du Roi: Légitimité et moralité royales dans les histoires de France au XVIIe siècle," *Revue d'histoire moderne et contemporaine* 21 (1974): 521–547; and "Les histoires élémentaires de la France au XVIIe siècle," *Revue de Marseille* 88 (supplément) (1971): 70–78.

31. The peak of historical publication in the seventeenth century occurred almost simultaneously with the trough in belles lettres in 1675–1690, and the peak in belles lettres occurred during the period with the lowest percentage of history books published. Why? Since history was considered a part of belles lettres throughout the early-modern period, these variations might perhaps be explained by the application of anachronistic notions of genre on Martin's part.

biographies of individual kings—the same family-history genres that had prevailed since Suger's revival of the individual biographies of French kings. The structures of dynastic history and royal biography remained so immutable that we scarcely need give them a further look in this book.

Tyvaert's statistical studies have confirmed Bloch's brilliant intuition about the continuities of political beliefs and knowledge of the past from the medieval centuries down through the early-modern period. In this vast literature it was, of course, the divinity of French kings that struck Bloch the most, but he perceived these continuities as more general: "La manière d'agir et de sentir de la majorité des Français au temps de Louis XIV, sur le terrain politique a pour nous quelque chose de surprenant et même de choquant."[32]

And shocking it is to imagine so many different writers over so many decades working independently of one another, but coming up with the same histories. This makes us uneasy. We search for the exceptions and the differences; in fact, we exaggerate them in order to preserve our sense of what it means to be a writer of history. We wish to cry out that new research must have changed the ways in which Charlemagne and Philip Augustus were portrayed—after all, a historical revolution had occurred in the sixteenth century.[33]

The twentieth-century historicist looks for origins and changes rather than continuities and celebrates the writer-scholar who "deepens our knowledge" of the past and thereby revises or alters the interpretation of it in some manner. But what would happen if Tyvaert were to apply his method of research to historical writing about George Washington, Thomas Jefferson, and Abraham Lincoln over the last century? We immediately think of the differences in interpretation, but modern historians also have made a great effort to communicate to the living the words and deeds of American national heroes. In practicing the art of writing history, seventeenth-century writers never seemed to question the desirability of facilitating the discourse between the dead and the living.[34] This function of the writer of history was, perhaps, the

32. Bloch, p. 344.

33. Donald Kelley, *The Foundations of Historical Scholarship* (New York, 1970). Kelley discerns the foundations of modern historical scholarship but in his conclusion also recognizes that these did not undermine the use of the *ars historica*. In addition to the works about French historical thought in the sixteenth century cited here and in Chapters I and II, see Yves-Marie Bercé, "Historiographie des temps modernes . . . ," *Bibliothèque de l'École des Chartes* 124 (1966): 281–295.

34. Religious reformers and philosophers inveighed against the pursuit of *gloire* and as a result offered powerful critiques of the function of his-

one most explicitly recognized by the ancients—passages from Cicero, Plutarch, and Quintilian immediately come to mind—but it pervaded and infused humanist historical thought as well. As long as men, families, and even institutions felt a need to recall their ancestors and search out new ones, writers would feel the attraction of *gloire*.[35] Indeed, the writers themselves, unlike their monkish predecessors, developed an all-pervasive need to be remembered after their own deaths. The *vitae* of sixteenth-century men of letters bear within them the structure of *haults faits* appropriate to the identity of writers. Today the names of scholars under whom historians studied, their good record as teachers, and their military service are still those virtues mentioned—the biographies of deceased historians in the *American Historical Review* being an apt contemporary example of this continuity.

The *Ars Historica*

The more learned the writer, the more familiar he was with biblical, ancient, and Carolingian literatures; and when writing history this learning prompted him to compare or parallel the deeds of the dead with those of heroic-historical persons presumably familiar to the reader. David, Solomon, Alexander the Great, Caesar Augustus, and Charlemagne frequently were paralleled with the Capetians.[36] In other cases the erudition of a particular monastic writer or his humanist successor resulted in very arcane paralleling.

----

tory. Immortality among men was such an accidental thing, Montaigne said; Chapter 16 of Book 2 is a critique of the pursuit of *gloire*. With this Calvin and his followers would have agreed; cf. Davis, p. 96. Calvinism and Stoicism had profound affinities in their disapproval of remembering the dead or of celebrating their virtues. Catholic reformers were divided on this issue, with some reproaching the pursuit of *gloire*, almost as if a mercantilist principle operated to fix an individual's immortality. When the *dévot* of the seventeenth century expressed his desire to be buried in an unmarked grave (La Reynie is an example), he hoped that his scorn for *gloire* on earth would enhance his *crédit* for *gloire* in Heaven. In this sense, Calvinism and Stoicism acted as arguments against carrying on the primordial function of history: facilitating discourse between the dead and the living.

35. See Arthur O. Lovejoy's deft exploration of this vast topic in *Reflections on Human Nature* (Baltimore, 1961), pp. 157 ff.

36. Richard W. Southern, "Aspects of the European Tradition of Historical Writing, I: The Classical Tradition from Einhard to Geoffrey of Monmouth," Royal Historical Society, *Transactions* 5th ser., 20 (1970): 173–196.

Like the eulogist whose task it was to celebrate the accomplishments of the deceased and raise him to a place of honor in the French pantheon, writers of history summed up his character in a portrait that would lend significance to a life already familiar to their readers or listeners. The *ars historica* is the congeries of devices used by writers and speakers to accomplish this purpose. As primordial ways of thinking and writing in Western civilization, the paralleling of deeds, the summing up of the significance of the deceased, and the praising of worthy examples of conduct had been codified, as it were, by the ancient rhetoricians. Knowledge of classical rhetoric led to an enrichment and refinement of the techniques comprising the *ars historica*, especially since a greater knowledge of Antiquity seemed to make possible the pursuit of immortality on earth through history.

The *ars historica* of the Middle Ages had generally yielded only literal parallels and narratives of *gestae*. Virtues and vices were summed up; examples of each were given from the lives of those deemed worthy of being either remembered or defamed. The philological and linguistic achievements of the sixteenth century led to a perception of the richness and complexity of ancient histories and rhetoric, and writers hastened to apply their new learning to the writing of history.

Conceits, those implicit images of the great that writers construct beneath the explicit narrative of someone else's life, owed much to an increased understanding of Plutarch's achievement. Familiarity with his techniques permitted writers to add psychological characteristics and qualities of mind to the portraits of individuals that hitherto had been only typological.

Though Alexander the Great's name might not be mentioned, the Plutarchian elements in his portrait were borrowed by early-modern writers and attributed to the portraits of French kings and great nobles. The historical effect was the same as the sculptural effect in Bernini's monumental equestrian statue of Louis XIV.[37] Beneath the features of Louis XIV the attuned eye perceives Alexander's features—or what were thought to be Alexander's. Typological portraits have, of course, gone out of fashion in more recent centuries, for biography has become a genre reserved largely for the exploration of an individual's unique qualities. The same is not true in social history, where the search for the characteristics of the typical peasant, slave, merchant, and so forth frequently results in the creation of conceits that confirm or refine

37. Rudolf Wittkower, "The Vicissitudes of a Dynastic Monument: Bernini's Equestrian Statue of Louis XIV," *De Artibus Opuscula XL: Essays in Honor of Erwin Panofsky*, ed. Millard Meiss (New York, 1961), pp. 497–531.

stereotypes from literary and visual sources. In the early-modern period such conceits had the effect of preselecting the themes (*topoi*) for narratives that would be drawn from the available evidence about the life of a particular king. With the exception of the *érudit*, the writer of that day had as little respect for the unique features in the life of an individual as the contemporary historian inspired by the social sciences when he searches for the typical in the study of human behavior.

While attempting to understand how the typological elements in history may be used to motivate individuals, Johan Huizinga coined the phrase (in translation) "historical ideals of life."[38] After describing how Charles the Bold's education had contributed to his early death as a result of an excessive emulation of Alexander the Great, Huizinga goes on to ask whether the young Germans dying in 1914 while striving to emulate their ancestors in the Teutoburger Forest were not motivated by a similar use of history. Huizinga's answer is obliquely affirmative. Early-modern writers had little doubt about their moral duty to facilitate the education of the young by manipulating them through the teaching of "historical ideals of life."

Topoi, those general truths applicable to all men in a similar situation yet true of a narrative about a specific time and place,[39] became for all writers the favorite device refined and developed from the *ars historica*. In the prose of a mediocre writer such as Charles Bernard, the *topoi* thunder from the pages, creating a heavy *histoire sainte et moralisante*. In Jean Racine's prose they are used to transgress the boundaries of time and place in ways that add both psychological and moral dimensions to any subject. Let us illustrate how *topoi* work by giving an obvious example from military history. When the historian in the seventeenth century remarked that the commander slept soundly on the night before a major battle, he almost certainly included this *topos* in order to convey a moral inference: the commander believed his war to be just and was certain of victory. Indeed, seventeenth-century writers used this *topos* so often that it lost most of its effect for more sophisticated readers and critics. In the eighteenth century the gradual liberation from the use of *topoi* borrowed from the ancients signaled the decline of classicism. Still, it is possible to suggest that some commanders who had read military history strove to convey

38. *Men and Ideas*, trans. James S. Holmes and Hans van Marle (New York, 1959), pp. 77–96.

39. See Struever, *passim*; and Peter France, *Rhetoric and Truth in France: Descartes to Diderot* (Oxford, 1972), Chap. 1. For ancient rhetoric, see George Kennedy, *The Art of Persuasion in Greece* (Princeton, 1963); and *The Art of Rhetoric in the Roman World, 300 B.C.–A.D. 300* (Princeton, 1972), *passim*.

the impression that they had slept soundly before combat. The general's orderly may have watched to see that the commander did in fact sleep soundly and would pass word to the watch, who passed it on to the troops, perhaps contributing to a regiment's pluck as it moved forward against the enemy at dawn.

Topoi were not always used explicitly to convey a virtue or a vice, but they served to build up a general impression of strength, weakness, or whatever. And upon reading about this particular *topos*, humorous as it is, some modern scholars might in fact retort that Napoleon really did sleep well before battle, as did Robert E. Lee—and as Winston Churchill slept soundly after learning that he had become prime minister. Empirical evidence may add something to a *topos*, but its chief purpose remains the revelation of something about the character of the individual to whom it is related.

In addition to *topoi*, early-modern writers resorted to inserting *sententiae*—that is, opinions or commonplaces—into their narratives to a far greater extent than their medieval predecessors. These truths that apply to all times and places may deal with individual moral actions, politics, military conduct, and so forth, but they are always included in such a way that the subject being discussed in the narrative confirms the truth of the sentence. One of the principal contemporary measures of the skill of writers of history during the sixteenth and seventeenth centuries involved their ability to include sentences in such a way that the reader scarcely realized he was being instructed in a general moral truth while reading about a specific incident exemplifying that truth. The works of Livy and Tacitus became the models for how sentences should be incorporated, and these ancient Romans' own sentences were relentlessly pirated by their admirers.

In modern English and American prose, commonplaces are easy to discern because history is habitually written in the past tense. Since the sentence is stated in the present tense, it stands out for the reader—perhaps one reason why it has tended to go out of fashion in writings in those languages. In French, however, where the use of the present tense is far more prevalent in history, sentences can be discreetly inserted into the narrative.

The stylized quality of historical prose in the early-modern period resulted in large part from the use—or overuse—of these devices. Ancient rhetoric seemed to provide ready solutions for the problem of conveying moral significance from the past to the present. Later writers would jumble sentences or disobey the rules for their use established during the classical era of French prose, and still others used them for an irreverent or satirical effect. Today one rarely finds French historical prose in which they are not present. When, in 1966, Pierre

Goubert wrote: "Le Roi [Louis XIV] venait de célébrer son soixante-dixième anniversaire, âge rarement atteint à cette époque, âge qui, même au XXe siècle, sonne l'heure de la retraite définitive pour tous, sauf pour les hommes qui se croient providentiels,"[40] we know that he was talking as much about Charles de Gaulle (who was seventy-six years old at the time) as about the Sun King. The decline of the pre-occupation with remembering the dead is so considerable in the twentieth century that Goubert added an allusion to the twentieth century to make the parallel obvious.

In the seventeenth century the more popular the history, the more explicit and obvious the parallels, conceits, *topoi*, and sentences. Writers carried on the earlier tradition of adding a tag "comme a fait Alexandre," to ensure that the reader grasped the parallel. The more learned the history, the greater the knowledge of ancient literatures required to understand the writer's purpose. The use of the *ars historica* may have resulted in denuding the dead of their unique qualities and distorting events by a kind of reverse anachronism, that is, a filtering of events in the early-modern centuries by and through the perspective of Antiquity. As Hans Baron remarked:

> The classicism which had gradually emerged by the end of the Quattrocento was a synthesis of originally opposing trends; it was a prototype of the relationship to antiquity known in the sixteenth and seventeenth centuries in many Western countries, until, on a larger scale and with even more momentous consequences for the modern mind, it reached its final phase in France in the age of Louis XIV. In all these various developments we ultimately find a humanist classicism willing to employ the ancient model as a guide in building a new literature with a new language in a new nation.[41]

This would be so down to and beyond the quarrel between the Ancients and the Moderns of the 1690s, for calling into question the standards of greatness from Antiquity was not the same as calling into question *all* standards of greatness.

The Writer and Dependency

In twentieth-century American, the word artisan connotes someone who makes something with his hands, a shoemaker or a tailor. In twen-

40. *Louis XIV et vingt millions de Français* (Paris, 1966), p. 194.
41. *The Crisis of the Early Italian Renaissance*, 2d ed. (Princeton, 1966), p. 353.

tieth-century France, *artisan*, one possessing a creative skill, has not
lost its parentage with *art*, *artifice*, and *artiste*. In French one can still
properly refer to Jean Monnet as the *artisan* of the European community. The writer whose art it was to praise the dead and educate the
young through the written word might, like an artist, practice his craft
in a number of genres or mediums, but the end product was the same.
He worked for pay and protection, and these varied according to his
talents. To increase opportunities for commissions and favor, the writer
had to develop nothing short of an ideology about his services, and he
would integrate that ideology into royal biographies and family histories.

Within this vast framework of dependency,[42] I explore the careers
of five writers whose bonds to the Bourbon kings were formalized by
both monetary remuneration and offices. Here the effects of these
bonds on historical thought are more discernible than in works written
by those who had either declined or never received royal favor. Appointment as *historiographe de France* or *historiographe du roi* signified the king's bestowing an honor, a dignity, and a title upon a subject.
Like other titles it became part of a writer's name or public identity.
How did holding the office affect the writing of history? Were the
works of the historiographers more propagandistic than those written
by nonofficeholders? Were their histories more absolutist, less aristocratic, or even less robe than those of other writers? These questions
lead directly to the general problem of the function of histories in
early-modern societies: the remembering of the dead and the teaching
of the young.

If the celebration of the actions of dead kings is accepted as a definition of propaganda, the results quickly appear too broad to yield any
other political or cultural features about the past than the conflicts
between nation-states and between republics and monarchies as forms
of government. Very quickly we realize the impossibility of deciding
what is propagandistic and what is not, unless it is possible to discern
the conscious acts of a writer who knew he was publishing a work
intended to influence public opinion in an ideological way.

42. And that of those seeking a mode of thinking outside of dependency.
See as an example the dedication to the anonymous *Histoire de France* published by Abraham in 1581: "Je me suis persuadé ne pouvoir mieux adresser
ce labeur qu'à vous [the king], qui comme Lieutenant de Dieu en terre, ne
le representez moins en bonté et faveur envers tous: qu'en puissance de
maintenir ceux qui d'une gaie et franche volonté s'offrent à vous faire tres
humble service. Non toutefois pour en tirer honneurs, richesses ou autres
avantages que chacun recherche avec tant de peynes et prochains hazards."
The work is attributed to La Popelinière.

Instead of taking this approach, I hope to capture the feelings and expressions of dependency among writers. Related to this, of course, is the need to search for the ideological origins of the modernist perception that the historian must be independent from remuneration and service if he is to write a completely balanced or allegedly objective history, the subject of Chapter II.

Marc Bloch observed that there was nothing particularly medieval about an individual's search for a protector.[43] Seeking patrons for monetary and psychological support continues actively in contemporary political and university life, with the resulting personal and ideological overtones or shadings in the writing of histories. The contemporary separation of the rights of citizenship and nationality from professional life permits scholars in history to believe themselves independent. We include clientage in historical discourse about national and local politics, while ignoring it in university life and the study of historical thought. Historians in France express few scruples about their students' habit of expounding and elaborating the theses their mentors have put forth. Anglo-American historians quake at the thought, though this by no means indicates that historical scholarship in the English-speaking world is free of mandarinism.

Holding the office of historiographer royal made the bonds of service and fidelity more overt than the ties that customarily develop between men of power and men of the pen in the twentieth century. Be that as it may, it is very difficult to find the line of demarcation separating the effects of dependency from those of ideological commitment in historical thought. National identity permits historians to use the plural pronoun, we, when describing the collective actions of their nation. This is what Racine did when France was at war. In internal political affairs, however, Racine could never use a plural pronoun—any more than Colbert or Louvois could—for all political acts in French political culture stemmed from the king alone or were done in his name. Partisanship and *esprit de parti* were well-known characteristics of historical thought in the *Ancien Régime* and may often be refracted through the writings of pensioned authors whose works have a Gallican, absolutist, princely, ultramontane, or parlementaire bias.

A historiographer royal had to please his patron-king or chancellor —if either of these bothered to pay attention to his work—and avoid offending great nobles and prelates. The modern writer, beginning with Hume and Voltaire, depended on the public, rather than on patrons, for self-esteem and income. Income from the sale of books took the place of pensions. But in the seventeenth century lesser historians

43. *Feudal Society*, trans. L. A. Manyon (Chicago, 1961), p. 147.

than they had already tasted the bittersweet experience of publishing, only to find that their unsold books remained on some book dealer's shelves. Dependency on the public? Writing history to please and instruct the public ranks high among the ancient commonplaces that early-modern writers knew and repeated.

The whole range of possible dependency systems now becomes apparent: through their works writers could attempt to please kings, princes, parliaments, and publics.[44] What in classical political thought are the forms of government included a political dependency (pension versus market) for the writer of history, a dependency that might or might not affect his recounting of the past. And patronage was so much a part of every society in early-modern Europe that writers scarcely perceived the ideological significance of viewing public dependency as the logical complement to republican political cultures and royal patronage as the complement to absolutist monarchies. The bureaucratization of patronage that occurred under Louis XIV must, therefore, be defined as the primary expression of that form of government as it affected the writers of history. Our repugnance for Ludovician political culture is chiefly derived from our modernist historical viewpoint, which is a child of republican forms of government—Florentine, Venetian, British, and Dutch.[45]

The five writers whose careers and works are scrutinized in this book include the obscure and the famous, mediocre and brilliant stylists, social climbers, eccentrics, the imprisoned, and the heretical. What they have in common is their tendency to emphasize eloquence over learning; none was an *érudit*.

Charles Bernard was a courtier whom Louis XIII liked personally

44. And it was here that the invention of printing provided the greatest impact to free writers from the bonds of patronage.

45. I particularly like Ranke's way of putting this genealogy: "Die allgemein wirksame, und allgemein gelesene historische Literatur ist, wie im achtzehnten Jahrhundert von Frankreich, so im sechzehnten und dem grössten Theil des siebsehnten hauptsächlich von Italien ausgegangen. Die italienische Historiographie hatte sich an der Geschichte der italienischen Republiken gebildet, und unter dem Einfluss des wiedererweckten Studiums der Classiker in Form und Inhalt zum Wetteifer mit denselben erhoben; sie hatte dann, als die Republiken in die allgemeinen europäischen Angelegenheiten verwickelt wurden, ihren Blick über diese ausgedehnt und sie in ihren Kreis gezogen; als endlich in dem unselbständig gewordenen Italien nichts Bedeutendes mehr vorkam" (*Französische Geschichte vornehmlich im sechzehnten und siebzehnten Jahrhundert* [Stuttgart and Tübingen, 1852–1856], vol. 5, p. 3). See also William Bouwsma, *Venice and the Defense of Republican Liberty* (Berkeley, 1968), Chap. 1, and pp. 140 ff.

and appointed historiographer royal. Charles Sorel was unsuccessful as a courtier, turned novelist, and finally became a conscientious historiographer after having inherited the office from his uncle. François Eudes de Mézerai, son of a Norman physician, *libertin*, and mediocre poet, had the bizarre habit of carrying a candle when seeing guests to the door in broad daylight. Paul Pellisson-Fontanier, a Huguenot from a robe family in Languedoc, was imprisoned for his fidelity to Nicolas Fouquet and converted to Catholicism before being named historiographer. The last example, Jean Racine, was a Jansenist, the son of a tax farmer, and a playwright, who became historiographer royal.

Through the study of their careers I hope to show how political, social, religious, and literary influences affected and in many instances determined the ways history was written. This story is not one of innovation; none of the five historiographers discussed here is worthy of being placed in the pantheon of the fathers of modern history. Quite the contrary. I hope to reveal the normative intellectual, ideological, and social constraints in which the historiographers lived and wrote.

Not *all* the historiographers, of course. That special group of the *érudits*—the Godefroys, the Duchesnes, the Dupuys, Etienne Baluze, Charles Du Cange, and so on—also appeared on the rolls of royal appointments, in most cases as historiographers, sometimes as librarians;[46] but the functions they carried out for the state differed from those of the more rhetorically inclined historiographers discussed here.

Now it is time to let the *gens de lettres* speak for themselves, and there is no better place to start than with Budé's discursive way of addressing Francis I about the services he, other writers, and history might perform for princes and French political culture.[47] Two centuries later, very late in the reign of Louis XIV, writers would be echoing his words, though in a different style. The synthesis of the *ars historica* and service to the Crown, as summed up by Budé, was destined to have a very long life.

46. The *érudits* who were religious are underrepresented, Jean Mabillon, the Benedictine, and such Port-Royalists as Le Nain de Tillemont being obvious examples.

47. Useful introductions to the literature on political culture are Lucian W. Pye, "Introduction," *Political Culture and Political Development*, ed. Lucian W. Pye and Sidney Verba (Princeton, 1965); and Robert C. Tucker, "Culture, Political Culture, and Communist Society," *Political Science Quarterly* 88, no. 2 (June 1973): 170–190.

Chapter I
Men of Letters:
Sixteenth-Century
Models of Conduct

*I*T is a commonplace to assert that the dignity and self-awareness of men of letters increased during the Renaissance. Sixteenth-century biographies, autobiographies, portraits, and collective biographies of authors testify to a sharper identity for men of letters than had been known in the late Middle Ages. This self-consciousness is also evident in the titles these *lettrés* bore and in the flood of correspondence they exchanged with one another. Their funeral orations and epitaphs reveal their pride in being men of letters. Yet, apart from general remarks and some pioneering articles,[1] research on the *lettrés* as a self-conscious social identity has been scanty. What identities or

1. The succinct way in which Jacques Le Goff describes the social ambience of humanists is pertinent here: "Le milieu de l'humaniste, c'est celui du groupe, de l'*académie* fermée et, quand le véritable humanisme conquiert Paris, il ne s'enseigne pas à l'Université, mais dans cette institution pour une élite: le *Collège des lecteurs royaux*, le future Collège de France. Son milieu, c'est la cour du prince. Au sein même de la querelle philologique qui l'opposa à Leonardo Bruni, Alonso Garcia semble en avoir eu le pressentiment: 'L'*urbanité* désigne pour vous cette *humanité* qui tant par les paroles que par les gestes va au-devant des honneurs. On désigne sous le nom d'*urbains* ceux qui ont pris l'habitude de fléchir le genou, d'abaisser leur capuchon, de refuser la préséance et les premières places même entre égaux. Mais ceux-là nous, nous les appelons *curiales* ou si ce mot te déplaît car il a un autre sens en droit civile, et si tu me permets d'user du langage vulgaire, nous les appelons *courtisans* et l'*urbanité* nous l'appelons *curialité* ou pour employer un mot du langage chevaleresque nous l'appelons *courtoisie*' " (*Les intellectuels au moyen âge* [Paris, 1960], p. 181). See also Robert Mandrou, *Des humanistes aux hommes de science* (Paris, 1973), pp. 42–51; and the pioneering study of the history of nonroyal humanist patronage, Eugene F. Rice, "The Patrons of French Humanism," *Renaissance Studies in Honor of Hans Baron*, ed. Anthony Molho and John A. Tedeschi (Florence, 1971), pp. 687–702.

models of conduct influenced the lives of men of learning and eloquence in sixteenth-century France?

This chapter offers nothing conclusive on this vast subject; but, to
provide a framework for understanding the lives and careers of seventeenth-century historiographers, it is helpful to begin with a glance at
what men of letters after 1600 believed to be the history of their predecessors.[2] The fact that these models of conduct were biographically
historicized is significant and helps us discern the social elements in
these models. Younger men of letters could look back to their older
and more established counterparts, using them as sources of inspiration
and guidance in learning how to cope with patrons and with rivalries
among fellow men of letters.

Their identity as men of letters was a supplemental layer of
consciousness and action. In addition to being men of letters, they
were statesmen, prelates, monks, clerks, professors, physicians, lawyers,
judges, courtiers, and seigneurs. Yet the merging of one's identity as
a literary and learned man with other identities ought not to be considered a conclusive indication that the influence of the first upon any
given individual was somehow less important, less real, or even less
forceful. Indeed, daring to pursue a career as a man of letters included,
as a near prerequisite, the assumption of more properly social, religious,
and professional roles. Although not quite sufficient for admission to
the elite circles where learning and the pursuit of eloquence flourished,
playing such roles was a virtual necessity. Their identity as men of
letters acted as a powerful determinant for the thought and behavior
of some of the great, and some of the mediocre, figures in the *monde
des lettrés.* From what other perspective might a man of letters hope
to determine the significance of his own literary creations? Some *lettrés* needed more immediate recognition (despite refrains about immortality being their concern), a feeling of belonging to a group that
was more appreciative of their learning and eloquence than the literate society at large. Such encouragement from already recognized
men of letters helped create the elements of a general identity for men
of letters.

2. Under *ordres du tiers éstat* Charles Loyseau lists: "Pour l'honneur
deub à la science, j'ay mis au premier rang les gens de Lettres, dont les
Romains ne faisoient point d'Ordre à part, mais les laissoient meslez dans les
Trois Estats. . . . Or nos gens de Lettres sont divisez en quatre facultez ou
sciences principales, à scavoir, la Theologie, la Jurisprudence (sous laquelle
je comprend le droit Civil et Canon), la Medecine, et les Arts, qui compren-
nent la Grammaire, Rhetorique, et Philosophie" (*Traité des ordres* [Paris,
1665], Chap. 8, p. 75).

A reputation for learning and eloquence could be fostered by recognition from patrons, by compliments from already established men of letters, and by public acclaim. A growing reputation was manifested when one was the subject of gossip, was invited to speak and give opinions on learned and stylistic questions, and sold more books. Some writers feigned not to take their reputations seriously; others took them much too seriously; and still others recognized how fickle and unfair the reputations established within the *monde des lettrés* could be. Flattery, inflated reputations, political influence, wealth, regional and monastic solidarities, and clerical infighting were among the many factors affecting reputations. Yet for generation after generation identity as a learned or eloquent man continued to attract individuals heeding the call of the muses.

How did the spread of printing, an increasing reading public, expanded educational opportunities, and religious controversy affect the identities of men of letters and the way their reputations were made? To attempt to answer this question would lead us far beyond the limits of an introductory chapter. What is significant, however, is that, all these changes notwithstanding, until the mid-eighteenth century relatively simple, almost archaic definitions of learning and eloquence continued to constitute the identity of the man of letters. And in this the writers of history were no exception. To be sure, an elaboration of the notions of learning and eloquence occurred during the sixteenth century, but the *monde des lettrés* still tended to remain a separate identity as long as the respect for Antiquity so characteristic of both humanists and classicists continued to provide a common foundation for learned culture.[3]

3. In sketching the origins of the "New Ideal of the Artist," Rudolf and Margot Wittkower suggest that the lives of artists in Antiquity served as an "archetypal case that stimulated imitation in the Renaissance" (*Born under Saturn: The Character and Conduct of Artists* [New York, 1963], p. 1). Could not the same be said for men of letters? Pasquier mentions that ancient writers wrote in order to gain mention in each other's books (Dorothy Thickett, ed., *Choix des lettres sur la littérature, la langue, et la traduction* [Geneva, 1956]). Budé uses the terms *gens de lettre* [sic], *gens scavans*, and *doctes et eloquans* synonymously in the *Institution du prince* (Claude Bontems, Léon-Pierre Raybaud, and Jean-Pierre Braucourt, *Le prince dans la France des XVIe et XVIIe siècles* [Paris, 1965], *passim*). Finally, there is something so delightfully scornful about Kathleen Davies's description of the way humanists behaved vis-à-vis one another, and as a group, that it evokes the behavior of other groups of men of letters in other times who seem to convert their contempt for the larger political culture into feelings of intense loyalty and support for like-minded writers: "There is the well-known fact that the humanist cliques formed themselves into little mutual

As men of letters increasingly gossiped about one another through-out the sixteenth century, and as they began to write autobiographies and biographies of one another, there was a growing tendency to evoke such information in the critical discussion of any writer's thought. The result was the rise of a new critical perspective upon historical thought. Medieval historical criticism, a neglected genre, rarely included re-marks about how an individual's personality, his identity as a man of letters, or even his social status, might have influenced the manner in which he recorded the past. By the late sixteenth century, however, the identity of the man of letters and his political participation in the affairs of state or his dependency could become a powerful critical comment brought to bear on historical thought. This development, after 1560, and its subsequent decline in the seventeenth century, leads us to the search for what men of letters after 1600 believed to be the history of their predecessors, and what they may have known about the relationships between earlier men of letters and their historical thought.

Budé's Career as *Exemplum*

Sixteenth-century men of letters were an inspiration for their succes-sors, as well as something of an embarrassment. Perceived as pioneers of the new learning, the *doctes* and *éloquans* living before 1600 served as models for their successors. While firmly believing that the writer-heroes of Antiquity had remained unequaled, writers of the seven-teenth century expressed little doubt that the scholarship and eloquence of the sixteenth century had already been surpassed. Accompanying the quarrel of the Ancients and the Moderns was the belief that real progress in learning and eloquence had been made from the sixteenth to the seventeenth centuries.[4] Yet, the models of conduct and the hon-ors received by their forebears were in no way denigrated by the *doctes* and *éloquans* after 1600. Quite the reverse. So often depicted in heroic terms, such men as Budé, Jacques Cujas, Pierre de Ronsard, Guillaume

admiration societies, from whose utterances it is extremely difficult to dis-engage not only what was the actual truth but even what they genuinely thought about one another" ("Late Fifteenth-Century French Historiogra-phy as Exemplified in the *Compendium* of Robert Gaguin and the *De Rebus Gestis* of Paulus Aemilius," Ph.D. dissertation, University of Edinburgh, 1954, p. 225).

4. See below, p. 179 (n. 25), for Chapelain's views on this question; and as explored in a pioneering article by Hans Baron, "The Querelle of the Ancients and Moderns as a Problem for Renaissance Scholarship," *Journal of the History of Ideas* 20 (1959): 3–32.

du Bellay, Clément Marot, and François Rabelais were pluralized—*les Marot, les Budé*—and were held up as *exempla* in a pantheon to inspire all men of letters.

Seventeenth-century men of letters looked back upon Francis I's reign as the beginning of a golden age of learning, eloquence, and patronage. Hundreds if not thousands of dedications in books, speeches, and paintings include the *topoi* about how learning began to flourish under Francis. As Mézerai put it, after summarizing Francis's acts on behalf of learning: "En un mot il mérita le glorieux surnom *de Père et de Restaurateur des Lettres et des Sciences.*"[5] The academic oratory of the seventeenth century interwove the Francis I *topoi* and those about Cardinal Richelieu as founder of the French Academy, asserting that moments of literary greatness occur simultaneously with the presence of powerful, generous, youthful monarchs and great patrons.[6]

Royal entrées during the sixteenth century had already helped establish the models for combining verse, history, and painting to laud Francis as a patron of learning, and when the Parisian town crier went through the streets announcing that king's death, one of the royal attributes shouted out was, "Père des bonnes lettres."[7] The King's patronage of belles lettres had become legendary even before his death; seventeenth-century men of letters would merely repeat the *topoi*.

The integration of belles lettres and men of learning into the symbols and realities of power in French political culture had its origins in the centuries preceding Francis I's reign, but for the entire early-modern period his reign served as a model for what that integration should be. Recognition from the public jostled with recognition from the state for learning and eloquence in a courtly model of conduct. Any attempt to separate public from princely recognition prior to the mid-eighteenth century therefore implies that connections could exist between *chose publicque*, that is, polity-centered monarchy, and men of letters, as opposed to connections between the prince and the man of letters. Yet, such connections were never explicitly elaborated, even in the thought of Jean Bodin and of Lancelot Voisin de La Popelinière, where they appeared fleetingly. Thus, as long as writers of history could with approval evoke the Francis I *topoi*, writers could barely

5. *Abrégé chronologique ou extrait de l'histoire de France* (Paris, 1690), vol. 2, p. 475.

6. See below, p. 173 (n. 11).

7. Harry Levin, *The Myth of the Golden Age in the Renaissance* (Bloomington, 1969), provides a general introduction to the place of the golden age in sixteenth-century thought. See also Jean Jacquot, ed., *Les fêtes de la renaissance* (Paris, 1956), pp. 11 f.; and Ralph Giesey, *The Royal Funeral Ceremony in Renaissance France* (Geneva, 1960), p. 11, n. 4.

perceive that contradictions between public and princely recognition were possible.[8]

As part of a larger social form, the integration of letters and power belonged to the courtly ideal of life. The patron's way of recognizing the value of learning, and of the *docte* and *éloquan*, was founded upon the ideal of personal intimacy and dependency between men of power and men of letters. This courtly ideal became reality to a certain extent under Francis I, as well in many lesser courts of great noblemen or of such royal officials as the chancellor, and even in the households of prominent bourgeois. It had been a reality under earlier kings and under the Burgundian dukes as well, but the enhanced identity of the man of letters inevitably led to a more explicit definition of relations between men of letters and patrons. During the sixteenth and seventeenth centuries the increase in the size of the royal households—chiefly of the king's household, but also those of the queen, the royal brothers and sisters, and other relatives—and the probable increase in the number of court pensions would indicate that the courtly ideal of personal recognition from the patron was becoming increasingly real and institutionalized.[9] No king or great nobleman could ever quite fulfill the ideal of intimacy with the learned and the ideal of respect for eloquence that men of letters had defined for him; but mere expression of interest in poetry, music, history, and grammar usually sufficed to transport men of letters seeking recognition to boundless admiration for patrons. Instead of emphasizing the autonomy of the creative act, which became fundamental to the writer's identity after 1800, the man of letters at court expressed a willingness to accept criticisms of his work and would incorporate the revisions suggested by his patron and by men of letters who had already found favor. Like the portraitist who turns to his sitter for suggestions on how to improve the likeness, sixteenth- and seventeenth-century men of letters accepted the commissions of their patrons and their criticisms as well. Like artisans, men of letters sought to fashion their works to conform to the tastes of the prelates,

8. This is not to argue that there were works that earned princely approval although they were scorned by the public, and the reverse. The issue is the writer's perception of both, until a delineation of princely and public interests became possible in France later in the sixteenth century as a result of a firmer understanding of the meaning of *polis* in Aristotle's *Politics* and of Machiavellian political thought.

9. The actual numbers in attendance and the degree to which they could claim accessibility to the prince and his *familiers* at various royal courts fluctuated from reign to reign, but prior to 1660 princes' and kings' reputations for accessibility were more significant than the number of men of letters actually at their courts.

nobles, and royal patrons to whom these works would be dedicated. Though Francis I was not known for voicing opinions about literary and historical matters, his sister, Marguerite of Navarre, undeniably played the role of the active and critical patroness with a skill that inspired admiration in the *monde des lettrés*.

No *érudit*—least of all Jean du Tillet, Étienne Pasquier, and Pierre Pithou, and their seventeenth-century successors—applied his very considerable talents as researcher-into-the-origins-of-things in an attempt to find out whether the Francis I *topoi* about patronage were in fact true. Did Francis give larger and more numerous pensions to the *doctes* and *éloquans* than Charles V or Louis XII? In many of his works, and more particularly in his *Institution du prince*, Budé expressed curiosity about the real value of pensions bestowed by patrons upon men of letters in Antiquity,[10] and he implied that pensions in Antiquity were much greater than those given by Capetian or Valois kings. The *érudits*, his successors in historical scholarship, did not, however, pursue the strategy of holding up Antiquity as a model for the patronage of belles lettres. Growing national sentiment and Francis I's own patronage may explain why this route was not pursued.

Did the sense of inferiority vis-à-vis the Italians, especially strong among the first generations of men of letters, make them reluctant to probe the record of royal favors? Recognition at court, without the social standing of courtier, may have provided an identity so ambiguous that its origins could not be researched. In a society in which social groups, religious commitments, roles, and functions were quite precisely defined and were overtly identifiable by vestimentary conventions, special manners, forms of address, and perhaps even gestures and physical features, this omission of the history of the origins of French literary patronage by the *érudits* reveals how elusive and dependent upon the court their models of conduct were. Still another explanation deserves mention. The *érudits* all held royal offices. They were councillors, librarians, secretaries, or judges holding any one of these or other offices. Such offices gave them more status in the political culture as a whole than the simple quality of "man of letters." The more courtly (*sans office*), and perhaps less erudite, men of letters appear to have been little attracted to research-into-the-origins-of-things. Thus, a hierarchy of titles within the *monde des lettrés* may have existed and may have been reflected both in the type of historical inquiry each man of letters undertook and in whether he tended to view his own talents primarily as learning or as eloquence. Imagine a man of

10. *Institution du prince* (in Bontems, Raybaud, and Braucourt), p. 87.

letters in royal service without any office whatsoever. Imagine how naked he must have felt vis-à-vis other men of letters holding offices. How would he dare explore the past of an identity that was in no way his? He would be wiser to turn his talents to panegyric.

And seen from the perspective of the society as a whole, the court, like the later salon, lacked the solid and overt vestimentary conventions and institutional foundations that gave an identity to the clerical, aristocratic, and perhaps bourgeois cultures,[11] which were older and very firmly established. Courtly culture would be an amalgam of all three and a repudiation of some elements in each. Its social and psychological foundations in what Roland Mousnier has called the *fidélités* is apparent.[12] Men of letters sought to "give themselves" to their patrons, to be under their protection. Daniel Poirion's observation about fifteenth-century poets captures the aspirations of early-modern men of letters in general: "Le poète fait souvent don de lui-même avec une insistance parfaitement justifiée dans cette société qui repose encore sur des liens personnels de service, de dévouement, de fidélité, et de loyauté."[13] Even though Budé appeared at Francis's court, as did other *doctes* and *éloquans*, and served in his government, he dared not dress as one of the young seigneurs in the royal circle of intimate courtiers. Yet, according to the courtly ideal, the prince ought to enjoy the company of men of letters during his leisure hours. The usual visual image of the two together emanates from the interests of the *doctes* and *éloquans*: a book is being presented by a man of learning and eloquence, upon his knees before his patron, who is seated on what may almost be described as a throne, if he is a king.[14]

11. For a provocative thesis on the relationships between clerical, aristocratic, and courtly cultures, see Georges Duby, "The Diffusion of Cultural Patterns in Feudal Society," *Past and Present* 39 (1969): 3–10. His definition of models of behavior as "exemplary types of human achievement" bears within it the implication that such models include names, themes, and actions that occurred in the past; thus they are not fundamentally different from Huizinga's "historical ideals of life." See Françoise Piponnier, *Costume et vie sociale, la cour d'Anjou au XIVe–XVe siècle* (The Hague, 1970), p. 39, for evidence of princely gifts of clothing to men of letters.

12. *Les institutions de la France sous la monarchie absolue* (Paris, 1974), pp. 84 f.

13. *Le poète et le prince: L'évolution du lyrisme courtois de Guillaume de Machault à Charles d'Orléans* (Paris, 1965), p. 117. For a very valuable overview of these questions, see Felix Gilbert, "The Humanist Concept of the Prince," *Journal of Modern History* 9 (1939): 449–483.

14. See the reproduction of the well-known miniature depicting Budé's

Accounts by men of letters of their reception by the prince were naturally highly laudatory of the prince, who was described as interested in learning. What the kings personally thought of this obsequious and often pedantic discourse is difficult to discover, but Henry III's attempt to establish rules for the conversations at his table reveals both a cynicism about the enterprise and a belief that the history spoken there was vapid and hence incapable of disturbing the royal dignity and digestion. Henry was supposed to have had Polybius and Tacitus read aloud to him; one wonders if men of letters were not a little jealous of those ancient authors because of the hearing their works received at court.[15]

In an age when the *érudits* were beginning to search for the origins and pristine qualities of virtually every role and function among social elites, their failure to study men of letters and patronage, and the elusive nature of their identity, make us pause before selecting terms with which to prepare an analysis that is anything more than descriptive. The danger lies in being too quick to narrow the definitions to "historian," rather than "man of letters," or to "courtier," rather than "clerk"; for both sixteenth-century men of letters and their heirs in the seventeenth century continually referred to themselves in such very general terms as *doctes*, *éloquans*, and *sçavans*. To evoke the Francis I *topoi* was certainly to assure a favorable response among both *docte*

---

presentation of the *Institution du prince* to Francis I in Donald Kelley, *Foundations of Modern Historical Scholarship* (New York, 1970), frontispiece. Does the dog, paws crossed and gazing at Budé, symbolize fidelity? For other scenes depicting men of letters presenting their books to late medieval kings, see Claire R. Sherman, "Representations of Charles V of France (1338–1380) as a Wise Ruler," *Medievalia et Humanistica* n.s., 2 (1971): 83–96; and Millard Meiss, *French Painting in the Time of Jean de Berry* (London, 1967), *passim*.

15. Francis I's meals with men of letters are touched upon in Roger Doucet, "Pierre Du Chastel, grand aumônier de France," *Revue historique* 133 (1920): 230. Regarding Henry III's attempt to regulate the discourse at his meals, the keeper of *hôtel* accounts records: "S. M. désirant manger en repos et se garder de l'importunité qu'elle reçoit durant ses repas, défend désormais qu'en ses disners et souppers personne ne parle à Elle que tout hault et de propos communs et dignes de la présence de Sadite Majesté, voulant Icelle que, particulièrement à son disner, que d'histoire on parle et d'autres choses de savoir et de vertu" (Louis C. Douët-D'Arcq, *Comptes de l'hôtel des rois de France aux XIVᵉ et XVᵉ siècles* [Paris, 1865], p. ix). Georges Grente quotes Davila about the reading of Polybius and Tacitus at court in *Jean Bertaut* (Paris, 1903), p. 28.

and nonlearned readers.[16] What was adequate for contemporaries ought to serve us well enough in this instance.

Moreover, what would be served if it were made known that little patronage had really existed over the centuries or that Francis I had not been all that generous or familiar with men of letters? Confronted by a dedication containing the *topoi* about Francis, the reigning monarch might pull his purse strings even tighter if an *érudit* found that Francis had been niggardly with men of letters. The researches of Claude de Fauchet and Pasquier, like the essays and poetry of Ronsard and Henri II Estienne, belong to a general search for great literary monuments of the past, a search carried back into the origin of belles lettres in Gaul and Capetian France.[17] They may express curiosity about authors and patrons, but their sole aim is to place the Francis *topoi* into a more general, ameliorating perspective. Celebratory in tone, Pasquier's *Recherches* acknowledges the great accomplishments in literature and learning made by the men of Budé's generation.

Thus, when seventeenth-century men of letters looked back to their predecessors, it was for the purpose of finding a golden age, or the beginning of one, in which patronage, particularly royal patronage, had been great. Instead of constructing a complete genealogy of men of learning from the remote past down to their own day—as they insisted upon doing for kings, royal officers, municipal, provincial, and parlementary officials, and so forth—they were generally content to evoke certain well-known individuals, whose careers and works they depicted in heroic terms. In this way Guillaume Budé became a part of the golden-age *topoi* dealing with the reign of Francis I. His reputa-

16. An alternative explanation should be mentioned. Since there was virtually no ideological controversy about the Francis *topoi* or about the status of men of letters, the *érudits* were not prompted to undertake research. A related point is Pasquier's assertion that the history of the founding of the Collège de France would demonstrate that Francis, not Budé, had come up with the idea in the first place (*Les recherches de la France* [Paris, 1665], p. 794). In the face of the almost numberless assertions that kings were personally responsible for so many initiatives in the patronage of letters and the arts, how do we explain the mechanism by which early-modern men of letters allowed the prince to receive credit for what they had in fact suggested or accomplished? The rivalry among men of letters, whether contemporaries or across generations, may have unconsciously led to attributions of royal initiative in order to tarnish the *gloire* of someone else in the *monde des lettrés*, hence Pasquier's emphasis upon royal initiative in appointing the *lecteurs royaux*.

17. The recent general work on this subject is Claude-Gilbert Dubois,

tion among the *doctes* and *éloquans* had assumed heroic proportions before his death in 1548.[18] Although it may not have functioned as a powerful historicized model of conduct for writers during the seventeenth century, in the reign of Louis XIV his name was still among the earliest and most prestigious of those great men of learning and eloquence included in the French pantheon.[19]

As the Petrarch of France, Budé endeared himself to later generations of men of letters through his life, his works, and his reputation as a man of learning and a successful promoter of learning before the King. Like Francis I's reputation as a patron, however, his career was not scrutinized to find out just how successful he had been at gaining pensions for himself and for others. Rather, succeeding generations of men of letters debated the significance of his political functions as ambassador.[20] The importance of this debate will become clearer later. Men of letters seem to have shown no desire to learn about his shortcomings or tarnish his image as a learned man who had earned recognition from his king and from the other learned men of Europe.[21] Throughout later French literary history, Budé would be described as *un des nôtres*, a national cultural hero. That his career and achieve-

Celtes et Gaulois au XVIᵉ siècle (Paris, 1972), *passim*. The historical scholarship of the legal humanists on cultural and linguistic topics remained largely at the level of testing and refining, and in some cases refuting, the patriotic assertions of the Pléiade poets. See Jacques Poujol, "Etymologies légendaires des mots France et Gaule pendant la renaissance," *Publications of the Modern Language Association of America* 72 (1957): 900–914.

18. "Depuis longtemps [before his death] l'homme était devenu un symbole: lui-même s'est prêté à l'idéalisation de son personnage" (Guy Gueudet, *Actes du VIIIᵉ Congrès de l'Association Guillaume Budé* [Paris, 1968], p. 602).

19. Louis Moréri, *Le grand dictionnaire historique* . . . , went through numerous editions. That of Paris, 1699, begins the article on Budé by describing his offices as "*conseiller du roi*" and "*maître des requêtes*" and then says: "[Il] est un de ces grands hommes qui a le plus fait d'honneur à son pais par son érudition et son mérite" (vol. 1, p. 577). If Moréri may be considered the more "popular" of the late seventeenth-century encyclopedia writers, Pierre Bayle may perhaps be considered closer to the opinions of the *érudits*. For Bayle, Budé "a été le plus savant homme qui fût de son temps en France" (*Dictionnaire historique et critique* . . . [Rotterdam, 1697], vol. 1, p. 689). Bayle refers to him as "notre Budé" throughout the article, which may indicate not only a national bond of loyalty but also a more personal one as fellow *homme de lettres*.

20. The controversy is summarized by Bayle, vol. 1, pp. 690 f.

21. Bayle's article is laudatory. If Budé's Latin was *rude*, it was owing to the inferior Latin teachers in the France of his day.

ments served as a model for emulation is suggested by the frequent expressions of praise for him.

Early sixteenth-century writers could still believe that ancient Gallic peoples had as ancestors the eloquent Greeks and that among these ancestors were numerous eloquent men equal in rank to the greatest of the Roman writers.[22] The growing national consciousness and the achievements of the men of Budé's generation fed the movement to heroicize Budé, Rabelais, Ronsard, du Bellay, and Marot. The laudatory biographies of the early *doctes* and *éloquans* are so well known that only two will be mentioned here as an indication that such biographies could function as "historical ideals of life." They are Louis Le Roy's *Vita Budaei* (1540),[23] at once a laudatory biography and an exhortation to young men of letters to follow Budé in the path of learning; and Pierre Galland's *Petri Castellani Vita* (1552),[24] another sincere effort to convince readers to model their lives upon that of a recently departed man of learning. All across Europe the laudatory biography, or panegyric, was a genre dear to humanists writing about earlier humanists. Such texts permit us to chart the development of a growing self-awareness among men of letters, a self-awareness that had not existed in medieval society. The *topoi* about learning, the active life, and familiarity with the great varied according to ideological conditions prescribed by the political cultures of which they were a part. Le Roy and Galland both celebrated the familiarity that Budé and Pierre Du Chastel shared with Francis I, implicitly claiming that the courtly ideals about respect for learning shown by the great, and about participation by the *doctes* and *éloquans* in the active life of government, had been realized under that monarch. The *déjeuners* that Francis held for the learned were offered as proof that royal recognition of learning had really happened; and, in a sense, both Le Roy's and Galland's works resemble advice books on how a young man who has only intelligence, patrons, and learning, and not aristocratic birth or military accomplishments, ought to conduct himself at court.

Recognized as leaders among the *doctes* and *éloquans* at court, these men of learning had attracted younger men of letters seeking favor and thus had served as direct models of conduct for their disciples. Competition developed among aspiring young authors at Francis's

22. On the history of the myth about the literary achievements of the Gauls, see Dubois, pp. 49 f.

23. Werner L. Gundersheimer, *The Life and Works of Louis Le Roy* (Geneva, 1966), pp. 60 f.: "It is in the light of his persuasive aims that his idolatrous praise for both Budé and Francis I may best be judged."

24. Doucet, pp. 1 ff.

court, all of them seeking recognition by Budé, Du Chastel, and other men of letters with established reputations. Mastery of ancient languages; personal conduct; and abilities as editors, translators, poets, and panegyricists were of great importance when Budé, Du Chastel, and members of the royal family came to determine the degree of recognition the king should bestow upon any one individual.

Existing evidence would probably be insufficient to permit a complete reconstruction of the dependencies linking the younger men of letters to their elders. Yet the *vitae* of Budé and Du Chastel alone reveal enough about these dependencies[25] and the consequent recognition and pensions for us to infer that a structure of clientage for men of letters had already developed among the partisans of the "new learning" during the reign of Francis I. The personal bonds—that is, bonds based upon the dependence of the younger and less reputed *doctes* and *éloquans* upon older colleagues with established reputations—conformed to the general model of courtly behavior. Great noblemen, and noble ecclesiastics in particular, had their clients among the younger men of letters at court. These younger men often sought to be pleasing and to render service to all the *gros personnages* in attendance upon the prince; but as the reputation of an individual became known publicly, it also usually became known that he was under the protection of the chancellor, or some great nobleman, or the king himself. As the star of a relatively unknown young man of letters brightened, did the powerful rush in to offer their services as patrons? Le Roy and Galland reveal that Budé and Du Chastel prided themselves on their familiarity with every promising young man of learning.

By no means as complex and bureaucratic as the system created by Jean Chapelain and Colbert after 1660, the courtly dependencies among Francis I's men of letters nevertheless were sufficiently well developed to establish patterns of favor among *doctes* and *éloquans*. Could combat among men of letters in the lists for royal recognition, or for recognition by the chancellor or some other *gros personnage*, be avoided? In the seventeenth century the principal way of avoiding such competition lay in withdrawing to the country and enhancing one's reputation by carrying on a brilliant correspondence with those who had succeeded Budé and Du Chastel as brokers of royal patronage. This

25. Including the patrons who first presented Budé and Du Chastel to the court, notably Chancellors Guy de Rochefort and Antoine du Prat. The role of the chancellors as intermediaries between the prince and men of letters, jurists, and university professors merits further research. The point of departure is provided by Hélène Michaud, *La grande chancellerie et les écritures royales au XVIe siècle* (Paris, 1967), pp. 23 ff. See also Gundersheimer, p. 10.

was the solution favored by Jean Louis Guez de Balzac;[26] he may have been influenced by several notable *doctes* and *éloquans* of the sixteenth century who had withdrawn from court life in this manner.

As a distinct model of conduct with its interlocking and hierarchical dependencies, the courtly ideal for men of letters ought not to be defined as conflicting with clerical or aristocratic cultures. Very few elements of monastic, university, or aristocratic life were rejected by the *doctes* and *éloquans*. Some exceptions readily come to mind. For clerical culture the rejected elements were more often philosophical and stylistic than social or religious, but throughout the *Ancien Régime* men of letters wearing cassocks presented themselves at court—testifying to the continuity in the relationships between clerical and courtly styles of life.

It would, however, be intriguing to test the possibility that the *vitae* of sixteenth-century men of letters led to the development of a structure of attributes that was similar in function to those attributes given French kings in histories of France. Tyvaert's method might well be applied to a collection of the most frequently republished *vitae* of men of letters in an attempt to discern whether changes in these attributes occurred[27] or whether they remained relatively constant. Learning and eloquence are attributes. In biographies of men of letters they are rarely defined but are instead merely stated as part of an *exemplum*. We are reminded of the structure of royal attributes—piety, justice, military courage, and patronage of men of letters—discerned by Tyvaert. The later collective biographies, notably those by François Grudé de La Croix du Maine, Antoine du Verdier, and André Thevet, which appeared almost simultaneously in the early 1580s, provided the bulk of the general knowledge that seventeenth-century men of letters would have about their predecessors.[28]

26. See below, p. 157.

27. See above, pp. 15–17.

28. The integrations of medieval writers (Pasquier referred to the chroniclers as "nos bons vieux pères") proceeded rapidly after the Pléiade and the legal humanists almost simultaneously threw off the cloak of reverence for Italian learning and letters. Inspired by Fauchet and Pasquier are La Croix du Maine, *Premier volume de la Bibliotheque qui est un catalog general de toutes sortes d'autheurs qui ont escrit en françois despuis cinq cents ans et plus jusques a ce jour d'huy* (Paris, 1584); du Verdier, *La Bibliotheque . . . contenant le catalogue de tous ceux qui ont escrit, ou traduict en françois, et autres dialectes de ce royaume ensemble leurs oeuvres imprimées et non imprimees . . .* (Lyon, 1585); and Thevet, *Histoire des plus illustres et scavans hommes et leurs siecles* (Paris, 1584, reprinted Paris, 1970). By "illustres" Thevet meant chiefly conquerors and kings from Antiquity

Related to the question of whether a structure of attributes for men of letters did indeed exist is the problem of the degree to which the genre of the *vita* impeded the inclusion of more personal information about men of letters, negative judgments about them, and unflattering or ignoble acts they may have committed. Roger Doucet seems mystified by the paucity of information about the personal life and conduct of Du Chastel.[29] His observation reminds us of the criticism so frequently made about the lack of personal ancedote or human qualities in humanist biographies of French kings. Were not the classicist definitions of what is worthy of being recalled at work in both the *vitae* of kings and the *vitae* of men of letters, effectively excluding the more personal elements because they were unedifying?

From the perspective of seventeenth-century political culture, it is the attribute of dependence upon the patron that deserves exploration. My research on the *vitae* has admittedly been cursory, but I have found no attributes stressing the desirability of independence from patrons. During the upheavals of the later sixteenth century, individuals critical of despotism, absolutism, and the royal court would condemn men of letters who flattered princes in order to promote their own *gloire*.[30] Yet the courtly ideal itself, with its psychological component of the dependence of the *doctes* and *éloquans* upon the patron, was not subject to extensive examination and criticism.[31] Although objections may have been raised about the actions of a specific patron or court—even a royal

---

to his own day; and under "scavans" he included Alcuin, Peter Lombard, Saint Bernard, Saint Thomas Aquinas, John Duns Scotus, Gerson, Pierre d'Ailly, Avicenna, and Averroes, extending the category even to Gutenberg! For earlier examples see John W. O'Malley, "Some Renaissance Panegyrics of Aquinas," *Renaissance Quarterly* 27 (1974): 174–192. See also Nathan Edelman, *Attitudes of Seventeenth-Century France toward the Middle Ages* (New York, 1946), pp. 90–93; and Claude Longeon, *Une province française à la renaissance: La vie intellectuelle en Forez au XVIe siècle* (Saint-Etienne, 1975), pp. 555 ff.

29. Doucet, p. 214.

30. Notably in the *Tragiques* of Agrippa d'Aubigné; see Françoise Joukovsky, *La gloire dans la poésie française et néolatine du XVIe siècle* (Geneva, 1969), pp. 294 ff.

31. One way of clarifying these issues might be an attempt to discern whether the *érudits*' increasing awareness of medieval administration facilitated a resolution of the contradiction between *fidélités* and offices as it had been defined in Cicero. Also at work is a Protestant sense of duty—particularly in writing history, but very possibly in government as well—powerfully evoked by Donald Kelley, "History as a Calling: The Case of La Popelinière," *Renaissance Studies in Honor of Hans Baron*, ed. Anthony Molho and John A. Tedeschi (Florence, 1971), pp. 773–889.

court—succeeding generations of men of letters persisted in passing down the same courtly model of conduct to their heirs.

Although the writers of the seventeenth century believed that Francis's patronage had created new possibilities for men of letters, many of these men remained quite immured in clerical culture. Others spent their lives as royal officials or were in some way nominally affiliated with the legal profession; still others practiced medicine or, as noblemen, avoided anything that might be considered a profession, preferring to make military service their way of life. Yet the models of conduct for clerical and robe culture would coexist with that of the court, although both the *doctes* and the *éloquans* would become increasingly attracted to the courtly model. When the need for recognition was particularly strong, or when the court seemed to be offering little recognition, men of letters would attempt to band together and found academies. With their protectors, charters, and rituals, these academies partially satisfied the need for recognition and protection felt by men of letters who had either virtually severed their ties with clerical or robe culture, or who were aspiring to a higher social status than clerical and robe identities could provide. Movements to found academies occurred when social and religious conflict disturbed the functioning of courtly culture and when Louis XIII himself paid almost no attention to literary matters.[32] Nor should the founding of academies be defined as anticourtly. Quite the contrary. More of a supplement to existing identities and patronage than a substitute for them, the academies offered recognition for learning and eloquence. This recognition in turn increased and systematized the patron's power, while protecting members from the often intense conflicts among patrons. The key factors were dependency and royalism as they shaped the writing and function of historical thought.

Writers and History in the *Institution du prince*

Budé's *Institution du Prince* was not published until 1547.[33] By then it's authors own activities during the preceding years had already in-

32. Frances Yates, *French Academies in the Sixteenth Century* (London, 1947), Chap. 12.

33. Louis Delaruelle, *Guillaume Budé, les origines, les débuts, les idées maîtresses* (Paris, 1907), pp. 199–220 and 228–245; and Madeleine Foisil, "Guillaume Budé," *Le Conseil du Roi de Louis XII à la Révolution*, ed. Ro-

fluenced the formation of models of conduct for men of letters. Nevertheless, the *Institution* confirmed and reinforced what was already known about Budé's efforts to increase royal patronage of learning and eloquence.[34] The *Institution* constituted Budé's most succinct statement about how both kings and men of letters could benefit from royal patronage.[35]

If read at all during the seventeenth century, the *Institution* must have appeared a crude and self-serving appeal for money and recognition. During that century the Pléiade's movement to purify French grammar and remove from the vocabulary all "base" words—including allusions to money—would eventually culminate in a change in sensibilities within courtly culture. Budé's frequent allusions to pensions and to the size of pensions in Antiquity, combined with the generally self-promoting tone of the *Institution*, would have made the work seem vulgar in Versailles. Nevertheless, though the tone and nuances used to evoke the delicate issues of money and titles changed from one century to another, the *Institution* and the actual patronage sponsored by Richelieu and by Louis XIV have many affinities.

As an exhortation about the advantages of an association between men of letters and the prince, the *Institution* reveals Budé's view of the ideal relationship between men of letters and men of power. The usual themes common to the mirror-of-princes genre, notably the moral obligations of Christian kings, are scarcely mentioned. Budé displays his classical learning to convince Francis I of the advantages to be gained from associating men of letters to his person. The arguments are supported by historical evidence culled from the Bible and from ancient Greek and Roman sources.

Did not Maecenas, Alexander the Great, Solomon, Vespasian, Caesar, and Caesar Augustus grant pensions to men of letters and recognize the value of learning and eloquence? The implication is that if Francis wishes his name to be raised to a rank equal to that of the great rulers of Antiquity, the patronage of belles lettres is indispensable.

Similarly, Aristotle, Quintilian, Athenodorus, Virgil, Horace, and Plutarch are mentioned as having received patronage. The great rulers and great men of letters are not always paired directly. Budé may have recognized that such a pairing would weaken his argument, for he

---

land Mousnier (Paris, 1970), pp. 277–292. There were three different editions in that year; cf. Bontems, Raybaud, and Braucourt, p. 3.

34. The theme appears in *De Asse*; Delaruelle, pp. 159 f.

35. Budé returned to these themes once more in the preface to his *Commentarii linguae graecae* in 1549. See David O. McNeil, *Guillaume Budé and Humanism in the Reign of Francis I* (Geneva, 1975), pp. 89 f.

would be obliged to match a relatively obscure ruler with an illustrious man of letters, and vice versa. The undisputed fame of the persons mentioned forms the skeleton of his loose, historicized structure of literary patronage in Antiquity.

In France, he points out, patronage has declined to a remarkable degree since Antiquity, for: "Se depuys le commancement des roys de France il y eust eu gens scavans et éloquens en France, et que les roys eussent fait estime d'eulx, la nation francoyse fust autant estimée que nulle autre après les Romains. Car les Francoys ont fait de grans choses qui n'ont pas bien esté mises par escript, au moyen de quoy on n'en fait compte aujourduy, néant plus que des cronicques de France qui se font par les moynes de Sainct Denis."[36] In this brief statement Budé sums up the history of the dire consequences of inadequate patronage, announces a program for the future, and reveals the inferiority he feels vis-à-vis the literary achievements of Antiquity. The assertion that this decline had not been caused by the lack of illustrious deeds on the part of the French nation, but rather by the lack of talented writers to record them, already had a history; and over the next two centuries this assertion would be repeated in numerous prospectuses for histories of France.[37]

Budé blames the Monarchy for the French failure to achieve recognition as having accomplished *grandes choses*, and he appeals to Francis to correct this sorry state of affairs by awarding pensions and recognition to men of letters.

In Budé's description of the Middle Ages the golden-age *topoi* are merely reversed.[38] The absence of royal patronage is given as an explanation for the mediocrity of medieval historical writings. Budé seems blind to the possibility that men of letters themselves, or clerical culture as a whole, might be responsible for these failures. His eyes are fixed on Ancient Rome as the measure of all achievements, both literary and political. In the *Institution*, Budé does not take the trouble to discuss the inadequacies of aristocratic and bourgeois patronage; he takes such inadequacies for granted, owing to both his belief in a prince-centered historical thought and his faith in the efficacy of antique models as a means of instructing the young Francis. In the *De asse* he had scolded aristocratic patrons who had supported Italian men of letters, which he saw as a betrayal of French letters;[39] but here he relies on the power of the names of Alexander, Aristotle, Caesar, Virgil, Horace,

36. Budé, *Institution*, p. 90.
37. See below, p. 66.
38. Budé, *Institution*, p. 90.
39. The complaints about patrons who have supported Italian men of learning are cited by Delaruelle, p. 163.

and Caesar Augustus to convince the King that patronage of letters is an indispensable complement to military conquest, and that, combined, the two can assure immortality.[40]

In discussing Jacob Wimpheling's historical thought, Frank Borchardt remarks that his "heroes are all either emperors or scholars."[41] The same may be said for Budé's biographies in the *Institution*, although the men of power and the men of letters of the Ancient World whom he discusses would not have unanimously accepted the Germanic definitions of "emperor" and "scholar." Our attention is caught by Budé's easy use of the term *gens de lettre* [sic] for the poets, philosophers, historians, and rhetoricians of Antiquity. The projection of this definition upon Antiquity reveals Budé's willingness to lump all men of letters together when describing and justifying their functions to a man of power. This mechanism of projecting sixteenth-century models of conduct upon the past and of bringing kings, emperors, and ancient men of letters forward from Antiquity as *exempla* to instruct Francis was the central characteristic of premodern historical thinking, with all of its survivals and resurgences still apparent in the twentieth century.[42]

For Budé the subjects of historical thought scarcely extended beyond the actions of men of power and the interests of the *doctes* and *éloquans*. Budé never once points out any possible objections to these relationships, especially as far as the dependent relationship of letters to power is concerned. His failure to see the dangers of dependence upon the prince resulted from the coherent and self-contained vision of monarchical political culture in which he had been raised and in support of which he bent his great learning. Yet he made some harsh assessments of Louis XII's policies; hence he must have believed that his prince would be open to views about past and present politics and would not remove him from favor. A prince would always be threat-

40. The program announced in the *Institution* was not original with Budé. Gaguin's appeals for recognition almost fifty years earlier, as we shall see in Chapter II, contain many of the same themes. The monks of Saint-Denis were less to be scorned than pitied, but how could Budé really believe that royal support had been lacking for these monks?

41. *German Antiquity in Renaissance Myth* (Baltimore, 1971), p. 101. Hannah Gray touches on how Petrarch and his successors looked upon Cicero's oration *Pro Archia* as a "sacred text" because a passage in it "celebrated the role of letters as bestowing glory upon subject and author alike, maintaining that letters provide the best, even the exclusive vehicle of immortality for men, deeds, and ideas" ("Renaissance Humanism: The Pursuit of Eloquence," *Journal of the History of Ideas* 24 (1963): 503.

42. J. H. Plumb, *The Death of the Past* (Boston, 1970), *passim*.

ened with isolation from political and social realities unless he had
"livres parlans de régime de peuple et de l'office de roy" about him,
enabling him to learn about those subjects who were not courtly
familiers. These and other *topoi* regarding the dangers of courtly life
for the prince give the *Institution* a broader significance than that implied by the central theme—that is, the advantages that men of power
gain from having men of letters in their service—yet these *topoi* all
hinge effectively on the presence of men of letters at court. Who would
give such advice to the prince in the event that Budé and others like
him were excluded from the royal presence?

When Budé describes the advantages of associating men of letters
with the court, he relies almost entirely upon the *topoi* concerning the
value of historical knowledge for those who govern. Knowledge of the
previous actions of men of power and of the customs of various peoples may contribute to "vertu et prudence, laquelle [congnoissance] est
nécessaire aux roys plus que à nulz autres, et elle se acquiert par ex-
périence, par exemples, par enseignemens des gens scavans du temps
passé, et par la lecture des histoires avec le bon sens et jugement naturel."[43] Budé is so earnest about the value of historical knowledge for
governing that he includes some flowers for Francis I to ponder immediately.[44] Through these flowers from the past we can perceive the
problems that Budé expected the young King to encounter. It was with
intense dedication to the service of his prince that Budé searched the
past for knowledge that would help Francis. Were the flowers that
Budé offered already part of the mirror-of-princes genre, that is, *topoi*
on the art of governance? Or had Budé, with his erudition and his
knowledge of Greek, found new flowers to present to the King? Some
of them, notably the discussion of Persian (Budé admired the Persian
Monarchy) and Carthaginian customs involving capital punishment of
rebellious great nobles, have a chillingly immediate and absolutist tone.[45]
To answer the questions of whether or not these were in fact new con-
tributions to the mirror-of-princes genre would take us far beyond the
boundaries of this study. But the flowers do indicate Budé's attempt

43. *Institution*, p. 139.

44. *Ibid.*, p. 91.

45. Budé admired the harsh laws against rebels, because severity permitted the prince to grant dramatic acts of clemency. This argument in
favor of harsh laws against rebellious nobles deserves investigation from
the perspectives of (1) its place in absolutist political thought, (2) its place
in jurisprudence, and (3) its place in the context of antiaristocratic thought
on the part of bourgeois and barely noble royal officials (*ibid.*, p. 100). See
Dora M. Bell, *L'idéal éthique de la royauté en France au moyen âge* (Geneva, 1962), Chap. 9.

to reach into Francis's mind by demonstrating his awareness of the critical issues affecting princely *majestas*. He does this behind a veil of historical knowledge, but the implications are no less explicit.

Throughout the *Institution* the motivational devices implicit in the *exempla* are effectively worked out to encourage the King to pursue his star by emulating the heroic rulers of Antiquity and by relying upon the services of men of letters to immortalize him. A man of letters, when given pensions and recognition, "récite honorablement et par hault style, les gestes et mérites des roys dignes de loz et de gloire."[46] This service of immortalizing the actions of princes and nations, Budé implies, may be performed solely by men of letters. He does not encourage Francis to attempt to write his own history. The *topos* that Alexander the Great preferred to have his notable actions forgotten, rather than have them recorded by "gens à faire non suffisans,"[47] is included to exhort Francis to take very seriously the dual foundations of immortality: heroic actions and patronage of belles lettres. The emphasis upon *hault style* reveals Budé's understanding of and sincere admiration for the *ars historica*, that legacy from the rhetoricians of Antiquity that had inspired humanist movements throughout Europe during the Middle Ages.[48] Quintilian's and Cicero's notions of the functions of historical thought are specifically referred to and held up as ideal principles for writers to follow.

Moreover, at no point did Budé suggest that the writers of history should attempt to instruct by recording the mistakes of those great men whose actions constitute history. Thus he lent his enormous prestige and personal conduct to the humanist rhetorical movement of his own day that fused panegyric, biography, and history into a single didactic literature about past heroic deeds of heroic men.[49] To Budé's mind, the principal historical work of Greek and Roman history was written

46. Budé, *Institution*, p. 79.

47. *Ibid.*, p. 86.

48. For a discussion of the tradition of the *ars historica*, see Girolamo Cotroneo, *I trattatisti dell' "Ars Historica"* (Naples, 1971), *passim*. A more general perspective is developed by Richard W. Southern, "Aspects of the European Tradition of Historical Writing, I: The Classical Tradition from Einhard to Geoffrey of Monmouth," Royal Historical Society, *Transactions* 5th ser., 20 (1970): 173–196.

49. Budé seems not to have distinguished between the classical genres of history and biography. Christopher P. Jones observes that "Polybius had distinguished biography from history as a field closer to formal laudation, in which the writer was bound to magnify the actions of his subject" (*Plutarch and Rome* [Oxford, 1971], p. 88).

by Plutarch, some of whose works he had already helped to popularize by translating from Greek to Latin.[50]

Alexander, Caesar Augustus, and Pompey are described as without blemish. We find none of the *topoi* included by medieval writers when they wished to be critical of Alexander.[51] The encouragement of war that pervades the first part of the work is tempered by allusion to the virtue of administration as exemplified by Augustus,[52] and to the "sérénité de renommée sans aucune nubilosité de vergongne et de reproche"[53] evident in Pompey's *gloire*; but it is Alexander who always serves as the measure for *gloire*. While condemning outright conquest, Budé equivocates about recovering territories to which France had claims. The possibility of war with Germany, that state with solid limbs but a weak torso, led him to warn of atrocities that German soldiers might commit should they invade France; but he adds that it "seems desirable to have the Empire joined to the realm as it used to be."[54] Budé attempted to discern Francis's preoccupations and to bring the lessons of history to bear on them.

The psychological dimensions of the Budean oeuvre confirm his attachment to the Plutarchian mode of instructing the young by parallels and portraits. Through these "historical ideals of life" drawn from ancient kings, he sought to instruct the young Francis in the same manner used by the tutors of Charles the Bold to encourage their pupil to emulate Alexander.[55] Budé makes no attempt to balance either Christian or ancient moral thought against the lessons of history. Indeed, it seems to have been his explicit purpose not to do so. The allusions to prudence are just that: exhortations to behave in a certain way, but with-

---

50. *Institution*, p. 81. He describes Plutarch as a *domestique de Trajan*. No denigration is meant by this description; the phrase ought probably be translated as "servant of Trajan" in the early-modern English sense that has survived in such expressions of courtesy as "your obedient servant."

51. George Cary observes that he was able to find only two unfavorable references to Alexander in medieval books of *exempla* and that both were about Alexander's alleged encounter with Diogenes. The anti-Alexander *exempla* of the Middle Ages derived from a theological tradition condemning the king for his arrogant pride (*The Medieval Alexander* [Cambridge, 1956], p. 157). Budé does not include a Diogenes *exemplum* in the *Institution*.

52. *Institution*, p. 112.

53. *Ibid.*, p. 130.

54. *Ibid.*, p. 116.

55. Johan Huizinga, "Historical Ideals of Life," *Men and Ideas*, trans. James S. Holmes and Hans van Marle (New York, 1959), p. 77.

out explicit historical examples that might convince the King of the benefits of prudence. In mirrors of princes, the balances between moral and historical arguments are always difficult to assess; but the degree to which moral arguments are supported by historical examples offers a clue to the fundamental tenor of a work. Historicized morals are more edifying than those that are not historicized. Budé never once presents an example of kingly, Christian piety for Francis to emulate. The only French monarch discussed at all is Louis XI, whose policies Budé admired.

Budé's research unearthing flowers from the past definitely had been determined by his preconceptions of the knowledge the prince *ought* to desire about the past. Take, for example, Budé's elation at discovering what he thought to be the correct interpretation of Aristotelian justice in a monarchy. It matters little whether Budé correctly understood Aristotle; his enthusiasm over the discovery is the more interesting because he believed that he had found a bit of historical knowledge to be employed in enhancing royal claims to render justice above and beyond that of the regular courts of law.[56]

Returning to his thought regarding the usefulness of patronage, it is also significant that Budé stresses the benefits of eloquence over those of learning. The *Institution* includes arguments for the financial support of the hours of labor doing research, but the tenor of the work stresses the immediate benefits that eloquence will bring to Francis. At one point, in a brief and brilliant description of eloquence, Budé proposes what would one day become the entire linguistic and rhetorical reform of the Pléiade and their classicizing disciples.[57] Budé was incapable of imagining that either learning or eloquence might go astray in a patron's service; yet his blindness, or his inability to conceive of learning outside the framework of courtly culture, appears to have elicited no comment from such later men of letters as Pasquier and Bodin.[58]

Seen as a whole, the Budean ideal of the dependence of the man of letters upon a patron, and his arguments in favor of placing both learning and eloquence in the patron's service, could serve as a model of conduct for the generations of men of letters appearing after 1540.

56. *Institution*, p. 80.

57. *Ibid.*, p. 89. "Eloquence est une science qui peut honnestement, haultement et suffisamment parler de toutes choses, c'est assavoir des petites choses promptement et subtilement, des moyennes doulcement et gravement, des grandes haultement et magnificquement et en manière que les escoutans s'en émerveillent."

58. See below, p. 76.

Although such a career and way of thinking were not typical, it was Budé's great success and renown, rather than his obscurity, that make the Budean model atypical. Were there other alternative or anti-Budean models for young men of letters to emulate? Each genre brought with it special elements; no budding poet could identify completely with Budé, but on the issue of dependency upon a patron, there would be near convergence of views. The views on patronage held by the poets of the Pléiade, and their historicization of these views by evoking the Virgil–Caesar Augustus *topos*, are too well known to require elaboration here.[59]

Yet Budé could scarcely have foreseen how this early sixteenth-century model would be refined by later generations. The changing fortunes of the *grands* and the rise and decline of a robe culture would lead men of letters to enhance the definition of *gloire*, that is, recognition that only the prince could bestow upon a man of letters. This inflation of princely recognition would reinforce the Budean model rather than undermine it. Who but the prince could bestow ultimate favor on this earth? Budé may have been incapable of asking this question, but his career reveals that princely recognition may have been even more important to him than recognition by the most eminent among his fellow men of letters.[60] With all its contradictions, shifts, and ambiguities, the Erasmian distance from powerful political cultures may not have been consciously rejected by Budé; he may simply have been incapable of perceiving it.[61] France, not Christendom, constituted a sufficient sphere of action and recognition for him.

59. Antoinette Roubichou-Stretz, *La vision de l'histoire dans l'oeuvre de la Pléiade* (Paris, 1973), Chap. 1.

60. On Budé's own courtly behavior, we ought not take his scornful remarks about court life too seriously (McNeil, p. 97). What prevented him from withdrawing from court? The courtier's remarks about the *ennui* and corruption of the court are *topoi* that remind us of men who either seek power or have it and who allude to their own retirement as something they desire above anything else. In early-modern courts, the expressions of repugnance to court life helped prepare a courtier psychologically for the disgrace that might fall upon him at any moment. Need we recall Budé's treatise on hunting (McNeil, p. 6), crude though it is as a work of courtly literature, if we wish to emphasize his desire to be courtly? See A. J. Krailsheimer, *Rabelais and the Franciscans* (Oxford, 1963), p. 3.

61. Erasmus remarked in a letter to Gaguin that the essential qualities of a historian are *fides et eruditio*, not *eloquentia et doctrina* (Myron Gilmore, *Humanists and Jurists: Six Studies in the Renaissance* [Cambridge, Mass., 1963], pp. 87 ff.). On the question of whether a writer ought to include evidence of cowardly or immoral acts committed by the person he is de-

Learning and Eloquence

For the subsequent generations of men of letters, the excitement generated by philology and the application and adaptation of classical
rhetoric to French would create whole, virtually self-contained philosophical and linguistic movements that expanded almost beyond recognition the rather humble notions of learning and eloquence familiar
to Budé and his contemporaries.[62]

Out of these preoccupations of the Pléiade would come the challenge
to write histories in which the skills of the rhetorician almost single-
handedly could be relied upon to give France a history on the Livian
model. The excitement generated by this challenge is difficult for us
to measure. We are accustomed to thinking of rhetoric as essentially
a given or almost constant, unchanging element in a culture. Thus we
find it difficult to assess the excitement, power, and outright intellectual arrogance that rhetoric was capable of generating when associated
with a linguistic movement aimed at "purifying" both the Latin and
the vernacular tongues used by the entire *monde des lettrés*. The claims
of the *éloquans* that "research" would be almost superfluous may seem
absurd to us; and if we must be shocked into the realization that philology, which seems so attractive to us, might appear a poor stepchild
in this movement, it is useful to recall the arrogant claims of twentieth-
century structural linguists that they can create a new past without
philology.

Among the *doctes* a passion developed to discover more and more
choses curieuses about the past, and they attempted to convey to their
readers the sheer pleasure of unearthing hitherto "unknown" historical
facts. The elaboration of this philological approach on the basis of
already familiar texts, and subsequently on all others, led some men of
letters to lash out at rhetoric as hostile to truth. As philological preoccupations increased, the *doctes* showed an increasing desire to publish integrally the texts of ancient times, especially since all the while
the *éloquans* were robbing them of the possibility of narrating their
findings in the honest, if "impolite," prose to which they were accustomed. The *éloquan* would scorn the antiquarian as pedantic, while the
docte could only reply that the history written by the *éloquan* was full

---

scribing, Erasmus favored their inclusion, arguing that these could be just
as instructive as heroic acts. See J. B. Maguire, "Erasmus' Biographical Mas-
terpiece: *Hieronymi Strideonensis Vita*," *Renaissance Quarterly* 26 (1973):
265–273.

62. Paul Zumthor, *Langue, Texte, Enigme* (Paris, 1975), *passim*.

of falsehoods. It will not be my purpose here to demonstrate the linkages and cleavages that developed in the *monde des lettrés* as a result of these rhetorical and philological movements; but it is useful to suggest that these movements tended to create two subgroups within that world. Both could look back upon Budé as a common ancestor, and both could still pursue the courtly ideal that his career represented. Indeed, most, if not quite all, of the senior and most respected men of letters—whether rhetoricians or *érudits*—were in the royal service as historiographers, librarians, or archivists, sat in royal law courts, or were included on the pension lists of the royal households.

Kings and chancellors, faithful perhaps to the lessons taught by Budé and by their own humanist preceptors, continued to offer pensions and titles to both *doctes* and *éloquans*. The intellectual sophistication prompted by rhetoric and philology may have created tensions in the *monde des lettrés*, but these tensions did not fundamentally alter relationships with the Crown or with French political culture. In the course of the sixteenth century it became apparent that the sophistication and talents of both *doctes* and *éloquans* could serve the needs of the prince.

In their near obsession with panegyric, the *éloquans* attempted to satisfy the increasing curiosity of French readers and to meet their need to identify with the prince's *gloire*. This growing reading public eagerly snatched up printed matter dealing with the *gestes* of the French in the remote past, with ceremonies at court, and with the military actions of the ruling prince. The rhetorical movement itself reinforced a public demand for eloquent history. A growing national consciousness, supported by increased literacy and the availability of printed books, sustained what was perceived as the noble literary genre, a genre that had been much admired by the ancient Greeks and Romans.

The function of the *doctes* was to supply precise documentary evidence about the past that might bear favorably on current political and ecclesiastical conflicts. In some instances these conflicts focused upon the exact interpretation of some political, constitutional, or ceremonial right; in others they were of a more general nature, as exemplified in Théodore Godefroy's synthetic work on the entire ceremonial of the French court.

The research into hitherto unknown or unread documents—chronicles or royal charters, for example—pushed the origins of the major European institutional-diplomatic controversies further and further back in time and had the effect of refining them by adding layer upon layer of documentation to very old differences of opinion between French kings and other contenders for European dominance, principally the popes and the emperors. To the great benefit of historical scholarship, the *doctes* and the diplomats who presented their evidence in actual negotiations never seem to have realized that expanded and ever-better historical evidence would not assure France's victory either in a court of law or in negotiations among states. Thus the process of digging up masses of hitherto ignored evidence on such subjects as the early Church, the Franks, or the Carolingian Empire continued, in the hope that such research would undermine the adversaries of French claims.

French ministers and kings, certainly Richelieu and Louis XIV, watched this process from a distance and probably had little confidence in it as an arm for advancing French prestige.[63] Though recognizing the necessity for such research (other sovereigns had researcher-historiographers doing similar work), when it came to formulating policies, these statesmen preferred to rely primarily on direct negotiations pragmatically determined, or on threats and guns, rather than on historical footnotes. Though historical precedent remained a first line of defense, as the seventeenth century wore on, fewer and fewer diplomats and sovereigns took seriously the legalistic outlook that had predominated during the sixteenth century; they believed less and less that historical knowledge of the origins of claims or conflicts could contribute to the resolution of differences among states. Indeed, if we attempted to assess just how significant the works of the *doctes* were to Richelieu and Louis XIV, we would find that both men were far more interested in and committed to the nonerudite writers of elegant history, especially those attempting to write in such a way as to gain a large reading public.

The *curiositez*[64] published by the *doctes*, either as documents published in extenso or as excerpts in pamphlets promoting French claims, also served to keep the numerically small but politically significant international community of scholars and jurists friendly to, or at least informed about, current French diplomatic and ecclesiastical politics. In France this group was significant politically during the sixteenth century. After Richelieu and the writers he sponsored—Théophraste Renaudot and the *Gazette*, the Academy—and the flood of Mazarinades, the influence of the learned upon the more general reading public declined steadily.

63. When it suited his aims in negotiations, Richelieu would cite historical precedent, including the works of such *érudits* as Jean du Tillet. See Pierre Grillon, ed., *Les papiers de Richelieu* (Paris, 1975), vol. 1, p. 85.

64. For an introduction to the meaning of *curieux* and *curiositez*, see Louis A. Olivier, "Curieux, Amateurs, et Connoisseurs, Laymen and the Fine Arts in the Ancien Régime," Ph.D. dissertation, The Johns Hopkins University, 1976, Chap. 1.

Yet the Monarchy's need for learned historical research persisted throughout the century.[65] Every political and religious controversy had its historical dimensions, and there was always at least something of a public to be influenced by historical evidence. This need assured the continuity of scholarly research throughout the century; indeed, it preoccupied several historiographers for most of their lives. The vast bulk of edited chronicles, learned introductions, summaries, and dictionaries published by the Duchesnes, the Godefroys, the Dupuys, and —though he never was a historiographer royal—even Jean Mabillon, had only tangential political-legal significance for their sovereigns; but this was not for the *érudits'* lack of trying. Like government-sponsored research in more recent times, much of the work had no political or ideological significance. However, since their authors had sought to be as authoritative as possible by publishing texts instead of mere accounts of their findings, the works of the erudite historiographers would contribute to the rise of numerous essentially apolitical debates among scholars, debates that would last for centuries.

Though included on the pension rolls in exactly the same fashion as the others, these erudite historiographers received their appointments at least in part out of recognition for their learning. Great compilers of knowledge who were known for their command of ancient languages, philology, customary laws, and genealogy, they often gathered in the royal library and gradually constituted an almost self-contained group of researchers. The volumes upon volumes of research notes they left behind, and their correspondence with other savants, permit the reconstruction of the historical questions preoccupying seventeenth-century scholars, but they rarely shed light on such questions as the exact way these men were selected or with whom they communicated, prior to the rise of Colbert. Yet the facts that in several instances brothers held similar posts as historiographers and librarians royal and that in the case of the Duchesnes a son succeeded his father suggest that these posts were filled more after the manner of a *charge*, or office, than by direct royal favor. Indeed, it is doubtful whether Louis XIII or Richelieu had any familiarity with the researchers whom they sponsored. But in an age when upheavals at the royal court could lead to the disgrace of many courtiers, there is an impressive continuity of appointments in this little group, for most if not all of its members continued to serve for life. Were they still part of the *monde des lettrés?*

65. For a thorough exploration of the relationship between scholarly research, diplomatic negotiations, and pamphleteering, see Joseph Klaits, *Absolutism and Public Opinion: Printed Propaganda under Louis XIV* (Princeton, 1976), p. 74 and *passim.*

In the tradition of La Croix du Maine and du Verdier, but specializing uniquely in works of French history and geography (he was also *géographe du roi*), in 1618 André Duchesne published his *Bibliothèque des autheurs qui ont escrit l'histoire et topographie de la France*.[66] This comprehensive historical bibliography represented the most methodologically advanced work of its kind for historical studies; and the author was certainly an *érudit*. Yet if we explore the work carefully in hopes of finding a clear boundary between the *doctes* and the *éloquans*, we shall be disappointed. The organization is mainly determined by chronology and subject matter. It begins with Gallic and Frankish history and follows the dynasties of French kings through Louis XIII. Here, in roughly chronological order, are the works of ancient authors (one almost hears the Latin resounding in Duchesne's choice of the word "autheurs"), of such medieval writers as Saint Martin of Tours or Alcuin, and of more recent authors such as Nicolas Gilles, Paul Emile, and on down to Scipion Dupleix, a historiographer contemporary with Duchesne. The works of all these authors are lumped together because they narrate French history, or some part thereof.

Next comes a section entitled "Meslanges ou Pièces Particulières," in which we find Jean du Tillet's principal works, du Haillan's *De l'Etat et succès des affaires de France*, Claude de Seyssel's *Grand' Monarchie de France*, Bodin's *Six livres de la république*, Pasquier's *Recherches de la France*, and du Moulin's major works, as well as those of Corrozet and others.[67] At the beginning of his book Duchesne tells his readers that he is going to include both "the good and the bad" books. He offers particular words of praise for Fauchet, Pithou, and Godefroy[68] and implies that their works are more authoritative on certain questions than some of the older works. Nevertheless, the definition of history shared by all members of the *monde des lettrés* has been allowed to determine the categories developed by Duchesne for this

66. I am using the "second edition augmented by more than two hundred authors" (Paris, 1627). Duchesne's publisher was Sébastien Cramoisy, who also published Godefroy and a number of other royally sponsored authors. Were all works published by Cramoisy cited or given preferential treatment by authors attached to him? Duchesne provides some evidence to confirm this supposition. His eagerness to cite the works of his fellow historiographers is also very evident. The solidarity of office seems to have won out over critical perspectives, notably in his emphasis upon the works of Scipion Dupleix.

67. *Bibliothèque des autheurs*, pp. 118 ff.

68. In the section of the book devoted to works on the royal prerogatives.

collection. Narrative works are placed first in the book. The category "Meslanges ou Pièces Particulières," in which Seyssel and Bodin rub elbows with du Tillet and Pasquier, is not the exclusive province of the *doctes*, for although their works include knowledge about the past, their principal intellectual perspective focuses upon philology.

If more evidence is needed concerning the persistent hold of humanistic rhetorical principles upon the organization of historical knowledge, it is to be found in the category of works on chivalric orders and in the "Vies, Eloges, et Oraisons." The works cited in the latter category are hagiographical and panegyrical and can indisputably be classified among the works by the *éloquans*, along with those narrative histories by Emile and du Bellay. There is no evidence to suggest that Duchesne felt constrained to include these works; he expresses his enthusiasm for the more *docte* works and for those by Dupleix and Godefroy, but he views all the authors and works dealing with France as constituting a whole in which the *bon et mauvais* bear no apparent relationship to methodological differences. His *Bibliothèque* concludes with chapters on ecclesiastical and provincial histories. Duchesne was not one to attempt to separate learning from eloquence; one of his own works was a translation of Juvenal's *Satires*. Although purely literary works are listed less frequently among the works of seventeenth-century *érudits* than among those of their forebears, this should not be interpreted as a rejection of the rhetorical principles and notions about history enunciated by the *studia humanitatis*.

After Denys Godefroy, Théodore's oldest son, had spent many years in royal service as historiographer charged with the task of copying and editing charters from the archives of recently captured Lille and Ghent, he proposed to Colbert in 1667 that a new general history of France be prepared. True to humanist conventions, he wrote a prospectus describing the qualities essential in a general history:

> Une des choses qui semblent les plus dignes des glorieux desseins et belles actions de Louis XIV, serait de faire travailler à une histoire générale de France qui contiendrait très-exactement et fidèlement les gestes les plus mémorables de tous les Rois de glorieuse mémoire ses prédécesseurs. La louange très-légitimement due aux hautes vertus et fameux exploits de tous ces héros rejaillira beaucoup sur la vie admirable de notre monarque. C'est sans doute un ouvrage de grande entreprise que l'on n'a point veu jusques à présent dans la perfection qui est à désirer; en quoy l'on peut dire que des nations estrangères ont quelque avantage sur nous. Mais une seule personne ne peut suffire à un si impor-

tant labeur. Il faudroit choisir quelque nombre des plus intelligens
en cette science pour y concourir et contribuer ensemble.[69]

Budé would not have been able to recognize Louis XIV on the basis
of this passage, although dynastic time might have enabled him to es-
timate when in the future a king bearing that numeral might appear;
and he would almost certainly have been able to infer that the particular
king to be praised was French, since the long list of kings called Louis
had already reached twelve in his own day. But Godefroy's proposal
would scarcely have surprised him. Budé had emphasized that through
royal patronage the *plus doués* must be encouraged to write history;
Godefroy's phrase is *des plus intelligens*.

Budé would, however, have had some difficulty following the argument when Godefroy further suggests acknowledging a division of
labor between those "qui ont le talent d'écrire le plus élégamment" and
those who are "les plus scavans et curieux dans les recherches de
l'antiquité," and favored that the two be brought together in a collaborative effort. Some refinement in the meanings of *éloquans* and
doctes is apparent since the days of Budé, but Godefroy perceives both
groups as still a part of the same *monde des lettrés*. Marin Cureau de La
Chambre (Mézerai's close friend), Jacques Cassagne, Louis-Isaac Le
Maître de Sacy, Pellisson, "and others" are proposed for doing the elegant writing, while it is suggested that Amable de Bourzeis, Charles
Lecointe, Christophle Justel, Antoine d'Herouval, Claude de? Denis de?
Sainte-Marthe, Louis le Valois, Duchesne, Baluze, Jean le Laboureur,
"and others" do the research.[70] It is tempting to assert that the Godefroy
prospectus reveals more than the still strong, single identity of men of
letters in the 1660s. It provides a clue to how the *doctes* could claim
that greater numbers of men of letters were needed to accomplish the
tasks set before them by philology, while the *éloquans* remained re-
strictive and asserted that fewer men were required. Godefroy mentions only four *éloquans* but gives nine *doctes*.

Though their identity as men of letters remained vague when
compared with that of the professions, and though both the *doctes* and

69. Addressed to Colbert, 23 November 1667. Denis-Charles Godefroy-
Ménilglaise, *Les savants Godefroy* (Paris, 1873), pp. 171 f.

70. *Ibid.*, p. 172. See George Huppert, " 'La Liberté du Cerveau': Notes
on the Psychology of Erudition," *Mélanges en l'honneur de Fernand Braudel*
(Toulouse, n.d.), vol. 2, p. 275. "The real distinction is between *érudits* and
littérateurs." For the *doctes* of the reformed Maurist Benedictines and their
works, arranged as exemplary biographies, see Filipe Le Cerf, *Bibliothèque
historique et critique des Auteurs de la Congrégation de Saint Maur* (The
Hague, 1726).

the *éloquans* continued to approach the Crown in much the same manner as their predecessors of more than a century earlier, in the end the *doctes* would learn how to relate the expansion of knowledge to bureaucratic growth in the state. In Godefroy's day royal officials still respected the *doctes* and *éloquans* equally, for they had been raised to accept the humanist world-view about the power of "pure language" and historical thought to edify readers and listeners. Budé and his heirs had performed their tasks well.

Chapter II
The Historiographers Royal

THE inscriptions on portraits and the titles after a name on wills, epitaphs, marriage contracts, and title pages of books constituted a code of honors and identities in postmedieval French society. Properly interpreted, this code may be made to reveal the structure of social realities and the aspirations of the men of letters who became historiographers. Although many portraits bear no inscription at all, whenever the sitter's name was inscribed, his titles and arms were almost invariably included. This suggests that once the name was given, the code of honors required that the titles also be included because they formed an integral part of the name. Indeed, were we to explore the code up and down the hierarchy of French society, we might discover a pattern in how these titles were integrated into the name itself.

Officers and Courtiers

Bernard de Girard, sieur du Haillan, offers a good example of a historiographer whose noble status and political rights were integrated directly into his name. The old family name of Girard, probably of nonnoble origin, was supplemented by *sieur du Haillan*.[1] Other titles incorporated into one's name revealed the degrees of perfection of noble status and political rights, ranging from *seigneur de* and *comte de* on up to the highest titles of the peerage and princes of the blood. No

1. His name is recorded thus in the "Dons du Roi Henri III," *Archives historiques et littéraires* 2 (1890–1891): 329, for 29 May 1581. If there is doubt about the relationships between personal identity and portraits, it is useful to recall how Cujas's successor on the law faculty, Imundus Merillius, had the portrait of Cujas removed from his room (where he taught? where he slept? where he did both?): "On disait alors qu'il était en train de réfuter Cujas, mais que le Prince de Condé le lui avait défendu, ce qui prouvait que sa réfutation était sure . . . pour ce motif, il avoit aussi enlevé de sa salle le portrait de Cujas qui y était suspendu (c'est ce que nous disent ses pensionnaires)" (Elie Brackenhoffer, *Voyage en France, 1643–1644*, ed. Henry Lehr [Paris, 1925], p. 156).

man of letters who became historiographer during the sixteenth and seventeenth centuries bore any title higher or any more integrated into his name than did sieur du Haillan. None performed more prestigious political assignments for the Crown. But if du Haillan's status appears to put him at the bottom of those nobles whose titles could be completely integrated into the name, he was nevertheless superior in status to all the others whose titles of nobility could not be so perfectly integrated. The historiographers who purchased an office such as *conseiller du roi* gained nobility in the process, but that nobility was less perfect than du Haillan's. To be sure, the historiographer who became a *conseiller* placed that title immediately after his name on all his portraits, his will, his *rentes*, and so forth, but the degree to which *conseiller* became identical with his name remained less perfect than in du Haillan's case, for the latter could let the Girard slowly disappear over time. There might be occasions when a *conseiller* would be addressed in public as *Monsieur le Conseiller*, with the name of the office substituted altogether for the family name. While indicating political rights, that title also bore connotations of recently acquired nobility.

Among the titles that were very imperfectly integrated into the name we find *secrétaire du roi* and *maître des requêtes* in addition to *conseiller du roi*, and these were the titles that most of the historiographers bore. Still further below, without noble status, were the advocates, procurators, notaries, physicians and surgeons, holders of posts and degrees, and persons with regular and secular ecclesiastical affiliations. None of these individuals was lifted into the second estate, and no one bearing one of these titles as his highest honor could by reason of his office consider himself an active participant in the affairs of state. Service in a provincial estate (Nicolas de Peiresc's portrait by Claude Mellan includes *senator acquiensis* as part of his name) or in an estates general does not always appear to have qualified someone as an active participant in the affairs of state, but the *monde des offices* included the humblest *seigneur* because he was endowed with political rights. Budé claimed that a courtier, or someone merely in attendance upon the king but holding no office, should not be considered an active participant in the affairs of state, because his political right was totally dependent upon the pleasure of the prince.

Genealogists and social historians have proved many times over that the hierarchic code of names occasionally became jumbled or was consciously and willfully distorted. Some titles were added, others deleted; Norman and perhaps other customary laws permitted individuals to add to their names the names of fields they owned (Mézerai); but despite these adjustments and distortions, the code reveals the places in the body politic held by men of letters.

What interests us in the code as it applied to historiographers is not so much their status but the nature and degree of political rights with which their titles endowed them. Present-day historians too often neglect to mention the political rights indicated by the various titles in the code—or the absence of such titles. It is therefore difficult for them to perceive the importance of the debates over the rights and privileges of royal councillors, for example in their battles with the parlement. We must remember that in addition to conferring status, noble rank, no matter how imperfect, allegedly included a degree of authority over others, a sphere of power upon which no one might infringe. For Charles Loyseau, a nobleman was an officer whose rights were directly related to the degree of perfection in his nobility. If a courtier was not also an officer of some sort, he did not possess political rights, for he served merely at the pleasure of the prince. The patron-writer relationship explored in Chapter I could never be completely adjusted to the implicit political distinctions between an officer and a courtier. A courtier could never integrate his favor into his name—unless his patron-prince granted him some title or office that could be listed as a title.

Criticism of historical thought was, if anything, a neglected genre during the Middle Ages. It rarely appears to have included a discussion of a chronicler's individual qualifications to write history. During the fifteenth century the more courtly writers apparently did not conceive of accusing a confrere of lacking qualifications for writing about the past owing to lack of personal political authority or experience. The assertion that proximity to men of power, acceptance of money, or receipt of other favors engenders flattery and adulatory history is so much a part of contemporary historical criticism that its origins have scarcely been explored.[2] This is because such criticism lies on the frontier between ideology—a living, contemporary critical perspective—and historical thought. The same was true in the sixteenth century in the discussions about a historian's qualifications for writing the truth about the past. How could a man of letters who had never been in battle write a military history? How could a man of letters capture the essence of debates in council if he had never attended or participated in a council of state? An officer—in this case anyone who was noble—was less dependent upon the prince because he possessed his own

2. Dorothy Thickett, "Introduction" to a collection of Pasquier's letters in *Choix des lettres sur la littérature, la langue et la traduction* (Geneva, 1956), pp. vii–xxxii. See William Bouwsma, *Venice and the Defense of Republican Liberty* (Berkeley, 1968), p. 140, for a discussion of the equation noble status = active participation in politics as a prerequisite for writing history in a republican political culture.

sphere of authority. Was the result a more truthful account of the past?

Here, in its rudimentary form, we find the beginnings of a critical perspective on historical thought founded upon the identities and rights of the writers themselves. This nascent critical perspective may be found among those robe ideologists whose thought derived from an Aristotelian mode of analyzing the distribution of powers and dignities within the body politic. From this perspective the French *chose publicque* could be perceived as a mixed government containing elements of all three of the desirable forms of government—a polity in some kind of balance. The exploration of ways to write a polity-centered history is a subject beyond the scope of this study, but it is important to note that, for writers such as Pasquier, Bodin, and La Popelinière, the effort called into question the courtly model of paying writers without political rights to prepare narratives of the past.

A history of the *chose publicque* would not be solely or even perhaps primarily a history of the royal family. A history written by someone in the pay of the prince could not be relied upon to include the history of all the constituted powers in the *chose publicque*. The probing for a clearer understanding of what a French republican history might be resulted in a discussion of the qualifications of writers of history. Was not the writer obliged to participate actively in the affairs he was describing in order to write truthfully about what had happened? The heirs of the courtly perspective would deny that active participation in the events they described was necessary, yet they always were content to write French history as if it were solely the history of a royal family. The problem for the writer who departed from the perspective that the whole republic was his subject lay in finding a way to integrate the political functions and duties of great nobles, estates, and corporations into the royal family history without falling into the trap of searching for their origins—since, thanks to the *érudits*, the search for origins always seemed to culminate in writing a history of the dependencies of all these persons and groups upon the Crown.

And because so many men of letters were of low birth and therefore not entitled to participate actively in affairs of state, the writing of French history from a republican perspective came to naught. By 1620 the critical perspective enunciated by Pasquier and Bodin would be virtually forgotten. With the *paulette* in 1604 and the increased rush to purchase office and nobility, political discourse slowly ceased to include the idea that money corrupted justice and the pursuit of historical truth. Before centering our attention upon the historiographers, however, we must attempt to gain one more general perspective on the *monde des lettrés.*

Donald Kelley has referred to the inordinate respect for the knowledge of Antiquity and its effects upon the historical thought of the sixteenth century. In addition, the *studia humanitatis* may also have acted as a brake on the specialization of fields of knowledge and on the creation of careers whose function was the writing of history.[3] From the past the *monde des lettrés* had gleaned only two models for relating knowledge to careers: that of Antiquity and that of medieval universities. The latter held few attractions for humanists. The classical model presupposed active participation in public life, with the exception of those few men who very dramatically had withdrawn or been excluded from active political life. Cicero, Virgil, and Plutarch remained the exemplary careers from Antiquity. Thus the classical heritage that had so effectively undermined the authority of Sorbonne logic, as institutionalized in the universities, may at the same time have been a constraint upon the learned community's ability to create new careers for its members. The writer of history remained just that, not a statesman-historian; the consequences of this fact form the framework for a study of the historiographers.

Within the judicial and fiscal administrations, the tiniest jurisdictions and functions seemed capable of almost infinite subdivision to yield new offices, titles, incomes, and duties. In 1515 there were just over four thousand royal officials; by 1665 the number had risen to more than twenty-seven thousand.[4] This growth suggests what could be done by zealously enterprising royal officials eager to sell offices. Although it created fewer new careers than the state, the Church founded new religious orders with increasingly specialized charitable and educational functions and devotional practices, thus creating possibilities for expanding and increasing the variety of careers open to literate members of society.[5] Though influential in both the state and the Church, the *monde des lettrés* was not very effective at converting new knowledge into careers in the state or Church, or careers into new knowledge. Put another way, the growth in the number of universities and *collèges* during the sixteenth century was like the growth in state official-

3. Donald Kelley, *Foundations of Modern Historical Scholarship* (New York, 1970), p. 302.

4. For estimates of the number of royal officials, see Roland Mousnier, *Le conseil du roi de Louis XII à la révolution* (Paris, 1970), p. 17.

5. There appears to be no study of the French Church as a "bureaucratic phenomenon." For some suggestions about how such a study might be developed, see Richard Newton, "Port Royal and Jansenism," Ph.D. dissertation, University of Michigan, 1974.

dom when a new parlement was established. All members of the new court exercised the same functions and bore the same titles as their colleagues in older parlements. But the *monde des lettrés* failed to generate its own panoply of new officials with new titles endowed with new functions—the whole resulting from an ever-increasing subdivision of already established functions. By founding specialized chairs, notably in Greek and Hebrew, the Collège Royal did open up some posts for disciplines that had not previously been recognized; and the new *collèges* also stimulated growth by permitting teachers a certain specialization of knowledge. But by comparison with the creativity of the state, the learned appear to have been painfully backward in expanding careers based on specialized knowledge.

Historiographers of France and of the King

The term *historiographe* became known in a century rich in the creation of new words with classical derivations. But did it bear within it any meaning that was not already found in the old word *croniqueur?* Only in the sense that it became associated with the offices—or "duties," in the Ciceronian sense—of *historiographe du roi* and *historiographe de France*.[6] The duties of the one were to record the principal events of the prince regnant, of the other to write the history of France. As an office it was not part of the royal household, as were the *lecteurs, bibliothèquaires, précepteurs,* and *traducteurs.* For one to be granted the honor of attendance at court, a title to be listed in notarial acts and printed on title pages, a pension (not always paid with regularity), and a claim to being part of a long tradition of servants of the state could count for a great deal in the *monde des lettrés.* With the possibility of participating in the state, one's opportunities for personal immortality might be enhanced, an almost obsessive factor in the minds of men of letters raised in the *studia humanitatis.*[7]

6. Emile Littré, *Dictionnaire de la langue française* (Paris, 1863–1872), "historiographe," cites from the *De la différence des schismes* (1511) of Jean Le Maire des Belges: "Comme le droicturier office et debvoir de tous bons iudiciaires, cronicqueurs et historiographes soit de monstrer par escriptures et raisons apparentes et notiffier à la gent populaire les vrayes et non flateuses louenges et merites de leurs princes . . . à ceste cause, je, qui suis le mondre et le plus jeune de la vocation des dessus nommez iudiciaires et historiographes."

7. Perhaps the best succinct summary of the foundations for nonmilitary *gloire* elaborated in the sixteenth century is provided by Françoise Joukov-

Writing in the 1640s, Charles Sorel began his discussion on the office of historiographer with the assertion: "Il n'y eut jamais d'Estats bien policez où l'on ne prist le soin de faire écrire d'un ordre consecutif toutes les choses qui s'y sont passées."[8]

The immemoriality of the function (except among barbarians) had been evoked before, and it would echo across the seventeenth and eighteenth centuries to justify the surprisingly wide variety of functions of erudite and literary-historical careers. The argument of immemoriality, we know from other contexts, was used frequently in early-modern historical thought, but the supposedly immemorial subject generally had to take on an ideological significance before philological research into its origins would begin.[9] For the historiographers the claim remained just that, a claim, because their office never became part of an ideological debate. Instead, the habit of perceiving numerous classical historians as "official" historians persisted right down through the seventeenth century. When Richard Simon began to speculate upon how the Bible had been redacted, he asserted that the Hebrew nation had "Ecrivains Publics" who were especially empowered to record the memorable events of their own time and make epitomes of the older histories kept in archives and that the Bible was just such an epitome.[10]

The immemoriality argument did not assert that there had been a continuous line of historiographers beginning with the reigns of Priam, Francus, or Pharamond. Yet French men of letters were unwilling to admit to the barbarian status of their ancestors. Here the *studia humanitatis* came to their rescue, for were not epic poems and "vieux romans" also histories?[11] The debate over genres—rather than over the "truths" contained in works, irrespective of genres—would preoccupy many

---

sky, *La gloire dans la poésie française et néolatine du XVIᵉ siècle* (Geneva, 1969), p. 195.

8. Printed along with the *Histoire du Roy, Louis XIII* (Paris, 1646), B.N., Rés. fol., L^{b36} 32.

9. The primary example of this phenomenon was the debate and research over the origins and nature of the Frankish constitution and the Gallican Church; see Kelley, *passim*.

10. *Histoire critique du Vieux Testament* (Rotterdam, 1680), p. 4.

11. La Popelinière, in criticizing other writers who had asserted that the poets were the first historians and in trying to discern another perspective on the origins of history, ended up relating it to a theory of the origins of language: "Ainsi les [Greek] poëtes comme ceux qui premiers ont escrit, donnerent matière aux orateurs, historiens, philosophes, et autres de les ensuivre et surpasser en toutes occasions" (*Histoire des histoires* [Paris, 1599], p. 138). For a later sequel in this debate, see Jean Chapelain, *De la lecture des vieux romans*, ed. Alphonse Feillet (Paris, 1870).

érudits down into the eighteenth century. The less learned men of letters would view Einhard as Charlemagne's historiographer, and Joinville as Louis IX's, while the Saint-Denis chronicles would be accepted as "monuments" of an age when *bonnes lettres* occasionally received some encouragement from a royal patron.[12] The vagueness of this evidence disturbs us. Yet, as in the case of Budé's unwillingness to apply his philological skills to the relationship between men of learning and men of power, we may once again be faced with a subject that was a virtual taboo for all but such exceptional members of the *monde* as Pasquier, Bodin, and La Popelinière.

For our curiosity, however, it is interesting to note that no one quite knows what Rigord meant when, circa 1200, he referred to himself as "regis Francorum cronographus."[13] By 1400 the same Rigord was described in a text of Saint-Denis as a "croniqueur dudit roy Phelippe Auguste et non pas de ladite église de Saint Denis, et est office royal, car il est ordonné par le roy, fait serement au roy et livrée à l'ostel du roy comme officer."[14] Here all the claims of the later historiographers were present. Gabrielle Spiegel and Bernard Guenée[15] provide a genealogy of historiographers from the late thirteenth century down through Robert Gaguin, whose attempts to be named historiographer reveal the functions of the office in the late fifteenth century.[16]

Upon learning of the death of Jean Chastel, the previous historiographer, Gaguin addressed an eloquent appeal in 1478 to the royal chancellor, Pierre Doriole.[17] The *gloires* of French arms and piety had

12. See below, p. 132.

13. Gabrielle M. Spiegel, "Studies in the Chronicle Tradition of Saint-Denis," Ph.D. dissertation, The Johns Hopkins University, 1974, p. 331; and Henri-François Delaborde, "La vraie chronique du religieux de Saint-Denis," *Bulletin de l'Ecole des Chartes* 51 (1890): 96.

14. Spiegel, p. 92.

15. *Ibid.*, pp. 339 ff.; and Bernard Guenée, "Histoires, annales, chroniques: Essai sur les genres historiques au moyen âge," *Annales, économies, sociétés, civilisations* 17 (1973): 1012 f.

16. As a pioneer among humanists, Gaguin aroused interest among men of letters about other men of letters, their lives, teachings, and works, in his *Epistolae*. See Marcel Bataillon, *Préréforme et humanisme à Paris* (Paris, 1916), p. 383. For biographical information see Louis Thuasne's "Introduction" to *Roberti Gaguini epistolae et orationes* (Paris, 1903).

17. Kathleen Davies, "Late Fifteenth Century French Historiography as Exemplified in the *Compendium* of Robert Gaguin and the *De Rebus Gestis* of Paulus Aemilius," Ph.D. dissertation, University of Edinburgh, 1954, pp. 71–76. It should be recalled that though Gaguin's special claim to favor had been his Latin history, his *Mirouer historial de France*, an updated, abridged, and translated version of the *Compendium* . . . prepared by Pierre Desrey

been recorded by earlier French writers, but only in the vernacular. Gaguin proposed writing a history of the French Monarchy in Latin. To support his appeal he argued that, though the great men of Greece and Rome had accomplished memorable acts, their reputations had been further enhanced by the embellishment of those acts as recorded by writers. Were not the actions of the French every bit as heroic and memorable, if not more so, than anything accomplished in Antiquity? The breakdown had occurred in the recording of the *gestae*, not in the significance of the *gestae* themselves. Writers would continue to use this argument until the overt quarrel between the Ancients and the Moderns in the late seventeenth century.

Just why the French national heritage would be enhanced if recorded in Latin is never explored by Gaguin. It was taken for granted by some of the first-generation humanists. Lacking a sense of self-consciousness about the relationships between events and the language used to describe them, Gaguin simply states that French had been an inadequate vehicle for recording memorable events. Claude de Seyssel would eventually sort out the confusions of languages and events and assert that "langaige" itself, rather than a superiority of Latin over French, would enable writers to enhance events.

Quoting the favorite *topos* from Martial when raising the ticklish subject of pensions, Gaguin asked: "Who would labor at writing history without the inducement of reward?"[18] This question would preoccupy the *monde des lettrés*, for they often dared not claim to gain personal immortality by recording the *gestae* of such illustrious men as the kings of France. The officeseeker humbled himself before men of power. Dedications to "gros personnages" (Budé's term), written in the hope of receiving money, made little mention of a writer's hopes of gaining immortality by writing the *gestae* of the great. Might the *gros personnages* conclude that immortality could be sufficient payment? In their dedications, writers seeking a courtly intimacy with the great could scarcely allude to their own personal hopes for renown, for immortality was, in a sense, the "product" they were offering to prospective patrons.

Despite eloquent appeals and the success of his *Compendium*, Gaguin

---

and published in Paris in 1516, had several editions and was probably more familiar to sixteenth-century readers than the *Compendium* . . . itself. For an analysis of national sentiment in Gaguin, see Mireille Schmidt-Chazan, "Histoire et sentiment national chez Robert Gaguin," in Bernard Guenée, ed., *Le métier d'historien au moyen âge* (Paris, 1977), pp. 234–300.

18. Davies, p. 73.

was not appointed historiographer. Many writers suffered the same disappointment. The techniques used to inform the *monde des lettrés* that one was vying for the appointment would be refined over the years, and dedications to chancellors and kings would become more subtle, but the *topoi* regarding the function of the office remained the same, that is, to record in embellished fashion the memorable events in the life of the prince regnant and in the French Monarchy.

Among the numerous writers who held offices and received pensions under Louis XII, several contributed works that expanded these *topoi* into methodological outlooks. Foremost among them was the Savoyard Claude de Seyssel, whose *Louënges* of Louis XII and writings in defense of the *Louënges* recovered and applied to French history the thought of the ancient rhetoricians about panegyric.[19] Seyssel did not institute something new, but he gave the French the terms and conceits to describe what they had been doing, or trying to do, all along when they sought to record *haults faits*. Seeing this tendency as derived from patriotism rather than hope of personal gain or rhetorical inspiration, he states that writers "voulans gratifier aux François, en toutes choses, qu'ils ont congneu estre à leur loüenge et honneur, n'ont pas obmis à mettre en leurs commentaires, et magnifier de langaiges, ce qu'ils ont peu. Et les choses qui estoient à leur desavantaige, ont teües, ou par quelque art, et couleur, desguisées, et amoindries, ainsi que ont accoustumé faire gens que tel mestier font."[20] Seyssel's defense of panegyric is not derived from the usual humanist claims that great men and their deeds deserve to be immortalized. Instead he insists that, act for act, Louis XII had expanded the realm more than any king since Charlemagne. Seyssel's sense of the limitations of *langaige* led him to offer a comparative analysis of the expansionist accomplishments of

---

19. Jacques Poujol's "Introduction" to Seyssel's *La monarchie de France* (Paris, 1961), p. 31: "Le panégyrique de Philippe le Beau [by Erasmus] inaugurait ainsi un style politico-littéraire qui ne sera que trop utilisé après Erasme: la louange hyperbolique et la flatterie à l'antique. Si habitués qu'ils fussent à l'adulation qui s'étale dans les Miroirs du Prince médiévaux, les contemporains regimbèrent parfois devant cette conception qui érigeait la courtisanerie en système et en faisait l'instrument idéal de tout réforme politique. . . . Lorsqu'il entonnait le louange du roi de France, Claude de Seyssel avoit donc un illustre garant." See also Jack H. Hexter, "Claude de Seyssel and Normal Politics in the Age of Machiavelli," *Art, Science, and History in the Renaissance*, ed. Charles Singleton (Baltimore, 1968), pp. 389–415.

20. Claude de Seyssel, *Les louänges*, in *Histoire de Louis XII*, ed. Théodore Godefroy (Paris, 1615), p. 20.

French kings, a kind of political science placed in the service of his historical narrative of praise.

In answering those who criticized him for excessive praise of Louis XII, Seyssel developed a defense based upon his knowledge of classical rhetoric. Familiar with some of the literature about genres, he pointed out that the panegyric had been a respectable literary form in Antiquity, thus implying that if the ancients had used it, it behooved contemporaries to do so as well. And then, had not the "Saints Pères," that is, the popes, permitted themselves to be praised?[21] Seyssel's efforts to legitimate panegyric may be partly ironic. His critics were largely Italians whose political allegiances had provoked them to take up their pens against both Louis XII and Seyssel.

Expressed in a combative and vigorous style, Seyssel's arguments on behalf of the "new" genre may simply have been an explicit statement of something the *monde des lettrés* took for granted; but such an able defense of panegyrical history by so powerful a figure at court may have speeded up acceptance of this genre by virtually all men of letters. Seyssel's works reveal that the process of refining and sophisticating genres in the light of ancient and modern Italian rhetoric had already reached an advanced stage by 1500. Medieval writers had been virtually unaware that they were writing a literature of praise; now, with the help of the categories and techniques of Quintilian and Poggio, they could do a better job of it. Other signs of these influences may be found in the works of Mellin de Saint-Gelais, Jean D'Auton, and above all Paul Emile.

By the late sixteenth century the delineation of functions for the *historiographe du roi*, who wrote panegyric about the prince regnant, and the *historiographe de France*, who wrote the entire history of France beginning with Priam or Pharamond, had been made explicit in their titles. In the reign of Louis XII the title had been simply *historiographes*, but the specialization of genres was already beginning to appear. It would never become complete; historiographers of France would occasionally write about the prince regnant, and vice versa.

Though he later gave up history to try his hand at poetry, Jean D'Auton is good example of a historiographer who wrote about the reigning monarch.[22] During the reign of Louis XII many men of letters received pensions and minor household offices from the Crown and from great ducal families. While D'Auton was accompanying Louis on the Italian campaigns, Paul Emile was working on the *De Rebus*

21. *Ibid.*, p. 163.
22. René-A.-M. Maulde la Clavière, "Introduction" to D'Auton's *Chroniques de Louis XII* (Paris, 1889), p. xxvii.

Gestis, his Latin narrative encompassing all of French history, finally published in 1516.[23]

D'Auton's understanding of the principles of ancient rhetoric remained superficial and mechanical. He knew that only the most important events, that is, battles and ceremonial occasions, ought to be recorded. His modern editor, René Maulde la Clavière, describes the *Chroniques de Louis XII* as "lourd et boursouflé" and offers as an explanation the fact that these were official accounts.[24] Already at work in D'Auton, however, is the attempt to write a historical narrative in which his own personal curiosity, public and private gossip, and the mundane events of camp life would be kept to a minimum.[25] This tendency to exclude ignoble events in order not to clutter the narrative of noble or memorable ones would pervade historical writing over the next two centuries, and the espousal of this tendency by writers who barely understood humanist principles of historical writing would make their narratives dull reading.[26] Only in the eighteenth century would French historians, less caught up in emulating the ancients, break out of this mold and realize that the inclusion of mundane events could make their texts more interesting and contribute an aura of veracity to their claim that these were eyewitness accounts.

In the grip of humanist principles, historical writing would, however, be fractured into three virtually distinct genres: the topically organized works such as Pasquier's *Recherches de France*, the personal memoirs, and the historical narratives.[27] The tyranny of ancient rhetorical principles is most apparent in the works of such writers as

23. Davies, *passim*.

24. Maulde la Clavière, p. xxxv.

25. This is not to imply that he was entirely successful. Despite his effort to do so, D'Auton seems to have experienced real difficulty in discerning noble from ignoble actions.

26. See below, p. 116.

27. On Pasquier's awareness of the innovations of genre in the *Recherches*, see George Huppert, "La naissance de l'histoire de France: Les *Recherches* d'Estienne Pasquier," *Annales, économies, sociétés, civilisations* 23 (1968): 74. The principal innovation was to incorporate passages from sources directly into the text. Marc Fumaroli remarks that history as a genre in the seventeenth century has many affinities with the epic, whereas the memoirs have the "sens moraux, tout d'abord: faculté de se souvenir, et aussi image que la postérité garde d'un grand homme. Sens concret ensuite: un mémoire, dit Furetière, c'est un écrit sommaire que l'on donne à quelqu'un pour le faire souvenir de quelque chose." This could be something that men of lettres might employ in writing history but that as such was not noble in form and therefore not history. See Fumaroli, "Les mé-

D'Auton. The *rhétoriqueurs* and their classicizing heirs created narrative pictures of events. The geographical summaries, the descriptions of fortifications and troop placements, the names of officers, and the courses of the battles read like laboratory reports. Though not informed by Louis XII of diplomatic negotiations or military strategy—in short, lacking the details that would have permitted him to write about the "ressorts" of actions (it is doubtful that he would have done so had he been given such information)—D'Auton produced an early landmark in humanist historical writing. The calligraphed copy that D'Auton presented to the King was placed in the royal library, where it has remained to this day.[28] Like the works of so many other historiographers, both medieval and early-modern, D'Auton's chronicles were private works written for the king and his heirs and had no public or propagandist function. They were not known to the outside world until Godefroy included portions of them in the *Histoire de Louis XII*, which he published in 1615.

Paul Emile's understanding of rhetorical principles apparently was more profound.[29] Working over the familiar chronicles of French history to produce an eloquent narrative, he attempted to give France what Livy had given Rome. His task resembles D'Auton's in some respects, however, because the "judgments" made by medieval writers had to be either deleted or altered to conform to more Roman standards of comparison. He, too, strove to delete some of the clutter of daily life so that the genealogy of French kings and their *gestae* could be brought into relief. Pasquier judged it to be the best history of "our kings' " actions written prior to the publication of historiographer du Haillan's *Histoire de France* in 1576.[30]

The Fall of Pierre Paschal

In the later years of Francis I's reign, Pierre Du Chastel played the role that Budé had portrayed himself as playing, that of intermediary be-

---

moires du XVIIe siècle au carrefour des genres en prose," *XVIIe Siècle* 94–95 (1971): 10. The distinctions drawn by Fumaroli were already familiar to the *rhétoriqueurs* of the sixteenth century.

28. Maulde la Clavière, p. xxiii.

29. Davies does not address herself to this question directly, but Emile's influence on some of the leading men of letters of his day suggests that eloquence was his principal claim to recognition. See Pierre Bayle, *Dictionnaire historique et critique* (Rotterdam, 1734), vol. 2, p. 723.

30. *Recherches de la France* (Paris, 1665), p. 886.

tween men of letters and the prince. Appointed librarian after Budé's death in 1540, Du Chastel recommended candidates for appointment as *lecteurs* and *précepteurs* and played the coveted role of intimate with Francis in discussions of histories and other literary works.[31] Like Racine almost a century and a half later, Du Chastel read ancient histories aloud to the King and commented upon them. One of his protégés who would be very influential in the next generation was Michel de l'Hôpital,[32] from whose circle as chancellor many of the later sixteenth-century historiographers would be selected. Although Du Chastel was not himself a historiographer *en titre*, that post being held by Arnoul le Feron after Emile's death, he played the courtly role that humanists led by Budé had created for men of letters at court. His power as protector of younger men of letters appears to have been acceptable, for, like Chapelain under Louis XIV, he was very learned and could write eloquently enough to earn their respect.

When we look at seventeenth-century lists of historiographers, we find that these lists reveal no trace of the office prior to the appointment in 1558 of that very controversial figure, Pierre Paschal.[33] The regular pension for historiographers—twelve hundred *livres tournois* per year —continued to be paid Paschal until his death in 1564, despite the attacks upon him that began with Adrien Turnèbe's Latin satire in 1559. Returning from Italy with very good connections among the humanists and with the protection of Cardinal d'Armagnac, Paschal let it be known that he intended to imitate Paulus Jovius and write a "lives of illustrious men" for the French. This immediately elicited a flood of dedications to Paschal and allusions to him by men of letters hoping to have their biographies included. Noted for nothing except his "pur langage," as Pierre Nolhac termed it,[34] Paschal was appointed historiographer with the support of Cardinals d'Armagnac and de Lorraine, and—according to Ronsard—Michel de l'Hôpital. The disenchantment

31. Roger Doucet, "Pierre Du Chastel, grand aumônier de France," *Revue Historique* 133–134 (1920): 212–257 and 1–57.

32. *Ibid.*, p. 240.

33. Throughout the seventeenth century the *commis* of the various ministers compiled research notes on titles, pensions, and offices to help them in the preparation of royal correspondence. Little research was done on the historiographers, which indicates either how little litigation developed over the office, or how unimportant chancellors and secretaries of state considered the office to be, or both. An exception is B.N., mss. fr. n.a. 22216, fols. 212–216, which is a memorandum of pensions paid to historiographers beginning with Paschal in 1558. See La Curne de Sainte-Palaye's much more complete list, B.N., Fonds Moreau, 1518, fols. 90v–93v.

34. *Ronsard et l'humanisme* (Paris, 1921), p. 305.

with Paschal evident in the *monde des lettrés* reveals the patron-client relationship and rivalries, as well as the controversies that shaped the activities of a historiographer.[35]

A Latin invective by Turnèbe accusing Paschal of recalling his Italian experiences and using Italian literature as a standard by which to scorn the French was freely and venomously translated into French by Joachim du Bellay and appeared just a few months before the accidental death of Henry II in June 1559.[36]

The death of a king—indeed, the death of any patron—provoked a greater than usual state of nervousness among royal ministers as well as among men of letters. Patronage could be completely withdrawn in the shifting sand of regencies, for power would be transferred to men with different tastes and different clients and men of letters to "protect." In his haste to write an appropriate eulogy for the late King, Paschal may simply have disregarded the Turnèbe–du Bellay attack; but the rumors in the *monde des lettrés* spread until Paschal's reputation suffered. Ronsard contributed to this attack by writing a Latin invective against Paschal and circulating it to Pasquier and perhaps to others as well.[37]

Paschal had risen too rapidly; he had employed his Italian connections and Ciceronian rhetorical theories to very good effect. In the *monde des lettrés* the accusation of admiring the Italians could no longer go without comment, unless the admirer wrote with the greatest skill and won the esteem of his fellow writers. Evidently Paschal had been assigned some hack writing; he was also busy supervising translations of his own eloquent works into Spanish and Italian. During the 1550s these tasks may have been added to the responsibilities of historiographer, for Imperial-French and Protestant-Catholic rivalries stimulated pamphlet wars before an increasingly large reading public.[38]

The reasons for Ronsard's attack had not included Paschal's hack writing or any of the other functions of the historiographer. Indeed,

35. Some of the modes of constraint as well as advancement at work in the *monde des lettrés* appear in Nolhac's account of how Paschal was promoted by the men of letters and then disgraced by them. Obviously Cardinal d'Armagnac, Michel de l'Hôpital, Cardinal de Lorraine, and other patrons also exercised influence, but Nolhac's account of the Paschal affair suggests that around the great patrons there existed a barrier of relationships and outlooks. This barrier had been created by men of letters already in favor who could either promote or disgrace a young or little-known writer by the offhand favorable or unfavorable remark about his work.
36. Nolhac, p. 326.
37. *Ibid.*, p. 262.
38. *Ibid.*, p. 309.

Paschal had written so little that his very lack of productivity may have aroused contempt. A eulogy is referred to in the text, but it is not clear whether the work that prompted so much ire was about Mellin de Saint-Gelais or Henry II. Nolhac believes that the eulogy to which the invective refers was that of Mellin de Saint-Gelais and that Ronsard was piqued by the fact that Paschal had chosen to praise Saint-Gelais before his old supporter, Ronsard himself. Saint-Gelais's recent death may well explain why Paschal had decided to celebrate the dead before the living.

It is also possible that Ronsard's invective was prompted by Paschal's eulogy of King Henry II, a eulogy so admired by Catherine de Médicis, the royal widow, that she had commissioned eloquent translations into French, Italian, and Spanish and carried a copy with her as a memorial for the rest of her life.[39] Had Ronsard, poet *en titre*, become envious of his protégé's new-found favor in a moment of flux at court?

Ronsard's attack is directed specifically against Paschal. It does not include criticism of the function of historiographer or of the courtly patronage that had earned him the post. Ronsard seems most upset at Paschal's Ciceronianism. After arguing on behalf of using various ancient authors as models, he accuses Paschal of borrowing phrases from Cicero and Jovius in a eulogy. The allusion to Jovius probably led Nolhac to assume that the eulogy in question was the one honoring Saint-Gelais, but it is possible that one Ciceronian might employ the words of another Ciceronian in the eulogy of a king.

The accusation of lifting words and phrases appears in the middle of a discussion of Paschal's role as historiographer. Ronsard asserts that

39. *Ibid.*, pp. 33 ff. A further avenue that has been suggested but not really explored, because of the visual and aesthetic anachronisms supplied by readers in later centuries, are the rhetorical and aesthetic presuppositions that synthesized not only learning and eloquence, but also the visual harmonies manifested in the formation of letters in the printed type. Royally sponsored projects of learning and eloquence, like manuscripts in earlier centuries, were almost invariably printed with the "most perfect" type available and on the best available paper or vellum. Budé's *De asse* (actually an abridged version) was very probably the first book written by a Frenchman to be published in Roman type (Harry G. Carter, *A View of Early Typography up to about 1600* [Oxford, 1969], p. 79). Only the Italians had set both ancient and modern authors in Roman type before this daring act. The second book printed in Roman type was Seyssel's translation of Thucydides. Paschal's eulogy was printed by Vascosan and thus has an important place in the history of Renaissance printing, if not of printing in general. See Stanley Morison, *Four Centuries of Fine Printing*, 4th ed. (New York, 1960), p. 120, for a reproduction of a page from Paschal's *Elogia*.

either Turnèbe or Claude-Joseph Dorat would have been more suitable for the post, but he does not prefer them for their erudition or accuse Paschal of lacking erudition.[40] Whether Paschal in fact borrowed phrases from Cicero is not of particular interest here, but the accusation itself is interesting, for it reveals the pressure upon a man of letters who was expected to equal the ancients in eloquence and who had been promoted too rapidly and praised beyond the record of his accomplishments. If one aspired to write eloquent Latin by using ancient models, why not simply rearrange the syntax of sentences taken from the models themselves? The gossip recorded by Pierre de Bourdeille de Brantôme was that Paschal was lazy and had summarized years and years of French history in a few pages.[41] Both of these accusations, like Ronsard's accusation of plagiarism, were related to the rhetorical movement as it affected the office of historiographer. Accusations of laziness or lack of accomplishment would echo down through the centuries, for men of letters would apply to Paschal's successors, that is, to "their own," standards of productivity never applied by royal officials and kings. Surrounded by those of his fellows who held no office, Paschal was expected to dominate the *monde des lettrés* by his productivity and his eloquence.

When Ronsard sent his invective to Pasquier, his young protégé, the latter replied in the typically obsequious manner of an "unknown" writer addressing someone who was already eminent. In addition, Pasquier included a French translation of the invective for Ronsard's approval,[42] another practice typical of young writers who *faisaient la cour*. To make it even clearer that he was on Ronsard's side, Pasquier referred to Paschal's "inepties" and called him a "grand monstre" and a "dangeureuse beste." Paschal soon found himself friendless in the *monde des lettrés*; his disgrace was virtually complete, though his pension continued until his death in 1564. Indeed, with the help of their friends and clients, such powerful writers at court as Ronsard could drive a fellow writer from court if not from office. Did historiographers

40. Nolhac, p. 267. They became friends again (Pierre Paschal, *Journal de ce qui s'est passé en France pendant l'année 1562*, ed. Michel François [Paris, 1950], pp. xxx ff.).

41. "Après avoir faict monstre de faire enfanter les montagnes, pour tout pottage, il n'a produit qu'un chétif éloge après la mort du roy, que j'ay veu en latin . . . voylà de quoy il a payé son roy et M. le Cardinal [Lorraine? Armagnac?] son Maecenas, et toute la France, qui en pensait avoir un plus beau et riche payement plustost qu'une quincaillerie" (*Oeuvres complètes*, ed. Ludovic Lalanne [Paris, 1867], vol. 3, p. 284).

42. Thickett, p. 9.

depend solely upon princely favor? Attacks against them often came from fellow men of letters.

Given this exchange between Ronsard and Pasquier over Paschal, it is not surprising to discover some echoes of it in Book I of Pasquier's *Recherches* and also in his *Pourparler du prince*, published together in 1560, the year of Paschal's disgrace. Pasquier alludes to the hazards confronting anyone who undertakes to write a history of "les temps modernes" and adds that these same hazards influenced him to study "anciennetez." [43] Certainly this was not the sole reason, and the storms of controversy over *anciennetez* could scarcely yet be foreseen. Paschal may have been a "dangeureuse beste," but there were lessons to be learned from his disgrace.

The *Chose Publicque* and History

In the law faculties, in the royal library, and among Chancellor l'Hôpital's circle of jurists, an inquiry was made in the mid-sixteenth century into the appropriateness of studying Roman law or of applying it to French jurisprudence. This inquiry led to a still more fundamental discussion of the nature of law itself, its relationship to the past, and the relationship of both to the *chose publicque*.

This inquiry has been admirably studied,[44] and there is little need to discuss it here except to note that it affected Pasquier's and Bodin's perspectives on history and the office of historiographer as parts of the *chose publicque*. After the publication in a single volume of the first books of the *Recherches* and the completed *Pourparler du prince* (1560), Pasquier's pursuit of *curiositez* would serve primarily in the movement to construct a historicized French national identity that did not have the royal genealogy as its axis. He might never have pursued this aim had he not explored the meaning of *chose publicque* as something outside the boundaries of the dynastic perspective that had hither-

43. *Recherches* . . . , p. 4.

44. Julian Franklin, *Jean Bodin and the Sixteenth-Century Revolution in the Methodology of Law and History* (New York, 1963), pp. 36–58; Kelley, pp. 116–148; Vittorio de Caprariis, *Propaganda e pensiero politico in Francia durante le guerre di religione* (Naples, 1959), pp. 257–317; J. G. A. Pocock, "The Origins of Study of the Past," *Comparative Studies in Society and History* 4 (1961–1962): 209–246; and Gerard F. Denault, "The Legitimation of the Parlement of Paris and the Estates-General of France, 1560–1614," Ph.D. dissertation, Washington University, St. Louis, 1975, pp. 463–479, for the definition of a citizen.

to served as virtually the only past integrated into French political culture. Bodin would be of more importance than Pasquier in these inquiries; his *Methodus ad facilem historiarum cognitionem* has been assigned a major role by J. G. A. Pocock in the effort to "bring history and jurisprudence back into concord, and restore the past to some sort of relevance to the present."[45] The publication of Bodin's *Six Books of the Republic* in 1576 was as much a signal of the exhaustion of all possible fresh approaches in this inquiry as it was a resolution of the issues that had initially been raised.[46]

The participants in this inquiry only rarely directed their arguments to such questions as how the identity of a man of letters or the career of a historian could influence their manner of writing history. Nevertheless, their views on these questions appear in the context of broader, more fundamental explorations into the nature of republics and law. Starting from similar, noncourtly points of departure, Pasquier and Bodin developed during the 1560s two quite different approaches to the problem of establishing stable republics. In 1560, Pasquier's perspective was already shaped by his robe and Gallican outlook, which prompted ever greater research into the origins of French institutions. Bodin attempted to test the classical definitions of forms of government, reworking them to construct a coherent theory of universal law and politics.[47]

By orienting their inquiries from the outset upon the nature of the *chose publicque*, rather than restricting themselves to the nature of monarchy, however, both Pasquier and Bodin would immediately place themselves outside the boundaries of those who stressed the dependencies of writers. Deciding to explore the relationship between the past and law and politics, within the general framework of ancient political thought, they found themselves not only beyond the pale of royal genealogy but also beyond the courtly late-medieval relationship between the *fidèle* writer and his patron. Bodin seems to have been unaware of the potentially earthshaking effects of this emphasis upon the *chose publicque* rather than upon the Monarchy. Political thought would have repercussions upon the notions of the function of historical thought as a means of legitimating existing institutions and would affect the very fabric of French national identity.

45. *The Ancient Constitution and the Feudal Law* (Cambridge, 1957), p. 11.

46. Julian Franklin, *Jean Bodin and the Rise of Absolutist Theory* (Cambridge, 1973), Chap. 2.

47. Franklin, *Jean Bodin and the Sixteenth-Century Revolution*, pp. 73–79. See also J. G. A. Pocock, *The Machiavellian Moment* (Princeton, 1975), p. 340.

Pasquier allows his readers of 1560 to know that he is completely familiar with the courtly mode of thought and action about seeking the protection of patrons, as articulated by men of letters. After remarking, almost casually, that history is the record of either war or peace and that administration has been omitted from all histories, he addresses himself directly to the role played by historiographers who receive payment from the prince.[48] He admits, or feigns to admit, that he does not know the effect such remuneration may have had upon historical writing. Though he boldly asserts that writers ought never to flatter princes, throughout Pasquier the quality of the prince appears as the determining factor in assessing the value of the history. If the prince is good, history written during his reign will be good. If not, not. Pasquier's hesitation about assessing the effects of remuneration on historical writing stems from his approval of such payments only if the prince is good. The good prince ought certainly to have "gens gagez pour l'embellissement de ses faits,"[49] for his "peuple" (not *sujets*) are very eager to learn all they can about him. Furthermore, it is undesirable that his *faits* be forgotten. Pasquier apparently could conceive of no alternative to royal patronage in order to assure the recording of history in a monarchy.

When the prince is bad, he will pay to silence knowledge of events; and if he wishes to present himself like a scarecrow before his subjects, he will attempt to keep secret that which the *peuple* not only want to

48. *Recherches* . . . , p. 4: "Et comme toute l'histoire bien digérée consiste principalement en deux poincts, dont l'un regarde la guerre et l'autre l'ordre d'une paix: qui est celuy (je n'en excepteray aucun) qui apres avoir quelque peu sauté sur les guerres, nous ait jamais discouru le fait de nostre police." The background for the discussion of the issues is provided by Pauline M. Smith, *The Anti-Courtier Trend in Sixteenth-Century French Literature* (Geneva, 1966), pp. 175 ff.

49. *Recherches* . . . , p. 5. "Je ne sçay comment ces salaires subornent chaloir au bon prince (car ainsi l'ay-je souhaitté) que l'on connoisse ses veritez? veu qu'il se doit asseurer que tout ainsi que nature l'a constitué au plus haut degré de prééminence que tous les autres, aussi l'a-t-elle estably comme dessus un theatre, pour servir d'exemple à ses sujets, lesquels par naturel instinct ont la veuë tellement fichée en luy, que comme s'ils eussent yeux perçans à jour les parois, entendent mesmes le plus du temps les plus petites particularitez de leur prince, et celles qu'il pense tenir plus cachées. Et certes ny plus ny moins que le bon prince deust souhaitter avoir gens gagés pour l'embellissement de ses faits: au rebours celuy que nature a procrée pour n'estre qu'un espouventail à son peuple, s'il se remiroit quelques-fois, deust grandement redouter de se voir peint de toutes pieces, et donner argent pour se taire, à ceux qui ont l'esprit et la plume à commandement" (pp. 4–5).

know but eventually will learn. In a similar vein, since the good prince presumably does not encourage flattery, it does not flourish. But what is the difference between flattery and "embellissement des faits"? Pasquier's remarks about both are *topoi* frequently found side by side in the *ars historica*; and since he does not comment upon them directly, we are left to presume that he wished to convey only the conventional meanings. What primarily interests him are those "natural" characteristics of monarchy in which the behavior of princes, men of letters, and the *peuple* are ineluctably bound together.

After these warnings against flattery and the behavior of bad princes, Pasquier asserts, albeit conditionally, that it is desirable for princes to pay historiographers: "il semble qu'il seroit requis qu'un bon prince, tout ainsi qu'il entretient à sa soulde capitaines et gens d'eslite pour la protection de soy et de son pays, aussy afin que ses faits ne tombassent en l'ingratitude des ans, eust à ses gages historiographes aguerris, et aux armes, et aux bonnes lettres."[50] In addition to eloquence, military prowess is, therefore, the primary and sufficient quality required of a historiographer. Pasquier's attempt to derive a military foundation for the payment of historiographers is a very significant element in his thought about the conditions that make *choses publicques* stable. In his *Recherches*, however, he takes us no further than this. We are left with speculations about how he thought the reading public might move from the *Recherches* to the *Pourparler du prince*, incorporated into the same volume but with its own title page. These remain speculations, however, and it seems desirable not to clutter this cursory exploration of Pasquier's thought with a theory of genres that might posit a logical relationship between the two texts.

In the dialogue that is the *Pourparler du prince*, Pasquier attempts to synthesize the older mirror-of-princes genre with the much more speculative search for the foundations conducive to stable *choses publicques*. The *escholier* argues in favor of the princely patronage of history and literature: "Quelle plus grande utilité que la lecture des histoires? desquelles, ny plus ny moins que la femme par la glace du miroüer prend conseil de sa bien-seance, quand elle se met en public, aussy estant icy un prince, comme sur un eschaffaut, exposé à la veuë du peuple, se mirant aux exemples des autres grands personnages, apprend tout ce qu'il luy convient faire."[51] We are already familiar with popular curiosity, but until then Pasquier had not suggested that when princes go before the public they should deliberately mirror themselves in the examples of other great personages. The *escholier* asserts that princely

50. *Ibid.*, p. 4.
51. *Ibid.*, p. 873.

speech through letters and history is the cement of the *chose publicque*. What would a monarchy be without this *langage*? It would be nothing, a body without a soul; and it is for this reason that seigneurs—and, by implication, princes—leave money for the writing of histories and that they found schools and universities. The *escholier* evokes Alexander; Pyrrhus; Hannibal; Scipio Africanus, with Polybius at his side; Julius Caesar, who ended liberty in the Roman Republic; Augustus; Béranger of Provence; Raymond of Toulouse; and Francis I and his sister, Marguerite of Navarre, as exemplifying all the desirable results—in other words, eloquence—of literary patronage.

The *philosophe* does not bother to refute this notion that eloquence is the foundation of princely government. His Stoic-Christian perspective permits him to castigate any and all who are preoccupied with the things of this world; one certainly ought not to praise someone who is still alive. How may a prince best pursue the "contemnement de ce monde"? [52] As we might expect, Diogenes is held up as an *exemplum* against an Alexander preoccupied with accumulating riches and power (but not *gloire*).[53] And are not Diocletian and Charles V, the Holy Roman Emperor, to be admired and emulated for abdicating their power and retiring from worldly cares? [54]

The *curial* (Pasquier admires this old word for *courtisan*) starts by scolding the *escholier* for beginning his speech with a "grande levée de rhetorique," thus implying an ancient, rhetorically inspired argument against the use of rhetoric.[55] The *escholier* had used overly common commonplaces. Then the *curial* asserts that military force, rather than eloquence, is the foundation of political stability. After noting that Cyrus, Romulus, and Tamerlane knew no letters, he then asserts: "Il est certain que toutes les republiques bien ordonnées prirent leur premier advancement par les armes, et lors qu'elles embrasserent les lettres, commencerent à s'aneantir." [56] The grandeur of a prince rests on his laws and armies, not on his patronage of letters. Should he cease to be preoccupied with "promotion et grandeur," as expressed in extending his realm, will the monarchy long survive?

The next speaker is the *politicque*, who explores all the arguments made by his predecessors. The dichotomy between arms and letters is not so much refuted as related to more profound, stabilizing influences within the *chose publicque* than the one or the other. Into this speech, a speech much longer than the others, Pasquier incorporates many of

52. *Ibid.*, p. 879.
53. *Ibid.*, p. 877.
54. *Ibid.*, p. 878.
55. *Ibid.*, p. 879.
56. *Ibid.*

the typical mirror-of-princes topics not yet mentioned by previous speakers. The *escholier* had not really asserted that the prince would learn to govern better if he patronized men of letters, yet Pasquier has the *politicque* refute this argument.[57] History, in particular, is something that is "fort chatoüilleuse," in fact, so ticklish that the prince cannot possibly rely upon it as a source of truth.

The critique of the courtly function of the historiographer is directly related to his inability to offer the prince the truth about the past. Furthermore, in addition to all the difficulties in finding out what actually happened at a battle, "il faut que tu flattes le prince auquel tu es plus tenu, ou duquel tu as plus de crainte. Et posé que tu n'en attendes bien ou mal, les premières faveurs ou defaveurs des personnes qui tombent en nostre esprit ont telle puissance sur nous, qu'elles les nous font quelquesfois haut loüer, ou terrasser à tort et sans occasion."[58] Had not Commynes diminished the significance of Louis XI in order to increase that of Louis XII? Had not Paulus Jovius misinterpreted the results of the French invasions of Italy by sidestepping the fact that the French had won the battles?

The *politicque* asserts that princes may waste too much time on literary matters. Let them read Plato's *Republic*, Cicero's *De Officia*, Horace's *Satires* and *Epistles*, Ovid, Catullus, and Petrarch, but by all means let them avoid Roman law![59] Then, as if realizing that he has pursued an argument too far, the *politicque* asserts:

> Parquoy je suis presque forcé de dire (et en petille qui voudra) que les lettres prises simplement, sont choses indifferentes: d'autant, et qu'avec elles, et sans elles, plusieurs bonnes republiques se sont long-temps entretenuës. Et si l'on vit autrefois la ville d'Athenes florir parmy une affluence de philosophes: vous eustes, et la Republique de Sparte, et celle mesme de Rome par l'espace de quatre cens ans, et la Seigneurie de Venise, ne faisans grand conte des lettres, mais vrayement soucieuses d'une plus grande science. Parce que toute leur estude consistoit à induire le peuple à l'obeissance des Magistrats.[60]

The distinction between letters, which flourish in monarchies, and the more profound learning found in republics did not alter the role of either in *choses publicques*. Pasquier may thus approach the Aristotelian notion that language or changes in the style of oratory play little

---

57. *Ibid.*, p. 885.
58. *Ibid.*
59. *Ibid.*
60. *Ibid.*, p. 884.

part in changing a government from one form to another.[61] In the thought of Pasquier in 1560, history could not be relied upon as a source of knowledge, nor ought it to be defined as something that could undermine the foundations of political stability. His *curiositez* included in the *Recherches* were offered neither as a source of truth nor as a subversive force on behalf of a political cause.

This does not mean that the *Pourparler* was devoid of a political message. Quite the contrary. Pasquier strongly favors the maintenance of a balanced, or "mixed," monarchy in which the prince, peers, parlements, and *peuple* each has its powers and in which each strives to maintain the *chose publicque* in ways not detrimental to the powers of the others. Did he believe that the survival of the French *chose publicque* in its present form would be affected by what men of letters wrote about its past? Where historical arguments are brought to bear, the result is more directly related to events taking place in 1560. Ought one to believe that Alexander the Great's conquest of Persia was a result of Greek military prowess alone?[62] How could an army of thirty thousand men conquer such a great kingdom unless Darius's subjects had already been angered by the fiscal extortions of their kings? And had not high taxes weakened the Italians' will to resist the French invaders under the command of Charles VIII?

The *Pourparler du prince* is thus relatively easy to interpret on one level; but an attempt to construct Pasquier's theory of the relationships among language, historical thought, and the transformations of *choses publicques*—say, from monarchy to despotism—would require reading into the text more than Pasquier had intended. The assertion that letters are "indifferent" in these great transformations does not negate everything the *escholier* had enunciated about a monarchy's dependence upon letters, or the *politicque*'s statement that republics depend upon *plus grande science*, or the belief that both depend upon military power. Indeed, some thirty years later, in a letter to Scévole de Sainte-Marthe, a master rhetorician if ever there was one, Pasquier again remarks that monarchies are founded upon military strength and that they end when letters become their main support.[63] But in the interval

61. It ought to be the aim of the orator to adapt his discourse to the particular "end" of the government in which he lives in order to be effective, but this practice in itself does not constitute a cause for the transformation of governments from one form to another, except in democracies, where the "growth of the art of rhetoric" fosters demagogues who attempt to win popular favor by attacking the rich (Aristotle, *The Politics*, trans. Ernest Barker [London, 1946], Bk. V, Chap. 5, pp. 214–217).

62. *Pourparler* . . . , p. 889.

63. Thickett, p. 58.

between founding and decline, the sources of change are not letters or history, but the other characteristics of monarchy—for example, the *peuple*'s natural curiosity about the affairs of their prince. Though the Wars of Religion prompted Pasquier to explore the effects of preaching upon the *peuple*,[64] and the results of favoring the establishment of court preachers, they do not appear to have led him to define the office of historiographer any more explicitly than he already had in the first pages of the *Recherches*. Nor did the civil war lead him to explore the relationships between letters and changes in the French *chose publicque*. Instead, in the famous Book VII of the *Recherches*, dealing with the history of French literature, he gives much of the credit for bringing France out of a literary nonage to her kings, namely Charles V and Francis I.[65] At another point, however, Pasquier asserts that the court's influence upon the French language is corrupting and artificial.[66] This leads us to infer that Pasquier may never have fully perceived the entire range of differences between *chose publicque* and monarchy. Yet he was nonetheless a great pioneer in the attempt to discern these differences.

Let us leave Pasquier—and his Pléiade friends—and review Bodin's thought about the relationship between historical thought and a historian's social and political identity. Pasquier's robe and Pléiade affiliations were compatible with his Gallican turn of mind. He observed the segment of the *monde des lettrés* that sought favor at court and knew its members and their thoughts about history. Certainly he would have subscribed to the notion that active participation in political life may enable a writer to understand more clearly the political life he narrates as history, but his own personal achievement was integrating the history of the *monde des lettrés* into history, which until then had really only included politics, princes, and the pious.

By contrast, Bodin appears as a modern Cicero, an orator and statesman who addresses himself to the critical issues facing the body politic. The thought characteristic of law faculties and of ancient rhetorical theory prevails throughout his early work; neither the Palais de Justice nor the king's chamber becomes his exclusive purview.[67] For Bodin,

64. *Recherches . . .* , p. 559.
65. *Ibid.*, pp. 598–610.
66. See Thickett, pp. 89 f. For his insistence that words and their usage should come from the *peuple*, see p. 66. His opposition to employing noble language is grounded in his belief that it weakens the didactic authority of history. "Il n'est pas dit que je vous doive seulement servir des faits memorables qui se sont passez par la France. Les mots et sentences dorées [sic] d'uns et autres, ne sont de moindre instruction" (*Recherches . . .* , p. 512).
67. The most authoritative and thought-provoking introduction to the

the pursuit of the origins of French national consciousness would be an insufficient foundation for an understanding of the worth of history or the mechanisms for distributing power in republics.

Bodin alludes to writers of history who accept remuneration and implies that the critical perspective of such men is altered as a result. Set against his insistence on active participation in the affairs of state as the primary precondition for writers of history, this insistence on the corrupting influence of money may be the logical pendant to a negative definition of civic participation itself. Indeed, the Aristotelian civic perspective that infuses all of Bodin's political and historical thought led him to perceive money as the corrupting agent of the balance of the three forms of government constituting an ideal republic. Bodin explains Jean Froissart's critical perspective as having been perverted by English money while he was a prisoner. What better example of the antithesis between mercenariness and citizenship? Not until the eighteenth century would the notions of a special civic-republican consciousness of the type elucidated by Machiavelli be clearly articulated in French political culture; but in pointing out the nefarious repercussions that taking money has on historical judgment, Bodin touched upon a mode of thought that would have powerful reverberations in Anglo-American political culture over the next two centuries.

As a rhetorician, Bodin did more than simply follow classical prescriptions about the organization and expression of thought. The rhetorician's art infuses the thought of the *Methodus*, in the fashion later found among classical writers of the seventeenth century. Arguments, phrasing, *topoi*, examples, and noble rather than base words are harmonized to achieve a balance of *eruditio* and *eloquentia* that will stimulate reason and emotions in just the right proportions needed to convince the reader. The tone is almost never earnest or pedantic. Thus the relentless pursuit of the preconditions for dispassionate historical thought is sustained, and the *Methodus* provides an example of a balanced work of history. Bodin offers a model for writing history while discussing how others have written it.

What is the significance of the identity of a man of letters or of his role in society for determining the value of his historical thought? In the resumé of all the functions in a state, the emphasis is upon their harmony and civil discipline, which "directs literary matters too: for example, the interpreters of divine and human law and those who are called sophists by the ancients, and later, in a single word, grammarians

---

Methodus studies now is Donald Kelley, "Development and Context of Bodin's *Method*," *Jean Bodin*, ed. Horst Denzer (Munich, 1973), pp. 123–150.

—the rhetoricians, I say, poets, grammarians, philosophers, and mathematicians. The ancients properly called this training architectonic, because it prescribes laws to all masters of all arts that they may direct their activities to the common good and not foment troubles to the disadvantage of the state."[68] Bodin stresses the distinctions among offices that carry power (*imperium*), those that confer honor, and those that receive remuneration; yet his illustrations of each make no allusion to the office of historiographer or to any household title.[69] The courtly ideal of service to the prince, praised by Budé, is tacitly condemned here, for it is not included in what is offered as a complete description of society. Beyond this, Bodin offers some critical perspectives on what the historian's identity should be, but he implies that none of these is sufficient.

The *topoi* about active participation in politics through holding powerful offices or at least through observing situations where the "gravest concerns of the state" are deliberated, is the principal critical perspective that Bodin offers to distinguish good historians from bad.[70] Those lacking experience in politics and war are limited in their ability to write history, just as the statesman, unless he has had considerable time for travel, cannot learn the science of government without books: "And it came about, I know not how, that men who were occupied with war and the administration of affairs avoided writing, while those who habitually devoted more time to letters, taken captive by their snares and delights, could hardly ever be enticed from them. Indeed, very often it happened that nations which had long cultivated arms lost strength and force of spirit after they became interested in literature."[71] The historical genre is not singled out as the genre par excellence by

68. *Method for the Easy Comprehension of History*, trans. Beatrice Reynolds (New York, 1945), p. 33. The critique of the rhetorical theories current in his own day should not be construed as evidence to exclude Bodin from having been interested in and having played a part in the debates over language and rhetorical theory. Quite the contrary. This evidence suggests his desire to contribute to these debates and perhaps impose his views on other writers. A point of departure for further investigation into Bodin's sense of the limits of language for capturing reality is Myron Gilmore, *Humanists and Jurists, Six Studies in the Renaissance* (Cambridge, Mass., 1963), pp. 35 ff.

69. *Method* . . . , p. 33.

70. *Ibid.*, p. 43. See also John L. Brown, *The "Methodus ad Facilem Historiarum Cognitionem" of Jean Bodin: A Critical Study* (Washington, 1939), *passim*, for a still valuable perspective on Bodin's general philosophical preoccupations.

71. *Method* . . . , p. 41.

which men of power learn about politics. History offers no more lessons than jurisprudence or philosophy.

As if to put this critical perspective to work and separate himself completely from the habit—so prevalent throughout the *monde des lettrés*—of laying on compliments about fellow men of letters, Bodin almost completely abstains from giving a word of praise to anyone. Budé is mentioned several times but only to point out the errors about Antiquity to be found in his works. Alciato is mentioned without praise, as are many other men of letters from the past, men usually given a word of praise by their fellows, who looked back to them as towering figures of learning. This point of view, of course, sustains his argument that recognition ought to be based on holding offices that confer power upon the holder. Guillaume du Bellay, a fellow Angevin (Bodin warns elsewhere against a historian's praise of a compatriot), is complimented,[72] and his office of viceroy of Milan is mentioned as an indication that he had really participated in the affairs included in his history.[73] Amyot is referred to as a man of the "highest erudition,"[74] perhaps a backhanded compliment for one who also claimed eloquence. In the discussion of jurists, Charles du Moulin is referred to as the "ornament of our college."[75] Yet none of these references reduces the importance of Bodin's emphasis upon active participation in politics. In the seven classes of citizens to be found in a republic, men of letters are given no separate category or distinction. The implication is clear that they ought to receive no special honors or offices in recognition of their learning or eloquence.

But if natural gifts and active political experience are desirable for historians, they are not absolute preconditions. Dionysius of Halicarnassus, the ancient historian most admired by Bodin for his serenity and balanced narrative, never held public office in Rome.[76]

72. *Ibid.*, p. 48.

73. *Ibid.*, p. 72. Du Bellay's tomb echoes this point, hence Bodin was merely summing up what efforts had already been made to depict him as the perfect man who had brought together arms and learning. Du Bellay's *gisant* is among books and armor, his right hand reaching for both books and sword. See Plate 6 in Elizabeth Armstrong, *Ronsard and the Age of Gold* (Cambridge, 1968), p. 160. La Croix du Maine, *La Bibliothèque* . . . (Paris, 1584), B.N., Q 59, p. 139, gave the epitaph: "Cy Gist Langey, / Qui de Plume et d'espée, / a Surpassé Ciceron et Pompée." Guillaume du Bellay was seigneur de Langey.

74. *Method* . . . , p. 90.

75. *Ibid.*, p. 5.

76. *Methodus ad facilem cognitionem historiarum*, ed. Pierre Mesnard (Paris, 1941), p. 194. The Reynolds translation, *Method* . . . , p. 44, is ren-

Second to political activity itself is temporal distance from the period about which a historian writes. Citing Aristotle, Bodin states that the most remote and most recent events ought to be avoided if a balanced account is to be made.[77] Bodin had already illustrated how this worked by criticizing Commynes for lauding Louis XI and by pointing out how benefits and familiarity with that king had led to this overly favorable treatment.[78] By contrast, Jean Le Maire des Belges's account of Louis XI is criticized for excessive harshness toward that monarch. Bodin prefers Paul Emile's account of the reign because it is the most balanced of the three.

The dangers run by the historian writing about his own time are obvious: "perturbationes," those emotions stimulated when a writer discusses his fellow countrymen and friends, are very difficult to control.[79] The implication is that political partisanship leads either to an excessively harsh narrative or to one that is overly laudatory; try as he will, the historian cannot avoid one or the other when writing about contemporaries.

A related matter is the historian's acceptance of money, which is merely an extension of excessive familiarity. In addition to his remark about Froissart, Bodin cites Leonardo Bruni as boasting about having received gifts from someone he had praised.[80] These nefarious effects can be mitigated if the historian avoids writing about his own time or attempting to discern the truth of past events on the basis of the records of early historians. He must also read the narratives of historians from different nations or historians known to have been in the enemy camp, if he is to balance praiseworthy and blameworthy evidence.

Bodin turns this general criticism of the historian's role into a more explicitly negative criticism of the historiographers when he comments that one cannot trust what kings write about themselves, for they al-

---

dered, "he held no political office." The more precise definition of political participation is: "I call a man thoroughly experienced in public affairs if he has shared in public counsels, executive power, or legal decisions, or at least has been privy to them. For in these three are involved the gravest concerns of the state. Yet he is even more skilled if he himself has ruled the state and still more expert if he has added to this practice the profound study of letters and public law" (*Method*, p. 43).

77. *Method* . . . , p. 46.
78. *Ibid.*, p. 45. For Commynes, see especially William Bouwsma, "The Politics of Commynes," *Journal of Modern History* 23 (1951): 315–328, for reasons why the *Mémoires* would have such powerful resonances throughout the sixteenth century.
79. *Method* . . . , p. 44.
80. *Ibid.*, p. 50.

ways boast about their exploits.[81] Then, facing the question of how a historian may use "untruthful" historians to write a truthful history, he quotes Megasthenes: "It is true that all authors who write about kings need not be accepted, but only the priests to whom is entrusted preservation of the public annals. An illustration is Berosus, who restored the whole history of the Assyrians from the annals of the ancients."[82] Put another way, official histories may include some truthful statements that cannot be found elsewhere; if these have been recorded by priests, they may be believed. Bodin does not describe such priests as historiographers; they are priests. He makes no allusion to the chroniclers of Saint-Denis.

Einhard's statements about Charlemagne are marred by excessive praise, as are Eusebius's about Constantine, Lebrija's about Ferdinand of Spain, Jovius's about Cosimo de' Medici, Philostratus's about Apollonius, Procopius's about Belisarius, and Staphylus's and Leva's about Emperor Charles V.[83] Bodin strikes down panegyric wherever it poses as history; the orator and the historian employ quite different genres. Through other *topoi* Bodin criticizes historians for "dissimulating facts," that is, for avoiding the inclusion of blameworthy material in their histories and, of course, for opposing the inclusion of judgments in history. If "all the facts" are included, he states, these will speak for themselves.[84] Though Bodin's mastery of the works of ancient and possibly of Florentine rhetoricians enabled him to delineate clearly the evils of panegyric in pursuing his ideal history, he remains almost entirely within the rhetorician's paradigm.

Should any doubt remain that Bodin is castigating the court historiographers, it is interesting to describe his enigmatic attack upon the author of a history of Henry II's wars with Charles V. Falling prey to *perturbationes* himself in this instance, Bodin declines to give the writer's name. Since the eighteenth century the writer being criticized has been thought to be François de Rabutin, who published a *Commentaire des guerres de la Gaule-Belgique entre le Roi Henri II et l'Empereur Charles V*: "The man (I omit his name) who related the wars of Henry waged with Emperor Charles V, making himself judge of both of them, surrounded the king with such fulsome flattery—or rather overwhelmed—that not even Henry himself could endure these

81. *Ibid.*, p. 47.

82. *Ibid.*, p. 47.

83. *Ibid.*, p. 45. See Girolamo Cotroneo, "Le quatrième chapitre de la *Methodus*," *Jean Bodin*, ed. Horst Denzer (Munich, 1973), p. 89, for the suggestion that Bodin is directly aiming at the historiographers.

84. *Method . . .*, p. 51. See below, p. 180, for Chapelain's and Richelieu's views on this question.

praises without disgust."[85] Jacques Le Long observed in 1719 that Rabutin's work did not seem to be excessively panegyrical but was instead
direct and honest. This assessment of Rabutin has been maintained down
to Henri Hauser, and yet no other work, either by title or by content,
appears to conform to the one described by Bodin.[86]

But we must remember that Rabutin's narrative had been selected for
embellishment by Pierre Paschal, the historiographer. Paschal sought
to render the French text in a Latin so pure that it would immortalize
the *gestae* of Henry II.[87] Ronsard had accused Paschal of plagiarizing
Rabutin's work. Bodin may have known of a manuscript by Paschal—
a manuscript that has since been partially or totally lost—in which
Rabutin's "honest" narrative had been transformed into the increasingly fashionable genre of panegyric.

Bodin points out that this "vir bonus"—in this context denuding him
of his office was very demeaning—has attacked Charles V, and he continues: "The good man does not understand how insult of this sort
flows back to his own prince, for whom it would be base to wage a war
with such an enemy, more base to be conquered by him, but most base
to contract any relationship by marriage."[88] Had not Francis I almost
married a sister of this same Charles V? Bodin asserts that Henry could
only have been disgusted by writings that described his imperial op-
ponent and relative in such ignominious terms. The elevation of one
prince necessarily lowered the other. Moreover, how could Henry be
considered a prince whose military victories were of heroic dimensions
if he had merely defeated someone base and of little stature as a prince?
Thus the ancient principle of heroic magnanimity and respect for the
heroic stature of the defeated is brought to bear on the panegyric as
a genre that distorts the truth about the past.

Would Paschal have been aware that by exaggerating Henry's *gloire*
he had laid a foundation for belittling him? Not enough is known about
Paschal to answer this question, but as a proponent of *pur langage* he
might well have attempted to revise Rabutin's text in such a way as to

85. *Ibid.*, p. 51.
86. *Bibliothèque historique de la France* (Paris, 1719), vol. 1, p. 395. Le
Long alludes to a manuscript that Paschal was preparing. See Henri Hauser,
Sources de l'histoire de France (Paris, 1909), vol. 2, p. 160, for a brief critical discussion of Rabutin's work. Guillaume-A.-A. Arendt noted that
Rabutin writes from an entirely French perspective ("Recherches sur les
commentaires de Charles Quint," *Bulletin de l'Académie Royale de Belgique*
2d ser., 6 [1859]: 241).
87. See above, p. 73. That Paschal was not going to rely entirely on
Rabutin is evident from his own *Journal, passim.*
88. *Method . . .* , p. 51.

portray Henry II as faultless. In his critique of the "good man's" history of Henry II's wars, Bodin appears more earnest than at any other point in the *Methodus*. Not that historians writing about princes are the only ones who tend to distort the outcome of battles. Though he does not mention that Cardinal Bembo was historiographer to the Venetian Republic, Bodin remarks: "In kindness to his fellow citizens he has written many things otherwise than as they actually happened, or else certainly Guicciardini is often to be charged with deceit."[89] The point in question involves Bembo's assertion that there were neither conquered nor conquerors after Fornovo, in reply to which Bodin quotes Guicciardini's definition of conquest and his description of the French success in putting the troops of the alliance to flight. The light and paradoxical tone derived from his own equanimity is temporarily put aside.

When discussing the pleasure and the utility of history, Bodin gleefully runs through all the usual *topoi*. The tone of the preamble raises doubts about whether he should be taken seriously. Parody might have been an appropriate way for an able and still relatively young writer (thirty-six years old) to make his mark. The pleasure of reading history is so great that it is capable of curing illnesses.[90] Is Bodin serious? If the *Methodus* did not include a number of quite extraordinary remarks about numbers, illnesses, and cohabitation of men with animals, we could be more certain that this passage should be interpreted as a joke.

The utility or function of history lies in its power to motivate the minds of men. Suleiman's ancestors had abhorred history; but when Suleiman undertook the first translation of Caesar into the vernacular, had not this knowledge prompted him to conquer Asia Minor and North Africa in order to unite these territories to the empire of his ancestors?[91] Had not Caesar himself attempted to equal Alexander? Would Alexander himself have won so many victories had he not attempted to model his conduct upon his knowledge of Achilles, gleaned from reading Homer each night before going to sleep? And for a less

89. *Ibid.*, p. 75. Paschal's own epitaph does not include his office of historiographer, but only that he wrote Henry II's history (*Scriptori Politissimo Antiquae*, in *Journal*, p. xxxvii).

90. "What is more enjoyable than to envisage their resources, their troops, and the very clash of their lines of battle? The pleasure, indeed, is such that sometimes it alone can cure all illnesses of the body and the mind. To omit other evidence, there are Alphonso and Ferdinand, kings of Spain and of Sicily: one recovered his lost health through Livy, the other through Quintus Curtius, although the skill of the physicians could not help them" (*Method . . .*, p. 12).

91. *Ibid.*, p. 13.

remote example, had not the reading of Commynes stimulated Emperor Charles V to attempt to equal Louis XI? Bodin's discussion of the utility of history falls within Huizinga's notion of "historical ideals of life," but are we to take Bodin seriously? His admiration for Plutarch is apparent at many points in the *Methodus*,[92] but these examples of "historical ideals of life" scarcely agree with the critical pursuit of balanced narrative written by dispassionate historians characteristic of the work as a whole. Scholars who place Bodin among the pioneers in defining a method for attaining historical objectivity may be attracted to the interpretation of this passage as a parody on the works of earlier rhetoricians who had practiced the *ars historica*.

The *Methodus* had its maximum impact upon Bodin's immediate heirs, La Popelinière, Jacques-Auguste de Thou, and Isaac Casaubon.[93] They pursued the program of writing dispassionately about the past, incorporating this aim into a definition of the historiographer's function in the state. A Protestant, and a *politique* by temperament, La Popelinière had dedicated early editions of his *Histoire de France* to Catherine de Médicis and Henry III at a time when Guisard strength at court would in all probability have prevented him from gaining recognition from the Crown. Then, according to G. W. Sypher's reconstruction,[94] La Popelinière's own Protestant confreres at La Rochelle objected to some passages in the *Histoire* as inimical to their cause. They forced the author to make a public confession and to undertake revisions.

During this period of upheaval, La Popelinière remained closely connected to partisans of Henry of Navarre, and it is clear that he hoped for eventual recognition from the first Bourbon king and an appoint-

92. *Ibid.*, p. 63, is the principal discussion of Plutarch as a historian.

93. *Ibid.*, p. 63. G. W. Sypher, "La Popelinière, Historian and Historiographer," Ph.D. dissertation, Cornell University, 1961, and "La Popelinière's *Histoire de France*," *Journal of the History of Ideas* 24 (1963): 41–54; Samuel Kinser, *The Condemnation of Jacques-Auguste de Thou's History of his own Time* (Geneva, 1967); and Alfred Soman, *De Thou and the Index* (Geneva, 1972). Casaubon's preface to his edition of Polybius is at once a brilliant, learned, and eloquent exercise that stresses the value of history for the practice of politics; see Mark Pattison, *Isaac Casaubon* (Oxford, 1892), pp. 197 f.

94. Sypher points out that La Popelinière's critics may have assumed, as did d'Aubigné, that La Popelinière was receiving royal pensions ("La Popelinière's *Histoire de France*," p. 51). Whether or not he actually received pensions is less significant for our discussion than the pursuit of high aristocratic (Anne de Joyeuse, Admiral of France) and royal patronage as indicated by the dedications.

ment as historiographer. The publication of three works in one volume
—the *Histoire des histoires*, the *Idée de l'histoire accomplie*, and the
Dessein de l'histoire nouvelle des François—in 1599 reveals both a continuing preoccupation with the problem of "balance" in history and
an increasing concern over the programmatic that was characteristic
of a man of letters in search of a patron and a possible appointment.
Gaguin's letters to Chancellor Doriole had revealed that the links had
already been established between the search for a patron and the writing of a prospectus offering both an "improved," that is, more eloquent,
Latin and a more "truthful," more chronologically satisfying, and less
"confusing" general history of France.[95] Gaguin had given only the
barest details of what he proposed to do. By the 1590s, however, the
programmatic possibilities had expanded enormously, and La Popelinière did not suffer from modesty when he proposed a "new" history
of France. His prospectus was enriched by Bodinian speculations, perhaps by the recent publication of Dionysius of Halicarnassus's writings
on Thucydides,[96] and by changes in the notion of the public as a result
of increased literacy and expanded publishing.

By 1700 the prospectus—those of Gabriel Daniel and Louis Le Gendre
are good examples—would be written with the virtually exclusive aim
of attracting public attention and intimidating other authors eager to
enter the competition of writing general histories of France.[97] During
the more than two centuries separating Gaguin from Daniel, the prospectuses of La Popelinière stand as monuments of what a "perfect
history" of France should be.

La Popelinière's observations about the office of historiographer indicate his almost religious belief in the notion that historical truth contributes to political stability. As early as the dedications of his *Histoire
de France* to Catherine de Médicis and Henry III, this Huguenot reveals
himself as a *politique* for whom the state can be the only foundation of
political and religious tranquillity. Then, the *Histoire des histoires*
makes explicit the implications of the *politique* position for the office

95. See above, p. 65.
96. The impact of Dionysius's historical criticism on late-sixteenth-
century historical thought is yet to be explored, but the editions after
1559 (the B.N. catalogue lists one by Aldus in 1560 and one by Friedrich
Sylburg at Frankfurt in 1586) indicate that this uniquely powerful work
about an ancient historian deserves to be investigated for its possible role
in the rhetorical side of the historical revolution.
97. Gabriel Daniel, *Deux dissertations préliminaires pour une nouvelle
histoire de France* (Paris, 1696), B.N., L[35] 118; Louis Le Gendre, *Essai de
l'histoire du règne de Louis le Grand jusqu'à la paix générale* (Paris, 1697),
B.N., L[b37] 68.

of historiographer. The marginal sentence that serves as the chapter heading, "Que la qualité d'historiographe de France soit si bien mesnagé qu'elle ne laisse tant soit peu de soupçon d'y estre corrompu,"[98] leads to a discussion of the needs of the state for a history of all the "notables particularitez" that have happened. La Popelinière is tentative about the motives that led Henry II and Henry III to appoint historiographers: "Ces deux princes semblent avoir judicieusement visé, ordonnant par forme de loy generale, l'honneur d'assister au Roy comme conseiller en titre d'office formé, et le profit pour luy fournir de moyens necessaires à concevoir, esclore, former, et produire au profit de l'Estat, les plus belles conceptions de leur esprit."[99] Unless this is done, and unless this function is performed in such a manner as to avoid all suspicion of having suppressed information, it is best that the writing of history be carried on without support from the state. Note how La Popelinière's description of the office seems couched in chancery form; such phrases as "conseiller en titre d'office," and "concevoir, esclore, former, et produire" are not those generally employed by the *monde des lettrés* to describe their sense of themselves or of their functions. That the historiographer should be a *conseiller* first suggests that active political involvement in the affairs of state should be either a prerequisite for the historiographer or his solemn right. How else can a historiographer really be informed about what has happened?

La Popelinière continues by making a public appeal for any and all documents and memorandums that would contribute to the "parachevement" of history; but he realizes that even this would be insufficient. He asks "His Majesty" for permission to be able to look for documents in places where he knows them to be, "and because the prince alone has the key to these places, it is necessary to speak to him and ask him to open them up."[100] La Popelinière's devotion to the writing of history was founded on an assumption that it was his civic duty to publish all the "notable particularities" of the French past. His sense of the public bore within it a notion that the public looked to him for the truth about the past. And who could be more interested in having the truth known than the prince? "Car comme ils [kings] representent tout l'Estat, aucun ne doit tant desirer que l'Estat soit au vray exprimé par l'Histoire. Et ce, tant par leur regard, que celuy de leurs sujets."[101] The notion that the state must be expressed in an accurate

98. *Histoire des histoires* (Paris, 1599), p. 376.
99. *Ibid.*, p. 377.
100. *Ibid.*, p. 380.
101. *Ibid.*, p. 377. La Popelinière's perception of the *politique* view rested squarely on his understanding of classical political theories about the

fashion through history increases the historiographer's civic responsibility beyond the range of the humanist didactic notions hitherto expressed in France.[102] Regardless of whether the "state is royal, popular, or aristocratic, very small, or very large,"[103] the writer of history
will need help in view of the complexity of the subject. To be sure,
La Popelinière adds that history is the "book of kings, princes, and
magistrates" (not uniquely of kings), and that the kings of Persia had
taught this to the Greeks and Egyptians, after which it was handed
down to Roman monarchs. Darius, Alexander the Great, Ptolemy, and
Caesar Augustus are suggested as providing a kind of genealogy of
focal points for history. Yet the immemoriality of the historiographer's
race is supported here by the notion of civic duty.

But, while a notion of *chose publicque* included civic presuppositions
that the writer of history should not accept money, other, more entrepreneurial men of letters were claiming in their writings to share
intimacy with the prince and access to secret documents. Indeed, what
could prevent a historiographer from claiming in his prefaces that he
had discussed affairs of state with ministers and had gained access to
secret state papers? An example of such entrepreneurialism is the Protestant, Jean de Serres, who in his 1600 edition of the *Inventaire général
de l'histoire de France* asserts that "Estant employé en grandes affaires
et dedans et dehors le royaume, j'ai eu l'honneur d'entrer aux cabinets
des rois et des princes, de manier les actes publicques des provinces et
communiquer avec les chefs des partis, pour apprendre de leur bouche
mesme et d'autres qui sous eux avoient l'autorité et l'entrepriese au
vray ce qui s'est passé."[104] De Serres had played a role in various negotiations conducted to end the civil war, but were such lofty claims

---

changes in the forms of government. "Ainsi tous estats se changent, non
seulement selon la rencontre des princes qui le [sic] gouvernent mais aussi
selon sa qualité propre et naturelle qui ne peut demeurer semblable"
(*L'amiral de France* [Paris, 1584], p. 85). The *parachevement* of history
must therefore be interpreted as a discernment of these changes within all
forms of government, which did not necessarily mean the formulation and
testing of laws that explain or reveal the nature of the changes in the forms
of government.

102. *Histoire des histoires*, p. 380.

103. *Ibid.*, p. 377. See Claude-Gilbert Dubois, *La conception de l'histoire
en France au XVIᵉ siècle* (Paris, 1977), p. 143, for a more extended discussion of La Popelinière's sociology of historians.

104. Quoted from *Inventaire général . . .* (Paris, 1600) by Corrado Vi-
vanti, *Lotta politica e pace religiosa in Francia fra cinque e seicento* (Turin,
1963), p. 250.

justified?[105] Since only Henry IV and his most influential councillors could really make such claims, we are left with only two alternatives. We must believe either that de Serres genuinely but naively thought that he had participated in the highest levels of government, or else that he recognized that such claims might enhance his prestige in the eyes of the reading public.

Thus, paradoxically, at the time when La Popelinière was elevating the historiographer's duty to one of civic, *politique* responsibility, his religious confrere may have been claiming a knowledge of affairs of state in order to make an already successful publishing venture, the *Inventaire*, even more successful. Like Bodin, La Popelinière warned of the dangers of accepting "faveurs mondaines," that is, money and gifts, that may lead writers of history to "dissimulate the facts."[106] Yet neither seemed aware of any commercial advantages to be gained by placing the title "historiographer" after the author's name on the title page and by claiming in the preface that the work was based upon the knowledge of state secrets. La Popelinière had paid for the printing of his own books and, alas, none became a commercial success; entrepreneurial devices may simply have been beyond his ken.[107]

Nor can the *mignons* be relied upon to write history. Those who have studied how to flatter princes (he does not blame the princes) will write panegyric, not history. Why have no good histories of France been written by Frenchmen? Because they have been either intimidated by Paul Emile's achievement or disgusted by it.[108] Whichever the case, the history of France can be improved only if access to documents is permitted and if the historian can talk with the king. La Popelinière's view of his own special role as historical conscience, or guarantor of historical knowledge before his readers, makes it difficult to conclude whether his recommendations were general ones or applied to him alone. In the final years of his life he received some royal support,

---

105. Charles Dardier, "Jean de Serres, historiographe du roi . . . ," *Revue historique* 22–23 (1883–1884): 291–328 and 28–75.

106. La Popelinière is very harsh on Froissart for having taken money from the English. He observes about the French historians who have discussed the Italian invasions, "peu y ont fait chose recommandable tant ils se sont estudiez à flatter les princes, et se monstrent au reste si peu judicieux qu'on n'en doit faire estat" (*Histoire des histoires*, p. 435).

107. Sypher, "La Popelinière's *Histoire de France*," p. 54.

108. La Popelinière notes that the "généreuse libéralité du roy François I" fostered the writing of all sorts of works and then goes on to lament the failings of his contemporary compatriots in writing history (*Histoire des histoires*, p. 438).

thanks to Sully, and his last work was a history of still another stage of the Italian wars that had long pitted France against Spain.[109]

This brief exploration of the thought of Pasquier, Bodin, and La Popelinière has not produced a description of the historian's office in the body politic; but the clues it provides contribute to and confirm some of the elements that have been revealed in the first part of this chapter. Is it correct to infer that the further a writer was removed from identification with the *monde des lettrés*, the greater would be his insistence upon active participation in the affairs of state as the single most important criterion for writing history?

Pasquier actively participated in the *monde des lettrés* and shared some of the assumptions about the need for a French history that could be compared with the great masterpieces of Antiquity. Bodin scorned the *monde des lettrés* from a senatorial perspective and raised doubts about rhetoric, unless the individual employing it had actively participated in affairs of state. With the exception of the usual *topoi*, the *ars historica* was of little use to La Popelinière, who asserted that not merely active participation in government but direct access to the prince were essential if one was to write the history of the state.

Together these writers confirm the impression that began to take shape after the discussion of Pierre Paschal's fate: namely, that a spectrum of qualifications for historians existed. This spectrum began with eloquence and erudition at one end and extended toward complete participation in the affairs of state at the other. At one end of the spectrum we have Bodin and La Popelinière, for whom panegyric was an almost natural result of the political condition of the man of letters; at the other end is Pierre Paschal, who set about rewriting Rabutin's narrative of a military campaign to make it conform to the canons of literary style established by the *monde des lettrés*. At one end is the view that the man of letters who had never commanded an army ought not to write military history and that the writer who had never actually wielded power had no business narrating the decisions of a council of state. At the other end is the world of letters, which would have exhibited little interest in the work of any historian heeding the views on the role of rhetoric voiced by La Popelinière, no matter how "truthful" the text might be. By pointing to the extremes, we may have discovered a congruence of the historian's identity and his sense of civic participation in the sixteenth century. The nuances within the spectrum were as numerous as the individuals who addressed themselves to the writing of history; and there were exceptions such as Jean de

109. Sypher, "La Popelinière's *Histoire de France*," p. 54.

Serres, who continued to write in the tradition of the medieval chronicle. Still, as a general rule, writers from bourgeois or barely noble social backgrounds tended to stress eloquence and erudition as central
to the identity of historians, whereas nobles and royal officials may
have tended to stress active political participation. Showing due respect
for all the elements of their identity, the writers of the sixteenth century adjusted these elements to conform to their own personal strengths
and weaknesses and to their political (and not merely their social)
status in the body politic. This spectrum may make it possible to shed
light on virtually every remark by contemporaries about the personal
life or works of a writer of history.

To search for the origins of the spectrum would take us far beyond
the range of an introductory chapter, but it is interesting to note that
the emphasis upon eloquence and erudition, as well as upon active participation in the civic life of the state, are in themselves *topoi* that cannot bear too close a scrutiny. The danger of perceiving them as conceits
is obvious.

The Humiliation of du Haillan

In the concluding part of this chapter, I shall touch upon some of the
more human and less dignifying aspects of a historiographer's life, in
order to suggest the contrasts that could develop between the hortatory
language about history and men of letters developed by courtly writers and the degrading circumstances in which a historiographer might
find himself.

After Pierre Paschal (d. 1564), the seventeenth-century record of
payments of historiographers of the past—the record is certainly incomplete—lists "Maistre Jean Bernard, sieur du Haillan" (the family
name of Girard is omitted) as the next individual having received payment. In 1572 and 1573 the sum received had been twelve hundred
livres (the equivalent of four hundred *écus*).[110] Du Haillan's income
was increased over the subsequent decades, but it is almost impossible
to discover whether these increases were granted in recognition of his
historical publications or for other services at court. Furthermore, du
Haillan encountered the greatest possible difficulty in actually collecting the payments authorized by the king.

Among the offices preceding the title of "historiographer" are "secretary to the Duke of Anjou and Bourbonnais," "secretary to the King
of Poland," "secretary to the king's chamber," and, after 1586, "royal

110. B.N., mss. fr. n.a. 22216, fol. 212.

councillor." Du Haillan had held the first of these offices in a household of one or another of Catherine de Médicis's sons. The most recent, and presumably the most prestigious, of these offices may have been purchased by the aging man in the view of bequeathing it to an heir. Did such offices represent "active participation in the affairs of state"? Or were they empty—without power or without civic responsibility? The overlapping of ancient Roman nomenclature upon feudal and then bastardized feudal household titles had enabled Bodin to draw a distinction between offices that conferred power and those that did not. From the courtly perspective, however, these titles all signified some degree of service to the prince and intimacy with him.

From other sources we learn that du Haillan did, in fact, carry out some delicate diplomatic missions in collaboration with other, more powerful officials.[111] Though never among the most intimate and powerful of royal councillors, he nevertheless had dabbled in the affairs of state. Indeed, in his histories he evokes this experience to suggest that his history is truer and more valuable for this reason.

In the royal instructions for payment signed by Henry III in 1581, du Haillan's other, nonhistorical services are enumerated, as are reimbursements for "voiages, charges et commissions."[112] Finally, at the end of the list of political reasons for payment, the document notes that he also deserves payment "pour avoir escript l'histoire des Roys de France où il a tellement travaillé qu'il merite d'en estre remunéré."[113] Thus we find no clear demarcation between political and historical-literary services rendered. They are all rolled into one and are worth one thousand *écus*—or possibly two thousand, for two payment orders for one thousand *écus* succeed one another at a brief interval. It is apparently impossible to determine whether this involved an administrative duplication or a double payment. More intriguing, however, is the fact that there is no indication of regular *gages* having been paid to du Haillan; rather, this single (or double) payment was for services rendered in various capacities over a twenty-two-year period. The sum does not seem very great when compared with the regular pensions on the household rolls granted to royal relatives, peers, and officers of the Crown.

Although I have not checked all surviving household accounts, those that are easily accessible reveal that the historiographers were not listed

111. Paul Bonnefon, "L'historien du Haillan," *Revue d'histoire littéraire de la France* 15 (1908): 642–696.

112. Paul M. Bondois, "Henri III et l'historiographe du Haillan," *Revue d'histoire littéraire de la France* 30 (1923): 508.

113. *Ibid.*

among those receiving regular *gages*.[114] Tutors, barbers, tailors, musicians, translators, and librarians seem to have been regularly inscribed on these rolls—but not the historiographers, because they were officers, not servants. Did the Crown choose to remunerate these men of letters by granting them a title and little else? There seems to be no evidence to suggest that they were honored by a swearing-in ceremony as one source suggests was the case in the fifteenth century. The persistent, indeed still increasing tendency of historiographers to include several dedications to a variety of prospective patrons in a single published work suggests that the title itself was still far from being a *charge*.

In the late sixteenth century, however, with the debates over the meaning of *offices* and *charges* and the elaboration of procedures over their hereditariness—of which the *paulette* of 1604 was only the culmination—the historiographers and their families probably began increasingly to view themselves as officers of the Crown.[115]

A great deal of research would probably be required to find out whether statesmen—men of letters such as Guillaume du Vair and de Thou, to name only two, perpetuated, in thought as well as in deed, the Bodinian perspective about the value of active participation in the affairs of state by writers of history. For the political culture as a whole, however, a title and acceptance at court would be considered as political participation. The Bodinian model was too elitist.

While these debates over the effects of venality on justice were going on, the links between office, inheritance, and wealth were quietly being forged by families eager to preserve their status and wealth. In Book IV of his *Traité des offices*, Charles Loyseau lists "les Maistres des Requestes, Conseiller du grand Conseil, Lieutenans de longue-robe du Prevost de l'Hostel, et selon aucuns, les Lieutenants de la Connestablie, Admirauté, et Eaux et Forests: il y a encore d'autres Officiers de lettres, comme les Gardes de la Librairie, et les Lecteurs du Roy."[116] Historiographers are not even mentioned, and the offices that resemble theirs are claimed "by some" to belong to this group of nonvenal offices, for Loyseau was unwilling to express his opinions decisively. *Gens de lettres* are described as part of the *collèges* and universities;

114. Eugène Griselle, ed., "Une liste alphabétique des offices de la maison de Henri II (1550)," *Documents d'histoire*, 1912, pp. 509 ff.; Eugène Griselle, ed., *L'état de la maison de Louis XIII . . . (1601–1665)* (Paris, 1912).

115. Roland Mousnier, "Sully et le conseil d'état et des finances," *Revue historique* 192 (1941): 69–86, and *La vénalité des offices* (Rouen, 1946), pp. 206–216; Raymond Kierstead, *Pomponne de Bellièvre* (Evanston, 1968), pp. 104–136; and John Russell Major, *Bellièvre, Sully, and the Assembly of Notables of 1596* (Philadelphia, 1974), *passim*.

116. *Traité des offices* (Paris, 1666), p. 336.

like printers, librarians, and bonded messengers, they are expected to obey the principal officers of the university.[117] The result of this debate had as great an effect upon the courtly ideal shared by men of letters as upon the judges who asserted that money and the inheritance of judicial *offices* would corrupt justice.

Upon Jean de Serres's death in 1598, his heirs appealed to the Crown for the right to nominate a candidate for his post as historiographer. Presumably that candidate would have paid them a sum of money for the recommendation.[118] Pierre Matthieu, who had been informed of his nomination as historiographer, appealed to the chancellor for speedy action upon his *brevet* because the candidate of the de Serres family might be appointed first. Why should Matthieu have been concerned? Several historiographers could be in service simultaneously. The possibilities that his *brevet* might be endlessly delayed in chancery and that his payments would be delayed if someone were appointed ahead of him were "embarras ordinaires" for men of letters in royal service, especially during periods of royal bankruptcy and confusion between the notion of office and courtly service. Venality and the right to bequeath offices to heirs eventually would remove the issue of corruption from the debates about participation in affairs of state. Those men of letters more inclined to be courtiers had never had qualms about taking money; they had not even bothered to refute the idea that mercenariness "corrupted" their ability to write "the truth" about the past.

During the reign of Henry IV it is apparent that du Haillan expected a regularly paid, annual pension as historiographer. The manuscript list of payments to historiographers notes that "Le Roy Henry IV par les lettres patentes du 18 octobre 1594 luy ordonna 2,800 écus soleil, pour sept années qui luy estoient deües à raison de 400 écus par an."[119] The sum of these payments indicates that by the late sixteenth century the

117. *Ibid.*, p. 475.

118. Pierre Matthieu to Bellièvre, 4 September 1603, B.N., mss. fr. 15900, fol. 508: "Il a pleu au Roy à vostre recommendation et de Monsieur de Villeroy de me donner un brevet d'historiographe de Sa Majesté, et d'agréer quelque dessein de l'histoire de son règne et de celuy du feu Roy que je luy fis veoir. Les héritiers de feu Monsieur de Serres prétendent faire renouveller les provisions qu'il avoit du mesme estat en faveur d'un professeur du Roy nommé Cazoy. Cela me constraint Monseigneur recourir à vostre justice, et vous supplier tres humblement de ne permettre qu'elles passent au seau, et d'avoir agréable que les lettres qui seront expediées sur mon brevet soient receues et scellés affin que je sois asseuré de la faveur dont le Roy m'a gratiffié."

119. B.N., mss. fr. n.a. 22216, fol. 113.

figure of twelve hundred livres per annum had become the regularly established pension for a historiographer. This remained the case, with some exceptions, until the reforms initiated by Colbert described in Chapter VI. How had this figure been reached? Perhaps a comparative study of the pensions of royal offices as well as of artisans, physicians, surgeons, musicians, and others performing service at court might shed light on this question; but on the basis of what we now know about patronage, it is tempting to assert that this figure had been pulled out of a hat by some royal *commis*. Whatever its origins, it placed historiographers in an immutable hierarchy; they became regularly paid royal officials, whether they produced books or not. The shift from the older courtly pattern of payment upon completion of a poem or book to that of regularly paid pensions seems to have had little effect upon productivity among the *érudits* or the *éloquans*. Instead, in the years prior to Colbert, productivity appears to have been influenced by the subtle pressures and sense of rank within the *monde des lettrés* itself.

The return to political stability under Henry IV did not, however, mean that du Haillan's pension would be regularly paid. Caught in between during the ministerial battles fought by Sully and Pomponne de Bellièvre, du Haillan was reduced to writing plaintive and then pleading letters to Bellièvre: "Mes affaires et mes debtes me pressent de telle façon que j'ay esté contraint d'envoyer expres mon lacquais vers Monsieur Rosni avec une lettre par laquelle je le suplie vouloir me signer une ordonnance de 600 livres restans de ceste demie année courante pour mes gages de historiographe de France."[120] Rudolf and Margot Wittkower have remarked that artists tended to feign dire necessity in letters to patrons, when in fact their financial situation did not warrant such pleas.[121] Du Haillan had previously expressed himself with vigor, and in print, about his sacrifices for the king. Nevertheless, erratic payments were a harsh reality for all men of letters—and for virtually everyone else receiving court pensions. Letters from dukes and peers, complaining about nonpayment of pensions, are preserved side by side with those written by historiographers, gardeners, and foreign statesmen.

Du Haillan's situation did not immediately improve. On 10 August 1603, he wrote another letter to Bellièvre, a letter that is familiar in tone as well as pleading: "Si Monsieur de Rosni [soon to be Duke de Sully] me traitoit bien je serois ordinaire courtisan, comme j'ay tousjours esté jusques au voyage de Savoye, et j'aurois ce bien d'estre pres

120. B.N., mss. fr. 15900, fol. 406. 21 November 1602.
121. *Born under Saturn: The Character and Conduct of Artists* (New York, 1963), pp. 255 ff.

de vous. Je luy ecris et le suplie de me signer une ordonance de dix-huit cents livres qui me sont deües de mes gages de l'année passée."[122] Was this sum, somewhat greater than the twelve hundred livres of a decade earlier, to be paid for du Haillan's services as royal historiographer? Or for his services as royal councillor? Or for both? Only through prolonged archival research might the answer be found. Although distinctions between *gages* and *pensions* had not yet become regularized, the former term was generally employed for all royal payments to officeholders, while the latter had more the ring of a household appointment, such as historiographer.

The *fidélités* extending down from chancellors and superintendents of finance could be disrupted by the disgrace of someone as powerful as Bellièvre. While du Haillan was having so much trouble wresting his payments from Sully, the latter was casting his eyes upon La Popelinière for the post of historiographer, with an assignment to write a history of the Savoyard wars.[123] The detailed archival research necessary to determine exactly what happened to du Haillan on the trip to Savoy scarcely seems relevant to the problem at hand. We have only to recall Bellièvre's ardent Catholic sympathies as undisputable evidence of the effects of ministerial rivalry, and perhaps even of Protestant and Catholic subparties within the *politique* sphere supporting Henry IV.

Not that du Haillan was disgraced in the wake of Bellièvre's "retirement." We learn from the manuscript pension list that on 30 September 1610, Louis XIII added eighteen hundred livres to du Haillan's pension as historiographer and that du Haillan continued to receive a pension until his death in 1621.[124] Henry IV had been assassinated on 14 May 1610. The increase in du Haillan's pension may have been granted out of a desire to compensate for years of nonpayment, or of underpayment, resulting from Sully's tightfisted control of patronage. Marie de Médicis had increased the number of members sitting in the Conseil d'en Haut, and it is just possible that an old ally or creature of Bellièvre's had recalled, or been reminded of, du Haillan's *fidélité*. Sully was forced into "retirement" the following year, which may not have distressed du Haillan. But an introductory chapter is not the place to explore how the historiographer may have revised his historical narrative in the light of the ministerial conflicts that had affected his career.

By now the need for more precise definitions of courtly conduct and of office is apparent, especially definitions of the sort that may be

122. B.N., mss. fr. 15900, fol. 379.
123. See above, p. 90.
124. B.N., mss. fr. n.a. 22216, fol. 113.

provided only through reconstructing careers and the related personal and political circumstances affecting them. As we turn from this admittedly sketchy description of the historiographers to the study of single careers, it may be useful simply to list all the historiographers *en titre*, 1580–1620.

While du Haillan was serving as historiographer (1572–1621), other names cited as receiving royal income as historiographers were: Nicolas Vignier, André Thevet, Gabriel Chappuys, Antoine de Laval, Georges Critton, Pierre Matthieu, Jean de Serres, Nicolas Prou des Cameaux, Théodore Godefroy, Scévole and Louis de Sainte-Marthe, and Scipion Dupleix.[125]

For Nicolas Vignier, the payment was made "pour les services qu'il avoit rendus au [sic] feux Rois et à sa Majesté [Henry III] à la recherche de plusieurs bons et rares livres et impressions d'iceux."[126] As we shall see, a historiographer apparently could be expected to do hack research into the history of dynastic claims and Gallican liberties and to eulogize the royal dead; he could be recognized for increasing the collections of rare books and editions in the royal library.

Among those writers and librarians receiving royal support for their historical works was Charles Bernard, a man of modest learning whose principal claim for being appointed historiographer was his ability to inspire a relaxed familiarity, if not affection, in the heart of Louis XIII.

125. *Ibid.*, fols. 212–216.
126. *Ibid.*, fol. 212 v.

Chapter III
Bernard and His History

THE career and works of Charles Bernard shed little light on the evolution of historical thought in early-modern France because little is known about his life and his histories were completely ignored at the time of their publication. His unique qualities prevent him from being described in any way as a typical man of letters, and yet he was a historiographer royal. His pamphlets and history, in their flatness and honesty, broke nearly every canon of literary taste when they were published, but they appeal to us as a straightforward, unembellished narrative. A first reading of his monumental *Histoire des guerres de Louis XIII* (1633) leaves the impression that the author was either lacking in intelligence or was attempting to parody the conventional standards of historical writing for his day. In fact, neither of these explanations is correct. A closer analysis of Bernard's works reveals a keen intelligence that was almost totally uninfluenced by the literary conventions of his time.

Charles Bernard, as we learn from the *Discours* written about him by his nephew, Charles Sorel, had a long career as a *lecteur* to Louis XIII, in other words as a courtier, before he ever came to write history. Thus Bernard's career is characterized by what could almost be defined as a reversal of roles: for instead of polishing his literary talents as a young man and seeking favor by dedicating poems to the prince and great nobles, he initially gained their familiarity and then turned to writing history. Bernard therefore seems to have been free from the worry that some rival man of letters would turn upon his work and make a harsh critique of his literary style. This disassociation from the world of letters permits us to delineate in which ways the intellectual, political, and literary tendencies of Bernard's day may have influenced historical thought in the 1620s. Bernard's career and work suggest that an almost iron tyranny of rhetorical standards was being imposed on history in the late sixteenth century. Put another way, the logical development of humanist literary and intellectual canons into classicism constricted history as a literary genre into something quite lifeless. Bernard's ignorance of these canons is remarkable.

Early Career

Apart from a few tax and *rente* receipts, Sorel's *Discours* is virtually the only surviving source about the private life of Charles Bernard.[1] It must be used with caution because Sorel had every reason to paint Bernard in a favorable light. Are the remarks about Bernard's childhood true? They are very interesting indications of the kind of personality that formed the pattern of behavior of a courtier. Indeed, Sorel's remarks may provide clues to the type of personality that sought intimacy with the *grands*, including the prince himself. One might imagine that had Budé been given the opportunity, he, too, would have had a "bon coeur" and enjoyed playing with children of aristocratic birth. If Sorel's remarks are put in general terms, they may be interpreted in three different ways: first, that they are simply descriptions of Bernard's childhood; second, that Sorel is in fact delineating a pattern of conventional social behavior that is also perfectly correct for Bernard; third, that Sorel is covertly describing his own fantasies or real-life experiences, while attributing them to his uncle. As we shall see in Chapter IV, Sorel took a genuine interest in the role childhood played in the individual's formative experiences, making his remarks about Bernard all the more interesting.

Born in Paris, according to Sorel, on 25 December 1571, of noble but in no way illustrious robe parents, Bernard was the oldest in a family of seventeen children. Only four of the seventeen seem to have survived childhood, which is one of the reasons Sorel gives to explain why Bernard's father was solicitous about the boy's education and introduction to aristocratic society.

Sorel believes that Bernard's father was chiefly responsible for his son's success at the royal court, because from an early age the boy had been "raised for some *haute charge*." The father alone, however, could not assure his son's success, and Sorel explains that Bernard was not only agreeable but that he "ne ressembloit pas à ceux que la timidité empesche de fréquenter de plus grands qu'eux, ou plutôt qu'un certain orgueil qui fait qu'il y en a qui veulent commander par les petits."[2] This ability to control himself and not seek to dominate those who

1. The unpaginated *Discours sur la vie et les escrits de Charles Bernard, lecteur ordinaire de la chambre du Roy Louis XIII et historiographe de France* is bound with Sorel's *Histoire du Roy Louis XIII* (Paris, 1646), B.N., folio, Réserve L^{b36} 32. It also includes the *De la charge d'historiographe de France*.

2. *Discours* . . .

were his age but had been born into socially superior families would be a valuable asset at court. As a result of his character, Bernard was sent on while still a child to "hanter les enfans des meilleures maisons." Sorel claims that in his childhood Bernard realized that friendship and intimacy with aristocratic children would serve him in the future; and since he lacked the pride that would have inclined him to domination over other children, young Charles was freely accepted into aristocratic households by parents and governesses. If these were indeed the traits that Bernard developed, it is not surprising that as an adult he could gain the favor of Pierre Jeannin, one of the royal ministers, and then of the King himself, and spend a life on the shifting sands of favor and disgrace as part of the royal household.

The next step in Bernard's development was his friendship with Philip II of Spain's disgraced minister, Antonio Perez, who had fled to Paris early in the reign of Henry IV. Sorel assures us that it was from Perez that Bernard learned many secrets about politics; and if this was indeed the case, Bernard could scarcely have had a better teacher about court intrigue. What is puzzling, however, if only for its absence, is the lack of any reference to the historical writings and personal letters published by Perez. Sorel either was exaggerating the intimacy that Bernard developed with Perez or else—rather than suggest that Perez may have taught Bernard how to write history—he preferred to omit the allusion, since Perez was a foreigner and any reference to a foreign influence on Bernard might have redounded negatively in an age when nationalism was acutely affecting French political culture.

There are no specific references to the offices or functions held in Paris by Bernard's father, but had these been in any way ennobling or distinguished, Sorel would almost certainly have listed them. This omission is devastating, for it suggests a family in which a boy is being raised to climb socially while his parents are almost frantically attempting to abandon their *roture* social origins. There is also a vague reference—and for this reason all the more suspect—to Bernard's ancestors having held high judicial "places" in Champagne and Burgundy. And yet, despite the fanfare about his social origins, his pensions, and the robe marriages for his children, Charles Bernard was never in a position to be accepted as truly of gentle birth. This fact is corroborated by evidence other than Sorel's *Discours*.

Number 302 in the series of *pièces originales* of the Cabinet d'Hozier, in the Bibliothèque Nationale, reveals the Bernards' pathetic struggle to move up in the aristocratic society of the *Ancien Régime*. Various financial transactions of the 1620s, probably the heyday of Charles Bernard's favor at court, describe him as "noble homme," "conseiller du

Roy," and "lecteur ordinaire de Sa Majesté." The title "historiographe de France" is added only to later documents.[3] In the welter of financial transactions everything seems to be going well. Indeed, some notarial acts link the Bernard children to other rising families: the Fouquets, Bullions, Aubespines de Chasteaneuf, Aumonts, Amelots, Guénégauds, and other robe families climbing rapidly in an age of massive venality of office.[4]

Charles Bernard died peacefully, believing that the nobility of his family had been securely established; but his son reached too far. In the search for false nobles carried out thirty years later by Colbert, the Bernard family was investigated and found guilty by the Crown, not of fraudulently assuming nobility but of adding the title of *écuyer*.[5] The son of Charles Bernard, also named Charles, had succeeded his father in the *charge* of *lecteur ordinaire* in 1627, but in the plea for clemency addressed to Louis XIV, no evidence or argument is put forth to justify the assumption of the title of *écuyer*. Royal service and an appeal to the generosity of the Sun King were the only claims the Bernards could make. At the bottom of the plea a secretary wrote: "The King has sent this plea to Monsieur d'Aligre, not wishing to act on it himself." The barrier between nobility and gentility may have been firmer in the late seventeenth century than anyone coming to maturity during the 1640s or 1650s could have suspected.

The principal doubt raised about Sorel's description of Bernard's life, however, concerns the degree of intimacy that Bernard shared with Louis XIII. Sorel claims that Bernard enjoyed virtually constant access to the King and was among the little group entitled to attend the *lever* and *coucher* every day. If this was in fact the case, why are references to Bernard so scarce in the memoirs written by other courtiers? And in Richelieu's correspondence,[6] for example, the one or two allusions to him suggest that Bernard was of no significance at all. Did Sorel attempt to increase Bernard's prestige by claiming that he was a familiar companion of Louis XIII, when in fact Bernard was not?

3. The *privilège* of the *Discours sur l'etat des finances au roy* (1614) refers to him as an "avocat en nostre Conseil et Parlement."

4. Roland Mousnier, *La vénalité des offices* (Rouen, 1945), *passim*.

5. B.N., mss. fr. 20922, fol. 2; B.N., d'Hozier 41, Bernard, 993.

6. In writing to the Duke of Guise, Richelieu encouraged him about the French readiness to battle with Spain, adding: "Par ce moyen, vous acquer-rez une si grande gloire que si M. Bernard n'est pas capable d'escrire, je m'offre d'en estre l'historien," which represents Richelieu's sardonic perception of the role of the historiographers royal (*Lettres, instructions diplomatiques et papiers d'Etat*, ed. M. Avenel [Paris, 1853–1877], vol. 2, 431, p. 658).

It is impossible to answer this question. Louis did have a small circle of intimate friends who were almost constantly with him and who were known to be nearly free of all political intrigue. As if needing a "family," which in fact his wife and children never provided, throughout his reign Louis XIII clung to the little private world that had peopled his nursery. The physicians, *lecteurs*, and such other intimates as the first Duke of Saint-Simon were never disgraced, because their relationship with the King was almost purely private. Yet if Bernard was among this group, it is curious that his presence did not leave more traces in the letters and memoirs of Louis's other courtiers. In any event, whether an intimate companion of Louis or not, Bernard was certainly at court sufficiently often to be able to observe the King's conduct; and, as we shall see, when Louis campaigned in the south against the Huguenots, Bernard accompanied him.

Virtually all young men, no matter how good their manners or how illustrious their social origins, had to depend on a patron in favor with the king if they wished to have the *honneurs de la cour* on a day-to-day basis. Only as a creature of some minister or favorite was this possible; otherwise those courtiers attached to other patrons discreetly excluded aspiring courtiers. Of course this did not happen if the king took notice of a young courtier and bade him stay; but with Louis XIII this happened very infrequently. In Bernard's case it was Pierre Jeannin, the aging but powerful minister of Henry IV and superintendent of finances after Sully's disgrace in 1611, who presented Bernard to Marie de Médicis and the boy King. A thorough search in Jeannin's correspondence might reveal the origins of their relationship, but in any event it is clear from the early tracts by Bernard that he was either already a client of Jeannin's or was writing tracts to gain his favor. In *Cléobule, ou l'homme d'Estat*, which bears no date, Bernard offers an apology to the monarch or, in this instance, probably to Marie de Médicis, for having a favorite as first minister: "Il luy est non seulement utile, mais necessaire, d'approcher de soy des gens, qui le soulageans luy façent recevoir l'honneur des choses qui arrivent à bonne fin . . . et qui portent en outre la disgrace de ce qui n'arrivant pas selon le desir et le voeu commun, pourroit apporter quelque tare . . . à sa reputation."[7] In this earliest of Bernard's writings, civil law and history are the two "columns" that sustain the state. Continuing in the conventional mode of thought about history, Bernard states that it is the "depot des actions honorables et de la reputation des princes; l'archive de leurs droits, celle qui leur enseigne à quel titre ils tiennent leurs estats, les interests qu'ils ont sur les autres, les pretensions des autres sur eux, les combats

7. B.N., L^b36 3533, p. 2.

et les guerres de leurs predecesseurs, les fautes et les avantages qu'ils y ont eus, l'establissement de leurs affaires pendant la paix; les traittés et les alliances, les seuretez et les infractions d'iceux; ce qu'on a baillé pour y parvenir."[8]

From these and other texts it is clear that Bernard had learned some *topoi* about history and had easily adjusted them to serve as an intellectual support for his career as writer for the Crown. Yet the literary refinements of the Pléiade had escaped him, for his concern seems to have been the ideas he expressed and not the literary style in which he presented them. In *Cléobule* it is impossible to determine to what degree Bernard was writing an apology for Marie de Médicis should she want to name Jeannin her first minister, and to what degree he was simply writing to support Jeannin. Indeed, the unity of these two purposes was the most important for Bernard, and it helps us to understand the making of a career as historiographer royal. *Cléobule* was a minor piece, just one among hundreds of pamphlets of this same genre, but it marked a political perspective that joined history to the service of the state and the writer to his patron.[9]

More interesting, not only for the ideas it presents but because it also illustrates a particular literary form that reflected increasing favor with Jeannin, is the *Discours sur l'Estat de finances au roy*.[10] Published in 1614, the text had probably first been written to instruct Louis XIII on fiscal matters. Had Jeannin, who was superintendent of finances at the time, actually commissioned Bernard to prepare the work? More probably, Bernard perceived that an avenue toward increased favor with Jeannin might lie in preparing a book of instruction for his prince. The work is in the mirror-of-princes genre. The description of revenues is clear and simple, evidently written to be read before a thirteen-year-old. The *sententiae* about the significance of finances for the well-being of the state are obvious and in most cases are supported by historical examples. Tacitus is a favorite source for Bernard, throughout the text, though there are also references to Lucretius and Strabo on how iron and copper had preceded gold as precious metals.[11] Since states are subject to "revolutions et changements," nothing contributes as much to their good order as sound finances. Vague mercantilist

8. *Ibid.*, p. 8.

9. Another tract, dated 1613 (*Conjonction des mères*, B.N., R 3089), reveals Bernard as something of a projector, for here he attempts to draw attention to his political capacities by proposing that a canal be built to join the Mediterranean and the Atlantic in order to further trade and thereby enrich France. The tract was dedicated to Jeannin.

10. B.N., L^{f76}39.

11. *Ibid.*, p. 5. There is an obvious literalism in his use of classical sources.

themes appear as well, for Bernard attempts to convince his readers that France may get along very well without importing anything, thanks to her fertile soil and her manufacturers.

But as is so often the case in the literature addressed to princes by an author who is a minister's protégé, emphasis is placed upon one particular policy or course of action. Indeed, when Bernard chose in this treatise to decry the devaluation of coinage as a solution to royal deficits, he may have known that Jeannin was also opposing this expedient in the Conseil d'Etat. Bernard had used a descriptive narrative of French finances, buttressed by historical references, to instruct his sovereign; but perhaps the principal motivation of the entire work had been to publish a pamphlet stating the arguments against devaluation. Then, too, why had Bernard chosen to publish his work rather than simply present it to Louis through Jeannin's good graces? Thanks to the invention of printing, the mirror-of-princes literary genre had become a vehicle for political controversy among the reading public at large, rather than among a limited number of courtiers and royal officials. The *Discours* therefore is one more example of the transformation of a very old genre into what had become in the sixteenth century a new vehicle for the exchange of ideas and opinions. If Bernard had not addressed his remarks on finances to Louis XIII, how might he have justified discussing what could only be defined constitutionally as the king's affairs? This little tract seems to have attracted no attention when it was published, but the lessons its author learned about presenting the king's affairs to a large public may have been useful when he came to writing about still more delicate subjects.

Yet Jeannin's favor was not the same thing as Louis XIII's. A treatise on finances certainly would not win the latter's attention. According to Sorel, Jeannin arranged to have Bernard serve as a courier between Louis and his army officers; and since there were many spoken messages as well, Bernard became known to the King and Marie de Médicis. Then, upon the death of Louis's preceptor, Fleurance Rivaret, Jeannin moved quickly to have Bernard named to replace him, but as *lecteur* rather than preceptor, since the King's majority had already been declared. From this point on, Bernard seems to have been in regular attendance at Louis's court, traveling with him and attending his entertainments.[12] It was Bernard, Sorel claims, who introduced Louis to printing, which the boy King enjoyed.

All the while, Bernard hoped for greater favor and higher office. But apart from one very minor diplomatic mission in 1629 and his

12. If a complete edition of Jean Héroard's *Journal* is ever published, we may learn more about Bernard's role at court.

appointment to the Conseil d'Etat, Bernard was no more than the King's companion. Then, in 1621, while accompanying Louis on the campaign against the Huguenots, Bernard was called in by the then all-powerful favorite, Charles d'Albert de Luynes, who suggested to Louis that Bernard be appointed historiographer royal to replace the deceased Pierre Matthieu. Were there other candidates for the post?

Bernard's appointment to the post of historiographer, described by men of letters as so illustrious and significant to the state, is an example of how the Crown typically viewed such appointments. By 1621, Bernard had won a reputation as a faithful courtier; he had never written any history, but he had, after all, become familiar with Louis XIII. His dependence on Jeannin had not been of the sort that made him a threat to Luynes, who had engineered the assassination of Concino Concini and had launched France in an all-out war against her Protestant minority.[13] As *lecteur*, Bernard may have demonstrated some mastery of the historical writings of Antiquity, but at the time of his appointment neither his literary nor his intellectual abilities had been proven. Matthieu's death had created a vacant post; what, to the minds of Louis XIII and of Luynes, could be better than to give it to Bernard, who had spent so many hours with the King, whose history he was now asked to write?

In the rural society of the seventeenth-century court, the lack of concern for expertise on finances and on almost any other matter save military experience suggests that patronage on the basis of literary merit did not develop, except through the influence of the *monde des lettrés* itself. Louis XIII had no one to play the role of Budé, nor did he have a Chapelain, as did his son. There was nothing atypical about Bernard's appointment. After all, previous historiographers had been no better qualified and had not even spent time at court; and none of Bernard's *éloquan* successors until Voltaire could claim to have written history before they were charged with writing just that. Bernard's fidelity to Louis XIII, and perhaps his ability to survive despite the storms of court intrigue, seemed all that was necessary.

Bernard's initial intention was to write a history of Louis's war against the Huguenots. This work, the *Histoire des guerres de Louis XIII . . . contre les religionnaires rebelles de son Etat* was not completed until 1633, the year in which an edition of perhaps as few as twelve copies was printed on magnificent paper with fine woodcuts, in folio.[14] It is clear that Bernard hoped for a favorable reception of this work

13. Alexandra Lublinskaya, *French Absolutism: The Crucial Phase, 1620–29* (Cambridge, 1968), Chap. 4.

14. The copy I used is B.N., Réserve, L^b36 20.

by the King and his ministers. He had paid the printing costs himself. Despite vague allusions to a much larger work about to be completed, a history of the entire reign, it is doubtful that by 1633 Bernard had completed as much as he claimed.

Sorel's explanation for Bernard's failure to publish a regular edition of this work is interesting, for it gives some insight into the influence of public taste upon the writers of history: "pour ce que le peuple demande tousjours des histoires complettes."[15] The commonly held belief that French history could be narrated only by complete reigns and not by topic or even by a specific war may account for the fact that no general edition of the *Histoire des guerres* was published. There are other possible explanations.[16] Bernard turned to writing an account of Louis's activities until 1635 and the declaration of war against Spain, but it is clear from the vagueness of the text that he had lost interest in his task.

There is no evidence to suggest that Louis XIII or, by 1633, the powerful Cardinal Richelieu, had quashed Bernard's plan to publish the account of the wars against the Protestants, yet the political climate may have partly determined the fate of Bernard's major historical work.

He was certainly not a creature of Richelieu's. In 1626 he had published a letter addressed to Marie de Médicis exhorting her to use her full influence to prevent her son from declaring war against Spain. This little tract, Bernard's most partisan political work,[17] probably placed him in the "Spanish party" at the court of Louis XIII. True, in 1626 that party was still inchoate, at least by comparison with what it would become under Michel de Marillac and Marie's direction in 1629–1630, prior to its demise after the Day of the Dupes.[18] But in other instances Richelieu demonstrated that he could remember the names and activities of those who had opposed him years before. In 1633 he may have recalled Bernard's letter to Marie, published back in 1626. Bernard's presence at court did not constitute enough of a threat for Richelieu to desire his disgrace; yet in this shady position of nonsponsorship by the Cardinal, Bernard's work on the wars against the Huguenots may simply have met the worst of fates: being completely ignored.

15. Sorel, *Discours*, p. 7.
16. The work was not written exclusively for Louis XIII or even for a handful of ministers; Sorel would presumably have known this.
17. *Lettre de C. B. pour engager à prévenir la rupture entre la France et l'Espagne* (n.p., n.d.), February 1626, B.N., L[b36] 2452.
18. Georges Pagès, "Autour du grand orage: Richelieu et Marillac, deux politiques," *Revue historique* 179 (1937): 63–97; and Georges Mongrédien, *La journée des dupes* (Paris, 1961), *passim*.

On the other hand, in his speech for the first estate at the estates general of 1614, Richelieu had insisted that neither arguments nor words, but only exemplary Christian behavior, would win back the Huguenots to the Gallican Church. The publication of a history of the military defeats suffered by the Protestants while Richelieu was principal minister could hardly be calculated to improve relations between the two religious communities. Richelieu was preoccupied with his "covert" war against Spain and hoped for the support of Louis's Huguenot subjects in this very perilous adventure. Whether or not he actually was responsible for the publication of Bernard's history, Richelieu would have been held so by the Huguenots as principal minister and architect of the victory of the royal armies at La Rochelle. And yet, in the massive publication of Richelieu's papers by M. Avenel, not a word or even a vague allusion to the small edition of 1633 appears.

Thus the reasons that prevented Bernard from publishing a full edition of his work are a mystery. Suppositions fall into two categories: political-religious and literary. Previous pro-Spanish inclinations and inopportune circumstances involving the Huguenots may account for Bernard's failure to publish, but there is no evidence to substantiate this reason. By contrast, the literary explanation—the popular demand for a complete history and the evidence that Bernard began to write a continuation of his history—suggests that these reasons may have held up publication. A further piece of evidence, again from Sorel, contributes to the historiographic-literary explanation: according to Sorel, Bernard's writings "n'ont pas la délicatesse de plusieurs de ce siècle." Bernard's literary style failed to edify his readers, and, even worse, he included digressions about the origins of the Protestant heresy and conditions among the peasants that were far too long to be appropriate in the history of a king. Sorel, as we shall see, should not have been the one to make these criticisms, for his style also failed to meet the standards of the men of letters and public at large in the mid-seventeenth century. But were these the reasons for the stillbirth of the *Histoire des guerres?*

One thing that neither a seventeenth-century king nor a minister could do was to assure the public acceptance of a work of literature. Royal or ministerial power could silence some writers who might otherwise publish satires; but the flow of anonymous pamphlets attacking all manner of literary-historical writing is testimony to the possibility that critics might attack any work of history, whether or not it had been sponsored by the Crown. This anonymity may not have been prompted entirely by fear. It may have been chosen by these critics out of a desire not to become known to other critics, much less to the author of the work being criticized. Whatever the reason, the magnificent type for a book of over six hundred pages was broken up after only a few copies had been printed.

In 1646, Sorel finally published the *Histoire des guerres* by inserting it as part of his general history of France. By then Louis XIII and the politicians at his court were dead. But again the work failed to attract attention from critics or gain public favor, which suggests that Bernard's weaknesses as a writer indeed explain the oblivion into which his work fell. There was no second edition.

We might think initially that his subject, the wars against the heretics, would be of interest to his contemporaries; and his account is unique for its richness and detail. Yet in the mid-seventeenth century, after decades of frustration and civil war, literate Frenchmen may well have begun to turn away from the entire subject of Huguenot rebellions. This attitude of wanting to ignore a source of conflict and hate coincided with the rise of a new Catholic sensibility during the first half of the seventeenth century[19] and may actually be related to the growing efforts quietly to exclude Protestants from all positions of power and from guild membership. By the time of the revocation of the Edict of Nantes in 1685, most literate Frenchmen seem to have convinced themselves that very few Protestants were still living among them and that with just a nudge they, too, might be converted to Catholicism.[20] Such a delusion may have had its origins in an unconscious unwillingness to read about wars with the Protestants as early as the 1630s. Bernard's subject could, therefore, have seemed more painful than timely to his contemporaries.

Nor did Louis XIII stimulate interest in the hearts of his subjects the way his father had and his son would. Coldly groping through life and doing his duty, Louis fulfilled neither the notion of conquering hero nor that of the cultivated patron of the arts that both writers of history and the literate public would so admire under Louis XIV. But perhaps his worst failing was his stammering and his inarticulateness, almost insurmountable liabilities in an age when letters and politics still placed great emphasis on the spoken word. The power of monarchy as an institution remained so strong that Louis XIII's conduct failed to stimulate widespread public criticism; but at the same time his very weaknesses also dampened desire to read historical accounts of his life. Bernard's history sheds light on the peculiar blending of political and literary cultures at a time when the *érudits* had already lost their larger public by continuing to write about pedantic subjects and before the

19. Cf. my *Paris in the Age of Absolutism* (New York, 1968), Chap. 7.
20. Jean Orcibal, *Louis XIV et les Protestants* (Paris, 1951); and Arie van Deursen, *Professions et métiers interdits, un aspect de l'histoire de la révocation de l'Edit de Nantes* (Groningen, 1960).

literary cult of the hero as epitomized by the plays of Pierre Corneille[21] could be historicized in writings about Louis XIV.

The *Histoire des guerres*

The rambling narrative of Bernard's *Histoire des guerres* defies simple categorization. A summary of personal observations about Louis XIII, it provides some clarification of the two conceits in which the history of a king could be written, for the author was unable to conform to either of them. Yet Bernard's misfortune stemmed not only from his mediocre ability as a writer but also from the fact that he had chosen to place Louis XIII in a conceit that was going out of favor in his time. This also partly explains why his work was ignored. Put another way, although Bernard and his contemporaries certainly agreed that the function of history was to edify and—when it dealt with a reigning sovereign—to immortalize, they did not develop a unique conceit in every decade or for every monarch in order to achieve these objectives.

By conceit I mean something more than just the image or central theme to be conveyed by the events occurring to one person. The medieval conventional conceit of sacerdotal kingship emphasized how the reigning monarch reflected the characteristics of all the members of a divinely chosen and supported dynasty of kings. The other conceit, implied since the time of Charlemagne but never fully developed until the reign of Louis XIV, depicted kings as universal heroes sharing qualities epitomized in the lives of Alexander the Great and Caesar Augustus. These two essentially different conceits were blended in almost every work of history; rarely if ever did historians write with only one of these in mind. The particular selection of *topoi* from one or the other reflected both the individual interests and sensibility of the writers and the political and religious climate of the time in which they wrote.

Just how these conceits, which involved quite different elements, became increasingly distinct from one another in the late sixteenth century is not for us to explore here. Yet it is clear that the more patriotic and religiously grounded sacerdotal conceit profited most from the rich lode of evidence unearthed by the legal humanists, whereas the heroic-universalist conceit was refined by the addition of psychological dimensions of individual motivation and literary taste wrought by men of letters, most notably the members of the Pléiade. The sacerdotal

21. Paul Bénichou, *Morales du grand siècle* (Paris, 1948), Chaps. 1–2.

elements of kingship attracted the *doctes*; the ancient elements, the *éloquans.*

During the last decades of the sixteenth century, the emphasis on dynasty and divine right lost favor or failed to satisfy a need for conviction and authenticity felt by descendants of the Pléiade and by some elements of the reading public. Then, too, such works as de Thou's monumental history, Pasquier's *Recherches*, and the elder Jean du Tillet's *Memoires et recherches* may have undermined the sacerdotal conceit by presenting precise evidence that cut kings down to purely human dimensions for both learned and literary readers. Not that these writers consciously sought to demolish the divine right of kings; but, rather, the French kings, with their blundering conduct, as often influenced by circumstances as by anything else, preserved too little of that aura of divine guidance conventionally evoked by the conceits found in the chronicles of Saint-Denis and such histories as those by Jean de Serres and Pierre Matthieu. De Thou's and Pasquier's histories may not have demythologized the French past in any strict sense, but for their more sophisticated public they may have come painfully close to doing so. In fact, though their contemporaries may not have realized it, instead of demythologizing French history, they placed great emphasis on myths about the *chose publicque* rather than on the divine character of French Monarchy.

In the late sixteenth century the attractiveness of the universalist-heroic framework became still stronger. The psychological elements in it satisfied the readers' needs for leadership, victory, unity, and a feeling of superiority. Sixteenth-century writers had not successfully historicized these characteristics in the lives of French monarchs, though the entire range of actions and emotions had been elaborated in verse. By the end of the sixteenth century *gloire*, or immortality among men, was not seen as the opposite of saintliness or Christian piety in kings, nor was it considered antithetical to dynastic claims of inherited superhuman qualities.[22] The reign of Louis XIII marked a hiatus in the extension of this conceit from poetry to history, though this extension occurred completely and almost monolithically after 1650.

When Bernard began to write his history of Louis XIII, he had the choice of depicting the King as a virtual institution through whom God worked, with very few biographical characteristics that were unique to Louis, or as an individual whose behavior conformed to the conceit about the conduct of Alexander the Great and Caesar Augustus. Bernard was neither sufficiently independent of mind nor per-

22. Françoise Joukovsky, *La gloire dans la poésie française et néolatine du XVIe siècle* (Geneva, 1969), Chap. 5.

ceptive enough to make a deliberate choice. Nor could he perceive
that, after the civil war, the Catholic Reformation, and the mood
created by the poets, the literate public would tend to find the heroic
framework increasingly in accord with its needs for history.

Bernard blended both conceits crudely and inevitably failed to attract a reading public at all, but this in no way should suggest that
he failed to convey in prose the image of kingship that Louis XIII
wished to have conveyed to his subjects. Furthermore, had literacy
extended to artisans, retail merchants, peasants, and farm laborers, his
peculiar blend of crude honesty and emphasis on the pious qualities of
devotion and constancy of leadership depicted in Louis XIII might
have attracted a large reading public. Bernard's style offended the overly sensitive men of letters who attended Parisian salons and were in
the vanguard of the movement to "refine" the French language and
taste; but numerically that was indeed a very small group in the 1630s.

Bernard did not know what he was doing. Unlike his nephew, Charles
Sorel, who genuinely tried to write a popular history of the French
Monarchy, Bernard believed he was writing a work that deserved to
be read by all Frenchmen, because they ought to know of the piety and
effectiveness that their sovereign, Louis XIII, had shown in quashing
a Protestant rebellion. In the general context of Bernard's own life, his
career almost fated him to stress the conceit depicting Louis XIII as
a divine-right monarch.

Regardless of the special synthesis of conceits, the result was, of
course, that certain events accorded with one conceit better than the
other. Almost before he began to write, Bernard was fated to produce
what could only appear as a depiction of a divine agent overcoming
the rebellion of heretical subjects.

Yet those among Louis XIII's individual traits that did not contribute to his portrayal as a French monarch or as a conquering hero
were rarely included in a work of history; and the more perceptive the
writer, the more coherent and in some ways suppressive the conceits
were allowed to become. The result was frequently an almost completely dehumanized portrait of a king, whose personal qualities were
never mentioned. Bernard allowed personal anecdotes to creep into
his work, thus violating the literary canons for history of his day. For
example, the fact that Louis liked to gather twenty-five or so of his
courtiers and soldiers and sing psalms and other liturgical music with
them scarcely contributed to his image as heir to Charlemagne or Louis
IX. If someone sang off key, Louis would break in to support the unfortunate singer with his own voice, an act the *éloquans* would have
scorned as too undignified to be included in a history.

Bernard had read the ancient historians, but he seems to have been incapable of perceiving the psychological aspects in their portraits. By nature more a Roman than a Greek, Bernard was attracted by laws and practices in such a way that in his work he plodded from truism to truism about the character of monarchical institutions. His thought is veiled by the evocation of *topoi* that are banal in the extreme, rendering Louis almost physically identical to the crown he wore. When Bernard does include elements from the heroic conceit, they have little psychological weight. The *topoi* about taking bad lodgings while on campaign, which is found frequently in Bernard, probably belongs to the heroic conceit; but since it is so banal, we scarcely notice it.

For Bernard, the maxims of political thought he had gleaned from Antiquity were to be accepted by his readers totally and almost unquestioningly, as if they were Bible verses. Through these *sententiae*, rather awkwardly inserted into the narrative, he attempted to edify his readers about the errors of heresy and the greatness of monarchy as an institution. Indeed, the mode of analysis that would create a divine-right conceit of Louis XIII implied a political philosophy, just as the conceit stressing the heroic qualities implied a psychology and a moral philosophy that could serve as a framework for selecting the themes and events of a sovereign's life history. Was Louis an individual with motivations and characteristics that somehow set him apart from other men? Bernard gives his readers little insight into the King's personality.

In the general development of seventeenth-century historical thought, Bernard's work must therefore be defined as a serious but clumsy effort to depict a reigning monarch by stressing his official and institutional powers and qualities. After Bernard there would be an increased tendency to portray royal personages solely through the conceit of the conquering hero. The attributes of monarchy that Louis XIV shared with Charlemagne and Louis IX would scarcely be noticed by Pellisson-Fontanier and Racine.

This shift from one conceit to another coincided with other changes in the political culture; but in no way did it break down the fundamental definitions and assumptions about the purpose of writing history. Perhaps the heroic conceit could not be historicized for the literate public in the figure of Louis XIII because society's preoccupations remained constitutional and religious during the decades following a terrible civil war.

From the date of its publication Bernard's history would be viewed as old-fashioned. The definitive shift from the divine-right to the heroic conceit during the 1630s and 1640s resulted from the synthesis of already developed tendencies in literature with the new, postwar religious expansionism of the state promoted by Richelieu, Mazarin, and finally Louis XIV himself. Throughout Louis XIII's reign, robe culture, the powers of the Parlement of Paris, and the powers of Protestants were all in positions of declining importance in the general political culture. Meanwhile, such *érudits* as the Dupuys, the Duchesnes, and the Godefroys carried on a brilliant program of publishing documents on regalian rights. These documents tended to sustain the claims of absolutism in ways that historicized and desacralized sacerdotal kingship.

For the literate public, especially in Paris,[23] critical thought about history was increasingly determined by the conceits that gained approval in the salons and in the newly founded French Academy. The development and refinement of the heroic conceit appealed to these groups from the beginning, and the historicizing of the Pléiade's notions of *gloire* and of the hero in a style free of pedantry and allusions to political controversy fulfilled their ideal of kingship. Interest in the divine-right or legal-constitutionalist aspects of French history would never be very great in this group of sons of robe officials, who were shying away from their social origins and their former interest in gaining greater political power through control of the legal system. If the political culture of the sixteenth century could be crudely defined as dominated by the robe, its successor in the seventeenth must be seen as a creation of that barely noble culture of the salons and the *honnête homme*.[24] Their historical thinking would more closely approximate that of the Abbé de Saint-Réal and Gatien de Courtilz de Sandras than that of Pasquier; the lines between *histoire*, or history, and *histoires*, or fiction, became almost totally blurred.

Thus historians, and the historiographer royal in particular, were confronted by a particularly difficult task after the theatrical successes of Corneille and Jean de Rotrou. Dare they write about a French king in such a manner that he appeared less alive or less heroic than those images of chivalric courage that had been received so enthusiastically on the French stage? After the *Cid* the historiographer royal's fundamental task was to write accounts of the lives of French sovereigns, attributing to them powers, psychological insight, and courage at least equal to that of the fictional portrayals on the stage.[25] Indeed, by ignoring Bernard's history of Louis XIII, the literary public implicitly de-

23. Henri-Jean Martin, *Livre, pouvoirs et société à Paris au XVIIe siècle* (Geneva, 1969), vol. 1, p. 46.

24. See Part IV of Carolyn C. Lougee, *Le Paradis des Femmes: Women, Salons, and Social Stratification in Seventeenth-Century France* (Princeton, 1976).

25. Not that Corneille violated the epic tradition of attributing the heroic qualities to the knight rather than to the king or emperor; Rodrigue is the heir of Roland, hence the play functions as an apology for the *grands*.

manded such history. The disparity between the edifying personality of Rodrigue and the sullen-humored Louis XIII must have been apparent to the younger men of letters of the 1630s. Bernard's portrait of Louis XIII, the work of an older man whose thinking about the Monarchy resembled that of the typical literate Frenchman of the late sixteenth century, was a hopeless failure for the generation of readers excited by the cult of the hero established by Corneille and Rotrou.

There was one discordant voice—Descartes—but there is no evidence that he read Bernard. What is significant, however, is Descartes's condemnation of the tendency to employ the heroic conceit, or any conceit at all, in historical writing: "Même les histoires les plus fidèles, si elles ne changent ni n'augmentent la valeur des choses pour les rendre plus dignes d'être lues, au moins en omettent-elles presque toujours les plus basses et moins illustres circonstances, d'où vient que le reste ne paraît pas tel qu'il est, et que ceux qui règlent leurs moeurs par les exemples qu'ils en tirent sont sujets à tomber dans les extravagances des paladins de nos romans et à concevoir des desseins qui passent leurs forces." [26] This critique of the *ars historica* is devastating; but, as we shall see, it had no effect on the historical writing of the historiographers royal, and perhaps no influence at all. Descartes's rejection of the *ars historica* was applied specifically to those works emphasizing heroic conceits. Since he never expressed much interest in laws, the constitutional foundations of the French state, or even divine-right political philosophy, it is impossible to infer what Descartes might have thought of Bernard's history.

That the ideology of monarchy in the reign of Louis XIV would follow the psychology of the *grandes âmes* also meant that the thaumaturgical elements of the Monarchy would be largely deleted. Bernard stressed precisely these themes, of course, and particularly the occasions when Louis touched subjects suffering from scrofula to cure them. In his account of Louis's life, Bernard stresses from beginning to end the King's support from God. As the agent of God, Louis has powers that no one else possesses. Has not Providence always looked with favor upon French kings since they first were strengthened by the Christian faith? Applying this to Louis XIII in particular, Bernard explains his triumph over the Huguenots: "Si la bonté Divine, par le soin ordinaire dont elle nous assiste, n'eust armé le bras le plus victorieux du Roy, le plus juste et le plus généreux de la Terre." [27] It is in this role as God's agent that Louis is depicted, and the essential elements of a divinely established and well-ordered monarchy are reiterated. Ber-

26. *Discours de la Méthode*, ed. Jules Simon (Paris, 1857), p. 5.
27. *Histoire des guerres de Louis XIII*, p. 2.

nard evokes the quarrel between Romulus and Remus to support his argument that monarchical power is indivisible; indeed, the honor and respect conferred upon royalty is destroyed by a division of powers: "Qui ne sçait que les Maires du Palais se sont acreus de ceste sorte, et par leur interposition des roys au peuple, ont empesché le respect des uns et le commandement des autres."[28] The element of divine favor is evoked in many different contexts, for if monarchy is indivisible, it is also something of a mystery: the king's actions and thoughts are never completely understood by even the wisest of his subjects.

In Bernard, Louis XIII is always surrounded by an aura of saintly or even Christlike conduct. And do not his subjects recognize this and respond to it? For Bernard the answer could only be in the affirmative. In a brief account of the procession of the Holy Sacrament in Sainte-Foy, a town newly conquered and removed from Protestant influence, Louis followed the "sacrament, bare-headed, and followed by princes, royal officials, the most eminent in his council, and many noblemen."[29] One senses that Bernard builds upon these essentially visual images just as Louis himself did. A presage of victory was apparent when the King decided to leave for a particular campaign on Palm Sunday, becoming a "vray figure des Palmes et des victoires qu'il acquerroit en ce voyage."[30] The inference, of course, is that, in the little villages through which Louis traveled, the hearts of his subjects, imbued with the festive spirit, would be moved to obedience and respect by the almost magical effect of seeing their king on horseback on that holiday.

Rebels flee upon hearing their master's name: "Nos Roys ne se qualifient pas seulement Roys de France, mais Roys des Français, des personnes aussi bien que de la terre, pour en monstrer l'auctorité. Puissance qui n'agit pas seulement sur les biens, mais aussi sur les inclinations et les courages de leurs sujets."[31] In this way Bernard explains the indecision and ultimate cowardice of Henry de Rohan, one of the Protestant commanders, who, he says, attempted to flee with his army at night by boat, "cherchans avec le vent et l'élément le plus déloyal du monde, leur salut que leur obeissance leur pouvoit donner et les mettre en la grace du Roy."[32] After citing a passage from Book II of Justin's *Historiarum Philippicarum* about how the authority of their masters had led rebellious slaves to flee despite the fact that they were armed, Bernard goes on to describe how the king's divine power can influence

28. *Ibid.*, p. 320.
29. *Ibid.*
30. *Ibid.*, p. 250.
31. *Ibid.*, p. 271.
32. *Ibid.*

the motivations and courage of his subjects. Bernard asks whether it was an act of God that led Rohan to abandon the rebellion and answers that it was the "effect de l'authorité du Roy." And yet this had not come about through Louis's personal valor, but rather through the institution of the monarchy itself. Here Bernard's use of the divine-right conceit almost crushes Louis the person under the weight of its power. Wherever Louis goes, and virtually whatever he does, it is *en roi*.

Rohan's surrender was, of course, less a result of royal intimidation than Bernard depicted it; in fact, Bernard even mentions that Louis gave Rohan six hundred thousand livres and reinstated him in all his offices and pensions in return for his obedience. But all this happens as if no personal quality of Louis had influenced Rohan. This is particularly interesting because after 1650 the historiographers royal would attribute similar actions to the personal influence or courage of the prince, and not to his powers as wearer of the French crown.

Therefore, from the viewpoint of seventeenth-century readers, the *Histoire des guerres* approaches a synthetic coherence to the degree that Bernard was able to portray Louis's conduct as consistent with the images and roles attributed to French sovereigns over the centuries. There is no doubt that Louis tended to conduct himself in harmony with those images in both his ceremonial functions and his personal life. As a result, Bernard's work could have conveyed truth to his readers, especially those who were familiar with the images of monarchy inherited from the Middle Ages.

There was much more to Louis's conduct, however, than could be conveyed through the divine-right conceit. Every day, especially while on military campaign, the King did more than hear mass and cure the sick. Almost unwittingly Bernard allows us to perceive that Louis was to some degree familiar with the elements of the heroic role that men of letters had so carefully refined in the sixteenth century. Bernard simply did not perceive the psychological elements, if they were in fact there, but included the more rudimentary and almost day-to-day aspects of a hero's behavior. A good illustration of this is the account of Louis's actions before an important military engagement on 15 April 1622.[33] Bernard states, apparently with absolute certainty, that the King did not sleep the night before the confrontation, but that after resting he rose between two and three in the morning, heard mass, dressed for battle, and was the first to mount his horse. Bernard recounts these details in a flat, undramatic prose, and yet almost all the elements of the ancient conceit about the conduct of a commanding officer on the night before a battle are present. In his own way, Louis was playing

33. *Ibid.*, p. 263.

a role as commander in order to maximize his impact upon his officers and troops; indeed, he may have been more familiar than his historiographer royal with certain aspects of the role to be played by a conquering hero.

In another instance, after an officer had disobeyed his orders and deserved punishment, his superior officer ordered him to reconnoitre the enemy lines that evening. When Louis heard of this he countermanded the order, explaining that instead of being punished the disobedient officer was being given an opportunity to earn *gloire*. Bernard comments flatly that Louis's decision to change the punishment, so that the disobedient officer could not by a quirk of chance earn honor, was in conformity with Roman law.[34] Here is a missed opportunity to describe Louis as a leader of men who comprehended their emotions and knew how to manipulate them in a context of the rewards and punishments at the sovereign's disposal.

Thus we can perceive, but dimly, that some of the impulses to heroic conduct existed in Louis, but that Bernard lacked the talent to make the most of them in his history. Just why Bernard remained so preoccupied with the sacerdotal and institutional roles of kingship is unclear, but a partial explanation lies in the specific theme of his work, the war against the rebellious Huguenots. The image of the king as a devout, clement, and indeed divinely favored monarch is very appropriate for such a subject. A talented historian might have created an image of mystery or mystical knightliness to accompany the conceit, but Bernard was unable to do so. On the one hand he recounts too much, on the other not enough. The details about Louis's clothes, his willingness to put up with bad food, or his ability to call officers by name could not really be inserted into the history so as to contribute to the development of an overall portrait of Louis. Bernard, who was a witness to so much, or at least claimed to be, failed to recreate those events in prose.

Nor is Louis's notion of the value of Bernard's history known to us. At one point during the campaign against the Huguenots, however, Louis prepared a statement about the conditions in his army and among his subjects in the devastated areas of the southwest, sent it to the "Queens"—his mother, Marie de Médicis, and his wife, Anne of Austria—and also commanded Bernard to insert it as a matter of record into his history.[35] This reference to the work at least indicates Louis's awareness of Bernard's project; and though of minor importance, it permits us to infer that in some way Louis was personally interested in

34. *Ibid.*, p. 331.
35. *Ibid.*, p. 136.

preserving the record of his own actions and in assuring his immortality through a written history of his life. Had Louis merely wanted a record of events, he could have ordered a secretary of state to prepare a summary; but he commanded Bernard to include these details in his history.

Bernard's *Histoire des guerres* may have been a failure for another reason. He always implies that Louis was making the decisions about affairs of state, even while still a boy, yet he refers occasionally to the influence on royal policies exerted by Marie de Médicis,[36] favorites, and other royal councillors. He conveys no coherent impression that Louis was the head of state, obliged to make political decisions. Favorites—the Concinis and Luynes—are barely alluded to and usually only after disgrace or death has removed them from political influence. But these bits of evidence contradict the assertion that the King is ruling. This vagueness would certainly have done little to dispel the almost paranoid visions of some parlementaires about the power of favorites, for in failing to be precise about who was actually conducting affairs, Bernard left room for the most dire interpretations of Louis's conduct. The parlementaires and great nobles interested in the distribution of power within the royal council learned nothing from Bernard. By contrast, the histories of Louis XIV convey the impression that the Sun King really governed and dominated both ministers and great nobles.

It was on the subject of religion, however, that Bernard's readers would have found him the most controversial. His account of the rise of the Protestant heresy was a conscious effort to depict the Huguenots as the violators of both Christian doctrine and French laws. It is particularly interesting as a source for what must be defined as nearly official policy about the Huguenots at a critical moment in their war for survival as a political minority in France.[37] True to the legists' method, Bernard believed that comprehension of the Protestant heresy required a description of its origins and its spread into France. After describing the unreformed Church, where the faithful felt abandoned by an inattentive clergy, the narrative turns to Martin Luther and what might be called like-minded reformers in France. The "spread" of heretical ideas was of great interest to Bernard. Attributing this spread to the favor that reformers enjoyed with two princesses who were closely related to Francis I and to the connivance of judges who with "trop de douceur" failed to punish the heretics sufficiently, Bernard found that the evil then infected the souls of the *grands* and principal justices. For Bernard, Protestantism began as an essentially elitist movement with tenets that were heretical: "Tous ces devoyez s'appelloient

36. *Ibid.*, pp. 61–70.
37. Lublinskaya, Chap. 4.

Lutheriens, non qu'ils suivissent entierement et universellement les opinions de Luther. Car quelques-uns renouvellent les anciennes opinions
des Vaudois des Alpes: d'autres suivoient celles de Wiclif, de Jean Hus,
de Zingle, de Carlstaid, de Melancton, de Bucer . . . car il n'y avoit
point encore de doctrine arrestée."[38] This served as an introduction to
a narrative of the influence of John Calvin—an "homme de grande literature" whose "opinions alloient bien plus avant que celles de Luther"[39]—and of the Wars of Religion. The royalist cause is not entirely
defended by Bernard, but for him it was not so much the errors of
Henry III, for example, as the effect of heretical ideas, that inflamed
France: "Tant dangereux instrument est celuy de la literature quand
il tombe en des personnes d'un esprit pervers, remuant, et d'une ma-
licieuse inclination."[40]

There were rebellious individuals in all parts of France, of course,
and Bernard believed that they were more influenced by pamphlets
than were the sober individuals who respected the authority of Church
and state. Beyond individual differences, the peoples of each province,
he believed, had different emotional characteristics, making some more
prone to rebellion than others. The peoples of the south were particularly excitable. They had not, for Bernard, respected the terms of the
Edict of Nantes, and only Henry IV's generosity had prevented an
outbreak of war.[41] Bernard does note, however, that the Crown pressed
the proselytizing of Huguenot regions, and he unconsciously assumes
that Henry IV would eventually have sought the recatholicizing of all
Huguenots. Henry had reestablished bishops in Navarre, but he had
granted them pensions from the royal treasury rather than oblige them
to attempt collecting the revenues of their dioceses. The people of
Navarre might rebel, for "Il est perilleux de venir d'un extreme à un
autre sans passer au moyens, et puis un peuple chaud et bouillant comme
celuy de ce païs, s'excite facilement à la remontre des grandes muta-
tions."[42] Nevertheless, Bernard implies that it would have been only a
matter of time before the newly installed bishops could have lived
on their own.

It scarcely seemed a political matter when the Crown pressed the
Huguenots, but when the latter continued to hold assemblies and levy
taxes after the King had forbidden them to do so, Bernard describes
these issues as political. For him the flagrant violation of this prohibition against assemblies constituted a threat to the state:

38. *Histoire des guerres de Louis XIII*, p. 5.
39. *Ibid.*
40. *Ibid.*, p. 6.
41. *Ibid.*, p. 40.
42. *Ibid.*, p. 61.

En quelque Etat que ce soit de Monarchie ou de plusieurs, les deliberations qui concernent le public, se devoit faire de l'authorité de ceux qui y commandent; ce qui s'y fait autrement, tient du monopole et de la faction, qui tend infailliblement à la destruction et au pervertissement de l'ordre qui y est estably: toutes assemblés y doivent estre suspectes, les corps, les colleges, les confrairies, y doivent donner de l'ombrage; la seule occasion de les souffrir dependant de la cognoissance certaine que peut avoir le souverain de ce qui s'y negocie et de la legitime permission qu'il concede de les tenir.[43]

Bernard was careful to document what he defined as the royal prohibition against holding assemblies; and then—like so many of his contemporaries, including Richelieu—he made it clear that it was the Huguenots' political and fiscal activity, in short, their rebellion, and not their religious faith, that had forced Louis to take up arms.

There were basically two kinds of Protestants: those who were in any event inclined to rebel, particularly the *grands*, and those who were sincerely and devotionally "égarés." His portrait of the latter is identical to the Crown's general position and reminds the reader of Richelieu's famous speech to the Estates General of 1614. Those who are full of faith are "digne de compassion, se perdans par une dureté de coeur, et par la malice d'autry. Mais ils ne se gagnent y par le fer, ny par la force, aussi n'est-ce point contre ceux-la que le Roy veut employer ses armes. Ce n'est point contre le corps de ceux de la Religion Prétendue Réformée. . . . C'est contre une rebellion formée qu'il entend faire la guerre."[44] Bernard thus clearly perceived that his function as historiographer royal was to record not only the King's actions but also the reasons given by the King and his councillors to justify them. The Huguenot responses to the Crown's arguments were not included, even on such an important issue as the right to hold assemblies.[45]

On the other hand, certain aspects of the Crown's policies and, an even more delicate matter, the conduct of the last Valois king, also constituted something of a test for Bernard. How could he write about Henry III's assassination of the Guises, acts that did not coincide with the sacerdotal conceit in which he had depicted French sovereigns? Had the King not founded the Order of the Holy Spirit, Bernard asks. Nevertheless, some aspects of Henry's behavior did not conform to the image of the divinely sustained, pious, not too deviantly religious

43. *Ibid.*, p. 86.
44. *Ibid.*, p. 127.
45. *Ibid.*, p. 44.

monarch that Bernard sought to use as an integrating theme for all of French history. After all, in the case of Henry III, "ses confrairies, ses oratoires, ses pelerinages le faisoient presque pancher à la superstition. . . . Dans l'innocence et la ferveur des devotions du Roy, l'on trouve de quoy le calomnier. L'on anime le peuple contre ses prétendues dissolutions et ses prodigalités. . . . Il n'a pas mesme une sincere confiance en sa Mère.[46] Bernard remained discreet. Hiding behind apparently careless references to what others had said, he managed to convey something of the character of Henry III.

The important point had been to assure his readers that Henry had been neither a heretic nor a king too favorable to the Huguenots. Similarly, the assassination of the Guises is mentioned, but Bernard rushes on to relate the lamentable effects of the meeting of the estates at Blois upon Henry's policies.[47] There is almost an implied cause and effect here, but Bernard hesitated. His naive manner of recounting events does not suggest that he was holding something back to avoid incurring royal disfavor. Indeed, had he been intellectually capable of such thought, he would have avoided remarks such as the criticisms of Henry III for lacking confidence in his mother. After all, his readers could instantly have jumped to the conclusion that by analogy Bernard was critical of Louis XIII for exiling his mother after the assassination of Concini in 1617.

This pattern of analogical criticism was a fundamental element in the historical thinking of early-modern France; so Bernard's failure to perceive what could and what could not be paralleled with contemporary political situations reveals his limitations as a man writing history according to the conventional standards for the genre applied by his contemporaries. Beyond this, Bernard's discretion and even his distortion of Louis XIII's life, and of Henry III's as well, were part of an outlook that had as one of its principal assumptions the belief that evil deeds, gossip, blunders, military defeats,[48] and the influence of favorites[49] do little to edify readers.

46. *Ibid.*, pp. 30–31.
47. *Ibid.*, p. 33.
48. The siege of Montauban in 1621, in which Louis failed to capture the city, elicits some soul-searching on Bernard's part, as it no doubt did for Louis as well. He describes the Conseil de Guerre in which the decision to besiege the city was made and notes clearly that Louis favored it (*ibid.*, p. 204). Since the raising of the siege was followed by subsequent victories, the overall effects of this defeat on the King's image is, from Bernard's point of view, minimal.
49. Bernard summarized a harangue given by a parlementaire of Toulouse

The wars, negotiations, and occasional searing comments about the conduct of the *grands* follow one another, page after page. Bernard includes *in extenso* the major acts of settlement between the Crown and the Huguenots, as if to imply that he knew that the official acts rather than his summary of them would lend a greater air of truth to his history and particularly to the contention that the Huguenots were always the ones to break agreements. His legalistic-constitutional approach to the upheaval was accompanied by an exuberant faith that the troubles were almost over.

And what better way to predict the end of the Huguenot rebellion than to anthropomorphize it and remark that it had reached old age in the reign of Louis XIII? Its birth had occurred during the reigns of Francis I and Henry II and its adolescence under Francis II; it grew in strength and vitality under Charles IX and reached maturity and full vigor under Henry IV: "La curieuse remarque qu'on a fait, que presque toutes les hérésies n'ont guère duré plus d'un siècle, nous promet que celle-ci aprochant de ce temps, réduite à la Veillesse, et grandement affaiblie par les justes armes de nostre Louis XIII." [50] One might doubt that Bernard could believe such a theory about a vast religious and social movement, were there not other indications of his belief that numbers and stars determined the destinies of men. In some passages Bernard seeks a purely literary effect and admits as much: "Les observations du ciel sont bien peu seures, le calcul en est bien incertain, et les jugemens bien trompeurs; il ne faut pas neantmoins obmettre cet ornement de l'histoire." [51] These astrological explanations for events are at times crude in the extreme, but since the historians of Antiquity had done as much, Bernard also inserted astrology into his history. After referring to the "grand comète" that crossed the sky in 1618 and mentioning calamities that would later be considered the beginning of the Thirty Years' War, Bernard comments that all this, and the Huguenot rebellion, "ne nous ont que trop fait sentir les rudes effets de ces météores." [52] In some instances Bernard's belief in the stars, and more especially in numbers, seems sincere. He is struck by the apparent coincidence of events and is haunted by the idea that there may be cause and effect between them.

Or was Louis the one who believed in such explanations for events?

---

against Luynes (*ibid.*, p. 233), but by the time Bernard published the *Histoire*, Luynes was safely dead.

50. *Ibid.*, p. 41.
51. *Ibid.*, p. 250.
52. *Ibid.*, p. 95.

A man who made a successful effort to die on the anniversary of his father's assassination and his own accession to the throne, Louis XIII could well have influenced Bernard's thought. Upon hearing the news that the English had sailed from the waters off La Rochelle, for example, the King, Bernard recounts, remarked that, as in the case of great men of Antiquity, the important incidents in his life had occurred on Friday: Henry IV's death, the Battle of Ponts de Cé, the capture of Saint-Jean, the first siege of Clairac, Soubise's defeat at the Ile de Ré, and "many other events." Bernard may simply have been reporting Louis's thought. It is impossible to distinguish Bernard's thought from the ideas he attributes to the King; but they probably shared a belief in numbers and the resulting correspondence between events.

His effort to make Louis XIII illustrious tended to depersonalize the King, but in this Bernard was no different from many other men of letters and even men of science of his generation. Bernard records with pleasure that, just as Galileo honored the reigning Medici prince of Florence by naming the "stars close to the planet Jupiter, which he discovered with the *lunette de Holande*," so Theologal had named his discoveries after Louis XIII, "comme les noms des grands princes de de l'antiquité avoient esté donnez aux grandes constellations."[53] Bernard's perception of the principles of rhetoric and of the cult of reverence for Antiquity rarely extended beyond such obvious *topoi*.

The long, convoluted phrases, interminable digressions, and especially the blending of "noble" subjects—battle, for example—with vulgar ones—a description of living conditions among the peasants, for example—also convey the impression that Bernard's historical writing belonged more to the sixteenth-century Renaissance than to the new literary style and intellectual sensibilities that were to be characteristic of the 1640s. After him, sacerdotal kingship disappeared from officially sponsored history.

53. *Ibid.*, p. 73.

Chapter IV
Sorel: A Novelist
Turned Historiographer

T H E *Vraye histoire comique de Francion* gave Charles Sorel literary notoriety long before he settled down to purchase the *droit de survivance* of his uncle, Charles Bernard, as historiographer royal. Born in 1602, the son of a minor robe official who had served in the armies of the Holy League, he grew up in the obscurity of a family with noble pretensions and enough wealth to permit one of its sons to become a man of letters. The family, which occupied a house on the rue Saint-Germain-l'Auxerrois, near the Louvre, claimed to descend from an old noble family of Picardy, the Sorel d'Ugny, which in turn claimed descent from an ancient Scottish clan, the Shorel of Kildare.[1] These claims should not be allowed to deceive us about Sorel's robe origins, nor should they be ignored. As is often the case with the families of seventeenth-century men of letters, sufficient wealth permitted some of its members to lead a life of leisure as *honnêtes hommes* and to imitate casually the manners of gentlemen. Sorel belonged to that group. The talents that he possessed as a writer of both fiction and history were reflected in his social aspirations; a genuine intellectual curiosity would lead him still farther beyond letters and history to write works of science and bibliography in which he attempted to summarize human knowledge.

A member of the Comte de Cramail's entourage in 1621, for several years Sorel attended court with his patron, hoping to be noticed and to gain royal favor. By 1626 it had become clear that he lacked the talent to please at court, and in that year he seems to have decided on a career of writing. Through writing history, Sorel could quietly pass his days in the company of kings, ministers, and great princes of the

---

1. The standard account of Sorel's life and works is by Ernest Roy, *La vie et les oeuvres de Charles Sorel* (Paris, 1891), p. 2. Roland Mousnier, *L'assassinat de Henri IV* (Paris, 1964), p. 184, points out the same scorn of the *gentilshommes* for the robe that appears in Sorel's novel. Sorel's personal quest for gentle status and his preoccupation with elevating his *charge* above those of the *historiographes du roi* suggest that this scorn for the robe may have emanated from personal feelings.

realm. A powerful urge for acceptance as part of the dominant aristocratic culture of the seventeenth century provided a psycho-social impetus to write history for almost all the historiographers royal of the seventeenth century.

It is impossible to determine why Sorel failed to gain attention at the court of Louis XIII, but his tendency to be farcical, apparent in the *Vraye histoire comique de Francion*, may not have served him in good stead. The circle of gentlemen around Louis XIII, led by the first gentleman of the bedchamber, Claude de Rouvroy, first Duke of Saint-Simon, made it extremely difficult for men of Sorel's inferior social origins to do anything but bow before the King. Bernard had at least succeeded in having his *charge* granted to Sorel, but he could not pass on to him an intimacy with the King, something that at this late date in the reign everyone had to achieve for himself. The cynicism that occasionally rises to the surface in the *Francion* may also suggest that Sorel lacked the blind subservience required to wait week after week to be noticed. He possessed independence and a sense of his own value, and because the need for money seems not to have preoccupied him, Sorel took his *charge* seriously by writing history regularly after 1626.

The success of the *Francion*, published pseudonymously in 1623, may also have prompted Sorel not to comply totally with the wishes of his patron, Cramail. After all, had he not already earned considerable renown in his own right? Sorel removed some of the most coarse and raucous language from the 1624 edition of the *Francion*, after which its popularity soared still more rapidly. There were at least fifteen editions of the novel during his lifetime, a success partly explained by the occasional chapters that Sorel added to recapture the public that had already read the book. The *Francion* appeared under the name "N. de Moulinet, Sieur du Parc, Gentilhomme Lorrain," whereas the *Avertissement sur l'histoire de la monarchie françoise*, which he published in 1628, appeared under his own name, with the added title, "Sieur de Souvigny."[2] Writing history could be a noble venture, but writing fiction clearly was, if not degrading, at least so dubious that anonymity was preferred.

When Sorel received the *survivance* of his uncle's *charge*, he had every right to believe that the pension of twelve hundred livres accorded to him would be paid in quarterly installments for the rest of his life. We do not know how much Sorel paid Bernard for the *charge*, so it is impossible to determine whether this was a good return on his investment. Granted the *charge*, like almost any other venal office,

2. Roy, p. 10. It is spelled Soigny in a *privilège* to publish his *Les droits du roi* in 1666.

as a result of Bernard's favor, Sorel could anticipate that the legal arrangements of venality of office would guarantee him both an income and higher social status. Careful to stress that he was the *premier historiographe*, Sorel would write about his *charge* and assert that it was as well established, if not as lofty, as those of the great officers of the realm, such as the chancellor and the constable—a claim that was, of course, absurd. The transfer of the office of historiographer royal had, however, become much more institutionalized, if not quite bureaucratized, than in the sixteenth century. Depending on the social status of the historiographer, favor at court had previously linked the position to the household; but in the heyday of venality during the reign of Louis XIII, individuals who performed service for the Crown attempted to convert their somewhat tenuous status into a veritable *charge*. This effort never quite succeeded, and the historiographers royal of the later seventeenth century found themselves once again mere members of the household and with no basis for a claim that their sons or nephews could inherit their *charges*.

When Sorel was appointed he had no reputation whatever as a writer of history. Nor were his political sympathies publicly known. Louis XIII may have asked Bernard about such questions as the Leaguish role played by Sorel's father, or where the young man's sympathies lay in the conflicts with the Huguenots or over relations with Spain; but it is doubtful if Louis or his chancellor ever took the trouble to do so. Appointing a person whose political positions were at least totally unknown to the reading public suggests the minimal significance the Crown attached to the post. Louis may never have known about Sorel's claims that his *charge* ranked among the highest in the realm or, if he did, he did not bother to disabuse him of this pretentiousness. The King had long since grown accustomed to having many of his subjects claim far more prestige and power than they possessed; he only bothered to cut them down when their claims led them to quarrel with one another. Nor is there anything about Sorel's early career and education to suggest that history had been of special interest to him. The college experience that he so brilliantly describes in the *Francion* may not be directly autobiographical, but it is nevertheless interesting to note the boy's passion for reading novels, which he sometimes referred to as "chevaleries."[3]

Intelligent, but very eclectic in his interests, Sorel set out to be a historiographer royal because he enjoyed both writing and the public that it gave him. Had he possessed a family link to holders of the *charges* of translator of foreign languages, royal librarian, or perhaps

3. *Vraye histoire comique de Francion* (Rouen, 1663), p. 154.

any other requiring some literary-scholarly endeavor, he might have adjusted his ambitions accordingly.

Charles Sorel's brief tract, "Traité de la charge d'historiographe de France,"[4] cannot be said to express any official definitions of the function of history from the Crown's point of view. Yet it is illustrative of the outlook of men of letters themselves, in this instance of one who has already earned appointment and who now turns to raising the prestige of his function. Sorel begins with the *topos* that all well-administered states have had writers appointed to record the events taking place—"toutes les choses qui s'y sont passées"—after which he continues by listing why this function is important. How else would we know the identity of the ancestors of the most notable individuals in the state and upon what rights they establish their *honneurs*? It is in history, Sorel continues, that kings may find the support for their scepters, and others may find the means of maintaining their fortune. Good actions are praised to give example to those who want to imitate them, and bad ones are condemned. The proofs of nobility may be found in history, the study of which is so great that both kings and the leading men in republics appoint men of great esteem to write history in order to be the "arbiters" of the renown of some . . . and the distributors of *gloire*. In this definition of the office, Sorel varies little from the typical *ars historica* notion of the utility of history. He never doubts the value of placing the writer of history in the service of the state. Then, as might be expected, after this justification of his function, he turns to a list of those who have performed this service for the French. Had the nationalization of the culture progressed to such a point that allusions from Antiquity had gone out of favor? Sorel was particularly eager to assure his *charge* in France, and for that reason he began his account with Einhard's role as historian of Charlemagne and then continued down the long list of writers and chroniclers whom he considered to have written in the service of the Crown: Nitard, of course, the monks of Saint-Denis, Alain Chartier, Gilles, Jean Le Maire des Belges, Paul Emile, Jean D'Auton, Denys Sauvage, and Pierre Paschal. Note the absence of Joinville, with whom Sorel certainly must have been familiar, and of Froissart, Commynes, and Gaguin, who despite their evident merit had written only as individuals and had not been selected or in some way sponsored by the Crown in their endeavors. Still, Sorel recognized that neither the appointments nor the functions of these writers were regular and that, above all, they lacked a succession from writer to writer.

Thus, for Sorel, it was in the reign of Charles IX that the appoint-

4. B.N., L³⁵ 89.

ment of historiographer of France became a regular *charge*, with an established succession beginning with du Haillan and continuing in Pierre Mathieu and Sorel's own uncle, Charles Bernard.

Beyond this—and it is a good illustration of the preoccupation with ranks and titles during the seventeenth century—Sorel's account of his office is mainly concerned with demonstrating the superiority of the historiographer of France over those who are merely designated historiographers of the king. The argument is tortured, the claims inordinately self-serving and pretentious. Concern with exclusivity, office, and pensions may have been stimulated by the social mobility engendered by the massive sale of offices during the 1620s and 1630s. During those years the traditional hierarchies in the law, guilds, and perhaps even universities and religious orders had barely survived the upheavals of the sixteenth century. And with mere bourgeois and tax collectors gaining nobility and prestige through offices all over France during the reigns of Henry IV and Louis XIII, the man of letters wondered about his place in the society and acted defensively by attempting to describe it as if it were a *charge*. Sorel's definition of a *charge* conveys the sense that it is a privilege and an honor transmissible from generation to generation, not a duty or service in the Ciceronian sense. And while enjoying the *charge* and attempting to enhance its status, Sorel nonetheless continued to seek other patrons.

In his long letter to Cardinal Richelieu, Sorel proposed dedicating to the Cardinal his early history of the Monarchy, that is, of the first two races of kings.[5] Beginning with the observation that all the recently published books are dedicated to the Cardinal, he notes that it is in commemorating the Cardinal's actions that writers can "faire un chef d'oeuvre de leur art." What can he, as an artisan, do to contribute to Richelieu's *gloire*? Since he has recently completed the first part of the history, he can think of nothing better than dedicating it to him. There is no mention of money, but if the Cardinal would simply encourage him by a *regard*, he might be able to work all the faster on the history of the third race of kings and thus reach that period when the Cardinal's own actions might be included in the history. Then there is the usual account of the inadequacies of already published narratives, coupled with the lament that in France the "faits d'Alexandre" or of the Roman consuls are better known than French history. In his conclusion Sorel points out that all those other works dedicated to Riche-

5. Undated, by 1631–1632? B.N., mss. fr. 23342, fol. 64. Published in the collectively edited *Mémoires du Cardinal de Richelieu*, Rapports, Société de l'Histoire de France (Paris, 1907), vol. 334, p. 283. I doubt that Richelieu gave him a pension over and above what he was already receiving.

lieu will not be durable, but that "les histoires vivent éternellement," especially when they are written with "vives raisons d'état et de ces sentences morales" included to stimulate the reader's interest. Illustrious though the *charge* of historiographer might be, it did not supplant or dispense with the need to seek patrons among the great. Nor did it command exclusive dedications to the king, at least during the reign of Louis XIII.

Sorel never claims that his knowledge of history might make him a valuable adviser to his prince; he seems not to have sought active participation in the life of Louis XIII's court, nor does he seem to have envisaged attaining the kind of intimacy that he claimed his uncle, Bernard, had enjoyed with Louis XIII. A shift in the relative importance of these claims to recognition occurred in the seventeenth century. The humanist ideal of the man of learning who advised his prince and shared intellectual interests had less appeal under Louis XIII. Indeed, the only group of writers to persist in the mirror-of-princes tradition were the reforming clergy during the reign of Louis XIV. For Jacques Bossuet and François de Salignac de la Mothe-Fénelon—the direct heirs of both the medieval ecclesiastical and the humanist scholarly traditions of service to the prince—the claim to be men of God sustained by the wisdom drawn from the lessons of history still marked the most powerful, if not the most radical, force in the political culture. Richelieu himself shared many of these characteristics.

The more secular men of letters, however, were interested in attracting the king's attention, not in instructing him. Couched in convoluted and plodding sentences, Bernard's or Mézerai's accounts of Louis XIII's battles reflected a desire to gain recognition from the King; but in reality neither had the ability to rise above more than a crude synthesis of contemporary literary canons and historical thought, whereas the somewhat later accounts of similar actions by Pellisson and Racine attained an aesthetic unity and perfection that made them ring false as history.

We may imagine the reading public and critics of historical writing in the seventeenth century as ranged together along a giant spectrum, with various segments of the public able to understand and appreciate different sorts of historical writing. The editions and heavily footnoted works of the erudite historiographers were at one end, with a very small public. Ranged along the middle were the historical works—neither very well researched nor very well written—of such men as Jean de Serres, Charles Sorel, and François Eudes de Mézerai, whose adjustment of the subject matter of their histories to please the larger reading public was rewarded by numerous editions of their works.

Then, too, these writers lacked talent as literary artists and could not write historical prose conforming to the literary canons established by Jean Chapelain and other founders of the literary aesthetic of classicism. Their choppy style, personal comments, gossip, and faithful inclusion of miracles and prodigious signs pleased the public; it was history *comme il faut*, that is, ridden with myths and full of boasting about the French.

Finally, at the other extreme of the spectrum we find the works of history—works by Pellisson, Racine, and others, including Bossuet himself—that met the standards of eloquence. Here the principles of ancient rhetoric had been comprehended and synthesized into a literary aesthetic that, when applied to historical writing, succeeded in conveying meaning and vitality to only a relatively small group of readers and listeners. Such eloquent histories were still frequently read aloud at court and in literary circles; indeed, they were declaimed.

At each end of the spectrum, then, we find the logical elaboration of the two principal tendencies that developed in the pursuit of erudition and eloquence, as each evolved into distinct but nonetheless connected seventeenth-century approaches to the past. Remember that when Sorel removed the "bas mots" from his novel, its popularity increased; the pursuit of eloquence seemed to accord with the campaign to have "everyone" read and enjoy French history.

Therefore, it is in this context of a certain freedom from a tradition of erudition and only a spare knowledge of rhetoric that Sorel's *Avertissement* takes on a special interest.[6] Conventional and innovative elements in the manner of writing French history are found side by side. The emphasis was, however, clearly on the innovative, on reaching as large a reading public as possible. Complaints about the lack of interest in French history or that men of letters know the number of Roman

6. Roy, pp. 340–345, claims that the fear of censorship turned Sorel away from archival research. None of the evidence of censorship cited by Roy refers to Sorel, nor is there evidence to suggest that Sorel considered becoming an *érudit*. His approach is conventional, that is, to write history from the works of other historians. And instead of a climate of censorship under Richelieu, a climate of debate developed as a result of the Cardinal's sponsorship of authors who wrote to counter pamphlets critical of his policies. The specific acts of censorship after 1624 seem to be no more extensive than during the previous period of strong royal government under Henry IV. Here we must remain tentative until there is more research of the type that Alfred Soman had carried out for the earlier period. See his *Press, Pulpit, and Censorship before Richelieu, Proceedings of the American Philosophical Society* 120, no. 6 (December 1976): 439–463.

consuls and emperors better than French sovereigns[7] add nothing to what is almost a genre in itself: writing about history to advertise and prepare the public for a big work on the subject. Sorel wanted to catch the public eye in this *Avertissement*, much as writers and publishers of history would do in the twentieth century. In order to do this he had to (1) accuse the reading public of its lack of attention to history, (2) denigrate the works of previous historians of France, and (3) promise to publish a history that would overcome these faults. Sorel claims that his history will be new. His promotionalism about the work and how in the future it will change the attitudes of Frenchmen toward their history is combined with a forthright claim about the value of his approach: "La jeunesse la lira aussi tost que des Romans, voyant que l'on y pourra apprendre de beaux mots, et que l'on y trouvera une diversité d'aventures. Les poëtes y chercheront des sujets pour leurs poëmes."[8] Sorel in no way felt inferior to the tradition of *érudits* who published ancient texts. His confidence in the value of his more popular approach to history seems to be forthright and genuine. By reading his history, foreigners will learn French—which he believes desirable—and they will also learn about the "célèbres actions" of the French Monarchy. But pedantic excursions must be avoided, and, above all, "Le peuple ne se plaist point à lire des histoires quelques véritables qu'elles soient, s'il n'y trouve quelque douceur qui soit comme un charme pour l'attirer et le retenir."[9] Sorel clearly believed that, if it was to reach a large public, his work would have to be not only truthful but agreeable as well. This perception of the public, and his adjustment of his writing to conform to this perception, provided a complete and self-conscious rationale for writing popular history that was at once compatible with the principles of ancient rhetoric revived by the humanists and with the aim to have a much larger public—the "peuple"—read history, an aim made possible by the invention of printing.

The denigration of his predecessors who wrote history was not personal, but sociological. Those Frenchmen "incapable of preaching or pleading, or of composing verses or elegant orations have for a refuge to be our historians, as if that profession did not require all the qualifications that characterize an accomplished author."[10] That writers of history had been defined as inferior in the hierarchy of letters may have troubled Sorel throughout his career. For social reasons—because writ-

7. *Avertissement sur l'histoire de la monarchie françoise* (Paris, 1628), p. 1, B.N., L[35] 89.

8. *Ibid.*, p. 34.

9. *Ibid.*, p. 36.

10. *Ibid.*, p. 7.

ing novels could not be ennobling—Sorel made a conscious attempt to gain the public recognition as a writer of history that he already had acquired as a novelist. The scientific and philosophical works he wrote after publication of his *Histoire de la monarchie françoise* in 1632 may have been motivated not only by an intellectual curiosity that history failed to satisfy, but also by his failure to earn acclaim, as we shall see, from his historical writings. Indeed, for Sorel the public response to any literary effort would always constitute the writer's ultimate success or failure. Having, in a sense, already acquired royal favor, Sorel did not write with an eye to increasing his favor with Louis XIII.

The reasons for the failure of his predecessors who had published histories of the French Monarchy interested Sorel. Their parochial emphasis on the institutions to which they were personally attached, and not on the lives of the monarchs themselves, fated writers to oblivion. Gregory of Tours is singled out to be criticized for his emphasis upon monastic history; for, Sorel says, instead of writing about the Franks, he writes about Frankish monks, "as if the history of the Monarchy were put in his book almost by accident."[11] But Sorel saves his most savage attack for the sixteenth-century predecessors, who "because most of the men have been *hommes du Palais*, they limited their [studies] to chicaneries."[12] His rejection of both monastic and robe historiography was above personal rivalry and may have been inspired by his own rejection of these two social forms of life, the intellectual segments of the first and third estates. But far from being unique, Sorel's criticism reflected the dominant mood of the political culture in the reign of Louis XIII. The emphasis on the controversies arising out of histories of monastic foundation and their privileges, or out of the constitutional and legal controversies so dear to the robe, offended Sorel's sensibilities and those of many other bright *honnêtes hommes* of his generation. Not that dealing with these subjects was dangerous owing to the possibility of censorship. Quite the contrary. For Sorel the mistake of the sixteenth-century historians in general had been that they "all contradict one another"[13] on these subjects. Sorel had had enough of controversy, and he believed that the reading public shared his fatigue with differing opinions.

The violence provoked by the Reformation and the Wars of Religion had run its course. Slowly the need felt for authority and consensus may have prevailed over a search for truth in historical writing. The *érudits* responded to this same mood by publishing texts, often

11. *Ibid.*, p. 8.
12. *Ibid.*, p. 156.
13. *Ibid.*, p. 32.

without much commentary, perhaps in subconscious recognition that not only would their own words be suspect but, more important, they also would fail to still religious and constitutional controversies. Claims that writers of history had sought the "truth" in their accounts had become commonplace in the sixteenth century; and since this search had apparently fed the flames of controversy and even violence, it had been devalued. On questions of their national history, the French wanted an account of their past on which they could agree, much as the English earlier had temporarily agreed about their religion in the theologically equivocal but faultlessly written *Book of Common Prayer*. Sorel attempted to respond to that need, as did many other historiographers royal throughout the seventeenth century.

Nor was Sorel proposing to write a history of France. Such an account would have to include descriptions of dress, construction, the founding of churches and *collèges*, and so forth.[14] Almost as if afraid of a particularistic detail, Sorel proposed to write only the "history of a state wherein one sees the succession of those who have commanded it. One must leave out countless details about what they did in their youth, and begin when princes ascend the throne."[15] Then, as if to be more specific, while discussing the significance of the founding of the monastery of Saint-Denis, he writes:

> Or si quelqu'un ne croit pas que la dedicace d'une Eglise ayt esté capable de faire descendre le fils de Dieu visiblement en terre, je ne veux pas faire partie avecque luy pour combattre toute l'antiquité. L'on me dira que les Moynes ont voulu persuader qu'il s'est fait plusieurs miracles à l'origine de leurs églises pour les rendre plus illustres, mais je me contante de ne les escrire point sans parler absolument du contraire. Chacun ne trouve pas bon que l'on refute ce que le peuple croid pieusement. Pierre Abeillard fut mesme excommunié autrefois pour avoir soustenu que ce n'estoient pas les reliques de Saint Denis Areopagyte qui estoient en France.[16]

Did Sorel deliberately want to confuse the issue of popular piety and the attitudes of educated contemporaries toward it with the Church's role as the guardian of those opinions and persecutor of those who challenged them? He seems to have been genuinely respectful of the beliefs of his ignorant compatriots; he nowhere implies, as Voltaire would a century later, that challenging popular piety might incite vio-

14. *Ibid.*, p. 55.
15. *Ibid.*, p. 54.
16. *Ibid.*, p. 133.

lence. Prudent on matters of church and state, Sorel attempted to write a history that would blur the edges of what had seemed irreconcilable conflicts. He wanted to write a history for "tout le peuple," as he put it, and he knew that to challenge popular religious opinion would prevent him from gaining the public acclaim he so desired. He hoped that his readers would find many "agreeable" things in his work. And, as if to summarize the commonplaces of the ancient rhetoricians about history, he added: "L'historien doit plustost estre porté au bien qu'au mal, et quoy qu'il soit obligé de declarer les mauvaises qualitez des Princes sans deguisement, si est-ce qu'il doit prendre plus de plaisir à raconter les bonnes, pource qu'elles ne servent d'exemple."[17]

This effort to write history in which the consensus of the French would be emphasized more than their conflicts extended beyond Sorel's thematic choices for his history to include a soothing literary style. He condemned the use of satirical nuances; "pointes," that is, phrases that could be interpreted in two ways—agreeably by the naive and reproachfully by the more sophisticated—had no place in such a history: "La beauté du langage d'un historien consiste en la force des mots, et en la naifve signification, et s'il veut avoir des pointes, il faut que ce soient autant de maximes d'estat."[18] By using commonplaces about the behavior of states ("science politique," as Sorel calls it), history would achieve the double purpose of removing grounds for future controversy and providing a general system of causation. Since princes hide the causes of their actions so well, Sorel asserts, the appropriately chosen maxim of state should be inserted to explain the causes of wars and other events whose origins are secret.

The research for his history obviously consisted of reading the previous histories, remembering the various accounts of the same events, and then choosing those that were the "most truthful" to comprise his own narrative. Where there is a disagreement between the "ancients" and the "moderns"—by which Sorel presumably meant historians writing in the remote past and those who had written recently—Sorel believed that it was his duty to give his own opinion. Thus, his personal sense of the creation of events in the past was very limited. Most of that work had been done by his predecessors, and when he complained about their contradictions and disagreements, it was not from a desire to denigrate them but rather from a feeling of frustration that they had not resolved all the difficulties. Whenever Sorel added his own opinion, it certainly was in order to blur conflicting conclusions about what had happened in the past. Only when he knew what he wanted

17. *Ibid.*, p. 171.
18. *Ibid.*, p. 201.

to say could he begin the difficult task of embellishing what he writes, what has never been embellished before.[19] Without the help of Providence, his history could never be completed, and, once published, Providence will preserve it: "afin que l'on voye combien sa Providence a paru dans les accidens passez, et combien il [Dieu] a tousjours favorisé nos Roys, et pour tout dire en un mot, afin que cela réussisse au bien commun de tout le peuple."[20] As an *avertissement* for a major work, Sorel's disarms by its honesty. His interests were literary. And since he was offended by the controversies that had preoccupied historians in the past, his aim would be to produce a past to which the entire French population could rally, be edified, and, still more, feel unified by reading it.

Just how typical was it for men of letters coming to maturity during Louis XIII's reign to flee controversy and, in a sense, to give historical foundations to the *politique* outlook? Throughout the sixteenth century, including the years of upheaval, writers had passionately described the Monarchy as the providential source of order, greatness, and unity in French society. Seen from this perspective, Sorel's historical thinking represents the continuity of one sixteenth-century strand of writing—broadly speaking, that of Paul Emile, François de Belleforest, du Haillan, and de Serres. A new element, however, was the decline of those whose works seemed to perpetrate disorder and historical controversy—those like de Thou, who kept writing history in such a way as to perpetuate partisanship and constitutional conflict. Regardless of whether de Thou was correct in recounting his own times, he seemed to inspire only contempt and censorship from the Crown. And he suffered oblivion, an even worse fate, among younger writers such as Sorel, who does not even mention him in his early works.[21] The question of whether the *paulette* had been promulgated as an edict according to the procedure of the chancery or in some other way by royal order—a subject of considerable interest to de Thou—was just the sort of chicanery disapproved of by Sorel. As the son of a robe official now busily establishing his credentials as a nobleman, he seems to have been revolted by the mental outlook of the lawyer-constitutionalist.

Other works of history, including Pasquier's monumental third vol-

19. *Ibid.*, p. 207.
20. *Ibid.*, p. 209.
21. Gustave Dulong dismisses de Thou and Agrippa d'Aubigné as having had no influence on seventeenth-century historical writing (*L'abbé de Saint-Réal, étude sur les rapports de l'histoire et du roman au XVIIe siècle* [Paris, 1921], p. 30). This seems difficult to accept, but references to their works or expressions of admiration for them as writers of history have not been found.

ume of his *Recherches de la France* published in 1616, also tended to provide underpinnings for French unity. The unifying force of culture, the French language and works written in it, and their authors, of whom all Frenchmen could be proud, also implicitly rejected the particularistic and controversial subjects that had pervaded the consciousness of some of the French literate elite during the Wars of Religion. The commonplace about the disputative and quarrelsome nature of the French was still included as part of the stereotype, but historians lacked the motivation to provide a demonstration of the presence of this trait in the national character.

The flurry of interest in the history of Gallican liberties was inevitable, what with the Venetian crisis of 1607 before their eyes; and at home the debate about whether to apply the articles of the Council of Trent and admit the Jesuits became controversies that stimulated historical scholarship and pamphleteering. These two different discourses had begun to flow together in the sixteenth century; the *érudits* of the seventeenth century would slowly move them apart by their works of scholarship. But even late in the reign of Louis XIV, the works of the *érudits* and the pamphleteering controversialists still had ideological-historiographical similarities.[22] In general, however, the historical interest in Gallicanism represented still another effort to emphasize the independence and, in a sense, the national solidarity of the French. Foreign influences—Genevan, papal, Spanish, or whatever—could be held as partly responsible for the decades of turmoil. The glorious triumphs over foreigners, the conquests of territory, and the careful recounting of French dynastic history and of the king's "rights" became favorite subjects for historians such as Sorel, who were writing for a large public, and even for some *érudits*, notably Théodore Godefroy.[23] As did the sixteenth-century statesmen they wrote about, historians implicitly accepted the notion that there was a relationship between foreign wars and civil wars.[24] Those of Sorel's generation had no difficulty in deciding which they thought the more reprehensible. They willingly praised wars of conquest, perhaps in the hope that, if such wars came, they would reduce the number of revolts led by princes, Protestants, and peasants.

With his emphasis on writing history that would be agreeable, and

22. Joseph Klaits, *Printed Propaganda under Louis XIV* (Princeton, 1976), *passim*.

23. See Théodore Godefroy, *L'ordre et cérémonies observés aux mariages de France et d'Espagne: Entre Louis XIII, et Anne d'Austriche* (Paris, 1627), B.N., L^b36 602.

24. Fernand Braudel, *La Méditerranée et le monde méditerranéen à l'époque de Philippe II* (Paris, 1966), vol. 2, p. 170.

having no antiquarian interests, Sorel would not need to devalue the search for "perfect history" as conceived by some of the sixteenth-century writers. He never pursued such an ideal. Neither ideological persuasions nor the love of adding hitherto unknown texts and dates to the canon of French history pressed him to go beyond reading the narratives of earlier historians. He saw no need to decipher ancient charters deposited in the Palais, that place he may have disliked because it symbolized the power and status of robe society. Later in life, when writing critical comments on past histories, he had words of praise for Pithou and his fellow antiquarians; but as a young man writing an *avertissement*, he seems not to have thought of archival research. Certainly such research was not seen as a necessity by Sorel and his contemporaries. The historical revolution of the sixteenth century had made no impact on the young historiographer royal writing in 1628. He read the histories published by the legal humanists, but he seems not to have viewed them as distinctly superior to those of their predecessors. Quite the contrary. They were full of chicanery, and he seems to have chosen deliberately to steer away from the subjects they had seen as central to the history of the French. Joan of Arc, for example, received no extended comment in Sorel's history; her career coincided with another moment of division and suffering that Sorel thought it better to deemphasize.

Sorel refused to write a history of the French, because that would have emphasized the particularisms and parochial jealousies that divided them. Instead, he proposed to treat the institution that united them: the Monarchy.

Unlike many of the sixteenth-century men of letters, however, Sorel did not stress the themes of glory and immortality earned by the French through their noble deeds. His knowledge of the rhetorical framework developed in praise of kings by the Pléiade must have been quite limited. His bawdy and lower-class *Francion* demonstrates his freedom from the cultural and intellectual preoccupations of the Pléiade. There would be little emphasis on edification and immortality in Sorel's history, and, as in Bernard's, where these are discussed, the humanist commonplaces about *gloire* are not synthesized with the personalities of French sovereigns. The vulgar anecdote would creep into Sorel's narrative, as it had into Bernard's; and just as Bernard had emphasized sacerdotal kingship, Sorel quietly emphasized the indispensable need for leadership among the French. This desire to escape from the loyalties previously given to estates, sects, monastic chapters, and courts of law, which so pervaded the *honnêtes hommes* of Sorel's generation, did not stem from the rhetorical traditions developed in the sixteenth century. For Sorel, the viable French past meant strong leadership from the Crown and obedience from subjects. The writers of his generation who were the heirs of the Pléiade placed the French past within the framework of classicistic culture and continually compared the ancients and the moderns. But not Sorel. More modest and perhaps ill-equipped to write in the grand manner, he would not earn public acclaim for his works.

Apart from counting the number of editions of a work after publication and perhaps recording the occasional critical remark found in letters by contemporaries, it is almost impossible to determine the response to a work of history published during the seventeenth century. Sorel's decades of historical writing were a time when pamphlet wars were still being fought and when the literary canons of the Pléiade and their successors were still being refined and established in literary circles. Thus, none of the national French histories written in the 1620s and 1630s, including that by Scipion Dupleix, won public acclaim. Editions of Jean de Serres still poured forth to satisfy the more popular market for French history. Sorel's *Histoire de la monarchie françoise* received very little attention and was not followed by a second edition.

After this failure, Sorel settled down to improving his knowledge of philosophy. He published occasional short pieces on behalf of the Crown's policies, for example, *La deffence des Catalans* (Paris, 1642),[25] an indication that he took his charge as historiographer seriously. But apart from these brief pieces, it is apparent that his interest was caught up by the works of Francis Bacon, Aristotle, and the ancient rhetoricians. An encyclopedic turn of mind is evident in some of the more philosophic works, notably *De la perfection de l'homme*, published in 1655. Sorel's desire to transmit knowledge to "all the French," like his desire to write a history of all the French, may have led him to attempt a synthesis of knowledge. His preoccupation with child rearing—including the benefits of breast feeding, for example—and with early education may have been related to an attempt to gain appointment as preceptor to young Louis XIV or some other princely child. But Sorel was curious intellectually; his works have the originality found in the autodidact who ignores the ways in which fields of knowledge are constructed. The blending of classical, mirror-of-princes, Baconian, and Cartesian thought is a personal one and hence not like those works of moral philosophy published by writers belonging to specific

25. He also defended the building of canals, as Bernard had done a half century earlier, and the superior rank of French kings over those of England and Spain.

schools of thought. Sorel simply read, thought, and wrote without testing his opinions on others, and he was greatly influenced by Bacon's thought.[26]

Still later in life, though it is impossible to know exactly when because the work was published anonymously as part of a collection of essays, Sorel attempted to sum up his views on history.[27] In their individuality and sincerity the results remind one of La Popelinière though less directly concerned with the problem of how historical truth may be discovered. Sorel was more sociological in his historical thinking than the Huguenot author of *Histoire des histoires*.

Some writers, Sorel asserts, who were paid by kings to write history, slandered their patrons to the point that their works were injurious to the posterity of those kings. Indeed, in such histories, monarchs are accused of crimes they did not commit. Sorel does not name names but presumably is interested in the distinction between someone granted a *charge* as *historiographe de France* and someone who was merely placed on the pension lists for having written history.[28] Sorel considered the *charge* both a privilege and a guaranty of probity. In the 1660s, Colbert tended to transform patronage into a commercial relationship, and Sorel may have been responding negatively to this tendency. The writer who produces is paid; the one who does not is stricken from the pension rolls. In the past the payment-for-production relationship now being favored by Colbert had led to calumny. Would it in the future? For Sorel, only persons possessed of *charges* could be relied on to record the actions of the prince.

In addition to his harsh criticism that the writing of history was being reduced to a virtual "putting out" system in which the entrepreneur selected the subject and supplied the memorandums to be used as sources, Sorel objected strongly to the appointment of a large number of poets as historiographers. Among the men of letters around Chapelain it was commonplace to hear that prose was easier to write than verse. From this assertion it was only a short step to the statement that a bad poet might well succeed if he applied his talents to writing his-

26. Richard Popkin, *History of Scepticism* (New York, 1964), p. 125. See F. Garavini, "Un ouvrage moderne: *La science universelle* de Sorel," *Le XVIIe siècle et la recherche*, published by the Centre Méridional de Rencontres sur le XVIIe siècle, (Marseille, 1976), pp. 225–236.

27. The volume is entitled *De la prudence*, B.N., Q 3421. Roy, p. 349, notes that Perrot d'Ablancourt had been named *historiographe du roi*. Perrot was never named to the post but was considered for it. See below, p. 192. This is not conclusive proof that these essays were all written at that time.

28. *De la prudence*, p. 45.

tory.[29] Sorel scorned these arguments and replied that the writing of history required special qualifications and talents not necessarily present in a poet.

In addition, although Sorel has compliments for Pithou and Duchesne, "la pluspart des Rechercheurs d'antiquitez ne s'estudient point à bien escrire n'y à composer des ouvrages complets."[30] Sorel sought a middle path between the rhetorically inclined and the erudite writers of history. His hostility to the appointment of *hommes de lettres* as historiographers[31] was so great that we must infer that he considered himself outside that identity.

Those to be appointed should be persons of "bonne naissance," well educated, and already established as writers of history. Sorel does not mention names, but presumably he was referring to François de Bassompierre when he observed that some writers of history had in fact possessed these qualifications but had given up because their efforts had not been remunerated. Sorel nowhere mentions active participation in the affairs of state as a qualification; if he was familiar with the civic perspective of the sixteenth century he did not mention it.

Though the appointment of poets was detrimental, and royal policies erroneous, Sorel saved his most bitter attacks for the influence of the *grands*. He credits their protection of men of letters as the compelling reason behind a royal appointment. The great nobles compete with one another to have the Crown appoint their favorite poets as historiographers and see that they are awarded pensions, regardless of their qualifications. The quality of a work of history does not determine its public reception; rather, its success or failure depends on the "crédit des autheurs" with the *grands*.[32] Sorel's position on patronage of history is a *thèse royaliste*. He was not critical of patronage as an institution, but his observation that the *grands* inflated the reputations of their literary clients in order to have them placed on the royal pension rolls coincides temporally with the post-Fronde crisis of the great nobility. Politically humbled, indebted as a result of their rebellion, and their own households in disorder, the princes turned to the Crown for places for their clients.

Moreover, Sorel asserts, neither the *grands* nor courtiers are in the least familiar with the qualifications necessary for writing different kinds of history. In the first place, it was wrong to consider a translator of the histories of Antiquity for appointment as *historiographe du roi*

29. *Ibid.*, p. 69.
30. *Ibid.*, p. 67.
31. *Ibid.*, p. 49.
32. *Ibid.*, pp. 49–53.

and expect him to write the history of Louis XIV.[33] This is an explicit allusion to Perrot d'Ablancourt, the translator of numerous classical works, who had in fact been considered for appointment as historiographer upon Chapelain's recommendation but who ultimately was turned down by Louis because he was a Huguenot.[34]

And yet Sorel stresses that anyone undertaking to write contemporary history must be entirely familiar with the "grand art de l'Histoire" —his way of saying the *ars historica*. His study of rhetorical theory had not led to an emphasis on language alone; he was neither an Ancient nor a Modern. From the general perspective of classicistic theories of history, Sorel could only be described as muddled.

But this was not all. Sorel added that another qualification should be "une certaine adresse d'escrire les choses les plus hardies sans qu'elles n'offencent personne, et il ne devroit paroistre ny medisant ny flatteur."[35] After this salvo on behalf of independence, however, Sorel descends into still another defense of his *charge* as more prestigious than that of the *historiographes du roi*.

The last source of contamination for history derives from the tendency of some writers to prepare *abrégés*, *narrations*, and *chronologies* at the specific request of book publishers.[36] It is surprising to find that someone who so eagerly pressed for the writing of a history to be read by all the French was unable to perceive that publishers were responding to the market demands when they commissioned *abrégés*.

After all these criticisms, Sorel proposes remedies. He suggests the establishment of a special academy for the writing of history. Members would be elected on the basis of their knowledge of languages, of the laws of rhetoric, and of politics—plus a "mélange d'autres disciplines." Their work would be carried out through the uninhibited discussion of each point or action of French history. A "directeur" would be selected from the membership to preside over the discussion and finally decide what phrases and facts would be included in a history of France and a history of the reigning monarch. His model is the French Academy and its dictionary project. Nor is it difficult to discern whom he thought would be selected for the directorship.

Like those who conceived the dictionary project, and like the sixteenth-century *érudits* who proposed models for "perfect histories," Sorel still thought a history of France could be prepared once and for all. The notion of historical scholarship as a process of deepening knowledge still had not been logically connected to a notion of the constant

33. *Ibid.*, p. 70.
34. See below, p. 192.
35. *De la prudence*, p. 70
36. *Ibid.*, p. 50.

revision of the general works of history written for the public. After repeating the central theme of all his thought about history—the need to have a history that everyone can learn—he finally gives us his purpose: "tous les François, de quelque condition qu'ils soyent, y puissent aprendre leur devoir."[37] One would like to be able to interview Sorel in order to discover what he meant by "leur devoir." It is tempting to assert that this theme appears as a result of the Fronde; but in his isolation and reflection, Sorel may have been reaching for an understanding of the function of historical thought that differed from or supplemented the function of remembering the dead.

A plaintive note appears at the end of the work. Describing himself and his career in the third person, Sorel remarks: "Chacun doit savoir qu'après avoir receu par plusieurs années les gages qui luy estoient attribuez à cause de sa charge, enfin ils luy ont esté ostez entierement, sons qu'il en ait jamais pû savoir la cause."[38] What had happened? Prolonged research in the treasury rolls might reveal the answer. Had the financial crisis provoked by foreign and civil war led ministers to eliminate his *gages*? Sorel had no strong supporters at court, so he may simply have been left to enjoy his *charge* without remuneration. He does not seem to have sought an interview with Colbert; he probably had only contempt for Chapelain, whose opinion of Sorel may have been no better.

This study of Sorel's career reveals that although Sorel needed the money and resented the withdrawal of his pension, he believed sincerely in the value of writing a history of France and was motivated as much by the higher status conferred by a *charge* as by the money it brought. After all, he did not receive a *pension*, but rather, *gages*, like those of a parlementaire. Or so he thought.

Sorel, we know, had exchanged books with Mézerai. It is not clear that they ever met; but one of Sorel's works, which once was part of Mézerai's library, bears the inscription in Mézerai's hand: "Don de l'auteur, esprit très ingénieux et très sain."[39] The reasons for the compliment will become clearer in Chapter VII.

37. *Ibid.*, p. 63. See Soman's remarks on this subject, p. 442.
38. *De la prudence*, p. 76.
39. Roy, p. 346.

Chapter V
Patronage and
History from Richelieu
to Colbert

N Jacques Dupuy's correspondence with Nicolas Heinsius, the term "patron" is frequently used to indicate the relationship between a writer and someone who "protects" him.[1] Occasionally the term "homme honoraire" is used to denote the patron-writer relationship. No special terminology had been developed to distinguish the writers of history from other writers, though it is clear that, at least among the *érudits*, the genre of historical writing had been defined as one requiring greater independence from the patron than other genres.

The education of the aristocratic patron included within its curriculum of humanistic studies the ideal that a man of birth should respect learning and favor those gifted in the arts. By the mid-seventeenth century the blending of aristocratic and robe values resulted in an extension of the ideal of the patron to include virtually the entire governing elite. Prominent churchmen, princes, nobles, parlementaires, and that socially vague but politically and culturally powerful group, the royal ministers, in some sense all felt the social obligation to patronize the arts, including the writing of history. As might be expected, some of the most rapid social climbers and seekers of power set out to be the leading patrons; they may have felt less inferior with a coterie of *érudits* and poets around them as a screen to shield them from the glares of the great nobles. Fouquet's statement about Paul Pellisson-Fontanier —"Il s'est donné à moi"[2]—provides a glimpse of the strong psychological and social dependencies that the ideal of the patron bore in the political culture of seventeenth-century France.

Concurrently with influences in education and the society at large, equally powerful bureaucratic influences would culminate in the social

1. *Correspondance de Jacques Dupuy et de Nicolas Heinsius*, ed. Hans Bots (The Hague, 1971), p. 71, where Dupuy suggests that Ménage has made it known that he wished the term *patron* used in defining his relationship with Cardinal Retz.

2. Adolphe Chéruel, *Mémoires sur Nicolas Fouquet* (Paris, 1862), p. 426.

type of the *honnête homme*. In the decades when Bernard and Sorel were writing, the robe nobility saw its status and income increased when the venal *charge* spread to every aspect of life among ruling elites. Many writers had sought to formalize the ideal of patronage into a royal office with a fixed income that could be passed on from father to son. However, venality of office may have had less impact on the ideal of the patron for the generation of writers that began to come to prominence in the 1630s. Fleeing the robe and already tending to be *honnête*, they simply did not consider the social status of such an office to be commensurate with a writer's position in a predominantly aristocratic or would-be aristocratic society.[3]

The result was an increasingly elaborate development of dependencies. As a sort of bastard feudalism that appears to varying degrees in all social circles attempting to control or monopolize political power in a society, the dependencies of the seventeenth century were perhaps most extensively worked out by Louis XIII's minister-favorites. In the circle of families dominating the royal councils, this pattern of gaining control of the government by placing creatures in virtually every available office reached its apogee under Cardinal Richelieu. Through his creatures—Bullion, Bouthillier, Chavigny, and Sublet de Noyers—in the Council of State, Richelieu attempted to control all appointments and every aspect of the central administration.

As a patron of letters, and particularly of history, Cardinal Richelieu also attempted through his creatures to control the literary and scholarly activities of France. The Cardinal's "protection" of an author had a very explicit meaning; in a sense it signified that the writer was his creature. Through humanist propaganda, during the course of the sixteenth century, French kings had become recognized as the principal patrons of the realm. They did not always live up to that ideal. Too busy—largely because of their obsession with hunting—to take a personal interest in the work and welfare of writers, early-modern French kings frequently permitted the arts to languish. Routine pensions were granted, with chancellors often playing a significant role in granting benefices to *érudits*. But from the beginning the humanist cultural ideal of the patron had included the patron's personal involvement. Vaguely platonic, perhaps, but assuredly self-serving, this ideal could

3. The flight from robe status and values was such a general phenomenon in mid-seventeenth-century literary culture that it deserves increased attention from scholars. George Huppert, *Les Bourgeois Gentilhommes* (Chicago, 1977), delineates some of the features of a robe country-gentleman social group that would see its dignities and respect in the society diminished as a result of the swelling in its ranks brought about by venality of office.

be attained only when the patron-sovereign himself wrote verses or discoursed on all the favorite humanist moral and political topics.

The active patronage of letters was something Louis XIII could not accomplish.[4] His love of music was great, but the terrible psychological blows that he had sustained at the hands of his parents and physicians left him with a speech defect and an aversion for things involving speech-in-literature. At the same time, his brother Gaston; his mother Marie de Médicis; those rebellious princes of the blood Conti, Soissons, Condé, and Beaufort; the other princes; prominent ecclesiastics; and leading parlementaires all competed in the arena of patronage to establish their own networks of dependencies and a certain control over literary activity.

The intellectual, political, and to a lesser extent social values and beliefs of these groups varied widely. During periods when the prince did not attempt to establish dependencies in the *monde des lettrés*, writers of history could select from among various modes of political and intellectual values. Together the values and political beliefs of all these groups constituted the boundaries of the political culture. In a sense, diversity of viewpoints was circumscribed within the limits of diversity represented by these groups. The reign of Louis XIII saw a decline in the influence of the parlementaires as patrons, largely because their own sons rejected robe political and social values; the influence of the princes would have its ups and downs throughout the century.

A writer was permitted to have several patrons simultaneously. Nevertheless, a patron's protection tended to establish something like exclusive rights over the writer's work. The social and political positions of the nobleman's clients or of Richelieu's creatures in the royal councils were fixed by dependencies. In theory the writer felt more or less compelled to respect his patron's views. In practice this obligation was much less constraining than it might appear. What were the aesthetic or political views of the princes and other great nobles? Certainly not freethinkers, they were, along with some of the leading churchmen, probably the least ideologically coherent or systematic thinkers in the entire society.[5] By comparison with any other group—say, the doctors of the Sorbonne, the bishops, or the merchants—the princely society of the seventeenth century was heterogeneous and

4. Balzac recognized this in *Le Prince* and added that the conduct of wars and *affaires* does not leave the necessary time—an apology if ever there was one.

5. Robert Harding puts it well in *Anatomy of a Power Elite: The Provincial Governors of Reformation France, 1542–1635* (New Haven, 1978), *passim*.

rather open to nonconformist aesthetic principles and thought. Always enigmatic, and only rarely as articulate as Rohan, Cardinal Retz, and François de La Rochefoucauld, they prided themselves on a certain openness of views, especially on political matters, where they often were in open conflict with one another and with the Crown.

Not that patron-writer roles were explicit. Authors often served as secretaries to the great or as tutors to their children, positions that some of the greatest writers of the seventeenth century do not appear to have found demeaning. And just as the writers hoped to influence their powerful patrons on political matters, so the patrons frequently attempted to write good poetry or even, on occasion, good history. The correlation between those whom writers defined as leading patrons and those patrons who wrote poetry is extremely high. The humanists' educational and cultural program was never more triumphant than in the efforts of seventeenth-century princes, generals, ministers, bishops, cardinals, and judges to write verses "worthy of being read." The flood of memoirs, histories, and editions of elegantly written letters produced by the generation writing and governing from 1630 to 1670 attests to the power of the humanists' program of promoting a unitary political culture in which writers would flourish. The nexus of that political culture was the patron-writer relationship.

For historical writing some of the boundaries of this culture deserve to be pointed out. The wealthiest and most powerful patrons were either noble or royal. Not a few were princes. Thus it is not surprising to find in the histories a kind of consensus about how to depict the nobility. The princes' courage, their victories, marriages, alliances, and so forth, occupy a central place in the general historical literature of the reign of Louis XIII. It is also in this context that we perceive the full significance of the heavily footnoted genealogical histories of noble houses written by the *érudits*. Humanist writers may have shared a common assumption that patrons liked to read about their ancestors —but certainly not to learn of those ancestors' vices and defeats. Some of the *érudits* responded with pioneering works of scholarship to uphold what was, in effect, the princely program to influence if not dominate the society and the Crown of France.[6] Though the Duchesnes and Dupuys, for example, wrote primarily for the Crown, it is not difficult to find works about princely houses among their scholarly production.

Therefore, prior to Richelieu's campaign to humble the princes, an

6. As one example only, André Duchesne wrote genealogical histories of the houses of Châtillon-sur-Marne (1621), La Rochefoucauld (1622), Montmorency (1624), Richelieu (1631), and Béthune (1639).

office such as *historiographe de France* or a pension did not mean—in the case of very eminent *érudits* and such prominent writers as Chapelain—that the holder worked exclusively for royal patrons, and on royalist history.[7] There was certainly room for conflicting views and even for controversy in the histories of noble houses, yet the very choice of subject was a sign of the constraints imposed by the system of patronage. The plethora of histories of robe families in the seventeenth century was also a manifestation—albeit on a lower scale than that of such houses as the Montmorencies and Guises—of the development of competing groups within the single confines of the political culture. Less erudite, but faithful to the same humanist principles about the meaning and function of history, are the epic poems, notably Chapelain's *Pucelle*, where the hero, Dunois, the ancestor of Chapelain's principal patron, the Duke de Longueville, is given a leading role.[8]

Still less "historical" but perhaps for that reason all the more powerful in the duel between Richelieu and the princes was Corneille's *Cid*. It boldly set forth an ethic of conduct for the princes that placed them virtually above royal law as they pursued a heroic ideal. True to his usual practice of attacking his opponents for spurious reasons while concealing the real ones, Richelieu attempted to humble Corneille by unleashing his newly founded French Academy upon the *Cid*, on the grounds that it had violated the ancient stylistic rules about the unities. The Cardinal had already faced several princely rebellions before the success of the *Cid* and could not permit such a powerful statement about the behavior of the *grandes âmes* to go unanswered. On other levels, as we shall see with Mézerai, Richelieu was attempting not only to reply to the cultural and ideological advances of his opponents, but also to forge a permanent, institutionalized instrument, in the form of the French Academy, with which to maintain royal dominance over the political culture. How could he stem the tide of aristocratic resurgence?

With his sovereign virtually incapacitated in this regard, Richelieu had to begin by attempting to be a great patron himself. He was an *arriviste*, after all. For psychological reasons, as much as for prestige, writers with already well-established reputations—notably Jean Louis Guez de Balzac and the heirs of François de Malherbe, principally Chapelain—hastened to support the Crown and its powerful exponent, Richelieu.[9] By extending his protection to as many writers as possible

7. See below, p. 225.
8. David Maskell, *The Historical Epic in France, 1500–1700* (Oxford, 1973), pp. 141 ff.; and below, p. 159.
9. In the thinly divided worlds of letters and politics, Balzac was not

through the Academy, the Cardinal at least temporarily accomplished his purpose of establishing a counterforce against the domination of the political culture by the heterodox yet competing great nobles. Virtually all writers of history, the *érudits* with official duties as historiographers included, sought the favor of at least one *grand*. By "protecting" through his Academy a number of major writers such as Balzac, and creating others such as Chapelain and Mézerai, the Cardinal hoped to develop a coherent absolutist literary culture in which the king would be the entire focus of patronage and historical-literary interest. Together, Balzac, Chapelain, Richelieu, and to a certain extent François de La Mothe le Vayer, formulated this program, but the ideal of a unitary culture supported by the learned, cultured, and powerful had been a humanist creation. The Cardinal's contribution had been to institutionalize the ideal of an academy and channel the creative forces of his time into it.

Or was it François de Boisrobert's influence on Richelieu, coupled with the poet's desire to enhance his own reputation among men of letters, that led to bonds between the Cardinal and the *monde des lettrés*, bonds formalized in the Academy? To answer this question would take us far afield, though the research might reveal still another aspect of Richelieu's reliance upon his creatures. More significant for our purposes is the fact that once again the collaboration between a man of letters and a man in high office led to an expansion of patronage and an enhanced role for men of letters in French political culture. Boisrobert, a minor poet, affable, and respected by his fellow writers, played the role that Budé, Chastel, Ronsard, and others had played before him.[10] He spoke directly to the Cardinal about the qualities of various literary works and their authors, arranged interviews for writers with the Cardinal, and clearly promoted those whom he liked and judged the most talented. Richelieu certainly had his own literary tastes; but Boisrobert articulated them. Guez de Balzac defined Boisrobert's role as follows:

> Vous estes particulièrement necessaire au monde scavant, et à la République des belles lettres. Sans vous les orateurs crieroient sans cesse dans leurs harangues contre le Temps et contre les

---

unlike Bullion, who, though powerful and prestigious himself, ultimately accepted the status of being Richelieu's creature. The Cardinal refused Balzac's service. On Balzac's critique of the heroic ideal and his relations with Richelieu, see F. E. Sutcliffe, *Guez de Balzac et son temps* (Paris, 1959), *passim*.

10. On Boisrobert see Emile Magne, *Le plaisant Abbé de Boisrobert, fondateur de l'Académie Française* (Paris, 1909), *passim*.

Moeurs; et les ne feroient autre chose dans leurs vers que maudire les muses et Apollon. Les bons offices que vous leur rendez auprès de Son Eminence adoucissent leur mauvaise heumeur, et leur donne des pensées moins violentes. Tellement qu'à prendre les choses dans leur principe, il ne soit aujourd'hui ni panegyrique, ni ode, dont vous ne soyez le premier autheur.[11]

A flattering exaggeration, to be sure, but one that nonetheless establishes Boisrobert's role. Many years earlier Balzac himself had sought contact with Boisrobert and Richelieu, and they with him. Years and years of observation and personal experience lay behind his description of Boisrobert's role, and Balzac may at one time have kept Boisrobert's taste in mind when seeking the Cardinal's favor.

The long and tangled relationship between Balzac, Boisrobert, and Richelieu need not detain us here, though it illuminates the entire pattern of thought that a seventeenth-century writer might have about patronage and politics. Neither Richelieu nor Balzac was duped by the polite phrases they addressed to one another.[12]

By temperament Balzac scorned innovation in both erudition and rhetoric. Most of what his contemporaries considered to be learning, Balzac viewed as pedantry; most of the recent attempts at eloquence, he castigated as hyperbole. And yet he sought a broader perspective through which innovation in language might be understood and found it in Ancient Rome. Fond of quoting Cicero, fonder still of trying to understand the evolution of genres, he remarked about the laudatory speeches addressed to Richelieu: "Le nouveau panegyrique vole bien haut, mais les anciens panegyriques volent encore plus haut que luy. Ce n'est pas la France qui a commencé à parler avec excès."[13] One senses his repugnance for what is happening. Yet he seems captured or constrained by contemporary currents of style and language. Writing to Valentin Conrart, he observes: "Le mal est, Monsieur, qu'il y a en France certaines gens, mesmes honestes gens, qui veulent tousjours paroistre par la nouveauté. Ils ne veulent jamais parler comme font les autres hommes; ils ne scauroient appeller les choses par leurs noms propres. . . . Ciceron a creû, et quelques autres avant Ciceron, qu'en chaque langue, les poëtes avoient une langue à part, separée et distincte de la vulgaire. C'est peut-être en dire trop. Mais certainement ils ont des figures qui leur appartiennent en propriété, et qui sont tousjours

11. 15 October 1640. *Oeuvres complètes* (Paris, 1665), vol. 2, p. 716.
12. See William F. Church, *Richelieu and Reason of State* (Princeton, 1972), pp. 166 ff., and Pierre Grillon, ed., *Les papiers de Richelieu* (Paris, 1975), p. 234.
13. *Oeuvres complètes*, vol. 2, p. 569.

poëtiques."[14] The only comparisons Balzac seems able to make are with Antiquity, and in this he was a typical influential man of letters of his day. In the thought of someone so imbued with respect for the ancients, it is not surprising to find only classical oratorical thought about history. Indeed, at one point he observes that to discuss politics without including history is to make politics a "spectre creux et plein de vide," a venerable commonplace indeed.[15] But, instead of serving as the beginning of a discussion of historical method or political thought, his observation is merely a recommendation to the orator desirous of persuading his audience of the merit of a special course of action. To convince the audience, Balzac asserts, the orator must cite historical examples to support his proposal.

Balzac's frequently expressed hostility toward the social pretensions of the *robins*,[16] a hostility sustained intellectually by the reverence for Antiquity, scarcely permitted familiarity with, let alone respect for, either the scholarship of the legal humanists or the methodological works of Bodin and La Popelinière.[17] A learned nobleman and a nationalist, Balzac remained insulated from the sixteenth century by his own classicistic predilections and his repugnance for the social milieu that had produced the elite circle of learned and eloquent men of letters. The only breach in these walls appears in his thought about the relationships between military might and literature.

France of his day, he asserts, could not put an army in the field equal in power to the armies that fought in the Crusades, because too many men spend their time reading and writing, rather than practicing a military career[18]—a vague reminiscence of the idea that literature and martial courage are incompatible. And, like his sixteenth-century forebears, Balzac was contradictory about how remuneration for service affects the republic of letters. Claiming to have sufficient income for

14. *Ibid.*, p. 572.

15. *Ibid.*, p. 494.

16. Even when making a compliment, Balzac is ironic. He asked Chapelain to revise a sentence in his work and to change "Elle produira toujours des héros de robe longue, des Catons, des Scipions, des Cicérons. . ." to read "Elle produira toujours des lumières à la France, des Catons, des Scipions, et des Cicérons français." Heroes they were, but by rank; and they were not to be confused with heroes formed by victory on a field of battle (20 September 1643, *Oeuvres de J.-L. de Guez, sieur de Balzac*, ed. L. Moreau [Paris, 1854], p. 592).

17. He ranks Cujas along with Turnèbe and Lipsius among the great French men of learning, but he does not indicate familiarity with Cujas's works (Balzac, *Oeuvres complètes*, vol. 2, p. 454).

18. *Oeuvres de J.-L. de Guez, sieur de Balzac*, p. 72.

his needs, he nonetheless frequently hinted, through friends with connections in high places, that a gift of money would be desirable. On the other hand, Balzac was obsessed with judging the quality of other writers' works and resented it when a pension was granted to someone whose work he considered mediocre. Had not Henry III paid ten thousand *écus* for a speech that he, Balzac, considered worth only "dix quarts d'escus"?[19] The ideal of the patron as someone with whom one conversed about literature and philosophy attracted his attention no more than it did Sorel's. Some notions about a relationship between the quality of a literary work and the sum of the resulting pension appear from time to time in his correspondence. Had Balzac and Boisrobert been temperamentally capable of switching roles, Balzac might well have imposed the higher standards for rewarding authors. He seems to have reduced the question of the author's independence to monetary terms.

Balzac would one day refer to the dead Richelieu as a tyrant.[20] He may have momentarily forgotten how his own work, *Le Prince*, had been written to buttress the Cardinal's power.[21] And though referring to Richelieu as a tyrant, in almost the same breath, Balzac sought to ingratiate himself with Mazarin. His royal pension had ceased immediately after Louis XIII's death, and writing Mazarin was the only way to obtain its renewal. At this point, in a letter to Balzac, Chapelain described something that Mazarin had done, and Balzac immediately took offense: "Ce que vous me mandez du Cardinal Mazarin m'a degousté de ce que j'ay dit de luy et m'a osté l'envie d'en dire davantage en un aultre lieu, ainsy que j'avois résolu. Il ne fault que les sçavans se prostituent à tous les heureux. Il fault conserver l'honneur des muses hautaines et braves, et si la Cour vous fait tort, faisons luy justice, c'està-dire parlons véritablement et noblement (*modo tuto*) dans les discours que j'ay tout prests pour cela."[22] What wrong could the court do to writers? To Balzac's mind, it is the cessation of pensions; he seems not to fear either political persecution or censorship. What is intriguing about this passage is the threat to speak out truly and nobly. Here we discover, or rather rediscover in personal terms, those same thoughts about the withdrawal of patronage that Balzac had expressed earlier to Boisrobert. Patronage calms the bad humor of writers and renders their thought less violent; the personal effect on Balzac would simply be to speak out *modo tuto*. That great outburst of bad humor in printed

19. *Lettres de J.-L. Guez de Balzac*, ed. Philippe Tamizey de Larroque (Paris, 1873), vol. 1, p. 456.

20. *Oeuvres de Balzac*, p. 461.

21. Church, p. 167.

22. *Lettres de J.-L. Guez de Balzac*, vol. 1, p. 468.

form—Mazarinades—was still four years off, but Mazarin had already laid the psychological foundations for it by withdrawing patronage in 1644.

Balzac never carried out his threat to speak out; he went on pursuing a pension. His ambivalence and his contempt for himself, for potential patrons, and for other writers better remunerated than he are evident in his letters to Chapelain, the future intermediary between men of power and writers, whose task was recommending to Colbert writers who deserved pensions. After trying for a pension and failing, then recoiling at the thought of what he might have to do in order to gain recognition, Balzac drew back and asserted his independence: "J'ayme mieux ruiner mes petites espérances que de renoncer entièrement à ma liberté et faire le Sirmond ou le Chastelet."[23] Yet he went on seeking a pension. Balzac wrote Christina of Sweden, complimenting her for having attracted Descartes and Claude de Saumaise to her kingdom. Despite an invitation, in the end he hesitated to make the long voyage to Stockholm. His thought and career reveal a phenomenon prevalent throughout the republic of letters: a swell of intense feelings about patronage. As part of an entire social system, excessive patronage produced dire consequences; but too little produced anger and rebellion. There seemed to be no middle ground. Yet, in the meantime, Richelieu's Academy and pensions were promoting the Cardinal's *gloire*. Fouquet and Colbert would return to the Cardinal's policy in the 1650s.

The years between Richelieu's death in 1642 and the reestablishment of peace after the princely Fronde in 1652 were years of turmoil and financial instability for men of letters. Writers on the royal pension lists, including the *historiographes du roi*, often saw the sums promised them go unpaid or be severely cut as a result of the financial exigencies of war. The war against Spain had bankrupted the Monarchy. As popular revolts, judicial revolts, and finally princely revolts broke out during the Fronde, the relationships between patrons and writers became strained to the utmost. Flights of excessive loyalty to the patron princes, detached and silent cynicism, and such "baseness" as openly attacking patrons constituted the gamut of experiences open to writers during the turmoil of the Fronde.

Occasionally Cardinal Mazarin would make a dramatic gesture on a writer's behalf, but the task of piloting the Academy had fallen to Chancellor Pierre Séguier, a weak leader who was ultimately considered a Frondeur and for that reason disgraced. Nor did Anne of Austria play a successful role as a leading patroness, though the outburst of fidelity and support for her in the years immediately following

23. *Ibid.*, p. 472.

Louis XIII's death in 1643 suggests that her character traits may have made her miss an opportunity to exercise a dominant role with writers.

The inevitable result of the civil war was increased activity by the parlementaires and the princes. Their overall patronage of letters may not have increased dramatically in monetary terms,[24] but the void left by Richelieu's death clouded the horizons of those writers who had sought "protection" primarily from the state. Pseudonymous works, anonymous works, jockeying back and forth among patrons, quarrels within the Academy, and the peculiar synthesis of elitist and popular culture in the Mazarinades were all signs of the troubles among men of letters during the Fronde. Writers of history were in the forefront of these difficulties owing to the obvious ideological import of their works.

The fate of the annual pensions paid to the historiographers royal is suggested by evidence found in Colbert's records.[25] His summary of the pensions paid to the historiographers indicates that none was paid after 1644. This certainly does not prove that no pensions were paid during the Regency, but almost all the corroborating evidence that can be brought to bear on Colbert's records has proven them correct and complete. On the other hand, a list of pensions paid to *lecteurs, professeurs,* and *historiographes du roi* from the account of the Recepte Générale de Paris for 1649 seems to contradict Colbert's evidence.[26] The accounting procedure of "assigning" expenses to specific sources of income was an old one, and in this case the pensions may have disappeared from the Epargne because as a block they had been assigned to Parisian revenues. Does this mean that the historiographers were actually paid in 1649? Not at all. Munitioners, dukes, prelates, spies, and historiographers may all have shared the common fate of receiving orders for payment to be deducted from revenues that had long since been spent. If it in fact produced income in 1649, the Recepte Générale de Paris probably was paid to royal creditors who had been waiting for payment since 1645 or 1646. Once assigned to be paid from the *comptants* of the Epargne, payments authorized by the Crown became

24. It is regrettable that Jean-Pierre Labatut, *Les ducs et pairs de France au XVIIe siècle* (Paris, 1972), declined to treat the subject of patronage as an element in the aristocratic identity.

25. B.N., Mélanges de Colbert, 318, fol. 31 v. The *Estat au Vray* for 1 January–5 July 1658 (B.N., Mélanges de Colbert, 101, fols. 216 ff.) contains nothing about pensions for historiographers. It is possible that these pensions were paid in the second half of the year, but earlier they had usually been paid by quarter.

26. B.N., mss. fr. 23045, fol. 126.

exceedingly difficult to collect during periods of war and financial insolvency.

Jacques Dupuy's letters attest to this turmoil. Like so many other *érudits* or writers of verse, he hoped the Fronde would be forgotten.[27] The humanist mode of thought, which generally stressed that history should record only events worthy of remembering and should teach by examples that were primarily good, set the tone for the entire political culture of the 1640s and 1650s. There were, to be sure, Frondeurs who could not disengage from the ideological conflicts, as Mézerai's career testifies; but in general the sooner the Fronde was forgotten, the better. In September 1650, Dupuy wrote: "nos affaires publiques sont en un estat si fluctuant et incertain qu'il ne faut pas que vous vous estonniez si les lettres y font si peu de progrez."[28] Gilles Ménage left Retz's household; Jean-François Sarasin fled the country after the imprisonment of his patron, Conti, in Vincennes;[29] the Mazarinist attack on the princes forced Louis Bourdeloue to leave the country; and Chapelain inquired about whether he should flee because of his attachment to the rebellious Duke de Longueville.[30]

The turmoil of the Fronde left both the parlementaires and the leading great nobles humbled by the state. The flood of memoirs by the leading representatives of both groups attests to this fact, as does the distance the Sun King later kept between himself and these two anti-absolutist political forces that had almost brought about a monarchical revolution. The Fronde turned the men of letters increasingly toward the Crown as the sole source of patronage[31] and toward the French Academy as the principal center of literary and historical culture. The *érudits* had come through largely unscathed, faithful to the Crown; the other writers of history had peered into an abyss of confusion and violence that had made them long for order.

27. Dupuy to Heinsius, *Correspondance de Jacques Dupuy*, p. xii.

28. *Ibid.*, p. 71.

29. *Ibid.*, p. 59. Sarasin had previously been the *homme honoraire* of Chavigny (Chapelain to Balzac, 28 August 1639, *Lettres de Chapelain*, vol. 1, p. 488). This was, of course, merely another extension of Cardinal Richelieu's patronage powers, since Chavigny was the Cardinal's creature.

30. Dupuy to Heinsius, 7 May 1650, *Correspondance de Jacques Dupuy*, p. 61.

31. When conditions in France were at their nadir, Christina of Sweden beckoned men of letters and scholars to come. Several Frenchmen, including Naudé, François Blondel, Pierre Bourdelot, and Descartes (from Holland), answered the call, providing an important testimonial to the suffering, both physical and psychological, caused by the Fronde.

The result was a striking shift in the literature of praise away from the princes toward the young Louis XIV. Not that the great nobles ceased altogether to serve as patrons for men of letters. Their role would remain significant until the mid-eighteenth century, but it had been diminished; and with this came a shift in the intellectual and political dependencies of writers. From under the wings of the Grand Condé, Jean de La Bruyère would still satirize both the court and the city; but neither the patron nor the writer dared to be openly critical about Louis XIV or encourage young courtiers to emulate the heroic ideal of the princes.

In the mid-1650s, Mazarin began to take up the old habits of his predecessor, Cardinal Richelieu. Did he do this on Fouquet's advice? Or Colbert's? Throughout the years of turmoil, Fouquet and Colbert had made significant but sporadic efforts to influence the world of letters. Then, in 1656, a rather dramatic increase in the patronage of letters began. Quarrels among the clergy were still Frondeur in tone and political significance, and the Parlement of Paris had not been as obedient as Mazarin had hoped on several matters, mainly fiscal. Nevertheless, a thorough examination of the unpublished ministerial correspondence might well reveal that personal rivalries between Fouquet and Colbert were already present and that these, rather than the larger political problems, account for the sudden increase in the Crown's active involvement with men of letters. The Fronde had not prompted Mazarin's policy of favoring men of letters; the lesser tempests of 1655–1656 probably did not do so either.

A dramatic gesture initiated the new policy in January 1656, when Jacques Dupuy received the unexpected visit of Jean-Baptiste Colbert, then a personal intendant of Cardinal Mazarin, Colbert extended Mazarin's "grans compliments" to Dupuy and then offered him a benefice worth about five hundred *écus* a year. Before departing, Colbert handed the astonished Dupuy still another present, a silk purse containing two hundred gold *louis*! All Dupuy could do was express his thanks and request the opportunity to thank Mazarin personally.

In describing these events to Heinsius, Dupuy noted that his family had not been unknown to Mazarin and that during his late brother's lifetime the Cardinal had sent them his coach so that they might come and greet him. Years had passed, however, since Dupuy had seen Mazarin. The initiative of 1656, which brought them together again, is one of our most precious sources for reconstructing the encounters between men of letters and men of power.[32]

32. Dupuy to Heinsius, 4 February 1656, *Correspondance de Jacques Dupuy*, pp. 197 ff.

Accompanied by his erudite friend, Ismaël Boulliaud, whom he probably hoped would be named his successor as *bibliothécaire du roi*, Dupuy appeared at the Louvre several days after Colbert's visit. Clearly impressed by the *grands* whom he saw in a "galerie fort ornée et remplie de beaux tableaux," Dupuy was received with a handshake from Louis XIV, who happened to be present. Then Cardinal Mazarin came over to him, embraced him, kissed him on the ear, and announced that he was Dupuy's "serviteur." The event dazzled Parisian literary society. It marked Mazarin's commitment to the old *fidélités* established by the Crown, for the Dupuys had not been Frondeurs.[33] All this time, Dupuy remained reasonably in command of himself and was perhaps inwardly convinced that he deserved this recognition. Indeed, Colbert and Mazarin had conducted themselves in accordance with the ideal of a monarchy that recognizes the importance of men of letters.

But, as with everything involving Colbert, the motives for his policies never seem to be clear-cut. On 12 November of the same year he wrote Mazarin that poor Monsieur Dupuy was very ill and would soon leave vacant the benefice that had been granted him.[34] Colbert went on to ask that the benefice as well as the post of *bibliothécaire* be granted to his own brother, Nicolas Colbert. Mazarin granted his request, and a Colbert[35] became the principal administrator of one of the major scholarly libraries of France, a meeting place for French and foreign *érudits*. Had Colbert merely anticipated Dupuy's approaching death and built up the income from the post before placing his brother as

33. For a glimpse at Jacques Dupuy's role as royal librarian during the Fronde, there is Sarasin's letter to him of 7 April [1649?]: "Monsieur du Puy est tres humblement supplié de dire s'il juge à propos qu'un prince de sang prenne un brevet pour entrer dans le conseil. Si cela faict point de tort aux prerogatives de sa naissance et si c'est point asses que le Roy luy mande par une lettre d'y venir prendre sa place. S'il y a quelques exemples de la conduitte qu'ont tenüe les Princes du sang en pareil rencontre, il me fera la grace de me les citter. Il tiendra s'il luy plaist ce billet en secret . . . Sarasin, ce 7e apvril à minuict. L'affaire presse" (Archives des Affaires Etrangères, France, 803, fol. 299). It is a remarkable glimpse into the secret day-to-day role the *érudits* played in the government and into the continuing influence of precedent on administration and society, and not merely on the law courts.

34. *Lettres, instructions et mémoires de Colbert*, ed. Pierre Clément (Paris, 1861), vol. 1, p. 270.

35. See the studies of various Colberts by Jean Béranger, William Roth, and René Pillorget in Roland Mousnier, *Le conseil du roi de Louis XII à la révolution* (Paris, 1970), *passim*; and Jean-Louis Bourgeon, *Les Colbert avant Colbert* (Paris, 1973), *passim*.

bibliothécaire? Jacques Dupuy had no children, nor had his brother Pierre, who had died in 1651. The *charge* could thus be disposed of without offending the Dupuys' relatives or erudite friends, who would very likely have clamored for a Dupuy successor had there been one with claims to erudition.

But to be fair to the always enigmatic Colbert, other activities at that time indicate that the Crown was about to undertake an expanded policy of patronizing men of letters. Battle lines had still not been drawn between Fouquet and Colbert, but it is significant that it was also in 1656 that Paul Pellisson-Fontanier became a creature of Fouquet's. Pensions soon followed for all of Pellisson's old literary friends, among them Boisrobert, Sorel, Paul Scarron, Jean Ogier de Gombauld, and Jean Hesnault.[36] It would take some time for this group to come together around Fouquet, as would the Crown's search for younger talented writers; nonetheless, from the beginning Colbert, and perhaps Mazarin as well, recognized the potential prestige to be gained by so powerful a patron as Fouquet in a political culture that had lacked a policy of royal patronage since Richelieu's death. Ostensibly, of course, this patronage of letters, whether sponsored by Fouquet or by Colbert, was aimed at assuring the *gloire* of Cardinal Mazarin and Louis XIV. But the men of letters who received pensions through Pellisson and Fouquet soon began to sing Fouquet's praises.

Historical writing, never independent from the humanistic culture that continued to prevail and that stressed "pure letters" in all genres, was soon to be torn by still another duel among its patrons. From it Colbert and the young Louis XIV would emerge almost completely in command of patronage.

Some time between the last months of 1654 and November 1655, Colbert had secretly asked an old acquaintance of Mazarin's, Pierre Costar, for advice about those who should be granted pensions, especially for writing history.[37] With his genius for organization, Colbert undertook an elaborate and systematic assessment of the literary productions of both French and foreign writers. With one blow he eliminated the personal element from the ideal of the patron-writer relationship, for the value of the written work and the capacity to produce abundantly were henceforth the primary criteria for pensions. Costar produced his lists and evaluations. This marked the beginning

36. Chéruel, p. 436.

37. He may also have made the same request of Gilles Ménage at about the same time. Cf. "Mémoire pour servir à la vie de M. Ménage," *Ménagiana*, ed. by Ménage's friends (or Ménage himself?), 3d ed. (Amsterdam, 1713), vol. 1, n.p.

of a bureaucratization of literary culture and of artistic and scientific productivity that was manifested in the founding of additional royal academies. Since the initiative with Costar proved to be only a trial one and was displaced by a second effort when Colbert turned to Chapelain for similar systematic evaluations, we may overlook Costar's lists. But the seeds of a general cultural policy had been sown by the son of a merchant draper from Rheims.

History would never find a more fervent supporter than Colbert. Had the emphasis on history been in part a response to Fouquet's very apparent genius for encouraging poets and other primarily nonhistorical prose writers?[38] This question cannot be answered, but some light is shed on it and related matters when Colbert's long-term inclinations are stressed. The continuing, almost obsessive interest in gathering and preserving documents, and in sponsoring research about the institutions and offices of France and Ancient Rome, implies a profound commitment to a historical outlook. This eminently useful knowledge sustained Colbert's curiosity about the past. And, adhering to the ideals of the humanists, Colbert instituted a program for assuring the immortality of the sovereign: his *grandes actions* must be recorded by the most talented writers of his age. Colbert pursued this goal throughout the rest of his long and eventful political career as minister of culture in all but name.

But the turmoil among men of letters caused by the disgrace of their patrons had not ended. The religious Fronde culminated in Cardinal Retz's disgrace and exile to a country benefice.[39] Mazarin's death and the brutal arrest, trial, and prison sentence of Fouquet eliminated for writers the last major intellectual and political perspective that did not center on the royal family. In the years between 1648 and 1661, the robe political and intellectual perspective, shared by the princes, the princes of the Church, and the prominent ministers, had weakened; in a sense these groups were no longer considered appropriate patrons for cultural-political ideals.[40]

38. Such competition developed in other artistic matters, notably over the selection of architects. Cf. Anthony Blunt, *Art and Architecture in France, 1500–1700* (Baltimore, 1957), pp. 188 ff.; and Francis Haskell, *Patrons and Painters* (New York, 1963), p. 187.

39. See J. H. M. Salmon, *Cardinal de Retz* (London, 1969), *passim*; and Richard Golden, "The Godly Rebellion: Parisian Curés and the Religious Fronde, 1652–1662," Ph.D. dissertation, The Johns Hopkins University, 1974, *passim*.

40. The circle around President Lamoignon might be considered an exception, but instead of mere patronage, Lamoignon's interaction with men

This drastic reduction of options among patrons, with the king standing as the sole political ideal, occurred at a time when Louis was himself a model young king. From its beginnings in the late fifteenth century, humanism had included praise of a young prince as an integral part of its program of letters. The simultaneous diminution of social and political perspectives as represented by the decline of non-royal patrons, and the rise of a handsome and apparently effective young king, thus marked a turning point in French political culture. The Age of Louis XIV is shocking in its obsessive adulation of one man by and through all the literary genres. Our first reaction is that it was a violation of the humanists' program. A closer look suggests that it was its fulfillment, but that social and bureaucratic upheavals occurring in the late sixteenth and mid-seventeenth centuries undermined the broad and diverse intellectual and political foundations that humanism had possessed during the decades when the Guises, the Montmorencies, Cardinals Duprat and d'Armagnac, and parlementaires de L'Hôpital and du Vair had served as more than purveyors of money. The cultural ideals and political power that these individuals represented had been undermined in the Wars of Religion and would be destroyed by the Fronde.

Colbert found himself the principal purveyor of patronage in 1661 without quite knowing what to support and what to ignore. His inclinations were businesslike, to the point of wanting to speed up the production of historical writing with little consideration for quality. Apparently relying on Costar's advice, and perhaps on that of other old friends of Mazarin's, Colbert continued to place great emphasis on the writing of history. Though never losing his concern for production (in 1674 he would exhort the Academy to work double time on its dictionary),[41] he quickly learned how to rely on expert advice concerning everything from poetry to fortifications to gardening.

But this was not until after the incidents sparked by his sponsorship of Benjamin Priolo's Latin history of France, 1643 to 1659.[42] In 1662 the history of these years was still exceedingly controversial for the reading public, especially because some of the former Frondeurs, including *grands*, had rushed to the defense of the recently disgraced Fouquet. The tense political situation may have pressed Colbert to

---

of letters resembles more that of a holder of salons than that of a patron. Cf. Peter France, *Racine's Rhetoric* (Oxford, 1965), p. 26, for the observation that it was a milieu favoring the *Anciens*.

41. *Lettres de Colbert*, vol. 5, p. lvii.

42. Published in its completed form, the *Ab excessu Ludovici XIII de rebus Gallicis historiarum libri XII* (Paris, 1665).

speed up his efforts to have histories written to defend the Crown's triumph under Mazarin.

Priolo combined the qualities of a spy who would change sides for higher pay with those of a courtier, an imposter, and a hack writer. Claiming to be the descendant of an illustrious Venetian family, but in reality born at Saint-Jean-d'Angély in the province of Saintonge, the much-traveled Priolo had served Mazarin during the Fronde,[43] before joining the Frondeur, Condé. This turned out to be an unfortunate decision. Returning from exile in Flanders, with Fouquet's help Priolo slowly reintegrated himself into Mazarin's circles. Costar praised him for his literary style. Fouquet's arrest again left poor Priolo on shaky ground, but Colbert seems consciously to have decided that histories of the Fronde would be a good antidote to all the lamenting among men of letters and princes over Fouquet's arrest. It demonstrates the cold shrewdness that motivated Colbert, who did not hesitate to pose as a patron and to sponsor an ideological history of the Fronde for immediate political purposes. An analysis of Priolo's experiences under Colbert's "protection" makes it clear that none of Richelieu's devices for sponsoring politically inspired contemporary history had been forgotten.

Colbert's letters to Priolo are friendly in tone, though he does urge him to complete his history as rapidly as possible. Further monetary support would be forthcoming upon completion of the history based on the "mémoires" that Colbert had supplied him.[44] What were these *mémoires*? The *érudits*, including Pierre Bayle,[45] later concluded that, in accordance with the tenets of the humanist program for writing of-

43. Priolo's association with Longueville had begun when he accompanied the Duke to Munster. According to B.N., mss. fr. 25026, early in 1652 Priolo—variously described as Longueville's "intendant" and "secrétaire"—was sent by the Duke to "compliment" Mazarin and at the same time discuss with Gaston d'Orléans the possibility of signing a treaty of union with Gaston's faction (fol. 12). Priolo made several trips between the Duke in Normandy and the court, at one point remaining in Paris for two weeks of negotiations. In part owing to Priolo's bargaining strategy, in the end Mazarin agreed to all of Longueville's demands (fol. 62 v), thus bringing Longueville over to a surface neutrality, although behind the scenes the Duke contributed to the empty royal coffers in July 1652 (fol. 110). See also Mazarin's letter to Lionne (late 1650), in *Lettres*, ed. Adolphe Chéruel (Paris, 1872–1906), vol. 3, p. 689. I owe this information to Patricia M. Ranum.

44. "Lettres de Benjamin Priolo," ed. Philippe Tamizey de Larroque, *Archives historiques de la Saintonge et de l'Aunis* 4 (1877): 267–76.

45. *Dictionnaire historique et critique* (Paris, 1720), vol. 12, p. 331, "Priolo."

ficial history, they had been secret documents about the affairs of state to which only a minister might have access. But they may also have been rather specific instructions on how to ridicule certain nobles and clergymen, ridicule that would make the publication of Priolo's history something of a cause célèbre.

Priolo sent Colbert excerpts of his Latin manuscript so that the minister might judge its value for himself.[46] Could Colbert actually read and assess the quality of Latin prose? He may have had one of his *commis* supervise the work. While Colbert was making his decision to sponsor its publication, initially in a condensed version paid for by the Crown, Priolo went on writing and promising faithfully to adhere to Colbert's *mémoires*. He also described the style in which he was writing. At first he asserted that, in being brief at the beginning of his history, he was carefully imitating Tacitus; then, a few days later, he wrote to say that he was imitating Livy. One of Priolo's friends had told him that his style was "mitoyen," that is, between the styles of Tacitus and Livy,[47] a remark that would have scandalized the *doctes* of his day. But, as if this were not enough stylistic confusion, two weeks after having claimed to write in a Tacitean style, Priolo informed Colbert that the first five books of his history were in the style of Sallust. Still writing, a month later he announced that the entire book would be in the style of Quintus Curtius![48] While wallowing in these stylistic confusions, Priolo pressed on, reassuring Colbert that his history would emphasize the triumph of Mazarin over the trials of war, both foreign and civil.

There is no evidence to suggest that Colbert was the least bit troubled about which ancient history Priolo was imitating.[49] He reassured the author of his support and asked him to do nothing about the publication of his work without first informing him. After publication of the first book in 1662, poor Priolo found himself beleaguered on all sides

46. "Lettres de Benjamin Priolo," p. 267.

47. *Ibid.*, p. 267.

48. *Ibid.*, pp. 274 and 276.

49. That other ministers had grown anxious about the political implications of the work is clear from Priolo's letter to Colbert of 31 October 1661. Loménie de Brienne had asked that the entire manuscript be taken to Fontainebleau, while assuring the author that the Chancellor would arrange for payment of the publication through Cramoisi, the Crown's principal publisher (*Lettres de Colbert*, vol. 5, p. 444). This fact would intrigue Bayle and other commentators, but they never suspected Colbert's sponsorship of Priolo. It may also be that Lionne was merely verifying for himself what he and Colbert, as well as Loménie, had agreed to support (*Lettres de Chapelain*, vol. 2, p. 264).

and hastened to seek shelter behind Colbert's reputation. Indeed, the former bishop of Coutances, Claude Auvry, had stopped Priolo in the street and reproached him for being overly harsh on the clergy in his history.[50] The *grands* had also expressed their discontent in numerous ways.

Claiming lack of money, Priolo wrote his patron: "Ma famille est nombreuse. Les bouchers et les boulangers ont certaines inquiétudes qui les saisissent et qui ne me sont pas commodes pour bien remplir les fenestres de l'histoire qu'on continue à imprimer. . . . Mais pour l'amour de Dieu, ne me laissés pas, Monsieur, disputer avec les boulangers et les bouchers. Il n'est question que de graisser la poulie pour Monseigneur le duc Mazarin."[51] Thus, while his history was arousing partisan emotions, Priolo made it clear that he was willing to continue as long as he had Colbert's protection.

On 10 July 1662, Priolo announced to Colbert that he felt threatened by the Parlement of Paris, the members of which he described as pedants. He had written in his history that "jamais advocat ne valut rien," which had infuriated the judges despite the fact that he said it was a quotation from Sallust.[52] The storm over his history finally forced Priolo to cease publication,[53] but he continued to write and promised Colbert that he would go to Holland if necessary to oversee the publication of his history there. Eventually the entire work was published in both French and foreign editions and became the subject of considerable critical discussion. Bayle was fascinated by Priolo's career, possibly because of Priolo's Protestant upbringing and "conversion," but he also came to admire the "hardiesse" of this history, which had attacked the *grands*.[54] On the matter of Priolo's style, Bayle remarked that "les phrases de Tacite en fournissent presque toutes les couleurs," and that were it in French it would please the modern taste because it "is completely filled with characters, with portraits that are presently so much in fashion."[55] Unlike Colbert, however, Bayle was confused by Priolo's remarks about the styles of ancient historians and attempted

50. *Lettres de Colbert*, vol. 5, p. 282.

51. April 1662, *ibid.*, p. 281.

52. *Ibid.*, p. 285.

53. *Ibid.*, p. 235. Priolo had thought that he should give up his pension in order to reduce the animosity expressed toward him; but Colbert assured him that since he had received pensions from Mazarin, this tactic would be to no avail.

54. Denis-François Camusat remarked, "M. Bayle a beau avoir appuïé sur la grande sincérité de Priolo. Tout l'Europe en a jugé autrement" (*Histoire critique des journaux* [Amsterdam, 1734], p. 262).

55. Bayle, vol. 11, p. 331.

rather desperately and unconvincingly to make Priolo appear consistent.

Neither Bayle, nor a man of letters with Chapelain's education and leanings, could grasp the intellectual-political purview of such a man as Priolo. It never occurred to Bayle that a hanger-on, a sometime diplomatic agent, might be able to write a lively Latin history, though unable to distinguish the style and moral implications of one ancient historian from those of another. The *érudits*, and perhaps unconsciously Bayle in this instance, still considered the careful study of the ancients as the only way to learn how to write history.

Other little lessons can be drawn from Priolo's career and works. Could Colbert have turned to one of the writers whose literary reputation had already been established when commissioning a history that denigrated the *grands*? The humanists' program stressed that history should tell the truth, but it also insisted that the best way to do this was through narrating noble and virtuous actions, the good *exempla*, rather than stressing evil and vices. In 1660, Colbert had no one to whom he could turn—no Balzac, for example—no one with the *hardiesse* to attack the *grands*. He found in Priolo what Richelieu had found in François de Fancan, Jean Sirmond, and Mézerai: the young writer who would write history to undermine the aristocratic, parlementaire, and ecclesiastical ideals and to support the Crown. As we shall see, Chapelain—to whom Colbert would turn in 1662 for advice on whom he should select to write the history of Louis XIV's reign—expressed his outrage over a quip about Longueville that Priolo had included in his history.[56]

At almost precisely the time when Priolo was writing, the aristocratic ideal was being humbled by the Fronde and by the Frondeurs' allies, the Jansenists—represented by Blaise Pascal and Pierre Nicole—who wrote critiques of the *grands*; but a negative account of aristocratic actions written by reputable authors was out of the question. As Chapelain's career attests, their interests already lay in the praise of the young Louis XIV and in the strong desire to forget the Fronde.

56. Chapelain eventually began to assert that Priolo mixed up everything, but this was only after he had become outraged at Priolo's remark about Longueville. His earlier, favorable comments about Priolo must therefore be read in the light of the fact that they were both Longueville's clients.

Chapter VI
Chapelain and the
Royal Patronage of
History

THIS sketch of literary patronage during the decades of upheaval between Richelieu's death in 1642 and the beginning of Louis XIV's personal reign in 1661 leads us to the more specific study of the persons and bureaucratic habits that linked writers of history to the Crown under Colbert. The chaotic relationships forged by the ideological controversies and the competing *fidélités* of the King, Cardinal Mazarin, and the princes certainly appalled Colbert. Within months after sponsoring Priolo's history, and despite all the social and economic engineering that he was undertaking, Colbert set out to bureaucratize literary patronage. His major decision was asking Jean Chapelain for assessments of all writers capable of writing history, in order that the Minister and the King might grant pensions and their personal favor to the most talented among them.

Seen from a twentieth-century perspective, Colbert's decision appears an obvious one; but it was innovative in the courtly society of seventeenth-century France, as yet only beginning to perceive the future role of royal intendants and other bureaucrats. Colbert triggered a mania for the formal gathering of information and advice that extended to every aspect of the economy, civil administration, and culture. He also violated the ideal of the patron-writer relationship when he began systematically to determine the sums of pensions on the basis of the quality and quantity of the historical production. The humanistic ideal of the patron had stressed the advancement of *bonnes lettres*, but it had included no mechanical procedures for judging the quality of a literary work. The son of the merchant draper from Rheims wanted such assessments incorporated directly into the decision to grant or renew royal pensions to writers. Colbert could be impatient. He relied on the advice of experts, granting larger pensions to the "strong" and cutting off the "weak." Never before had there been such extensive bureaucratic organization of scholarly and literary activities; it would be refined and extended in subsequent regimes down to our own day. As we shall see, what had originally been a rather open, generous policy favoring writers became under Colbert one that was constraining and competitive.

Chapelain's role as expert adviser was not entirely new. Never recognized by the creation of a specific office, his role on occasion had been played—but never so systematically or extensively—by many other poets and historiographers royal who, like everyone else at court, pressed their sovereign or the royal ministers to award pensions or grants to disciples and friends. Chapelain's role was far more influential than this; its prototype was that played at the court of Francis I by that great pioneer, Guillaume Budé. Budé's campaign to convince Francis to patronize letters and enter the international competition for attracting reputed scholars to France[1] had been a remarkable victory. This campaign fundamentally changed the image of the Monarchy, as the ideal of the princely patron gradually displaced that of the sacerdotal kingship, and as language and culture supplanted religion as a central element in French nationalism. Chapelain and the writers of his and the following generation reaped the benefits of the increased status won by the great humanist-politician who had pleaded with Francis I for "good letters."

This great Valois and Louis XIV both managed to convey powerful images as patrons, thanks partly to the successful efforts of Budé and Chapelain.[2] Men of learning and letters could empathize with the political and cultural designs of these kings. Though dedications to each monarch differed in tone, they were filled with rapturous phrases about *gloire*. Because of Francis's and Louis's willingness to pose as royal patrons, the ideal of a unitary French culture equaling those of Ancient Greece and Rome could have meaning for those observers of political and court life, the writers receiving royal favor and recognition. Budé and Chapelain played their roles with enthusiasm. The recognition accruing from royal favor may have satisfied some personal need for higher status, especially for the commoner Chapelain, who, unlike Budé, never had an active political career.

Each enjoyed a high reputation among writers and scholars. Indeed,

1. One of the most notable and most familiar, perhaps, was his effort to attract Erasmus. See Jean Plattard, *Guillaume Budé* (Paris, 1923), p. 29.

2. The Monarchy's patronage of humanist writers had been minimal before 1520, a year that probably witnessed Budé's increased influence on patronage. See Claude Bontems, "Introduction," *Le Prince dans la France des XVIe et XVIIe siècles* (Paris, 1965), p. 5; and Eugene F. Rice, Jr., "The Patrons of French Humanism, 1490–1520," *Renaissance Studies in Honor of Hans Baron*, ed. Anthony Molho and John A. Tedeschi (Florence, 1971), p. 690.

their ability to influence the Crown had enhanced this reputation—and, in Chapelain's case, had inflated it beyond measure. Each was also politically engaged and, though certainly in different ways, was disposed to accept as fair and just almost anything that royal policy dictated. The political perceptions with which each was endowed permitted him a grasp of fundamental royal policies, even though in most instances he was familiar only with the surface political events. Neither man was consistently privy to matters of state; yet in his dealings with other writers who were less intimate with the King, Chapelain—and pehaps Budé—implied a greater knowledge of royal policies than he actually possessed.[3] There were, however, differences between the two men that may reflect either changing ideological moods within the society or the changes that frequently occur in the writings of a man like Budé, who at one point was all but disgraced and at another both in favor and influential. His relatively harsh criticisms in *De asse* of the Monarchy's previous social and economic policies and of taxes and tax collectors[4] are unparalleled in Chapelain's writings. In view of the shifts in personalities and policies from the reign of Louis XII to that of Francis I, it is not clear that Budé's remarks were interpreted by his contemporaries as critical of the Monarchy. But if Mézerai's experiences can be considered typical, it seems safe to conclude that by 1661 the range of criticisms open to a writer who wanted to gain or continue to maintain the favor of royal ministers had narrowed.

Did Budé and Chapelain use the same criteria when recommending scholars and men of letters to the Crown's attention? Since the primary focus here is on the seventeenth century, I have not studied Budé's recommendations, even to the extent that it is possible to do so. It is clear that Chapelain's criteria were his critical judgment of the authors' published works, his "connoissance" of their stylistic and scholarly strengths and weaknesses, and the promise of further works to come. These criteria, which from the perspective of the ideal of patronage seemed startling and lacking in humanity, served as the basis for Chapelain's recommendations to Colbert in his famous "Liste des gens de lettres vivans en 1662."[5] Chapelain's recommendations and the royal

3. In Chapelain's day the genre of letter writing included news about political and military developments; but Chapelain went beyond this, implying that he had information that was secret, rather than that available to the general public.
4. Louis Delaruelle, *Guillaume Budé* (Paris, 1907), pp. 173 f.
5. B.N., mss. fr. 23045, fols. 104–113; published by Denis-François Camusat, *Mélanges littéraires tirés des lettres de M. Jean Chapelain de l'Académie françoise* (Paris, 1749); and in Pierre-Nicolas Desmolets, *Continuation des mémoires de littérature et d'histoire* (Paris, 1726), vol. 2, pt. 1, p. 21.

bureaucracy would set in motion what must be defined as the largest and most systematic program for the support of historical writing and scholarship that the West had ever known. Before discussing in detail the "Liste" and its effects, it is worthwhile to look more closely at the career and intellectual presuppositions of its author.

Part of a generation of men of letters who sensed that they and their culture were accomplishing great things, Chapelain wrote in 1638: "Dans trente ans au plus tard la France se debarbarizera."[6] This conviction—held even by the skeptics whose thought raised doubts about nonhistorical knowledge[7]—was solidly grounded upon a historical perception of French cultural achievements over the previous century and a half. Knowing how the diffusion of humanist doctrines could lead to cultural greatness, to a truly golden age, Chapelain and the authors of his generation commented ceaselessly upon the revival of *bonnes lettres* that had begun just prior to or during the reign of Francis I. Never did a generation feel itself a more integral part of a historical movement about to reach its apogee. They saw themselves as standing on the shoulders of giants whom they praised continually: the great Budé, the Pléiade writers, and Malherbe, the founders of this cultural achievement. Du Bellay's *Deffence et illustration de la langue françoyse* (1549) had been the manifesto of this broad cultural movement to achieve a French golden age. Du Bellay's ideas were repeated almost endlessly in a literary culture that placed far greater emphasis upon the eloquent restatement of *topoi* than upon originality of thought. Did not France owe as much to Francis I as Rome did to Caesar Augustus?[8] Down to

6. *Lettres de Jean Chapelain*, ed. Philippe Tamizey de Larroque (Paris, 1880–1883), vol. 1, p. 268.

7. The assertion that skepticism among seventeenth-century thinkers undermined confidence in historical knowledge has never been closely examined. Though not our subject here, it is perhaps worthwhile to note that this assertion is based on the tenor of the works of such major writers as Montaigne and on La Mothe le Vayer's *Du peu de certitude qu'il y a dans l'histoire* (Richard Popkin, *The History of Scepticism from Erasmus to Descartes* [New York, 1964], particularly Chapter 5). That neither Montaigne nor the aristocratic culture that he represented placed much emphasis on historical knowledge or felt part of a historical movement is, of course, obvious, but it is not clear that this lack of historical-mindedness was derived from skeptical philosophy. In the case of La Mothe le Vayer, the problem would seem to lie in explaining the apparent contradiction between the title and the work itself, for the latter is really a quite conventional example of the *ars historica*. Was La Mothe playing the old game of attracting attention to his work by selecting a provocative title?

8. Françoise Joukovsky, *La gloire dans la poésie française et néolatine du XVIe siècle* (Geneva, 1969), p. 217.

the mid-eighteenth century it would be impossible to conceive of a period of cultural greatness unaccompanied by great political achievements. The two went hand in hand and were parts of the same thing, *un siècle heureux*, a golden age.[9]

Not crushed by the *gloire* of their immediate predecessors, though still feeling unequal to the great writers of Antiquity, the authors of Chapelain's generation confidently carried on their grammatical and stylistic studies—and especially work on the dictionary of the French Academy—to establish a pure language. Once free of "barbarisms" and ignoble words, an ordered, polite, and regular French language would be a creative force in its own right.[10] The movement carried along with it the germ of national unity and "true eloquence" in French. Respect for the writings of others based on stylistic consideration would transcend the baser inclinations that had previously motivated men to violent theological and political controversies. Form, order and harmony sustained by a wise and generous prince would pervade religious thought, philosophy, letters, and political action. Indeed, men of Chapelain's temperament believed that the political consequences of classicism ought to be freedom from the violent use of words in controversy, even literary controversy.

In the century of civil and ideological wars between 1560 and 1660, the movement in favor of eloquence may have been slowed down after the progress made under Francis I, but it had never been halted. Under Louis XIV the Crown at last seemed willing to respond once more to the humble supplications and occasionally passionate exhortations of authors to attempt to recreate a golden age. Writers were the sole individuals capable of recording great political achievements; political achievements worthy of record occurred exclusively during periods when there were authors with the talent to commit these achievements to paper. Though tautological and banal, this ideal is very significant. After 1660 it was the fundamental cultural-political presupposition of both writers and men of power. Eloquence, immortality, and *gloire* were tangible phenomena for Chapelain, Colbert, and, in his still formative years, Louis XIV.[11]

9. Bodin also believed that cultural greatness occurred concurrently with political greatness (*Methodus ad facilem cognitionem historiarum*, ed. Pierre Mesnard [Paris, 1941], p. 277).

10. This linguistic explanation for cultural achievement also had a long history. Suffice it to point out its central place in Voltaire's *Siècle de Louis XIV*.

11. The belief that "pure" language and political greatness coincided was not peculiarly French in the seventeenth century. This humanist tenet was shared by writers throughout Europe. To take a rather extreme case—

The ideal roles that a prince and writers of history might play were therefore well established before Louis XIV, Pellisson, Racine, and numerous other authors carried them out; Chapelain was a vulgarizer of these ideals and an arbiter of the styles in which they could be expressed on paper. The mood of confidence and even of self-congratulation among writers would generate further confidence in the achievements of men of letters.

The beginning of a personal reign always brought hope and promise, which men of letters—and perhaps Louis XIV's subjects—took more seriously than they should have. Chapelain argued that *gloire* was necessary if kings were to inspire veneration in their subjects and respect in neighboring states. This philosophy politicized the pursuit of *gloire* by removing it almost completely from psychological and moral considerations. Chapelain went on to raise the question of whether private individuals could acquire *gloire* at all. His hesitant "yes" in "Le dialogue de la gloire" (1662)[12] reflects a royalist extremism in which all individual behavior was implicitly defined as noteworthy, immortalizing, or *glorieux* if it emanated from a desire to please and support the prince. *Gloire* would presumably have been denied to rebellious great nobles and to authors who attempted to convince the prince to change his policies. The contradictions in this work and Chapelain's divergence from the extreme position that his "Dialogue" expressed were probably apparent to the few who read it. Never published, it nonetheless is an interesting testimony to Chapelain's thought in the critical year that witnessed the inauguration of a systematic program to patronize the writing of the history of Louis XIV.

The flights of enthusiasm for Louis and for his conquests, his buildings, and above all, his person, would last into the 1690s, when the mood among writers would change to one of despair.[13] Chapelain did not live to witness this brutal transformation, though its origins had already

---

for John Milton would have disagreed with Chapelain on many other issues —we find the English poet writing: "Where language is not cultivated, what does it mean but that the souls of men are slothful and gaping and prepared for any servility? Conversely, never have we heard of an empire or state that does not flourish so long as it cultivates its language and is proud of it." Protestant and English nuances aside, Milton's ideal of a conjuncture of great literature and political greatness is very similar to that of the French men of letters of his generation (quoted in Hugh Trevor-Roper, "The Elitist Politics of Milton," *Times Literary Supplement*, 1 June 1973, p. 602).

12. Georges Collas, *Un poète protecteur des lettres au XVIIe siècle, Jean Chapelain, 1595–1674* (Paris, 1912), pp. 343 ff.

13. The mood of despair contributed to Racine's inclination to remain

become apparent by 1672. In that year Chapelain observed: "Les nuits de guerre [read defeats] refroidissent les muses."[14] In the "pure" language of the late seventeenth century, men of letters used the term *guerre* almost exclusively for military actions that had an uncertain outcome or were outright defeats; all other military actions were considered conquests. Earlier in his career Chapelain had admitted that his country's fate on the battlefield either inspired or dampened his spirits and writing; he remained fascinated by every detail from the front and celebrated each victory.[15] Chapelain's earliest surviving correspondence, dated 1632, joyously alludes to royal victories over rebellious Huguenots.[16] When war with Spain broke out in 1635, he was quick to accept as causes the explanations that Richelieu had developed and distributed. Later he would hasten to help translate and distribute works written to support the shaky claims of Louis's wife to parts of the Spanish Netherlands in the War of Devolution, 1667. Yet there were some limits to the degree of his engagement in these royal enterprises. Unlike a spectator at a game who bemoans defeat, Chapelain now felt little gloom when the royal cause was in jeopardy. Disappointed but serene after having witnessed so many defeats, Chapelain typified the Crown's supporters among the men of letters who had been tempered by the Fronde. They were engaged and willing to help in the King's affairs, but they also may have been painfully conscious that their role in these *grandes affaires* was limited to writing about them. The sense of common purpose with the prince had been joined by a respect for the hierarchy of capacities and functions. Chapelain recognized the distances that separated his poorly heated study from the battlefields and the *cabinet du roi*.

The teachings of the ancients and the *gloire* of Louis XIV had been fused into one system of passionately held beliefs. Both Chapelain and Colbert often couched in religious terms their enthusiasm for the thought of Antiquity, whether expressed in Latin or translated into French. Instead of passing his hours in *oraison*, Chapelain read the ancients for a sense of direction and spiritual renewal. Gustave Lanson remarked that Chapelain had the temperament of an "*érudit du XVI*ᵉ *siècle*; he worshiped the ancients: he not only looked for the most per-

---

silent during the 1690s. Through the religious life expressed in his last two great plays and in his history, *L'abrégé de l'histoire de Port-Royal*, he would return to a search for order in French political culture.

14. 1 January 1672, *Lettres de Chapelain*, vol. 2, p. 768.

15. *Ibid.*, vol. 1, p. 1.

16. *Ibid.*, pp. 2 and 5.

fect forms of art in [their writings], he also sought from them all his moral and political principles, reading them as a historian, a grammarian, a philosopher."[17] The divinity, immortality, and majesty of this cult infused every aspect of his thought and action. Louis XIV could be seen only as the fulfillment of the heroic conceits revived from Antiquity.

Chapelain's references to the God of papal Rome are remarkably infrequent and conventional. Whether in letters to Colbert or to his most intimate friends, his enthusiasm was almost exclusively reserved for the divine figure who created Versailles and who had begun to "defeat Europe." Yet a charge of idolatry or blasphemy would not have perturbed Chapelain; the *dévot*, ultramontanist, or even pietist presuppositions of anyone who might make such a charge would have led him to discount it. Although he believed that the monarch possessed the ultimate authority on matters of religion and state, Chapelain did not accept the general implications of divine-right monarchy made fashionable by such younger contemporaries as Bossuet. Counting Jesuits, Jansenists, Huguenots, skeptics, and Frondeurs among his friends, he carried on with *bonnes lettres* as the single unifying theme in his correspondence. He was a frequent correspondent of persons who would not have shared his political views. Though Chapelain observed that men of good letters, including the Abbé de Saint-Cyran, could be arrested, he expressed no dismay. In later life he would be forced to witness the persecution of Jansenist and Protestant friends, yet never once in his voluminous correspondence is there a hint that he attempted to intervene on their behalf with his influential patrons at court. Indeed, this inaction may have been an integral part of the behavior of a seventeenth-century man whose various friends were irreconcilable enemies. Chapelain possessed the talent both to please and to inspire respect. He liked to sow compliments, reap them later on, and in general remain silent rather than write a slashing comment about an individual or his works.[18] The antithesis of the controversialist, and yet a powerful critic, Chapelain made enemies less through his weaknesses as a *politique* than through the failure of his poetry to sustain the high status commensurate with royal favor and his place in the Academy. Chapelain's efforts on behalf of historical writing and his views about the function of letters in political life were not apt to make enemies.

17. *Grande encyclopédie*, ed. Berthelot et al. (Paris, 1886–1902), vol. 10, p. 551, "Chapelain."
18. Antonin Fabre, *Chapelain et nos deux premières académies* (Paris, 1890), pp. 1 and 19; Collas, p. 76.

Historical Criticism

Chapelain remarked that he believed he had some talent as a *politique*. Exactly what did he mean by this? A person who understands *la politique* may himself be *un politique*. Chapelain applied the term both to himself and to entire peoples. In history the *politique* element of a narrative was the congeries of ideas that transformed events into a *corps d'histoire*. The interplay of institutions, personal motives and actions, and the long-term behavioral patterns of nations and families constituted *la politique*. One of the attributes of a good historian was his command of what Chapelain called the "théorie de la politique."[19] Enthusiastic about the *politique* element of Polybius's history[20]—another indication of his interest in the dynamics of social and institutional behavior, at least among expanding states—Chapelain was nevertheless most interested by the study of individuals in political life. He almost was given the opportunity for an active political life as a secretary to an ambassador, but either the terms were not quite right[21] or, as occurred when he was being considered for the post of tutor to Louis XIV, the opportunity evaporated in the mists of court politics.[22] No moral or spiritual constraints obliged him to live the life of a man of letters, but he would not accept a royal appointment that at the most would have conferred a minimal increase in status. Any appointment offered him had to satisfy his amour-propre, that is, his own conception of his public reputation and of his sphere of action as a *politique*. Put another way, although Chapelain himself did not succeed in being offered positions that he deemed worthy of his consideration, he was very ready to advance the names of others for service to the Crown. Indeed, he may have thought that his role in selecting historians was even more prestigious in the eyes of a group from which he coveted acclaim: his fellow men of letters.

It is difficult to conceive of a more appropriate mental and political outlook than Chapelain's for the role he began to play in 1662. He

19. *Lettres de Chapelain*, vol. 2, p. 275.
20. *Ibid.*, p. 634.
21. *Ibid.*, vol. 1, p. 20.
22. La Mothe le Vayer had first been proposed, but Naudé relates that Anne of Austria had excluded him because she "wanted a man who was married." This criterion presumably also eventually excluded Chapelain (*ibid.*, pp. 625 and 655). Cf. G. Lacour-Gayet, *L'éducation politique de Louis XIV* (Paris, 1923), p. 10. In the end a celibate, Péréfixe, was appointed.

possessed a coherent body of principles about what truly outstanding historical writing should be, a fine critical sense on matters of style, and a personal disposition to favor or to recommend to Colbert only those writers and scholars whom he considered the most qualified. History was indisputably the most difficult of all the literary genres. Chapelain pointed out that as a prose genre its chances of survival for thousands of years were somewhat less than for works in verse, and he quickly cited Homer's poems as an example. By emphasizing epic poems, however, Chapelain was actually defending his own decision to write his major work, the *Pucelle*, as historicized verse, as an epic. Might not works in epic form assure the Sun King's immortality a bit longer than would prose narratives? Chapelain gave no thought to how the invention of printing might have affected the odds for the survival of literary works in the minds of the reading public. So steeped was he in the thought of Antiquity that he dared not violate any of the "historical" conclusions suggested by the survival of works from Antiquity.

The continuity of themes and of critical observations over the thirty years spanned by Chapelain's correspondence suggests that this almost blind respect for the authority of Antiquity gave him the confidence to ignore the implications of recent publication in philosophy or rhetoric. He greatly admired Descartes, whom as early as 1637 he considered the most esteemed and eloquent of recent philosophers. Though Cicero alone, of all the ancients, may have been the equal of Descartes, Chapelain believed the latter possibly the more original thinker. After all, Cicero had merely "lent his words to the thought of others, whereas [Descartes] is adorned in his own thoughts, which are sublime and, for the most part, new."[23] Yet this respect for Descartes did not incline Chapelain to comment on Descartes's devastating critique of historical writing. Chapelain must surely have read *Le discours de la méthode*, yet Descartes's observation about the disastrous effects of depicting individuals in the past as somehow larger than life—in short, a critique of the outlook on the past that Huizinga defined as the "historical ideals of life"—is never touched upon by Chapelain or, for that matter, by any of his contemporaries.

On the shelves in Chapelain's magnificent library, where each book had been selected with care, stood Bodin's *Methodus ad facilem historiarum cognitionem*, Alciato's *Emblemata*, Poliziano's collected works, and some Pontanus and Poggio, as well as the major works of Pithou and Pasquier.[24] Though criticisms of the *ars historica* of an older generation

23. *Lettres de Chapelain*, vol. 1, p. 189.

24. *Catalogue de tous les livres de feu M. Chapelain*, ed. Colbert Searles (Stanford, 1912), *passim*.

could be found in these works, Chapelain evidently disregarded such criticisms.[25] He generally scorned the efforts of moderns to go beyond the ancients and seems to have especially disliked writing *about* history rather than writing history itself. Although it is obvious that he had not yet read Agostino Mascardi's *Dell'arte historica,* he commented to a friend: "Je souhaitterois qu'il [Mascardi] nous voulut monstrer dans un corps d'histoire de longue haleine la pratique de la belle théorie qu'il a donnée."[26]

The general implications of this criticism of theorizing cannot be derived from the text itself; but when viewed from the perspective of someone committed to the ancients, as Chapelain was, it sheds some light on the question of why the men of Chapelain's generation ignored, or failed to recognize as significant, the historical theories of their late-sixteenth-century compatriots. Since the progress of *bonnes lettres* had generally come to be perceived as a historical movement that began during the reign of Francis I, why should the prescriptions for a golden age be abandoned? Chapelain considered strict adherence to the literary-historical models and principles derived from Antiquity to be sufficient to bring forth a golden age. Why did he turn to the solemn compendiums of recent thinkers? Mascardi (and, subsequently, his French counterpart, Father Rapin, author of *Les instructions pour l'histoire,* 1677) provided little more than restatements of *topoi* derived from ancient rhetoricians. In a sense, therefore, the makers of classicism were blinded by this perception of the revival of *bonnes lettres* as a historical movement based on adherence to the principles of Antiquity. They did not comprehend the achievements of such forebears as Bodin and La Popelinière, who subconsciously attempted to break away from

25. Just the year before his death, the aged Chapelain attempted to answer some of Conring's questions about Bodin. The replies are pitiful, because Chapelain makes mistakes about the order in which Bodin's works were written, then corrects himself. He stresses his belief that Bodin was Jewish. Had Conring asked Chapelain about Bodin's religion? Chapelain also boasts about Bodin's "génie" and how he has brought honor to France, but Bodin's religion interests Chapelain most. One variant of a letter is interesting for Chapelain's impression about the Jewish community in France. Bodin's "mère luy avoit inspiré la créance, étant de ces Juives que leurs biens retiennent dans les provinces, qui s'y habitent pour suivre leur mari, étrangers principalement marchands Portugais qui s'y viennent établir. On en connoit particulièrement à Rouen plusieurs qui, pourvu qu'ils paroissent Chrétiens, et sans scandale, ne sont point inquietés par les Magistrats, dans la vue de ne pas affoiblir le commerce de la Ville" (*Lettres de Chapelain,* vol. 2, pp. 809, 825, and 832). Note how Chapelain implies that the status of the Jews in France is the same in his day as it had been in Bodin's.

26. *Ibid.,* vol. 1, p. 227.

the first principle of humanism: respect for the authority of Antiquity. Chapelain always commented politely about the theorists, but beneath the compliments may be concealed the suspicion that they were subconsciously challenging the authority of the ancients. This made him uneasy. How much better had Mascardi simply written a history of Florence with Livy as his principal inspiration!

Chapelain's reliance on the thought of the ancients was so complete, indeed so much a part of his sense of the meaning of history, that his more formal historical criticisms remind readers of what Lucian and Dionysius of Halicarnassus wrote about history. The tone is restrained; there is little effort to be precise or analytical. In short, the ancient rhetoricians were reborn in Chapelain. Probably unable to perceive rhetorical theory as separate from history, or even as merely one among many intellectual-philosophical congeries of ideas about language that had been inherited from Antiquity, Chapelain felt supremely confident in making "judgments" about history. At Auger de Mauléon's request he prepared a critical essay on Cardinal Guido Bentivoglio's *Historia della guerra di Fiandra.* Chapelain may have suspected that his work would be passed on to Cardinal Richelieu, for he took extreme care in preparing it. The Cardinal—through the poet Boisrobert, his secretary and "gray eminence" for contacting men of letters—made known to Chapelain his disagreement on the question of whether or not moral judgments should be included in histories. This question had been much debated by the humanists, especially after the discovery and publication in 1515 of Tacitus's *Annals.* Thus it is of interest that this debate was still very much alive in 1632. The question of including moral judgments had become a *topos* itself, of both stylistic and theoretical importance. As such it goes to the heart of the theory that the *ars historica* was moral philosophy recounting man's past actions. The exchange of correspondence about Bentivoglio's history discloses the contours of Chapelain's thought about history and reveals the *ars historica* as very much alive.

Following the principles of ancient rhetoric, Chapelain disarms the reader by first stressing the strong points of Bentivoglio's history. There is an implicit assurance that no vitriol will be used; the flattering remarks about Bentivoglio himself reflect the triumph of the humane and gentle tone of humanist letters.[27] There will be no scurrilous or *ad hominem* attacks after the manner of monks writing about something with which they disagree. Chapelain admires the balance between the significance of the subjects discussed and the number of words used to describe them. This was a clever and brief way of dealing with a cen-

27. *Ibid.*, p. 13.

tral issue in the *ars historica*, the issue of the hierarchy of "noble" or worthy subjects or actions to be described and the proportion of words in a history dictated by this nobleness or commonness. An imbalance between subject and number of words and a certain inclination to include "ignoble" subjects were two of Mézerai's weaknesses, as we shall see. Chapelain either was genuinely impressed by Bentivoglio's successful handling of this problem, or he simply wanted to be critical on other grounds.

The issues that Chapelain wanted to discuss were style, the use of speeches, and the inclusion of moral judgments. Indeed, Bentivoglio's style is criticized for employing the first person in the narrative, at least in part because this liberty should be available only to actual participants in the historical incidents recounted. In addition, new, affected words are present in the text, words that Chapelain dislikes and refers to as "cortigianesque." Himself a creator of new words, Chapelain apparently believed it a mistake to do so when writing history, because new words and the use of the first person both impair the achievement of a balanced Tacitean style. So confident about his control of Italian that he frequently advised Italian writers on stylistic matters, Chapelain goes on to compliment Bentivoglio for the "majesté négligente" of his sentences, which are "composés de périodes courtes et nerveuses, dont les membres sont divisés et tournés de son mesme air."[28] Writing in a Tacitean style had therefore been very clearly defined by the date of the founding of the French Academy. Chapelain found Bentivoglio's speeches to be superb, entirely infused with the genius of Tacitus. Nothing equals the quality of these speeches, he asserts, except those by Scipione Ammirato in his *Istoria Fiorentina*.

What really mattered to Chapelain, however, was Bentivoglio's decision not to include moral judgments. After asserting that Tacitus himself had rendered such judgments, Chapelain gingerly points a finger at "some persons who have prescribed that historians should only recount without being engaged" in making moral judgments. Here a "modern" tendency is implicitly singled out; but instead of launching a formal attack, Chapelain continues by asserting that the inclusion of moral judgments by Paolo Sarpi in his *History of the Council of Trent* and by Francesco Guicciardini in his *History of Italy* won these works their preeminent place as the best histories written in modern times. These two works alone are the equal of all those written in the "*premiers aages*"; thus Bentivoglio seems to be consciously breaking one of the prescriptions for a great historical work. If a historian does not interrupt his narrative to keep score of good and bad actions, he must

28. *Ibid.*, p. 4.

—Chapelain holds—nevertheless clearly state his position. Then, scoffing at Bentivoglio's assertion that Anne Boleyn's "impiety" had been responsible for the rise of "impiety" (read heresy?) under Elizabeth, Chapelain continues by declaring that there is every reason to expect better than this from so subtle a *politique* historian.[29]

Quibbles aside, Chapelain turns to what he considers the book's fundamental weakness on the matter of judgments, namely, the author's failure to establish what Chapelain calls a position of neutrality between the views of the Spanish and the Dutch combatants in the Flemish war. From its very first page, partiality for the Spaniards and Catholicism renders the work suspect to readers. Enunciated as a principle to be followed in writing history, this "neutrality" as Chapelain defined it was not, however, a definition of historicism in disguise. In accordance with the historiographical principles proposed by the sixteenth-century *politiques* to whom he was indebted on this matter,[30] Chapelain can merely appeal for "neutrality" and then elaborate a view of history delimited by the ideological confines of the state. In this instance Bentivoglio has failed to distinguish between the religious and the political causes of the Flemish war and to place those that were political above those that were religious. Philip II had carried out a "changement universel" in the Netherlands; "Spanish barbarities," not heresy or impiety, had provoked the revolt of the Dutch and the ensuing war. "Neutrality" could therefore be perceived as emphasizing political explanations for the war, since religion, "la rébellion contre Dieu," had not been the "cause primitive" of the war: "[Bentivoglio] auroist plustost reconnu ingenuement que la violence qu'ils souffroient les avoit précipité dans l'hérésie que de poser pour fondement que l'hérésie les ait porté au souleuvement contre leur prince."[31] The "vices" of the Spanish should have been included and, in order further to redress the balance, the strengths and virtues of the estates and of William the Silent should have been emphasized.

Chapelain's notion of "neutrality" had provided him with a critical perspective on Bentivoglio's pro-Spanish and pro-Catholic views. Yet it had in no way freed him from the *politique* context of neutrality, which in this instance meant that revolts should be seen in political terms alone; the religious motives of men were either secondary to the

29. Nor was Chapelain the last to discuss the role of judgments in the age of classicism. See particularly Hugh M. Davidson, *Audience, Words and Art: Studies in Seventeenth-Century French Rhetoric* (Columbus, 1965), pp. 43 ff., for a discussion of Rapin's views.

30. Vittorio de Caprariis, *Propaganda e pensiero politico in Francia durante le guerre di religione* (Naples, 1959), *passim*.

31. *Lettres de Chapelain*, vol. 1, p. 16.

political or of no significance for history, because religion had become a matter of personal conscience for the *politiques*.[32] We should not be surprised that that historiographical perspective remained very much alive during the years of Richelieu's greatest power—for its political corollary had been the keystone of the Cardinal's policy toward the rebellious Huguenots at La Rochelle—and appeared in the Peace of Alais. In his *Histoire des guerres de Louis XIII*, Bernard had argued in the same vein, claiming that the Huguenots had to be defeated as rebellious subjects rather than brought to the stake as heretics. Chapelain states the *politique* doctrine succinctly in his general statement about history: "Je tiens pour moy, que l'histoire est instituée seulement pour l'utilité de la vie civile, et qu'on y doit regarder le vice moral, pour le rendre odieux, et la Vertu, sa contraire, pour en persuader l'amour aux peuples. . . . La bonne religion, qui devoit bien plustost avoir ce privilege, n'est pas si heureuse. Chacun appelle la sienne la meillieure et l'on ne prouve rien à son ennemi de diverse créance, lorsqu'on prend ses argumens et ses moyens sur la fausseté de ce qu'il croit."[33] For Chapelain, neutrality can be defined only as the moral and ideological framework established by rivalry among states.

Initially Gallican and then *politique*, the position that Chapelain defended caused him to regret only that religion had lost its primacy over men's lives. He experienced no spiritual turmoil as a result of his allegiance to, if not his faith in the state. Chapelain's *politique* position might seem out of date to men of later generations or, worse, would appear to be a regression from a position of historical relativism freed from the confining statist ideologies; yet in the 1630s, political reformism based on the spiritual unity of Christendom and the repression of heretics still found ardent defenders in France. The Day of the Dupes had not silenced the voices of the party of the Counter Reformation.[34] Chapelain believed that the stability and the fate of the Monarchy hung on the life of one man, Richelieu, whose "grande ame est trop necessaire à cet Estat et Dieu a trop de soin de cette monarchie pour croire qu'il souffre qu'elle soit privée de celuy qui en est l'unique soustien."[35] Failing to pursue the unity of Christendom and French religious diversity circumscribed the *politique* position. The only alternative was unequivocal support for the state and an eagerness to employ history on its behalf. Seventeenth-century authors recited the *topoi* about the

32. The anti-Spanish sentiment reflected in the critique suggests that Chapelain's notion of neutrality was very state-centered indeed.

33. *Lettres de Chapelain*, vol. 1, p. 16.

34. William F. Church, *Richelieu and Reason of State* (Princeton, 1972), pp. 212 ff.

35. 26 October 1633, *Lettres de Chapelain*, vol. 1, p. 52.

utility of history as an instrument for instruction in virtue, in much the same manner as choristers in Notre Dame might sing a litany about God's favor on France after the birth of a dauphin. If such *topoi* had actually served during the sixteenth century as a critical scheme for a different perception of the past, they no longer had such a function by the time Chapelain put them on paper. Endlessly repeated throughout the early-modern centuries, the *topoi* of the ancient rhetoricians, echoed in Chapelain, possess approximately the same magical qualities as the truth recited in the mass or in the *pater noster*. Through uncritical acceptance and a kind of comforting support for a literary-intellectual enterprise that could not bear close scrutiny, the rhetorical principles so dear to the humanists had become articles of faith legitimated by their antiquity.

More significant, the emphasis on stylistic matters in historical criticism, to the almost complete exclusion of political and religious issues, permitted authors of Chapelain's generation to forge a political perspective out of their insistence on *bonnes lettres*. The pursuit of eloquence had subtle political consequences. Those who pursued *bonnes lettres* avoided the use in historical writing of invective, *ad hominem* attacks, "impolite" words, and arguments that smacked of the bookishness of the Sorbonne or the Palais. They thought that the utility of history would scarcely be advanced by controversy; therefore it was better to stress the good deeds of past monarchs and the pursuit of a new golden age.

When Boisrobert informed Chapelain that the Cardinal did not agree with some aspects of his critique, especially on the issue of including moral judgments in history, it became obvious that a second letter would be necessary. This time Chapelain addressed Richelieu directly. The Cardinal's remarks can only be inferred from Chapelain's reply, but Chapelain appeared convinced that there was a fundamental difference of opinion between them.[36] His reply is interesting because it reveals another side of humanist thought about history: its effects on the reader.

Partisans of the ancients like Chapelain had a difficult time discussing audiences and reading publics, for Cicero and Plutarch offered them little guidance about the effects of printing. Rhetoric was a neutral

36. Richelieu clearly was better at logic than Chapelain, and their disagreement may have arisen from the fact that Chapelain had criticized Bentivoglio for failing to include moral judgments and then had proceeded to write a critique about what could only be considered obvious and clearly stated moral judgments about Dutch rebels. Richelieu was inclined to make criticisms of others' thought by just this sort of "plain" logic.

device, a system of devices for facilitating expression and for convincing listeners, not readers. Unlike polemicists of every proclivity, who quickly grasped the importance of printing and glimpsed some of its consequences for the formation of public opinion, Chapelain could not really come to grips with the changes occurring in the reading public as a result of the rise of literacy and printing. Richelieu had long before grasped the dynamics of molding public opinion and had instituted policies that culminated not only in answering polemics written against his ministry but also in explaining as effectively as possible his policies and their history. Chapelain, by contrast, remained negativistic and elitist.[37]

Moral judgments must be included in history, Chapelain argues, because the "commun" or "ordinaire des hommes" is incapable of profiting from history unless such judgments are included. "Le raisonnement n'est pas un bien public; peu de gens le possedent."[38] Historians must therefore state in their narratives what is good or bad action. Chapelain does not imply that entire populations would or should be reading history; unlike Bernard or Mézerai his views are far more elitist.

On the one hand, Chapelain's argument appears merely an adaptation of the familiar one about the inability of the *commun* to understand religious matters sufficiently to permit them to read the Bible. As the Tridentine fathers had recently reminded Christendom, the unlearned Christian, the Christian lacking in reason, might err in his faith if he were to read the Bible. Similarly, how could the *commun* profit from reading history if moral judgments were not included? There is an admission on Chapelain's part that the *commun* will indeed read history, but he still seems fearful of the conclusions they will draw from it if vices are not clearly pointed out. The possible alternative was to write history that consisted solely of recounting the virtuous actions of men in the past, an alternative that became the dominant mode of historical writing in the seventeenth century.

On the other hand, Chapelain's argument may reflect the disenchantment experienced by a mild-tempered man of learning in an age recovering from the tempests of popular and religious controversies. Throughout Chapelain's thought runs a yearning for a harmonious, unitary political culture where theology, politics, and history are synthesized in one pure language. This yearning may have been implicit in his attitude toward the effects that history had on the *commun*. Though

37. Cf. Davidson, p. 43, for a discussion of Rapin's attempt to define audience in an elitist way by stressing the culture of the *honnêtes gens*. Chapelain might well have agreed with Rapin on this point.
38. *Lettres de Chapelain*, vol. 1, p. 36.

Chapelain gives no hint of a fear of the *commun* in his letter to Richelieu, his commitment to history as an instrument of civic utility leads him to attempt to define how it should be written in order to edify and unify a people. If the *commun* is not helped to understand the past by reading history, an opportunity to edify it has been missed.[39]

In other instances his comments about history were less narrowly French, either in implication or in subject matter. Peoples, he thought, differed; and on the matter of understanding history, the French had to be measured against the Italians. The Italians possessed a greater understanding of *la politique* than other peoples,[40] while the Germans were not very subtle in that respect.[41] Would the French ever equal the Italians?[42] Chapelain was dubious. A great admirer of Enrico Davila, whom he considered equal to if not better than Guicciardini, the "best of modern historians,"[43] Chapelain based his historical criticism on an understanding of *la politique*. Italian historians could "penetrate intrigues" and see relationships between motives and actions better than anyone else. Chapelain admired this quality most, perhaps because it allowed him to be transported vicariously into the cabinets of heads of state, where momentous political decisions were made.[44] He had been eager to read Hugo Grotius, from admiration for his mastery of the art of writing in both a Livian and a Tacitean style and from a desire to grasp his *politique*.[45] The activist pose in writers of history appealed to Chapelain; the zest for politics in Polybius, Guicciardini, Davila, and perhaps even Mariana attracted him to these historians.[46] Unfamiliar with the world of precedents and the aura of such corporate bodies as the parlement, Chapelain did not respond to the *politique* historical perspective that these engendered. Like the polemical writers, he simply ignored them as if their works and *politique* were dead. In this he was representative of his generation. Sons of notaries —among them Chapelain—of lawyers, and even of judges turned away

39. Chapelain received portions of Bentivoglio's uncompleted second volume through an intermediary. Bentivoglio later made him a present of the completed second volume. Chapelain wrote the customary letter of thanks, containing nothing but praise and flattery for this powerful prince of the Church and his history (*ibid.*, p. 128).

40. *Ibid.*, p. 518.

41. *Ibid.*, vol. 2, p. 133.

42. Chapelain to Balzac, 20 November 1639, *ibid.*, vol. 1, pp. 529 f.

43. *Ibid.*, pp. 518 f.

44. *Ibid.*, p. 518.

45. *Ibid.*, p. 704.

46. On Mariana, see *ibid.*, vol. 2, p. 205.

from the robe preoccupations of their forebears. There were also back-sliders among the great scholarly families.[47]

Even more revealing of Chapelain's thought than either the formal or the more emotional responses to Bentivoglio are his letters to close friends. Balzac had suggested that Chapelain write history. Whether or not Balzac had been serious when making this suggestion, Chapelain felt obliged to explain to him why he had never done so. After the customary remarks about being inadequate to such a lofty task, Chapelain detailed exactly what he thought history should be. He pointed out the danger of an excessively florid style, which can transform history into a "pièce de théâtre," a "pièce de cabinet." The language of history must be sparse and possessed of a "gravité austère . . . presque tétrique qui luy semble seule digne de la vérité qui se présente presque toute nue."[48] These remarks can be recognized as commonplaces about history as a genre. Authors of the most flattering and embellished histories repeated them in their introductions. Almost as if he deliberately were trying to contradict himself, Chapelain continues by saying that if embellishments are called for, they should be like those in Quintus Curtius's history, which accord perfectly with the truth of the text and do not stand apart from it. Thus at every turn Chapelain remained a strict adherent to the thought of the ancient rhetoricians; he simply could not perceive history beyond the thought and examples of Antiquity.

Then, in a barely veiled comment about his own life work, the epic poem the *Pucelle*, Chapelain remarks that writing the truth "toute nue" about the past could have dire consequences. The "vérité ingratte" written by de Thou had attracted many enemies. This possibility did not appeal to Chapelain, whose personal conduct and pursuit of *bonnes lettres* had been part of an attempt to earn respect from everyone. His solution had been to write the truth about the past in verse form: "On est plus longtemps à ajuster les syllabes, mais on est moins longtemps

47. This was not a purely French phenomenon. Despite the efforts of Daniel Heinsius, his son Nicolas abandoned legal scholarship in order to prepare an edition of Ovid, which in turn received something less than complete attention (Hans Bots, ed., *Correspondance de Jacques Dupuy et de Nicolas Heinsius, 1646–1656* [The Hague, 1971], p. xxxvi). An even more painful situation occurred when the son of an *érudit* felt inadequate or was unable to sustain the family's reputation for learning. For example, Léon Godefroy urged younger members of his family to do what he personally could not do: face the *érudit* friends of his family in Paris (Denis-Charles Godefroy-Ménilglaise, *Les savants Godefroy* [Paris, 1873], p. 145).
48. 26 November 1638, *Lettres de Chapelain*, vol. 1, p. 325.

à examiner les vérités. . . . On se divertit et si l'on se peut promettre de divertir une postérité délicate, du moins on jouit des applaudissemens des vivans qui ne s'y connoissent pas si bien, et la vie coule sans procès et sans querelle."[49]

The long-range repercussions of the reception and subsequent suppression of de Thou's *History of his Own Time* in 1604 were constraining and intellectually intimidating for men of Chapelain's temperament and probably for bolder spirits as well.[50] De Thou had not only made enemies of partisans who might reasonably be expected to attack his views; he had also lost the "protection" of his patron, Henry IV. A *fidélité* had been broken. The *politiques* of the late sixteenth century may have perceived that, like religion, historical "truth" might have to be subordinated to the state in order to secure foreign and domestic peace and stability. The Wars of Religion had refracted the ideological-intellectual perspectives in which history could be written. Along with the clouds of reaction gathering over freedom to preach and teach had come the suppression of de Thou's *History*. Pasquier's remarks about the dangers of writing contemporary history seemed wise in retrospect. Chapelain considered the dangers of writing history so great that he attempted to write the truth about the past in verse form. He would nevertheless eagerly recommend that others write history.

Recommending Writers to Colbert

Barely a few weeks after the stir created by Priolo's history, Colbert wrote asking an acquaintance—Chapelain—for advice about a number of ideas that, if put into practice, might help assure Louis XIV of immortality. The principal implicit question was: who should be appointed historiographers royal?

Chapelain begins his reply to this question by defining what a history of the King's actions should be. The "motifs des choses" must be included; there should be prudent reflections and documents, or it will be only a "relation pure, sans force et sans dignité."[51] Such a history naturally will contain state secrets. Chapelain therefore recommends that it be kept secret until a time when its publication will prejudice neither the King's affairs nor those of his allies. A historian undertaking

49. *Ibid.*, p. 325. Gustave Lanson pointed out long ago that Chapelain had done very thorough research for the historical narrative of his poem (*Grand encyclopédie*, vol. 10, p. 551).

50. Samuel Kinser, *The Condemnation of Jacques-Auguste de Thou's History of his Own Time* (Geneva, 1967).

51. 18 November 1662, *Lettres de Chapelain*, vol. 2, p. 275.

such a task must be an "homme de bien"; he must have a command of political theory, military strategy, geography, chronology, and the manners and customs of other nations; he must also have read extracts from dispatches and treaties. In addition to all these requirements, he must possess the "talent naturel qu'il faut avoir du ciel" and a solid mind with years of experience in government, or at least in courtly life. Chapelain concludes his remarks about history by saying there is no one available who is up to such a demanding task, except, of course, Colbert himself. Then, perhaps without realizing that he was contradicting his prediction of a French golden age made thirty years earlier, Chapelain remarks that there are "few writers in this century who were worth something," but that perhaps some can be found who could write about the King's "miracles oratoirement"—in other words, prepare panegyrics about Louis XIV that were similar to Pliny the Younger's panegyrics about Trajan. Classicistic literary culture had not lost the fundamental distinction between history and panegyric; indeed, Colbert proceeded to commission "secret" histories of the King's actions, and *relations* that were clearly panegyrical in form. In fact, the Minister himself soon began to write history.[52]

From this influential letter—as well as from Colbert's decisions based on the assessments of the qualifications of ninety French writers contained in the "Liste des gens de lettres vivans en 1662 par ordre de M. Colbert" that accompanied it—a systematic policy of bureaucratizing the patronage of men of letters was set in motion. As always, Colbert's motives remain elusive. Short-term aims may have been uppermost in his mind; Fouquet's arrest had caused an outcry from all the writers who had been receiving pensions from him. His trial mobilized public opinion, and not a few writers pressed for Fouquet's release from prison.[53] The dispensing of royal pensions may have been perceived as a way of assuaging their discontent and of reducing the possibility that a literature of protest might reappear, this time attacking Colbert rather than the Cardinal.

The political implications of the long-range aims do not have to be ferreted out. Colbert and Louis XIV both sincerely believed in the principle that a great king should advance *bonnes lettres*. Louis was young, Chapelain told Colbert; therefore it would be quite proper for the King to sponsor writings that would assure him of a *gloire* that otherwise would come only when he was older. With such arguments, the *topoi* about the automatic attraction of writers to the truly heroic

---

52. Pierre Clément, ed., *Lettres, instructions et mémoires de Colbert* (Paris, 1868), vol. 5, p. lix.

53. On the question of Colbert's motives, see Collas, pp. 352 ff.

king or conqueror could be adhered to, and the sensibilities about remuneration for *louanges* could be respected. It is probable that neither
Chapelain, nor Colbert, nor Louis were duped, but the prescriptions
of the classical rhetoricians and humanists were being followed: engage
the best writers of an age to recount in prose the deeds of a great king,
and *gloire* is assured. The authors who had proffered such prescriptions to the men of power for well over a century probably never took
them as seriously and earnestly as Colbert did after 1662.

In his recommendations Chapelain has a good word to say about
everyone of "some merit" who has come to his attention. The tone of
the assessments is generous; when weaknesses are pointed out, there is
an implicit suggestion that the desired improvements will actually take
place. The absence of harshness and of *esprit de parti* is remarkable;
only Chapelain among the writers of his generation could have eval-
uated his peers with such detachment. Of the ninety French writers
whom he chose to assess, some already had well-established reputations.
Despite their merits, the Corneilles, La Mothe le Vayer, Honorat de
Racan, and Antoine Furetière, to mention only a few, could not be
selected to write a history of the reign. Either already preoccupied
with their own projects, too philosophically original,[54] or, in Furetière's
case, tending toward the satirical, none of these men would have been
the appropriate choice, despite their merits. Chapelain includes words
of praise for the *érudits*, whom he unhesitatingly includes among the
gens de lettres. Léon Godefroy and the Sainte-Marthes are complimented for their great learning and for the high quality of the works
they publish. There is not a word of criticism about either their work
or their literary style, almost as if Chapelain recognized that literary
style had little significance in works of erudition. As for Olivier Patru,
he is "renfermé dans les matières de jurisprudence; mais contre la
coûtume des avocats, il les traite très elégamment. . . . Il travaille peu,
parce qu'il veut trop bien faire."[55] Though the emphasis on productivity is rarely as explicit as in this instance, Chapelain indubitably
counted it one of the factors to be considered in selecting a historiographer royal.

Sometimes the comments are lengthy, at other times very brief. Stylistic concerns do not always predominate. For example, Henry Sauval
makes the mistake of embellishing his prose when the text calls for

54. *Ibid.*, p. 364, points out the consistency of Chapelain's views about
La Mothe's lack of originality by quoting Chapelain's observations on La
Mothe to Balzac. They are very similar to what Chapelain wrote Colbert.

55. Camusat, p. 235.

simplicity; but the "mille curiosités" included in the *Antiquitez de Paris* improve Chapelain's opinion of this author.[56] The term *curiosités* was applied to facts that Chapelain did not already know, that kind of "new" knowledge about French institutions and customs with which chroniclers and humanist historians had not deigned to clutter their narratives. Indeed, though Chapelain does not say it, Sauval must be seen as a worthy successor of Pasquier.

In Mézerai's case, the compliments are qualified. Chapelain quite naturally is circumspect concerning a writer who has held a royal appointment for years. The works that Mézerai has already published are good and his style "n'est pas non plus mauvais"—a kind of backhanded compliment. It is to be feared, however, that, in attempting to demonstrate that he is "free in his judgments," Mézerai leans toward the satirical and maltreats individual reputations when he wants to instruct his readers. In addition to these weaknesses, he "sets himself up as a severe judge of the plans and activities of the *grands* without asking himself whether he has the intelligence or authority to do so."[57] Such harsh criticisms may have signaled the beginning of Mézerai's downfall; henceforth the Monarchy of Louis XIV, unlike that of his predecessors, would often object to the outright attacks upon the great nobles and financiers that since Budé had been an acceptable mode of political criticism among writers in the pay of the Crown.

As for Pellisson-Fontanier, Fouquet's favorite *commis* and author of a very well-received history of the French Academy, Chapelain stresses his written style—"très beau, et très achevé."[58] Were Pellisson ever to devote himself entirely to literature, he continues, there is no doubt that he would become a writer of the "first order." Pellisson was a prisoner in the Bastille at the time Chapelain wrote this assessment. The fact that he had been Fouquet's *commis* and was now the bitter and captive enemy of Colbert did not prevent Chapelain from recommending him very highly.

Fine politique that he believed himself to be, Chapelain did not remain generous or vague about the question of who should be appointed historiographer royal. Weaving in and out of the assessments is a thread of argument pointing to only one man, Perrot d'Ablancourt. Described as the best of "our translators," d'Ablancourt had all the right qualifications except one. He knew how to narrate; writing speeches to be inserted into a narrative would not be new to him, nor would military

56. *Ibid.*, p. 196.
57. *Ibid.*, pp. 241 f.
58. *Ibid.*, p. 249.

matters. His style was the most "dégagé, plus ferme, plus résolu, plus naturel, son génie est sublime." [59] The sole difficulty was his lack of familiarity with worldly affairs.

Though ultimately a failure, Chapelain's sponsorship of d'Ablancourt reveals much about the personal patron-client relationships among men of letters, who, like men of power, perceived "protection" and advancement within a framework of *fidélités*. D'Ablancourt was one of Chapelain's creatures. Whether or not Chapelain had conceived the idea that d'Ablancourt translate Thucydides, it is clear that he thought he deserved credit and rather patronizingly wanted to share the *gloire* resulting from the success of the translation. [60] D'Ablancourt may well have made the initial overtures to Augustin Courbé, who ultimately published the translation; but it may be more than coincidental that this same publisher had earlier brought out the luxurious first edition of Chapelain's life work, the *Pucelle*, in 1655. Chapelain had strong entrepreneurial instincts when it came to finding publishers for authors, and d'Ablancourt may have felt a debt of gratitude for both the suggestion behind the work and its publication. The Thucydides had been dedicated to Louis XIV, another decision that may have been proposed by Chapelain[61] and that could only enhance d'Ablancourt's chances for acceptance by Colbert as historiographer royal almost a year to the day after the publication of the *Histoire de Thucydide*.

The decision came quickly. On 9 December 1662, Chapelain informed d'Ablancourt that he was about to be named historiographer royal.[62] The terms of the appointment are very revealing, for Chapelain and Colbert had agreed that whatever was written by d'Ablancourt should be "reviewed and corrected by the three of them together." Chapelain added that he had assured Colbert that there would be no difficulty over these terms, since d'Ablancourt already was accustomed to letting him read drafts of his work. A pension was promised, but the sum was not mentioned. D'Ablancourt seems to have been willing to accept these arrangements.[63]

59. *Ibid.*, pp. 237 f.
60. Chapelain to d'Ablancourt, 20 December 1661, *Lettres de Chapelain*, vol. 2, p. 185. Chapelain proposed that he translate Cicero's three philosophical dialogues next.
61. René de Kerviler, *Nicolas Perrot d'Ablancourt, 1606–1664* (Paris, 1877), p. 73.
62. *Lettres de Chapelain*, vol. 2, p. 277.
63. At first d'Ablancourt had not been very enthusiastic about the project. Was it the possibility of having his writing "reviewed" that restrained him? He had not realized that Colbert was the one actually recommending the appointment, and the inference that Montausier was sponsoring him

Chapelain had selected d'Ablancourt not only because of his talent but also because of the strong bonds between them. The older and more prestigious man of letters felt he could collaborate with d'Ablancourt and share in the *gloire* of writing the history of Louis XIV without actually doing the writing himself. Colbert also wanted to participate in this *gloire* and at the same time be sure that the history would be "correct." Thus this collaborative program to write the King's history resulted from the specific literary-political interests of Chapelain and Colbert; soon the King himself—as well as Octave de Périgny, Pellisson, and perhaps others—would be participating in the writing.

Everything seemed settled, but one person had not yet been consulted: Louis XIV. On 29 January 1663, Chapelain learned directly from Colbert that the King had opposed d'Ablancourt's appointment because he was not of the King's religion.[64] Chapelain later admitted that he had considered d'Ablancourt's Huguenot upbringing before recommending him, but that he had decided to ignore it because the Huguenots had solidly supported the Crown during the Fronde and because d'Ablancourt was a mild-mannered, eminently trustworthy individual whose writing would be "reviewed" in any case. Chapelain's letter of 31 January is an eloquent brief for d'Ablancourt, but the King had made up his mind.[65] In their conversation Colbert had asked Chapelain about Périgny's qualifications, and Chapelain had been forced to admit that he knew nothing about his worth as a man of letters. Even though he was not appointed, d'Ablancourt received a pension of fifteen hundred livres. Périgny was given the appointment and almost immediately began to develop what would be known as the *Mémoires de Louis XIV*, a work on which Colbert, Pellisson, Chapelain, and the King himself collaborated.[66]

With Périgny chosen as a collaborator on the royal history, Colbert could proceed to establish royal patronage of letters on a systematic basis. Listed among the architects, gardeners, university professors, painters, chimney sweeps, doorkeepers, and guardians of altar lamps—all carefully distinguished by category—in the accounts of the *surinten-*

---

may have disturbed him as much if not more than having his writing "reviewed" (Collas, p. 372).

64. *Lettres de Chapelain*, vol. 2, p. 287.

65. This was not the only time d'Ablancourt was denied a commission because of his religion. The Duchesse d'Aiguillon sought a historian to write the life of her uncle, Cardinal Richelieu, but d'Ablancourt was rejected as a Huguenot. The Jesuit, Le Moyne, received the position (Henri Chérot, *Etude sur la vie et les oeuvres du Père Le Moyne* [Paris, 1887], p. 397).

66. See Chapter VIII.

dance des bâtiments there appeared beginning in 1663 a list of gifts to be distributed to "savants et hommes de lettres français et étrangers."[67] Colbert had decided to draw a distinction between those who received gifts, or *gratifications*, and those who received *pensions, appointements*, or *gages*. Since the mid-sixteenth century the latter three terms had denoted payments to one who held an office or *charge*, a special designation, honor, title, or function to perform. After 1668 architects and painters, for example, were paid *gages* and *appointements*,[68] and the learned and men of letters were singled out for the special category of "gifts," whereas they had previously been paid *gages* or *pensions*.

Although it is impossible to discern exactly what Colbert had in mind when making this change, it may be that through the institutionalization of gift giving to men of letters, Colbert attempted to codify changes in the ideal of the patron and make a dramatic gesture that would draw the attention and support of men of letters to the Crown. The gift honored them but did not convey the notion that the recipient had a special task to perform or a place at court. The brief descriptions following each name in the accounts make this obvious. Titles disappear; there is no indication of Mézerai's or Godefroy's positions as *historiographes de France*.[69] They are simply listed as recipients of gifts.

To be sure, it is unwise to place too much emphasis on the use of the term "gift"; not every royal official, and probably least of all Louis XIV, perceived this shift from pensions to gifts as significant. But, seen in the context of Colbert's dramatic increase in the number of authors receiving pensions and his emphasis on productivity on almost every front, it is clear that the fundamental changes taking place in the ideal of patronage reflected changes in the state itself.

Under the old system of pensions in the *maison du roi*, a continuity of payments—if not for life, at least until the next war drained the royal treasury—had implied permanent status. *Gages* and *pensions* connoted steady payment by quarterly installments, year after year, for services performed on a lifetime basis.[70] With the new system of gifts—which

67. *Lettres de Colbert*, vol. 5, p. 466.
68. *Ibid.*, p. 455. Because they held ranks in a corporation—the University —professors and lecturers received *gages* (*ibid.*, p. 464). This is not to say that *gratifications* had not previously been employed. Quite the contrary. But a whole category, men of letters, had never before been given support in this way. See G. Couton, "Effort publicitaire et organisation de la recherche: Les gratifications aux gens de lettres sous Louis XIV," Actes du 6e Colloque de Marseille, *Le XVIIe siècle et la recherche* 6 (1976): 41–55.
69. *Ibid.*, p. 467.
70. Although pensions were often in arrears, this in no way meant that the positions for which they were paid were not permanent.

were promptly and dramatically paid either in the form of gold coins in silk purses or, in the case of foreign authors, by letters of credit, there was no indication that these gifts would be repeated in the coming year or any time thereafter.

Men of letters responded immediately to this shower of gold coins. Panegyrics, poems on the recovery of Louis XIV from a recent illness, and ponderous, overblown letters of thanks came pouring in to Colbert, who passed on to the King those that he and Chapelain considered the best. All the themes and flowers of the literature of praise that had developed during the sixteenth century[71] were reworked and piled one on top of the other to create what at best could be considered an artificial if not revolting edifice of vapid phrases.

The role of adviser could not be denied to an old man who had never quite recovered from the blast of criticism greeting the *Pucelle*. Chapelain basked in the white-hot rays of praise that pierced beyond the Sun King to enhance the reputations of Colbert and Chapelain. He had played a particularly important role in selecting foreign authors who were to receive gifts. His correspondence with Girolamo Graziani, Herman Conring, Johannes Casparus Gevartius, the younger Nicholas Heinsius, and Denis, the younger Vossius—which frequently included a personal letter with each letter of credit—[72] is a testament to Chapelain's successful effort to attract men of considerable reputation to respect and praise Louis XIV. The political consideration shows through all the allusions to Louis's "miracles" and "immortality." Chapelain wrote Colbert that "Entre tous les écrivains que Sa Majesté honnore de ses faveurs, ceux qui me semblent les plus dignes d'estre mesnagés sont les historiens, et entre les historiens ceux qui traittent des affaires présentes ou qui ont relations aux nostres. Vous le croyez ainsy sans doute, Monseigneur, et c'estoit l'opinion des deux derniers fameux cardinaux [Richelieu and Mazarin] qui ont fait le bonheur de la France.[73] In his last years Chapelain busied himself with such petty tasks as instructing an Italian writer about how to write dedications pleasing to Colbert and Louis and about how to have his books bound and packaged in a manner worthy of presentation at court.

The headlong dash to attract still more authors with international

71. See Joukovsky, *passim*. The similarities of themes and stylistic devices in literatures of praise may be evoked only in a general way, not studied in detail, for their repetition would be painful to both this author and his readers.

72. A letter in which Chapelain presented additional foreign writers to Colbert for *gratifications* is dated 18 June 1665, *Lettres de Chapelain*, vol. 2, pp. 401 f. It is typical of his way of assessing authors.

73. *Ibid.*, p. 466.

reputations to write the "history" of Louis XIV gradually was taken over by Colbert's powerful young *commis*, Charles Perrault, who had engaged an exceedingly bright and perceptive Italian, Vittorio Siri, to help him establish the proper lines of argument for historical works sponsored by the Crown. The bureaucracy assumed the annual preparation of lists of authors receiving gifts; the rise and fall in the amounts of these gifts reflect the careful attention given to productivity, stylistic merit, and the political character of the works and authors deemed worthy of support. Chapelain had contributed to the original "program"; in his last years his influence diminished.

Occasionally Chapelain still undertook something a bit less bureaucratic. He wrote an account of the campaign in Franche-Comté and submitted it to Perrault in 1670. The old man who had helped in the founding of the French Academy and who had been an adviser to Richelieu and Colbert thus participated in the new team brought together to help Louis XIV write his own history. In his last surviving letter, dated 22 October 1673, Chapelain enthusiastically commended Battista Nani's history, in which he recognized the "style of the Thucydideses, Xenophons, Sallusts, Titus Livies, and Tacituses, and in reading it I felt myself transported back to those happy times when prudence and liberty moved the pens of the true *politiques* and champions of virtue."[74] All his life Chapelain had pursued the art of creating a mood worthy of comparison with those created by the great historians of Antiquity. He died confident that others would write about Louis XIV in ways commensurate with the Sun King's greatness.

74. *Ibid.*, p. 839.

Chapter VII
Mézerai: A *Libertin*
Historiographer Royal

H E *libertins* of Paris—those unconventional, almost freethinking men of leisure and learning—came from varied social backgrounds but more frequently from the small but quite special *corps* of physicians and surgeons.[1] Men in the medical professions may have raised their children in some special way; or perhaps the study of medicine, combined with the secure social status and wealth of physicians and surgeons, developed in some of their children both a tendency to ask questions and a willingness to stand apart from the fashionable and conventional noble and bourgeois ways of thought and behavior. Eccentric, independent, and frequently very learned, the *libertins* constituted the closest thing to the modern notion of "alienated intellectuals." Their willingness to scandalize the conventionally minded, and their independence from prevailing social expressions of religious belief, provided an atmosphere for freethinking and critical attitudes toward the dominant political and social ideas of the midseventeenth century. In other words, if France possessed any thinkers in this period capable of criticizing the prevailing ideologies from a more secular and *politique* perspective, they were to be found among the *libertins*—and François Eudes de Mézerai would be among them.[2]

Though many of the *libertins* were born into medical families, we should not conclude that all sons of physicians and surgeons had *libertin* tendencies. A computerized study of the social origins of the *libertins* might well reveal a close correlation between libertinism and medicine, but a closer look at one family of surgeons reveals the dangers of such an approach. The Norman family of Eudes is a case in point.[3] Jean, the first of the three sons of a devout Catholic surgeon,

1. The standard work on the *libertins* is René Pintard, *Le libertinage érudit au XVIIe siècle* (Paris, 1943). On the *médecins* see vol. 1, pp. 80 f.

2. Pintard's description of Mézerai as a *libertin* is found in *ibid.*, pp. 280–283.

3. The principal source for almost all of Mézerai's early life is his early eighteenth-century biographer, Daniel de Larroque, *La vie de François Eudes de Mézeray* . . . (Amsterdam, 1726). Sympathetic and anecdotal,

was received into the Oratory by the great Pierre de Bérulle and spent
a long life actively preaching and writing as a leader of Catholic reformism; François, the second son, became a *libertin*, a historiographer
royal, and perpetual secretary of the French Academy; and Charles,
the third son, the "only one who married," carried on the family tradition and became a rich surgeon and bourgeois political leader in
Normandy. No lessons may be drawn from the study of the careers of
a single family, other than the necessity for caution when explaining
individual behavior on the basis of social and professional origins. The
future saint and the *libertin* in the Eudes family remained in contact
with one another throughout their lives, and the *libertin* historiographer
royal is said to have been grief-stricken at the loss of his *dévot* brother
when Jean died in 1680.

The *libertins* were almost invariably learned in ancient languages.
They dabbled in philosophy and theology, wrote poetry, and discoursed together on every conceivable grammatical, scientific, and political question; but in addition to "learning," they cultivated a reputation for what was thought to be "bizarre" behavior. Declining to dress
according to the latest fashion, feigning lack of interest in accumulating
wealth, they used *gros mots* and were anti-*précieux*, talked familiarly
with the *peuple*, and caroused together, sometimes in cabarets and with
women of ill repute. These sons of *bons bourgeois* and nobles refused
to adopt the ways of the *honnête homme*; their scorn for the affecta-
tions of courtiers became notorious. By ignoring or ridiculing social or
religious conventions, the *libertins* set out almost deliberately—and perhaps even collectively and consciously—to scandalize their families and
the bourgeois would-be noble society. Their critiques were gentle; not
affected by spiritual reformism, they went about refusing to be pious,
to fast, or to heed any number of the many social conventions associated
with revived Catholicism in the families of the *gens de bien*. Their
offenses frequently were very minor, their learning often so extensive
that they knew the boundaries of Catholic doctrine and therefore
protected themselves by avoiding heretical actions. Their reading of
Montaigne, Charron, and the ancient Stoics and Epicureans, and their
discussions with Protestants and neo-Platonists, combined with their

---

Larroque's biography forms the basis for the *libertin* accounts of Mézerai's
life. Some of his evidence, particularly on the matter of Mézerai's will, is
corroborated by other sources. See the mysterious letter written by Jean
d'Eudes to Colbert acknowledging the reception of an order to leave Paris
without delay on 15 April 1674, in E. Griselle, *Documents d'histoire* (1910),
vol. 1, p. 473.

"bizarre" social behavior, rendered them suspect to both Jesuits and Jansenists. Rarely developing a coherent philosophical system and unable to formulate a critique of either absolute monarchy or the hierarchical society that supported it, the *libertins* nevertheless created a malaise among elite groups and a milieu favorable to affected young people who were disdainful of the dominant modes of social behavior. They also tried their hand at writing *bonnes lettres*; but owing to stylistic inadequacy and their personal *bizarreries*, their works rarely won public acclaim. Indeed, Mézerai was the one *libertin* whose works did reach a large reading public.

Early Career

François Eudes—who took the name of Mézerai from a piece of land belonging to his family—was the seventeenth century's leading *libertin* writer of history; and it is in the context of the *libertin* that his career and work ought to be described. His early biographers have recorded his tendency to wear old clothes (he was said to have once narrowly missed being picked up as a beggar by the *archer des pauvres*)[4] and his decision to bequeath most of his wealth to his "dearest friend," the keeper of a cabaret; but his *libertin* proclivities became most apparent in his roles as historiographer royal and writer. During his own lifetime his unconventional behavior and his tilts with Colbert over the censorship of his historical works had earned him a reputation for independence and originality. Future generations, including scholars in the twentieth century, always held Mézerai up as the example of the historian who had valued his independence of thought and action in an age when absolutism was presumably stifling both.

After studying Latin and being smitten by a desire to write poetry while at the University of Caen, Mézerai went to Paris, where he sought the protection of his fellow Norman, Vauquelin des Yveteaux. Also something of a poet, and a former preceptor to the royal children, des Yveteaux's social nonconformity—he was inclined to dress peculiarly —may have left a lasting impression on Mézerai. While preceptor to the future Louis XIII, des Yveteaux had enraged the Parisian clergy, who attacked him for what they claimed to be weaknesses in his teaching. But Gédéon Tallemant des Réaux says of des Yveteaux: "On l'ac-

4. The convenient modern account of his life, which accepts Larroque uncritically, is Wilfred H. Evans, *L'historien Mézeray et la conception de l'histoire en France* (Paris, 1930), p. 78.

cusoit aussy d'aimer les garçons."[5] If true and known to the public, this may partially account for the clergy's attacks and perhaps for des Yveteaux's disgrace immediately after Henry IV's assassination. In this household reputed for the unconventional, Mézerai set out by writing verses and political satires; but if Wilfred H. Evans can be trusted, des Yveteaux sensed that the young man's talents might be better applied to history.[6]

At this point the young writer may also have participated in his first political controversy, thereby attracting Richelieu's attention. In 1631, during one of those stormy debates over Richelieu's policies carried on through a flood of anonymous pamphlets, Mézerai may have replied to one of the attacks by Matthieu de Morgues on the Cardinal.[7] The evidence is inconclusive. Larroque, Mézerai's eighteenth-century biographer, collected remarks about Mézerai from people who had known him and who asserted that "Sandricourt" was a nom de plume for Mézerai.[8] *L'ombre de Sandricourt* had been a minor salvo in the series of blasts and counterblasts by Richelieu, Sirmond, de Morgues, Hay du Châtelet, and others. It seems that in times of crisis Richelieu reached

5. Gédéon Tallemant des Réaux, *Historiettes*, ed. Antoine Adam (Paris, 1960), vol. 1, p. 138.

6. Evans, p. 40.

7. William F. Church, *Richelieu and Reason of State* (Princeton, 1972), pp. 205 ff.

8. Larroque, p. 25, asserts that Sandricourt is an anagram for Mézerai. He gives the titles of a group of Mazarinades but does not attribute *L'ombre de Sandricourt* of 1631 to Mézerai. Evans, p. 40, notes these attributions. It has often been pointed out that in part 3, p. 46, of *Le censeur du temps* (Paris, 1652), the author's age is given as fifty-five. Mézerai was only forty-two at the time. Moreover, "Sandricourt" seems to pay special attention to Marshal d'Hocquincourt's activities, whereas Mézerai seems never to have sought the Marshal as a patron nor to have expressed a particular interest in him. "Sandricourt" rarely makes arguments based on historical precedent, but then Mézerai did not belong to the legal humanist tradition that tended to do so. Also, in *Le censeur du temps*, part 3, p. 46, "Sandricourt" refers to Richard Knolles's *General historie of the Turkes*. . . . Mézerai's interest in Turkish history, as we shall see, may have already been established by the time of the Fronde. "Sandricourt" seems to have been a Frondeur without a party, a *politique* speaking out for the restoration of "good" government, the indictment of tax collectors, and the disgrace of Mazarin. Mézerai favored these policies, but any number of other Frondeurs shared these sympathies. A general analysis of the Mazarinades based on the study of policies and client systems, year by year, month by month, might reveal "Sandricourt's" party and possibly his identity; but such an effort would be enormous.

down to reward almost any and all men of letters who supported him, and during these years Mézerai received his first pension from the Cardinal.[9]

Then, perhaps through des Yveteaux's influence, Mézerai became a *commissaire des guerres*, a position involving minor administrative responsibility for supplying food and munitions to the expanded French army after the declaration of war against Spain in 1635.[10] This life evidently did not please him, for he settled down to reading and translating in the Collège Sainte-Barbe of Paris, circa 1637 or 1638.[11] The Marquis d'Asserac had asked him to translate John of Salisbury's *Policraticus*, which Mézerai published in 1640 under the title, *Les vanités de la cour*. The book seems to have received virtually no public attention, perhaps because the prevailing *cortigianesque* habits and ideals had greater appeal for readers than the sterner, less compromising program of the *Policraticus*.

Then came a translation of Grotius's *De veritate religionis christianae* in 1644, which also failed to attract public attention.[12] The prime reason may again have been lack of interest among the reading public; a translation had already appeared in 1636. The book never received the acclaim in France that it earned in Protestant countries, notably in England and Holland.[13] Owing to its silence on the matter of whether or not God was three persons, the Trinity, the *De veritate* may have been subject to censorship in translation; or, if Richard Popkin is correct, it and similar works may have been perceived by the Catholic evangelists as supporting their efforts to combat atheism and Pyrrhonism, for they attempted to prove the existence of God and the "truths" of the Christian religion.[14] However, the religious preoccupations of

9. *L'ombre de Sandricourt* attempts to refute de Morgues's charge that Richelieu had had Gaston d'Orléans's wife assassinated and attacks evil councillors, President Le Coigneux in particular.

10. Gustave Levavasseur, *Notice sur les trois frères . . . Mézeray* (Paris, 1855), p. 6, claims that Mézerai accompanied the armies on two campaigns into Flanders.

11. Georges Ruhlmann, *Cinq siècles au Collège Sainte-Barbe* (Paris, 1960), pp. 70–72. This study is almost entirely drawn from Larroque and Evans.

12. François La Mothe le Vayer later pointed out some of Mézerai's errors in translation, *Hexameron rustique* (Paris, 1670), p. 44.

13. The *De veritate* was originally published in 1627; these translations seem to come a bit late. The reasons for this tardiness deserve to be investigated.

14. *The History of Scepticism from Erasmus to Descartes* (New York, 1964), Chaps. 4 and 5.

the larger public lay elsewhere—in books of devotion, prayers, and the lives of the saints. Socinianism had never posed a major threat to Catholic doctrines in France. Thus Mézerai's translation of Grotius, like des Yveteaux's fideist and stoic "Institution du prince," a poem about the education of Louis XIII, failed to reach beyond the tiny groups of *libertins* and philosophers who carried on the skeptical tradition nourished by Montaigne's works.

As in all instances involving the public's response to a literary work, Mézerai's failure to gain public attention through his translations may have stemmed from causes other than intellectual and religious ones. The power of literary and stylistic conventions increased rapidly during the first decade of the French Academy's efforts to "purify" the French language, and Mézerai's works may have been victims of this effort. Apparently always attracted to popular phrases and *gros mots*, and unable to write in any style other than the *embrouillé* one of the sixteenth century, Mézerai in his translations may have offended those individuals sharing the new stylistic sensibilities propagated by the Academy.

Mézerai's failure to earn the respect of his fellow men of letters resulted from his inability or unwillingness to adopt the new "classic" French, laden with social and religious sensibilities that had been adopted by a newly ennobled courtly society but that offended the translator of a work entitled *Les vanités de la cour*. Incapable of abandoning the sixteenth-century tradition of writing in the pithy, popular, satirical, and jocular style affected by Rabelais, Mézerai found that his writings—including his famous histories—drew cruel critical censure from the pens of none other than his fellow Academicians. To make matters worse, after the deaths of the Dupuy brothers and of Conrart, his longtime supporter, Mézerai suffered almost complete ostracism from the circles of men of letters. Had he not previously been elected its perpetual secretary, the Academy might likewise have diminished his participation on the grounds that his writing lacked the politeness and polish of "pure" French.

Mézerai's *libertin* outlook, Frondeur sympathies, out-of-date tastes, shabby clothes, and—as Larroque suggests—"paresse" and tendency to drink too much wine[15] rendered him suspect to the polite society of both Paris and Versailles during the 1660s. He had even become something of an embarrassment to his friends.[16] Once he invited three of

15. Larroque, pp. 66 f. Whether or not the anecdote is Mézerai's cannot be authenticated, but he was supposed to have said that his gout came from "la fillette et de la feuillette," a pun that Larroque says is more worthy of the Halles than of an Academician.

16. *Ibid.*, p. 64.

them to dinner but they declined, claiming previous engagements. Soon afterward he found them strolling together in conversation in the Tuileries gardens. He was deeply wounded. More important, however, was the fact that—despite his contacts with the molders of the more polite literary style—Mézerai declined, or was unable, to change either his literary style or the subject matter of his histories to make them conform to the classicistic canons of taste. Even his history "sentoit le populaire," an offense more damning than any other for members of the Academy. In his massive *Histoire de France*, for which the *privilège* was granted in June 1643, it is perfectly clear that Mézerai labored to make his history eloquent and edifying; but despite his best efforts the results were judged crude by even his more intimate academic friends.

Mézerai had quite specific ideas about what to include in his history; and like many of the humanist historians before him, he set these down in a "Dessein d'une parfaite histoire."[17] Perhaps written to convince a royal official, François Sublet de Noyers, to grant him a pension, or perhaps to attract a publisher's interest, it summarizes his goals. One remarkable omission in his "Dessein" provides a clue to the thought and work of this *libertin*: there is no discussion whatsoever of the stylistic weaknesses of earlier histories. The theme that France lacked a well-written history had become so conventional that rarely did a seventeenth-century plan for a history fail to mention this lacuna. Stylistic matters had been Charles Sorel's principal interest.[18] Mézerai, however, declined to discuss such questions, and by that decision alone it may be inferred that he remained exceptionally independent from or uninhibited by rhetorical teachings. There is only a passing introductory phrase about the function of history for instruction, pleasure, and the satisfaction of curiosity; but the pedagogical themes so dear to the humanists and their heirs are not belabored. In fact, almost from the beginning it is possible to sense an element of irreverence in Mézerai's writing; for whether or not he said so explicitly, one unaltering aim

17. B.N., mss. fr. 20796, fols. 64–67. Evans, p. 70, concludes that this text was written after the publication of the *Histoire de France*, i.e., after 1651; but unlike Evans I find no internal evidence to support this conclusion. On the contrary, on folio 66, Mézerai proposes to write two volumes in folio, each with three hundred pages, divided into twenty-nine books. If he had already published the *Histoire de France* in three folio volumes, he would scarcely envisage redoing the project in two volumes. More likely, the original two-volume plan expanded into three volumes. Though he later reduced these into the *Abrégé*, in the "Dessein" Mézerai makes no reference to an effort at conciseness, nor does he mention having previously written a history.

18. See above, p. 139.

was to entertain his readers. Free of pomposity and preoccupations with the "nobleness" and "purity" of his language, Mézerai conceived his project in such a way that it could only be rejected by the Academicians and welcomed by the less self-consciously literary Parisians and the provincial reading public.

For Mézerai the weaknesses of the histories of France written by his predecessors were chiefly substantive: the names of illustrious families under the Carolingians had been omitted, and insufficient attention had been paid to the accomplishments of Frenchmen in "barbarous countries," notably while crusading. Furthermore, previous accounts of French history since the reign of Louis XI were inadequate, for they did not include state secrets, intrigues, and war plans—all of which Mézerai proposed adding. The history of the "origine, la fonction et la croissance et le déclin des grandes charges de l'Etat" should also receive more attention, and there was the customary proposal to "note exactly from time to time" changes in the language, customs, laws, manners, art of war, laws of war, founding of celebrated churches, and growth of cities."[19] Mézerai pointed out that these subjects had been discussed in earlier histories, but insufficiently; he proposed being more inclusive and bringing it all together into an "entreprise très glorieuse à la France et très agréable à tout le monde."[20]

Through these proposals, and still more specifically in the discussion of the number of pages and format of the volumes, Mézerai lets escape what had become a major preoccupation: how to attract a large reading public. He had a keen sense of what might make books sell and seemed willing to do almost anything, including the addition of miracles and prodigies, to appeal to the public. Like Sorel, he never seems to have been captivated by the desire to produce books that would please his fellow Academicians and impress the aesthetes at court through the artistic merit of the typography, etchings, and binding. On the basis of the "Dessein," Mézerai thought he could calculate how many pages his history should contain and how verses and engraved portraits of kings and queens, medals and coins, war machines and siege maps could be included to capture the readers' attention and perhaps satisfy the curiosity of those who could barely read. This entrepreneurial aspect of Mézerai's "Dessein" could not be completely realized. As with most research and writing projects, the final results were more modest, and the publishers reduced the number of plates to cut costs.

But all his life Mézerai was preoccupied with the question of how to reach a large public. Other members of the Academy, led by Chapelain,

19. B.N., mss. fr. 20796, fol. 65.
20. *Ibid.*, fol. 66.

hoped that an increasing number of Frenchmen would "purify" their language and lift themselves up to observe the canons established by the classicistic stylists. Mézerai took an opposite course and wrote his history to reach a large public without ever hoping to elevate the standards of taste. His motives may have been more pecuniary than consciously popular-literary. Indeed, from the "Dessein" it is clear that he planned to include as many family names as he could, plus two thousand coats of arms,[21] an already well-established device for increasing the sale of books in a society where nobles had a reputation for buying books that included the names and arms of their ancestors. Similarly, a discussion of *charges*,[22] the parlements, and the leading ecclesiastics would also expand the potential market; and the insertion of short summaries about the growth of provincial cities might attract the attention of leading robe and perhaps bourgeois families in the provinces. Mézerai did not openly declare that he planned to include these subjects in order to increase sales, but he already had considerable experience on how pithy and biographical subjects and visual effects influenced the sale of books.

In addition to what must be done to attract readers, Mézerai also emphasized one thing to be avoided. Although it would be "new," he asserts, to cite sources of previously unpublished material and contradictory evidence at the bottom of the page, he "would not amuse himself in *formes de procès* or controversies,"[23] apparently because he thought these did not please readers.

Mézerai's translation of Grotius's *De veritate* had been published by Pierre Moreau, a royal typographer who had designed typefaces to resemble handwriting. In an attempt to simplify the problem of learning to read, Moreau had developed a type that reproduced a stylized form of the cursive script prevalent in the 1630s.[24] But instead of attracting a large number of purchasers for Moreau's books, the inven-

21. *Ibid.*, fol. 66.

22. *Ibid.*, fols. 64 ff. Numerous works on the history of *charges* had appeared in the 1620s and 1630s, and Mézerai may have hoped to include material from these specialized works in his general history. For example, André Duchesne's *Histoire des chanceliers et gardes des sceaux de France* (1630), written with his son François's collaboration, contained material on a subject that had never been integrated into the national histories. Works by the *érudits* were Mézerai's favorite sources for enriching his narrative with *curiosités*, that is, facts and discussions of events not hitherto included in the great national histories.

23. B.N., mss. fr. 20796, fol. 66.

24. A page from one of Moreau's books is reproduced in Stanley Morison, *Four Centuries of Fine Printing*, 4th ed. (New York, 1960), p. 158.

tion actually reduced sales. Thus, after two or three attempts, Moreau returned to conventional Roman typefaces. The unconventional appearance of the printed pages may partially explain why Mézerai's translation of Grotius failed to please the public. And though there is no specific evidence to support this, the experiment may have affected the way Mézerai assessed the reading public, making him particularly interested in finding ways to attract readers. In his next publication, the first volume of the monumental *Histoire de France depuis Faramond jusqu'à maintenant*, Mézerai sought a publisher who shared his ideas about what a history should contain if it was to gain favor with the public.

The 1640s witnessed an explosion in the number of illustrated books published specifically for the luxury book market. Mézerai's history constituted something of a pioneering effort, for a publisher and his author attempted to capture the market through emphasizing the size of the volumes and the number of illustrations. Mézerai's historical narrative was very lengthy and, as we shall see, eventually limited sales of the entire history. But although the text was long, the full-page plate devoted to each French king, his queen, and medals and coins of his reign made an impressive array of "historical" material linked reign by reign with Mézerai's narrative. Copperplate etching had only very recently replaced the woodcut for illustrating folio-sized books. This proved an ideal medium for portraits, for a person's character could be conveyed through the subtle shading of face and expression. As never before, Mézerai's history permitted Frenchmen to study the character of their kings through these portraits.[25]

Nothing quite so grand or apparently so authentic had appeared prior to Mézerai's history. Though not on the list of royal printers, the publisher Matthieu II Guillemot was one of the most reputable in Paris.[26] He possessed the talent for coordinating, or being willing to have coordinated, both the artistic efforts sponsored by Rémy Capitain and those of the poet translator Jean Baudoin. He also obtained the right to reprint Jacques de Bie's plates of royal coins and medals. These had appeared in *La France métallique*, published in 1636 by Pierre Rocolet, another leading Parisian printer. Like Capitain, de Bie apparently had tried to make accurate copies of coins, seals, and medals from the originals.[27] Mézerai and his collaborators' claim to historical accu-

25. See Jeanne Duportal, *Etude sur les livres à figures édités en France de 1601 à 1660* (Paris, 1914), p. 277.

26. Cf. Georges Lepreux, *Gallia typographica* (Paris, 1911), p. 257, for a reference to Guillemot.

27. It would be interesting to pursue Duportal's suggestion (p. 277) that

racy was ingeniously supported by the device of omitting portraits for the Merovingian kings. The massive frames included in the section devoted to these kings, empty and accompanied only by a verse, must have prepared readers and viewers to accept the others as "true."[28]

In addition to these innovative visual materials—especially those pertaining to the queens, who had scarcely been included by earlier historians—eloquently rhymed quatrains appeared beneath each royal portrait. Jean Baudoin, Mézerai's friend and fellow *libertin*, had also longed to be a poet; and like Mézerai he had been obliged to admit an apparent lack of talent and had turned to translating to earn a living.[29] Like many earlier humanists, Baudoin and Mézerai collaborated to make the verses and the prose sustain one another.[30] The quatrains are an encapsulated rendition of the longer prose narrative, with each of Baudoin's lines containing a major theme, event, or attribute of the sovereign. The lines for Henry IV read:

> Fier et brave ennemy, doux et clément vainqueur,
> Grand Roy sans favoris, sans fraude, et sans vengeance,
> Par force ou par amour, je reconquis la France,
> Et de tous les mortels j'eus l'estime et le coeur.[31]

Mézerai's prose narrative expanded these themes. The result is a unified visual, poetical, and prose-historical work dealing with every French king, reign by reign. Sometimes Mézerai's narrative provides too many incidents or attributes to permit all of them to be subsumed neatly into a quatrain; but the simultaneous collaboration between the poet

---

de Bie had sought information about the authenticity of coins from the great Peiresc.

28. The favorite place for copying royal portraits was Saint-Denis, where, in a desire to elevate the abbey even higher in the ranks of sacred foundations in the realm, Louis IX had supplied a long row of tombs with effigies purportedly going back to Merovingian times.

29. For a brief and near-contemporary account of Baudoin's career, cf. Paul Pellisson-Fontanier and Pierre-Joseph Thorellier d'Olivet, *Histoire de l'Académie française*, ed. Charles-L. Livet (Paris, 1858), vol. 1, p. 238. His chef d'oeuvre was his translation of Davila's *Histoire des guerres civiles*, published by Rocolet, which appeared in 1644.

30. Evans, p. 49, states that some eighteenth-century critics asserted that Baudoin also collaborated in writing the prose narrative of volume 1. Throughout his career Mézerai was accustomed to consulting his friends, chiefly on matters of style; but there is no support for the assertion that he did not in fact write the narrative of the first volume. His willingness to recognize in the preface his debts to others should be taken at face value.

31. They are repeated in *L'Abrégé chronologique, ou extrait de l'histoire de France* (Paris, 1690), vol. 3, p. 278.

and the historian is evident. Similarly, from a manuscript copy of de Bie's work on coins and medals—covered with Mézerai's marginalia—it is possible to observe how the historian may have attempted to infer something about the character of a given king from his portraits, coins, and the iconography prevalent during his reign, in order to insert these inferences into his prose narrative.[32]

As the publication date approached, Mézerai undertook all the conventional steps taken by men of letters to secure royal approval and a pension. He prepared a dedication to Richelieu, but the Cardinal's death in December 1642 forced a change in plans. The double frontispiece of the book depicts a triumphant Louis XIII on horseback and contains a dedication to that king, despite the fact that he had joined Richelieu in death before the book was published.[33] Accordingly there is a second large illustration of Anne of Austria and her two young sons, Louis XIV and Philip of France, with a dedication to her as Queen Regent.

The second volume, dedicated to Chancellor Séguier, appeared in 1645, and the third and final volume, dedicated to George William, Duke of Brunswick, appeared in 1651. In the second volume, Mézerai is described as *historiographe de France* for the first time on the title page of a book, indicating that the first volume had earned him royal patronage and a pension.

Mézerai's search for a patron had been complicated by Richelieu's death and the resulting ministerial changes. An undated letter from Mézerai, apparently to François Sublet de Noyers, indicates that he made every effort to gain both Sublet's and Anne's favor.[34] By evoking

32. Evans, p. 48. One is reminded of Gibbon's preoccupation with the study of ancient coins during his tour of Italy, prior to writing his *Decline and Fall*. See Edward Gibbon, *Journey from Geneva to Rome*, ed. Georges Bonnard (London, 1961), pp. 165–171.

33. Tallemant des Réaux, vol. 1, p. 344, asserts that Mézerai presented Louis XIII with a copy of volume 1 of his history. Since Louis died on 14 May 1643, it is clear that the bulk of the printing had been completed before the *privilège* was granted in June 1643.

34. B.N., mss. fr. 12796, fol. 44. This letter prompts several factual questions. The principal subject is Mézerai's interest in writing the history of the Turks, a project perhaps begun at the instigation of Sublet de Noyers before his disgrace in the spring of 1643. The first volume of the *Histoire de France* had already appeared, for Mézerai refers to its favorable reception at court. Sublet, the sponsor of the royal printing works in the Louvre, is known to have sponsored several large-scale publishing projects, especially illustrated books. Had Sublet also played a role in facilitating Guillemot's arrangements for Mézerai's *Histoire de France*? The question has larger implications, since Sublet was a *dévot*, perhaps even a Jesuit. Cf. Ranum,

the status of Blaise de Vigénaire—who had the right to enter every-where and be "particulièrement des serviteurs" of the royal household —Mézerai hoped that he might eventually gain the same favor. Unfor-tunately, Sublet had already been disgraced by the time Mézerai wrote this letter. In March 1643, Louis XIII had abruptly removed him from his offices and had sent him packing. The emphasis on pleasing Anne of Austria throughout the letter indicates that it was written after Louis XIII's death and that Mézerai was naively seeking favor from a min-ister who had little if any favor at court. Still, Anne may have reached out to grant audiences to the minister whom her recently deceased husband had disgraced, for Mézerai writes: "Je m'assure Monsieur que vous n'avez pas oublié de marquer à la Reine que dans mon *Histoire de France* . . . je ne perds aucune occasion d'honnorer la memoire des pre-decesseurs de Sa Majesté, et particulièrement de Monseigneur son Père [Louis XIII] et de Monseigneur son ayeul [Henry IV]."[35] Mézerai ends his letter with a lament about his bad fortune, which "until now" has been more powerful than his writings and other actions toward ac-quiring favor.

If efforts to gain favor through Sublet proved abortive, he was more successful in approaching Chancellor Séguier, who sometime between 1643 and 1646 not only granted him a pension but also furnished him a place to live[36] and supported him for election to the French Academy, which had chosen Séguier as its protector after Richelieu's death. Henceforth the Chancellor's and Mézerai's careers would be linked.[37] The patron suffered repudiation by his fellow magistrates early in the Fronde and disgrace by the Crown as the Fronde worsened, only to be eventually reinstated in his high office. Colbert, Michel Le Tellier, and Louis XIV never had complete confidence in Séguier, because at one point he had faltered and gone over to the Fronde.[38] Séguier's political fortunes may offer more than a clue to Mézerai's own political wav-erings during the Fronde and perhaps to the turmoil and isolation that are evident in his later writings.

The third and last volume of the *Histoire de France* appeared while

---

Richelieu and the Councillors of Louis XIII (Oxford, 1963), p. 101; and Duportal, pp. 216–217.

35. B.N., mss. fr. 12796, fol. 44.

36. Evans, p. 68. Mazarin also gave him a pension.

37. The Séguier papers in the B.N., Paris, reveal very little about this relationship. Perhaps the correspondence preserved in Leningrad would clarify it. See Roland Mousnier, ed., *Lettres et mémoires adressés au Chan-celier Séguier, 1633–1649* (Paris, 1964), "Introduction."

38. Louis XIV, *Mémoires for the Instruction of the Dauphin*, trans. Paul Sonnino (New York, 1970), p. 34.

Séguier was in disgrace.[39] In order not to have it appear that he was completely abandoning the Chancellor by dedicating his work to another Frenchman, Mézerai addressed the book to George William, Duke of Brunswick, who already had a high reputation as a patron of men of letters.[40] Beneath the phrases about his new patron's knowledge of French culture—a reflection of Mézerai's strong national sentiments—and about the place that history should occupy in his "cabinet," there is a preoccupation with the effects of the Fronde on historical writing. George William may read his history dispassionately, for unlike the French he is disinterested. His sole desire is to learn about great events. The argument is strained. Furthermore, Mézerai asserts that George William's protection has freed him from the fear of displeasing his patron by speaking out firmly about the past, rather than disguising the truth.[41] The mood of volume 3 is sullen rather than detached. Mézerai could not avoid perceiving the Wars of Religion through the optic of the political upheavals of the Fronde. There is a sense of futility and of frustration at his compatriots' inability to remove the sources of revolt. An analysis of the three volumes as a whole might reveal Mézerai's increasing preoccupation with the social and ideological cleavages that were appearing in the 1640s. But instead of attempting to describe Mézerai's entire account of French history beginning with Pharamond, we shall look briefly at his narrative of the Wars of Religion in order to compare it with his much more widely read *Abrégé chronologique*.

Cynical, almost bitter, and yet judicious about the travails that France had undergone during the Wars of Religion, Mézerai wanted above all else a return to stability. Frondeur though he was, stability and order, indeed a return to the old order, was what he wished for his *patrie*. No social order is criticized as such, nor any religious group—except perhaps the Holy League, though here Mézerai is careful to seek political reasons for their conduct. A *libertin* committed intellectually to maintaining French institutions unaltered, he commends only those changes that would restore church and state to stability. Unlike some of his sixteenth-century forebears, however, Mézerai did not advocate a mere return to some pristine institutional and social arrangement that had existed before their "corruption." His cynicism, or perhaps his knowledge of history, prevented him from believing that a pristine French Monarchy had ever existed. The "innovations" that he abhorred were new taxes, venality of office, the procedure of farming out taxes, "weak-

39. The printing was completed in July 1651.
40. Evans, p. 50.
41. *Histoire de France* (Paris, 1651), vol. 3, p. iii.

ness" and corruption of the nobles, particularly new nobles, and corruption in the Church. The reader occasionally must infer these issues, since Mézerai avoided a straightforward assessment of the causes of the Wars of Religion.

His account of the crucial year 1588 begins by noting the great shortage of grain south of the Loire and the foul-smelling slugs that came out of the ground at night and devoured the seed. Had not the astrologers concurred that 1588 would be a year of momentous and strange events? That year had brought a great number of ill omens: tempests, earthquakes, women bearing twins five days apart, and, if one "believes those who come from the country, phantoms of fire had appeared in the air."[42] This mixture of omens and of perceptive observations about the effects of actions by one social group or another, or about the roles of various princes, the League, the King, and Catherine de Médicis reflects Mézerai's attempt to understand the causes of instability. He asserts, for example, that the invasion by the Spanish army "swelled up" the League party—giving Henry de Guise credit for something he did not deserve. Like Davila before him, Mézerai saw the rise of parties in the Wars of Religion as the ultimate source of the state's ruin.

In addition, the courtiers were filled with the "cursed maxims from Florence,"[43] and, while Henry III was busy studying Machiavelli, the Duke of Guise was reading Tacitus. The avarice of the tax farmers contributed to civil war as the council and other royal officials became increasingly partisan. The "fourmillière d'imposts" devoured the country, while those in the Estates General of 1588 offered solutions that had been appropriate in the fifteenth century but had been rendered inappropriate as a result of the Crown's dependency upon the tax farmers and the detested policy of increasing royal income by the sale of offices.

Public opinion was whipped up by the leaders of parties and the preachers, the latter being especially singled out for reproach when Mézerai included them in a list of those whom he considered seditious.[44] He was also very harsh toward the League Parlement, which he likewise deemed seditious. Cornered by parties, the King himself is not depicted as a suffering servant but rather as a dreamer[45] given to excesses of devotion and affection for favorites.

In addition to the general narrative, Mézerai keeps score of private actions, which he either castigates or approves. For example, the Che-

42. *Ibid.*, p. 478.
43. *Ibid.*, p. 2.
44. *Ibid.*, p. 592.
45. *Ibid.*, p. 567.

valier d'Aumale permitted "pillaging, insolences, and inhumanities" that history could not forget. By contrast, on several occasions François de la Noue is singled out and praised for his actions and solid royalism in speaking on the King's behalf at a moment of financial crisis and foreign invasion: "C'est en des occasions où il s'agit du salut de l'Estat, comme en celle cy, qu'est véritable cette maxime que nos biens et nos vies sont au Roy."[46] Mézerai's perpetuation in history of the memories of infamous and praiseworthy acts took courage, for at the time many if not most of those who had participated in the Wars of Religion had descendants bearing their names.[47] The climate of the Fronde may have strengthened Mézerai's courage to mobilize history on behalf of humanity and political stability by warning the perpetrators of violence and partisanship in his own day that their infamous acts might make their names infamous for all time.

While still at work on his history of France, Mézerai had also undertaken a narrative of Turkish history for the years 1612 to 1648. The reasons are apparent: his publisher needed help. Not only did Guillemot plan to publish a larger and more grandly illustrated history of France than any yet printed; he had also decided to produce a similar work on that perennially fascinating subject, the Turks. There would be quatrains, eulogies, prose narrative, and portraits of sultans; but this time, instead of beginning with an entirely new history, Guillemot arranged to republish Demetrius Chalcondyles's *Histoire de la décadence de l'Empire Grec et establissement de celuy des Turcs* in the translation by Blaise de Vigénaire.[48] The narrative had already been brought up to date once by a certain Thomas Artus, so Mézerai's task was to summarize the still more recent Turkish past.

The book may have been planned as early as 1642; Mézerai refers to it in a letter written between 1643 and 1645 to Sublet de Noyers, the founder of the royal printing works in the Louvre.[49] Mézerai does his best in this letter to ingratiate himself with Sublet, especially by point-

46. *Ibid.*, p. 640.

47. Tallemant des Réaux, vol. 1, p. 308, claims that Cardinal Retz destroyed part of a Brantôme manuscript that discussed his own grandmother in ways he deemed unfavorable.

48. For a general introduction to the works about the Turks available in French, see Clarence D. Rouillard, *The Turk in French History, Thought, and Literature* (Paris, 1938).

49. B.N., mss. fr. 12796, fol. 44. Sublet had already been disgraced when Mézerai wrote him, since there is no reference to Louis XIII in the letter. Mézerai naively overestimated Sublet's power during the Regency, though it is still possible that Anne of Austria may have remained in contact with this hardworking *dévot*.

ing out that Vigénaire, his predecessor on matters Turkish, had had the "droit d'entrer partout" at court. The implication is that Mézerai would very much like being granted the same honor.[50]

The current state of knowledge concerning seventeenth-century publishing makes it difficult to determine whether Sublet de Noyers had urged Guillemot to undertake the simultaneous publication of these two massive histories. An admirer of illustrated books, Sublet commissioned Poussin to do the artwork for new editions of ancient poets at about the same date that Guillemot launched Mézerai's history and the history of the Turks. This is a fact of more than passing significance, because it sheds light on the specific ways in which the Crown and the Catholic reformers cooperated to subsidize illustrated books.[51] If in fact Sublet was a patron of Guillemot, and through him of Mézerai, this might help explain why the publication of the Turkish history, in press three times, did not finally occur until 1650, with a second folio edition, this time published by A. Courbé, in 1662.[52]

The effort to launch both an illustrated French history and a Turkish history may have exceeded Guillemot's resources. To help assure success he acquired rights to Michel Baudier's pornographic and very successful *Histoire génèralle du serrail*, with its etchings of Turkish women. Baudier, himself a *libertin*, was a friend of Mézerai's; they may have collaborated in a publishing venture where the maximum was done to enhance sales. The Baudier was brought out to accompany and be bound together, if desired, with Mézerai's narrative of recent Turkish history.[53] The books were very slow to appear, however, and while some of the delay may have been caused by the authors and the engravers of the plates, it may in part have been owing to the need to use the capital from the sales of the first volumes in order to proceed with the later ones. Payments had to be made to the original publishers of

50. He also asked Sublet to point out to the Queen how he had lost no opportunity in his *Histoire de France* to honor the memories of Henry IV and Louis XIII (*ibid.*, fol. 544).

51. For a general introduction to these questions, see Duportal, pp. 216–218, and p. 229 on how Protestant books published in the 1640s were rarely illustrated or, if illustrated, bore only tiny figures.

52. All subsequent references are to this edition.

53. Michel Baudier became a more overt critic of ministerial government than Mézerai with the publication of *Toiras* in 1643. He possessed the talent to write about the Orientals in ways that confirmed the French perception of these people as "debased" by despotism. Baudier is a link between the sixteenth-century writers who held up the Ottoman Empire as an image of how France would be if her kings became as powerful as the sultans and Montesquieu's *Persian Letters*. See Rouillard, pp. 103 ff.

the earlier editions; and since the subjects were so popular, these fees may have been rather high.

The reader was to approach the Turkish history in the same manner as the French one: to study first the portrait, then the quatrains,[54] and finally the narrative. A kind of "art of memory"—neither very subtle nor very elaborate—infuses the structure of all of Mézerai's histories.[55] Little printed hands indicate especially exciting passages, proverbs are underlined, and italic type is used to set off official documents and royal speeches—devices supporting the conclusion that both the printer and the author made a studied effort to attract readers. Perhaps Guillemot or one of his typesetters had suggested these techniques; perhaps it was Mézerai himself. The "Dessein pour une parfaite histoire" had reflected a willingness to use visual devices to attract the general public; the publisher and the historian may have made a genuine effort to collaborate on both monumental histories.[56] Uninitiated readers could visualize and recall a crude outline of visual and political elements about each sultan and each French king.

In addition to these mnemonic devices, Mézerai did not hesitate to create a mirror in which the various groups in French society could see themselves. These verbal images invariably contain social criticism almost immediately recognizable to his more informed readers. The theme about the disastrous consequences for the state of promoting individuals too rapidly or too far above their social rank is reiterated almost as a refrain. Indeed, Mézerai seems to have considered this the principal weakness of the Ottoman political system, and he may have implied as much for France as well. Armies mutiny against the sultan when they are commanded by men of low birth; the praetorians of Ancient Rome, like the Mameluks, were a grave threat to the stability of the state[57]—perhaps an allusion to the pillaging armies commanded by royal favorites and Richelieu's relatives during the Fronde. Murad IV's male favorites are called "mignons"; they bring a life of debauchery to the sultan's court. But worse, since Murad had given them the highest positions in the state and commands in the army, their jealousies

54. The only difference being the addition of eulogies, an expanded version of the quatrains.

55. Frances A. Yates, *The Art of Memory* (Chicago, 1966), *passim*.

56. The total number of folio pages in the first edition of the *Histoire de France* is 3,568, not including prefaces and indexes. For more on the *Histoire* . . . see Phyllis Leffler, "From Humanist to Enlightenment Historiography: A Case Study of François Eudes de Mézeray," in *French Historical Studies* 10 (1978): 416 ff.

57. *Histoire générale des Turcs* (Paris, 1662), vol. 2, p. 39.

and eventual rebellions invariably created instability among the older, well-established families and within parts of the sultan's own "family."[58] In discussing the dynastic conflicts and power struggles that wracked the Ottoman state in the first half of the seventeenth century, Mézerai stresses both the immorality of the Ottoman court—Murad's death, he asserts, was the result of eating and drinking too heavily—and the dire consequences of family conflicts among members of the seraglio.

The role of the very powerful Queen Mother is emphasized in a way that could only evoke for French readers the "time of trouble" under the later Valois.[59] The military defeats, rebellions, assassinations, intrigues, and moral depravity of both the seventeenth-century Turks and the sixteenth-century French put their histories in parallel. Despotic social and political organizations—and not the fact that the Turks were heathen—resulted in the inevitable moral decay, violence, and military defeat. In fact, Mézerai is careful to tread softly on the religious differences between the French and the Turkish peoples, because, after all, the alliance between the two preserves Christendom. Over a third of his text[60] is a straightforward account of the diplomatic relations between the two states and an argument for their cooperation against the Hapsburg threat.[61]

Thus, while Mézerai could employ Turkish history as a lengthy metaphor to lament the sufferings of France in recent times, he could nevertheless staunchly defend French foreign policy in the Thirty Years' War. Since the reign of Francis I the French had sought to cooperate with the Turks in limiting Hapsburg power. The Crown may well have wished to see this perennial issue, with its moral and religious implications, supported by a historiographer royal. Whether or not it resulted from the orders of a royal official, Mézerai's history complemented the works of other historians writing in defense of the French Crown—including the *érudits*, whose work supported both dynastic claims and claims to temporal power over the Gallican Church.[62]

58. *Ibid.*, p. 164.

59. *Ibid.*, pp. 165 ff.

60. At least in the second edition. Volume 1 is dedicated to the Queen of Poland, a Savoyard princess, and Volume 2 to the Duke de Richelieu, the Cardinal's nephew.

61. *Ibid.*, vol. 2, p. 196, in which Mézerai asserts that he has received an account of diplomatic negotiations from the Dupuy brothers. This illustrates the cooperation between the *érudits* and the more humanist historiographers.

62. See any bibliography of the published works of Pierre and Jacques Dupuy.

Mézerai's work could only have been read as an attempt to undermine further the *dévot* party by justifying France's alliance with a heathen state against another Christian state.

The style of the Turkish history, like that of everything that Mézerai wrote, is blunt, lively, and awkward. The usual devices are present, including omens: an earthquake destroyed Mohammed's tomb at Mecca, and lightning struck so close to Davud Pasha that his shirt was burned though he remained unharmed.[63] These events may actually have occurred; but they are never integrated into the narrative and simply appear as signs or portents of the terrible times being described. Mézerai strains to sum up events and personalities. About Ahmed I he writes: "Il fut prince de grand courage, mais de très petit jugement; appesantez et presque hebetez par les excez de ses voluptez brutales; peu estimez de ses sujets, parce qu'il estoit malheureux, ayant receu de grands echecs par les Persans."[64] What Mézerai was observing with equanimity were the travails of another people whose political system had resulted in international humiliation and internal disorder.

Early French History as Criticism of Foreign Policy

Throughout his long career Mézerai was accustomed to lending drafts of his unpublished work to friends, asking them for criticism. This practice was characteristic among the men of letters of the seventeenth century, but unlike most of them, Mézerai kept some of the proffered criticisms among his research notes.[65] He not only saved these suggestions for revision but preserved his own marginal replies to his critics. Through studying these materials it is possible to establish the approximate intellectual framework of critical thinking about history in the mid-seventeenth century. The overwhelming emphasis on style helps us see how the most *libertin* of seventeenth-century historians responded to the current literary movement to "purify" the French language by rendering it free of Rabelaisian grammar and vocabulary.

63. *Histoire générale des Turcs*, vol. 2, p. 125.

64. *Ibid.*, p. 37.

65. Mézerai's notes merit a much more careful description and analysis than could appropriately be included in this book. The materials that belonged to La Popelinière should be viewed as an entity that was crudely but effectively integrated into the rather rudimentary chronological notes kept by Mézerai. A comparative study of these materials in B.N., mss. fr. 20796, might reveal the identities of some of the anonymous critics discussed below.

It is not surprising that Mézerai submitted his drafts to his fellow men of letters for criticism. He may have shown some of his work to the Dupuy brothers for critiques of his interpretations, but there is no available evidence to support this contention. Instead, the evidence implies that Mézerai's own primary preoccupation was to develop a style that would be agreeable to readers rather than be erudite and that consequently he sought the criticism of friends in the French Academy whom he knew well and respected. Through a brief analysis of these critiques, it is possible to perceive the stylistic disjuncture between the "purifiers" of French and men like Mézerai whose style represented continuity with the sixteenth century.

Mézerai's friends seem to have been capable of only one stylistic critical mode. Indeed, their remarks about his verses are similar to those about his historical narrative. For the dedicatory verses addressed to Louis XIII in volume 1 of his history, the spokesman for these friends remarked: "Cela est trop joué pour une inscription et trop commun. On a jugé qu'il ne falloit point mesler la justice avec la guerre en cette periode. Ce mot est trop fort. Ce mot ne se prend jamais, qu'en mauvaise part. . . . Il fault mettre un autre mot en la place de celuy, qui est odieux. On ne doit point conquerir des peuples, mais des royaumes. . . . Ce sens est bon et necessaire, mais il n'est pas dit assez noblement." [66] The tenor of the criticism is clear without reference to the specific verses that Mézerai's friends were discussing. The emphasis on polite language, the avoidance of strong words, and the subtle stress upon avoiding associations of justice and war, peoples and realms, reflect a stylistic sensibility at work to alter the meaning and significance of ideology in French political culture.

Much more succinct and representative of his views, however, is Mézerai's unpublished memorandum on French foreign policy, which he addressed to Louis XIV.[67] Probably written in 1667–1668, during the War of Devolution, it is nothing less than an analytical treatise on foreign and military policies.[68] Mézerai attempted to clarify the King's thinking and to persuade him of the dangers involved in basing any course of action on the alliance with England. He admitted that he had

66. B.N., mss. fr. 20796, fol. 54. The attribution in Mézerai's hand on the manuscript reads: "C'est le commentaire [?] de M. de la Chambre et de Sérisay [?] et trois autres de l'Académie sur l'Inscription de mon histoire au Roy Louis XIII."
67. B.N., mss. fr. n.a. 1249, fols. 146 ff.
68. One clue to the date is the phrase, "L'experience des deux dernières campagnes, où la flote d'Angleterre qui a tant cousté d'argent et de soings à la France et esté plutost un embaras qu'un secours à la nostre" (*ibid.*, fol. 151 v).

neither access to state secrets nor the *droit d'entrer* into the royal councils, but he showed a certain dignity of self and a trust that the King would take the trouble to consider his views. Did Mézerai actually send off a finished transcript to Versailles? The text, which is preserved among his personal notes, is covered with revisions, indicating that it received a great deal of attention from the author. The heap of surviving notes in the Archives du Ministère de la Guerre, the Archives Nationales, and various other collections of state papers in Paris may contain an as yet unidentified final copy of the memorandum that Mézerai worked painstakingly to prepare.

Its aim is to offer advice on policy, not on how policy might be expressed to affect public opinion. No emphasis whatever is placed on what might be considered an official function of a historiographer royal: namely, to write a history of events in support of the King's policy and for use as propaganda. Instead, the assumptions and analysis are reminiscent of the venerable tradition of advice literature that men of learning addressed to the king. Indeed, many of the arguments and assumptions about the conduct of monarchies, France's place in Europe, and the desirability of conquest recall those made by Budé in his *Institution du prince*.[69]

Beginning with the observation that France has great "puissance," Mézerai lays down three alternative strategies for the future. Since France was at war at the time he was writing, there is no discussion of whether there should be peace or war. Instead, the focus is on how much Louis might wish to conquer. He might choose to press "endlessly" beyond the Rhine and into Italy and Spain in order to "restore the Empire to the French House as it was under Charlemagne"; or he might choose to conquer territories as far as the Rhine, giving "à la France les mesmes bornes que la nature avoit données à l'ancienne Gaule"—that is, the Alps, the Pyrenees, the Rhine, and the two seas; or he might conquer only enough territory in the north to make the existing borders stronger.

These were the three alternative war aims as Mézerai saw them. Which one had Louis selected, or ought he to select? Mézerai did not answer this question. His principles were concise: "La sage politique est de se faire du bien à soy mesme et à ne pas faire du mal que pour n'en point souffrir."[70] The outcome of the war was what counted, not the number of victories won along the way. As Mézerai put it: "On a toujours remarqué dans les guerres que le dernier évenement est celuy qui regle tout, et qu'il seroit peu d'avoir gagné quatre ou cinq batailles

69. See above, Chapter 1.

70. B.N., mss. fr. n.a. 1249, fol. 149 v.

si on perdoit la dernière."[71] In his analysis of the three possible war aims, Mézerai stressed the extreme hostility that France would encounter from the Hapsburg Empire and even from the Turks were Louis to attempt a new Carolingian Empire and the hostility of the Rhinelanders to French expansionism if the King pressed northward and eastward. Indeed, by implication it seems that Mézerai only really considered the third aim—the strengthening and squaring-off of the northern borders—as practicable or operative. If such was the case, and I believe it to be, why then did Mézerai take the trouble to discuss the first two strategies? The research required to answer this question would take us too far afield, but it is nevertheless interesting to speculate that by going over the first two strategies and then concentrating on the third, Mézerai summarized or echoed the fundamental distinctions between the ideology of conquest and the explicit aim that was actually helping to shape the Monarchy's goals and hopes in the War of Devolution. The conventionality of Mézerai's analysis is striking. Here was a man learned in the history of French diplomacy and alert, though uninformed of the discussions taking place at Versailles; he could nevertheless still grasp the general contours of the affairs of state. And like the ministers and perhaps the King himself, Mézerai struggled to discern what ought to be done to prevent a war from turning into a defeat. His emphasis lay on the last battle to be won, not on all the previous victories and the *Te Deum* masses that Louis XIV ordered.

The precise recommendations and especially the warnings in the memorandum may not have been directly relevant, or at best they may merely have been redundant. Mézerai stressed the danger of establishing enclaves in Flanders that were difficult to supply in wartime and that also frequently included Protestant towns. This meant that in the years to come these towns might lean toward "them," that is, the Dutch, rather than "us," the French.[72] The Protestant reactions to the French invasion, as we shall see, also preoccupied Pellisson; but unlike that former Protestant, Mézerai tended to be more fearful for the future and certainly more cynical about the prospect of ever holding the Spanish Netherlands. His fears derived from a general concept of the way states and peoples behave over centuries, not from an observation of the responses of Flemish crowds to Louis XIV.

71. *Ibid.*, fol. 149 v. To support this contention, Mézerai alludes to Henry II's defeat at Saint-Quentin in 1557.

72. *Ibid.*, fol. 152. The prevalence of the language of "them" for other European names and "us" for the French army among seventeenth-century men of letters (cf. below, p. 314) sheds some light on the ever-increasing extension of national consciousness to the literate elites and perhaps below them to the *peuple*.

Mézerai was particularly apprehensive about one crucial element in French policy: the Anglo-French alliance. Such an alliance seemed almost unnatural to him. The two kingdoms had been at war off and on for the past five hundred years, during which the French had taken many rich and prosperous provinces from the English inheritance on the Continent. Through economic interests, Mézerai asserted, the English would always be ready to milk the French for their foodstuffs, paying them in money not up to its assigned value. Moreover, "Dans la guerre présente ils [the English] ne souffriront point que nous facions des progrès sur les costes de la Hollande."[73] The English recognized their interests, and these interests differed from those of the French. The alliance of two nations with such disparate humors and aims rarely succeeds: "Qui doute que les Anglois ne soyent les ennemis mortels de la France? Ils sont depuis cinq cents ans et ne cesseront jamais l'estre outre qu'on ne scauroit leur arracher du coeur le ressentiment qu'ils ont de ce que nous leurs avons osté cinq ou six grandes provinces qu'ils tenoient en France de droict patrimonial et hereditaire. L'empire de la mer qu'ils s'attribuent, et leur humeur orgueilleuse et insociable, et leur jalousie naturelle leur feront toujours regarder nos prosperités d'un oeil envieux et malin."[74]

Mézerai's Anglophobia seems remarkably strong, yet it is not surprising when placed in the general perspective of his historical thought. The *libertins* were strong nationalists; xenophobia about the Papacy, the Spanish, the Jesuits, and the English was a part of their European perspective. In Mézerai this anxiety was also strengthened by his fear of innovation in any and all manner of social and political relationships. Like the legal humanists who implicitly longed for a return to a simpler, more golden age, Mézerai resented changes in alliances. He seemed incapable of perceiving that England had temporarily become a client state of France.

As for the Dutch, "Si Sa Majesté n'a eu intention que de chastier leur insolence, il semble qu'ils sont assez rudement punis,"[75] which was Mézerai's way of favoring an end to the war. The French had conquered territory; the Spanish had been defeated; a basis for negotiation and a peace settlement existed. Mézerai could not quite bring himself to state this last point succinctly. Though this draft is incomplete, the argument leads to a recommendation that the King bring the war to an end. During the next war—perhaps owing as much to his own decline from favor as to Louis's decision to attack Holland—Mézerai

73. *Ibid.*, fol. 151 v.
74. *Ibid.*
75. *Ibid.*, fol. 151.

altered his perception of French foreign policy and in doing so believed he had to alter his definition of French national character.

In his last major work, the *Histoire de France avant Clovis*, first published in Amsterdam in 1682, Mézerai wanted to insert an attack on French foreign policy. He apparently could find no better way of doing this than to change his interpretation of the Frankish invasions of Gaul. As had been the case for some of his earlier works, he asked a friend to read and criticize the text.

The atmosphere of praise created by other writers, who described Louis XIV as a conqueror, was also more than Mézerai could accept. In addition, the war with the Dutch during the 1670s had gone beyond the military exploits of a young king and had become a battle for Europe in which the survival of the Dutch as an independent state had been placed in doubt. In historicizing this issue, Mézerai asserts that the Franks had invaded Gaul as much to oppose the Gauls themselves as to combat the Roman conquerors of the Gauls.[76] His critic balked. Were not the Franks greater enemies of the Romans than of the conquered peoples, that is, the Gauls? French sensibilities about their territorial rights in Gaul had, of course, been satisfied by the conventional nationalist interpretation that the Franks had driven out the Romans and had been in effect the liberators of the Gauls. Mézerai had rejected this interpretation out of a desire to emphasize the warlike and expansionist nature of the peoples whom the critic continually refers to as "us," the Franks.

Again, the critic rankled at Mézerai's use of the term "nation bellicose" for the Franks, because calling a people warlike did not seem "true praise." The critic could not conceive of a history of "his" people that failed to endow them with noble and positive attributes; "bellicose" could be misinterpreted.[77] Mézerai agreed to delete the offending adjective, but for reasons diametrically opposed to those of his critic. If "bellicose" could in any way be interpreted as praise for the Franks, he asserted, it must be deleted, for he did not want to praise them at all.

Once he had laid out the general characteristics of the Franks and had implicitly condemned their expansionism, he was confronted by the question of the continuity of these characteristics. At one point Mézerai chose the words, "jusqu'au règne présent de Louis le Victorieux." Did this, the critic pointed out, include Louis XIV's reign or exclude it? The phrase was ambiguous. Mézerai replied: "Non, non, il est ambigu et je le veux ambigu,"[78] meaning that the words could be

76. B.N., mss. fr. 20797, fol. 399.
77. *Ibid.*
78. *Ibid.*, fol. 398.

interpreted by a censor or a critic as including or excluding Louis XIV's reign; readers familiar with the historiography of the Frankish conquests would recognize immediately Mézerai's attempt to denigrate the warlike attributes of the French.

At one point the friend-critic finally began to glimpse Mézerai's purpose and lashed out: "L'historien n'est pas obligé de dire tout ce qui est véritable. Il suffit que tout ce qu'il dit est véritable, et il y a beaucoup de choses qu'il est obligé de dissimuler quand cela ne fait point de tort à la vérité ou intelligence de l'historien."[79] Perhaps in no other instance in the seventeenth century had a man of Mézerai's convictions and temperament observed how puerile was the force of ancient rhetoric, with its emphasis on writing the truth in history. Indeed, in his later career he found himself in opposition to his fellow Academicians and Colbert on this very question of how much truth a historian should recount.

The critique also included the usual stylistic queries. Mézerai had used the word "langage," which his critic described as pedantic and "peu français."[80] He was castigated for repeating the same word twice in one sentence and for writing "vrai ordre des années" instead of "vrai ordre du temps." He seems to have committed frequent violations of rhetorical convention by reversing word orders; at one point he had written "manners, customs, and laws," rather than the preferred order, "manners, laws, and customs."[81] In other instances the critic found his friend's stylistic faults so grave that he could not readily think of a way of repairing them. Lacking an ear for eloquent phrasing and hostile to the principle that "ennobling" words should always be selected over the language of common speech, Mézerai could not write prose that pleased his fellow members of the French Academy. And yet it was not for lack of trying.

Mézerai's correspondence is a record of his attempts to improve his style. He revised his works and strove to gain the respect of his critics. Thus, beneath the disparities between his writing and the changing stylistic conventions of his day lies the fundamental question of how to interpret this "failure" to improve his style. His inability to write "pure" French, his "bizarre" life style, and his criticisms of Louis XIV's policies were all integral parts of Mézerai's life and thought. Each of these elements reinforced the others; stylistic failures may have prompted an unconscious political and historical libertinism.

79. *Ibid.*, fol. 399. See also Jacques Barzun, *The French Race* (New York, 1932), pp. 116 ff.

80. *Ibid.*, fol. 417.

81. *Ibid.*, fol. 413. The critic does not specify his reasons, but they seem to emanate primarily from the sound of the phrase rather than from a hierarchy of manners, laws, and customs.

The Bizarre Academician

Mézerai's life and work are chiefly characterized by their continuity in an age when great changes were taking place in French literary and political culture. Nowhere is this quality more apparent than in Mézerai's tilts with other members of the Academy over the words deemed worthy of inclusion in the dictionary that body had agreed to prepare.

Upon Claude de Vaugelas's death in 1650, the dictionary was in danger of being abandoned altogether, for none of the leading Academicians wanted to undertake the tedious and time-consuming task of completing it. Conrart was too ill, it seemed, and Chapelain too preoccupied with the *Pucelle.* Thus, in a typical confraternal gesture, the members of the Academy turned to the recently elected Mézerai, appointing him to select the words that would then be either approved or rejected by the Academy as a whole.[82]

Just how well the project did in fact progress under Mézerai is difficult to determine, but almost from the beginning his "stubbornness" and views about language pitted him against the majority of the Academicians. Interminable disputes arose over principles of orthography, points of grammar, and selection of words; but during Conrart's lifetime his young friend Mézerai may have been protected from the full fury of his colleagues. There were several false starts, and only a certain arbitrariness on Mézerai's part led to the publication of the first edition in 1694. François Tallemant observed: "Il arriva enfin, au grand malheur du Dictionnaire, que M. de Mézeray se trouva mal satisfait de ses confrères sur ce qu'ils luy firent plusieurs fois de suitte éffacer toutes les phrases qu'il avoit apportées et que l'on ne trouvoit point seulement de bel usage, mais mesme de l'usage approuvé parmy le peuple. Il estoit pourtant persuadé qu'il les avoit consacrées en les mettant dans son *Histoire.*"[83] The trouble would always be that Mézerai had "bassesses dans le style" and apparently a genuine desire to include in the dictionary the expressions and words used by the *peuple* of the Halles. When his proposals were voted down, he would simply record them as approved.[84]

Mézerai served as secretary during Conrart's indispositions and exploited the position to make his views prevail over the opposition's. Chapelain and the other Academicians would become infuriated by such high-handed behavior but were powerless to prevent it.

82. Charles Beaulieux, ed., *Observations sur l'orthographe de la langue françoise* (Paris, n.d.), p. 37.
83. *Ibid.,* p. 38.
84. *Ibid.,* p. 39.

The secretary's function was to record the proceedings of the Academy. The position was "perpetual"; only death could remove the incumbent from office. The Academicians may already have had enough of Mézerai by the time of Conrart's death in 1675. He was, however, the logical choice. Yet only twelve members attended the meeting at which the election was to take place—not a quorum. At the next session Mézerai was recorded as having been unanimously elected; he personally recorded the election. It had been by voice vote, and no one had dared express his disapproval. Immediately after this election the Academy's first act was to change its rules from election by voice vote to election by secret ballot, providing still another indication of the opposition that Mézerai's conduct had inspired.[85]

In his various academic labors, Mézerai never developed coherent procedures for completing the dictionary. Hopelessly lost in revisions and sunk in spiteful lassitude after years of pursuing conflicting, even contradictory aims, he nevertheless continued as the principal compiler of the dictionary until 1672. Controversies raged over the project. Later these political machinations ceased in the face of Mézerai's stubbornness and his virtually complete control of the proceedings.[86]

Yet matters could not come to a head as long as Mézerai's personal patron and the Academy's protector, Chancellor Séguier, retained some control over nominations to vacant chairs. His death in January 1672 made it possible for Colbert to alter fundamentally the proceedings and general tone of the French Academy.[87] For the efficient minister the dictionary literally embodied French order and grandeur; he did everything possible to improve it and hasten its completion. After asking his assistant, Charles Perrault, to stand for election to the Academy, Colbert made it clear to the Academicians that the Crown wanted to exercise strong leadership in the Academy. Then, in order to press on with the dictionary, Colbert ordered that writing boxes, candles, firewood, and a clock be installed in the room where the Academicians worked,[88] to inspire them to work faster. As if these changes were not enough, a system of distributing silver *jetons* or tokens was instituted to provide a daily payment to each member attending the sessions.

With pressure from Colbert increasing, it soon became apparent that Mézerai would lose his control over the dictionary. Researching the

85. *Ibid.*, p. 72.

86. *Ibid.*, p. 97.

87. Charles Perrault, *Mémoires de ma vie*, ed. Paul Bonnefon (Paris, 1909), p. 96.

88. The Academy had been meeting in quarters provided by Séguier; now it moved to the Louvre, the residence of its new protector.

precise ways in which this was done would shed little light on Mézerai's career as a historiographer royal,[89] but the repercussions of this battle may have influenced his behavior during the last decade of his life. Isolated from the social activities and small talk in which the Academicians all indulged, Mézerai continued his arbitrary way of recording the academic minutes. Indeed, he recorded those decisions that he approved and ignored the others. He would respond to the isolation, if not downright ostracism, which he had at least in part brought upon himself, by seeking the companionship of a cabaret keeper on the edge of the city.

The stormy events of the 1670s in the Academy had been only the public aspect of a more private struggle between Mézerai and the dispensers of royal patronage. The carefully preserved minutes of Mézerai's letters to patrons and potential patrons record the adversities that a man of letters could suffer.[90] During the Fronde, numerous men of letters had almost frantically searched for patrons; and, like Descartes, Saumaise, and many others, Mézerai had sought and gained support from foreign princes. As early as 1652 he also sent Gaston d'Orléans a frank appeal for a pension in return for dedicating to him volume 4 of his *Histoire* (which never appeared).[91]

This casting about for a patron eventually led him back to Mazarin, for his Frondeur sympathies seem to have been less strong than his desire for money. Daniel de Larroque, his eighteenth-century biog-

89. Beaulieux, p. 21. The *Observations sur l'orthographe*, which Mézerai prepared and on which other Academicians gave their opinions, probably served to restore the influence of other members of the Academy over the preparation of the dictionary. Several members indisputably possessed a firmer grip than Mézerai on the linguistic and stylistic principles to be followed. The critics of this text—including Pellisson, Charles Perrault, and Chapelain—rejected Mézerai's work, while attempting to remain courteous and constructive (*ibid.*, p. 123).

90. The letters addressed to Sublet de Noyers, B.N., mss. fr. 20796, fol. 44, reflect the earlier state of affairs.

91. After admitting that in this volume he wished to "donner des marques de ma soumission [to Gaston] et de mon zèle ne passe pas par une preuve de mon indiscretion, ce qui redouble ma crainte c'est que depuis que j'ay eu l'honneur d'envoyer ce petit projet à Vostre Altesse, je n'y ai aucune nouvelles, et comme je connais le peu de mérite de cet ouvrage, j'ay fini de croire qu'il n'aura pas trouvé un acceuil favorable" (Paris, 7 September 1652, *ibid.*, fol. 293). This letter could have been addressed to one of the other princes, but a reference to a *palais* (Luxembourg?) suggests that it was intended for Gaston d'Orléans.

rapher, remarked about Mézerai's desire to accumulate wealth;[92] so did Charles-Auguste Sainte-Beuve.[93] Thus by 1653 or 1654, Mézerai had established a fairly intimate relationship with the Cardinal. He claimed as much in a letter written to Louis XIV rather soon after Mazarin's death in 1660. Contemporaries were always quick to assert that Séguier had been the source of Mézerai's twelve-hundred-livre pension and favor, but this may not in fact have been entirely the case.[94] He claimed that Mazarin had not only read his history but had taken the trouble to point out certain corrections that ought to be made in a subsequent edition.[95] The letter to Louis was an appeal for money, and it is tempting to assert that Mézerai was exaggerating his favor with Mazarin in order to impress the inexperienced King. But Mézerai asserts that Claude Auvry, Bishop of Coutances; Toussaint Rose, Louis XIV's personal secretary; and Jean de Silhon, Mazarin's secretary, would all testify to Mazarin's interest in the new edition of the *Histoire*. It is therefore virtually certain that Mézerai did in fact establish a relationship with the Cardinal, a relationship that was even more intimate and possibly exerted more influence upon his historical writing than had his association with Richelieu. Mézerai would never have dared appeal to Auvry, Rose, and Silhon about a matter that was untrue. After all, they had been very intimate and influential members of Mazarin's household and one of them, Rose, continued in the service of Louis XIV.

Throughout the 1650s and 1660s and right up to his death in 1672, Chancellor Séguier also continued to be one of Mézerai's patrons. In addition, in Séguier's circle Mézerai continued to play a minor political role as an informer, which may have provoked Colbert's suspicions.

92. Larroque, p. 93.

93. Charles-Auguste Sainte-Beuve, *Les causeries du lundi*, 3d ed. (Paris, n.d.), vol. 8, p. 229.

94. *Lettres de Jean Chapelain*, ed. Philippe Tamizey de Larroque (Paris, 1880–1883), vol. 2, p. 35.

95. "Aussy, feu Monseigneur le Cardinal, ne croyant pas indigne de ses soings une chose si importante à la gloire de Votre Majesté, et à l'honneur de la France, avoit bien voulu prendre la peine le lire et de considerer ces volumes, et ce grand génie aussy esclairé qu'infatiguable, ayant recognu ce qui manquoit à la beauté et à la symmetrie d'un si laborieux dessein, m'avoit ordonné de quelle sorte il en faloit reparer les fautes, et ce que je devois y adjouster pour le metre en sa perfection. A quoy ayant travaillé durant quatre ans suivant les ordres de S.E., et luy en ayant fait voir le nouveau plan, et une partie de la composition, il avoit eu la bonté de penser à m'obtenir un fond de Vostre Majesté" (B.N., mss. fr. 20796, fol. 280).

Indeed, on 10 July 1664, during one of the moments when Colbert's power—and through him the King's—was being challenged by the effects of canceling *rentes*, Mézerai was reporting to Séguier about the mood of the assemblies at the Hôtel de Ville.[96] This same political crisis may have hastened Colbert's plans to launch a vast new project granting regular pensions to men of letters.

Chapelain, in the memorandum on the qualifications of men of letters prepared at Colbert's request in 1664, was quite favorable to Mézerai, though he did not recommend him for the special post of *historiographe du roi*, which was to be created for someone who would help Louis to write his memoirs. Instead, Chapelain summed up what he thought to be the principal characteristics of the man and his work:

> Son stile n'est non plus mauvais; quoi qu'il pût être plus naturel
> et plus soutenu. Il y auroit à craindre qu'à force de vouloir se
> montrer libre dans les jugemens et dans les partis qu'il prend et
> qu'il épouse facilement, il ne panchât vers le Satirique, et ne fît
> tort aux particuliers en voulant instruire le public. Il ne paroit pas
> toujours équitable aux Puissances, et s'érige de lui-même en juge
> sévère des actions et les desseins des Grands, sans songer s'il
> a assez de lumières et d'authorité pour cela. C'est néanmoins le
> meilleur de nos compilateurs français.[97]

Acting upon this assessment and on the other recommendations, perhaps from Auvry and Rose, Colbert decided to grant Mézerai the highest pension (four thousand livres) to be received by any man of letters, French or foreign, in the great round of patronage donations undertaken dramatically in 1664. From 1664 through 1670, Mézerai continued to be the highest-paid writer in the service of the Crown.[98]

Why did he receive such a large sum? Colbert may have feared the pen of the alleged Frondeur, who had ties to Séguier and who controlled the preparation of the dictionary. A high pension might reduce the tendency to independent judgments that had worried Chapelain. On the other hand, the Fronde was past and Mézerai had shown no sign of insubordination once he had sought Mazarin's favor. An alter-

96. Evans, p. 66.

97. "Mémoire sur quelques gens de Lettres," Denis-François Camusat, ed., *Mélanges littéraires tirés des lettres de M. Jean Chapelain de l'Académie françoise* (Paris, 1749), pp. 240–242.

98. Chapelain received three thousand livres, and Denis II Godefroy received thirty-six hundred livres, second only to the pension granted Mézerai (*Lettres, instructions et mémoires de Colbert*, ed. Pierre Clément [Paris, 1868], vol. 5, pp. 466–480).

native explanation might be that Colbert—who sincerely believed in the importance of the Academy's project to prepare a dictionary for the increased *gloire* of French language and culture—may have increased the regular sum due a historiographer in recognition of Mézerai's labors on the dictionary.[99] The remarks after Mézerai's name on the pension lists do not support this second contention, however, since they refer only to compensation for his historical writings.[100] The question of why Mézerai's pension was higher than anyone else's may never be answered. It must nevertheless be borne in mind for the light it may shed on Colbert's behavior at the time of Mézerai's fall from favor.

L'Abrégé chronologique, ou extrait de l'histoire de France began to appear in 1667; the third volume, which turned out to be the last, appeared in February 1668.[101] The book had therefore been on the market for only a year when, according to Larroque, Colbert's son Seignelay reported that he had been pleased to learn about the origin of the gabelle, tailles, and other taxes from reading Mézerai. Colbert decided to read the passages about taxes himself, possibly suspecting something from his son's report. He found that Mézerai's account of the origins of these taxes did not accord with royal policy. Upon making this discovery, Larroque continues, Colbert requested that Charles Perrault go to Mézerai and inform him "que le Roi ne luy avoit pas donné une pension de 4,000 livres pour écrire avec si peu de retenuë: que ce prince respectoit trop la vérité pour exiger de ses Historiographes qu'ils la deguisassent par des motifs de crainte ou d'esperance; mais qu'il ne pretendait pas aussi qu'ils dussent se donner la licence de reflechir sans necessité sur la conduite de ses Ancêtres, et sur une politique établie depuis longtemps, et confirmée par les suffrages de toute la nation."[102] Although Larroque's account of the incident should not be trusted completely, it is supported by a letter from Mézerai to Colbert, dated 31 January 1669.[103] After humbly apologizing, Mézerai states: "Ce que

99. Beaulieux, p. 20.

100. For example, on the pension list for 1665: "Pour les ouvrages d'histoire qu'il a composés et compose journellement" (*Lettres de Colbert*, vol. 4, p. 469).

101. A *privilège* had been granted back in 1653. As with the folio history, Mézerai projected a fourth volume to bring the narrative down to his own day. Colbert's disfavor may have definitively discouraged Mézerai from preparing this fourth volume.

102. Larroque, p. 37.

103. Mézerai must have immediately written one letter of apology that has been lost. The 10 January letter is referred to as the second (*Lettres de Colbert*, vol. 5, p. 522).

m'a dit M. Perrault de vostre part a esté un terrible coup de foudre qui m'a rendu tout à fait immobile et qui m'a osté tout sentiment, hormis celuy d'une extrême douleur de vous avoir déplu."[104]

Colbert's "coup de foudre" had come either in late 1668 or in January 1669, at a time when Mézerai's control over the preparation of the dictionary had already begun to weaken. In this incident, all he could do was promise Colbert a corrected edition of the *Abrégé* that would, he assured him, quickly displace the first one in the eyes of the public. To be certain that no further mishaps would occur, Mézerai proposed bringing his corrected pages to Perrault before they were set in type: "C'est dans cette disposition, Monseigneur, que j'ay prié M. Perrault de vous assurer que je suis prest à passer l'éponge sur les endroits que vous jugerez dignes de censure dans mon livre . . . je veux employer tous mes efforts et si peu de talent que Dieu m'a donné pour faire connoistre à toute la terre que vous n'avez jamais fait de créature qui soit à vous par un attachement plus véritable."[105]

The oral reprimand transmitted by Perrault had alluded to Mézerai's four-thousand-livre pension; but not until 16 March 1672—over two years after the incident—did Mézerai again write Colbert, ostensibly to thank him for his pension, but really to complain that it had been reduced from four thousand to two thousand livres.[106] In this letter Mézerai began by pointing out that Colbert had cut back on a commitment originally made by Mazarin, an argument designed to soften Colbert, who held the late Cardinal in great respect.[107] The letter is full of bitterness and self-pity; Mézerai reports that he has been working as rapidly as possible on the revised edition of the *Abrégé* and that he has been submitting his revisions to Perrault.

The conjuncture of events is apparent, for it was also in 1671–1672 that Colbert, through Perrault, had taken virtual control of the French Academy and had broken Mézerai's hold over the preparation of the dictionary. Still more revealing of the relationship between the Crown and men of letters is the fact that Colbert did not cut the pension until

104. *Ibid.*

105. *Ibid.*

106. *Ibid.*, p. 537. The cut appears in the lists for the first time under 1671, but presumably the pensions for that year were not paid until the first months of 1672.

107. B.N., mss. fr. n.a. 6237, fol. 38. His pension for 1661 is recorded as thirty-six hundred livres in B.N. mss. fr. 22216, fol. 216. We should recall that Colbert had served as Mazarin's *intendant* in the 1650s and was probably familiar with the names of those who had received pensions from the Cardinal.

the death of Mézerai's and the Academy's protector and patron, the venerable Chancellor Séguier, in January 1672. Mézerai had been left with no one to intervene on his behalf with Colbert, for he had alienated his colleagues in the Academy and through Séguier's death had lost his remaining support from the previous generation of ministers. Furthermore, in order to pay for the increased military costs entailed by conflicts with the Dutch, Colbert may already have begun to scrutinize every budget to see where savings could be made. Indeed, as a result of the war, the total amount allocated annually for pensions to men of letters—which had been averaging over one hundred thousand livres prior to the war—dropped to about eighty thousand livres for the year 1672 (paid in early 1673) and decreased still further to sixty-two thousand livres for 1674.[108] It is clear that Mézerai's pension was cut along with those of many others.

The second edition of the *Abrégé* appeared in 1672. It apparently pleased no one, least of all Colbert, for Mézerai's name disappears altogether from the pension list for 1673.[109] Larroque records the event: "Par malheur cela ne servit ni le public ni le ministre; le premier parce qu'il étoit sacrifié à la politique, et le second parce qu'il remarqua que l'auteur avoit plus pensé à pallier sa faute qu'à la réparer. Le mépris où tomba cette édition qui n'a pu encore s'en relever, auroit dû persuader à M. Colbert que les corrections étoient sincères."[110]

Bayle made essentially the same remark, adding that the first edition of the *Abrégé* is always much sought after and sells for more than the others, for it contains the censured material.[111] Mézerai's revisions had pleased neither Colbert nor the public, and he was dropped from all further royal subsidy. He had money enough, but the humiliation caused him to become increasingly "bizarre." The passages that led to so much difficulty deserve a closer look before we can attempt some general assessment of Mézerai as a historian.

A tradition at least as old as Budé's *De asse* had permitted men of

108. *Lettres de Colbert*, vol. 5, p. 582. It is interesting to note that royal building expenditures (p. 583) dropped at approximately the same rate as the pensions, again as a result of the war. Losing one's pension during wartime did not necessarily mean a break in the relationship. Claude de Bullion, Superintendent of Finances, took Chapelain's pension away, though the latter remained in favor (*Lettres de Chapelain*, vol. 1, p. 91).

109. *Lettres de Colbert*, vol. 5, p. 485.

110. Larroque, p. 39.

111. Pierre Bayle, *Dictionnaire critique et historique* (Amsterdam, 1730), vol. 1, p. 225.

letters to rail against the evils of the tax collectors,[112] and more especially the tax farmers, those *gabelleurs* and *maltôtiers* who provided the focus for so much hatred in periods of rebellion. But if this tradition had persisted down to the 1660s—which is dubious, in view of the very different political climate following the Fronde—it was still less brazen than what Mézerai presented. He pointed out the "tricks" used by French kings to collect taxes. The distinction between practices and rights was fundamental. The one may still tolerably have been open to criticism, but the other was not. Yet Mézerai's history of taxation was not so much constitutionalist or antiabsolutist as irreverent. He did not attempt to do the research that an *érudit* would undertake in order to find documents supporting his contention that tricks had been played on the French by their kings.

In his last years Mézerai fell into what Larroque calls a "profonde lassitude." Refusing to work despite the coercion of his publisher, he seems to have withdrawn from his few remaining contacts and associated almost exclusively with his friend, Faucheur, the cabaret keeper. When death overtook him on 10 July 1683,[113] his heart was interred in a special monument for that purpose in the Carmelite monastery of Les Billettes in the Marais. The epitaph read: "Icy devant repose le coeur de François Eudes de Mézerai, historiographe de France, sécrétaire perpetuel de l'Académie Françoise. Ce coeur, après sa foi vive en Jésus-Christ, n'eut rien de plus cher que l'amour de sa patrie. Il fut constamment ami des bons, irreconciliable ennemi des méchants; ses écrits rendront témoignage à la postérité de l'excellence et de la liberté de son esprit, amateur de la vérité, incapable de flatterie, et qui, sans aucune affectation de plaire, s'était uniquement proposé de servir à l'utilité publique."[114] The simplicity of this prose contrasts with the sonorous elegiac Latin verses found on the tombs of many of his fellow men of letters. Jules-Étienne-Joseph Quicherat observed about Mézerai that "there was something about him that was Roman, and of the philosopher of Diogenes's sect."[115]

112. For example, these themes of outrage against corrupt practices are reiterated in Postel. Cf. William Bouwsma, *Concordia Mundi: The Career and Thought of Guillaume Postel (1510–1581)* (Cambridge, Mass., 1957), p. 268. It is interesting to note that Postel also was affiliated with the Collège Sainte-Barbe.

113. Larroque published Mézerai's last will and testament, pp. 98–109. See the copy in B.N., mss. fr. 22222, fols. 220 ff.

114. B.N., *Cabinet des titres*, 1957, fol. 8. Evans, p. 82, does not include the name and offices in his transcription.

115. Ruhlmann, p. 72. See Charpentier to Huet, 30 August 1683, for an

Colbert, whose withdrawal of Mézerai's pension had greatly contributed to the historiographer's embitterment, died only two months
later.

---

early, if not the earliest account of the details about Mézerai's last will and
the anecdotes about the money he had sealed up in a paper that was to be
reserved for renting a place on the Place de la Greve to watch the first
hanging of a *gros maltotier* (B.N., mss. fr. 15189, fol. 76).

Chapter VIII
Pellisson-Fontanier:
From Protestant Judge to
Historiographer Royal

T H E predominant moral and political ideas about heroes and monarchy inherited from the sixteenth century[1] gave form to the literature of praise and the historicized cult of Louis XIV almost from the moment of his God-given conception and his birth.[2] The showering of compliments, the allusions to the stars and what they portend, and the variety of ethical and political teachings ranging from covert Machiavellism to neostoicism to refurbished medieval commonplaces, all sustained the ideal that the prince must set an example by his piety, charity, and justice. Though specific ethical teachings varied, there was universal agreement concerning the manner in which the prince should be taught and the definitions of his place in the world and of divine favor upon France.

The histories commissioned by Chapelain and personally paid for by Louis through Colbert were merely an elaboration of these conceits about princely conduct. The tendency to fuse the genres of panegyric and history had been built into a literary culture that revered the ancient rhetoricians. The classical age, like the humanist one before it, was made up of men working faithfully to fuse the literary and political cultures into one unified, coherent whole that would bring immortality to both writers and sovereigns.

1. Françoise Joukovsky, *La gloire dans la poésie française et néolatine du XVIe siècle* (Geneva, 1969). Note particularly the extension of the idea of *gloire* so that it may be compared to an "impérissable substance divine" (p. 583).
2. The best work on the literary culture and its relation to the Monarchy, and Louis XIV in particular, remains Georges Lacour-Gayet, *L'éducation politique de Louis XIV* (Paris, 1923), where the discussion of most if not all of the contours of humanist mirror-of-princes literature, the role of preceptors, and court politics demonstrates the continuities of sixteenth-century and pre-sixteenth-century patterns of elitist thought and action down to the mid-seventeenth century.

In the mid-seventeenth century centers of parlementaire and aristocratic thought and culture still survived, if somewhat diminished, and implicitly encouraged opposition to the absolutist views of monarchy and French society. Efforts at finding historical precedents to support the claims of the robe and the *grands* to power and status dwindled, however, because increasingly fewer members of the literate elite perceived French political culture in a constitutional perspective. Put another way, even if incontrovertible proof had been presented in 1630 to show that the Frankish kings had pledged to uphold the privileges of some assembly of their subjects, or those of a warrior nobility, such proof would scarcely have provoked a shift away from absolutism. History as the legal brief of the French constitution had few adherents during the century separating François Hotman from Henri de Boulainvilliers and Montesquieu; nor was research into the antiquity of the French language still aimed primarily at proving that French was as old as Greek or Latin, or equally pure in its pristine state. Long before 1600 interest had shifted to reforming and "purifying" the existing language, for reviving old French had never been a serious alternative. Histories of illustrious houses, towns, and parlements served to enhance the reputations of their members, but rarely did these accounts attempt to provide a foundation for an argument on behalf of limiting royal power.

More vital as a source for critical perspective on the Monarchy and on the histories that glossed over royal weaknesses was the intense partisanship caused by the ministerial turmoil during the reign of Louis XIII. The collapse of the party of the *dévots* turned such men as Matthieu de Morgues into embittered writers of contemporary history.[3] The historical genre and the politically partisan tract could be fused as easily as panegyric and history. Moreover, owing to the peculiar nature of ministerial government, the King was praised as frequently in the tracts written to oppose his policies as in the panegyrics written on his behalf, since the venom was aimed at such royal ministers as Richelieu and Mazarin, or such foreigners as Marie de Médicis and Anne of Austria. The more intense the partianship—and the Fronde is a case in point—the higher Louis XIV's actions and image were elevated above those of ordinary mortals, a phenomenon that began while he was still a boy.

Protestant parties and, to a lesser degree, the Jansenists, also pos-

3. William F. Church, *Richelieu and Reason of State* (Princton, 1972), part 3; and Donald A. Bailey, "Writers against the Cardinal: A Study of the Pamphlets which Attacked the Person and Policies of Cardinal Richelieu during the Decade 1630–1640," Ph.D. dissertation, University of Minnesota, 1973, *passim.*

sessed sufficient vitality to stimulate the writing of history from these political-religious perspectives, though by the beginning of Louis XIV's personal reign occasional works and tracts constituted the only attempts to recount the past from the perspectives of these parties. The Jansenists never subscribed to a revived historical account of the "ancient constitution," and parlementaires like Claude Joly never raised their heads above the Hotmanesque legal-historical framework to include providential elements about a pristine church in Augustinian times. The cleavages were deep within what has sometimes been viewed as a single robe-bourgeois, religious-political movement.[4] As we shall see, Protestant and Jansenist historiographies exerted their own peculiar attractions upon Bayle and Racine, but in no way did they provide a generally accepted critical perspective on the King or his policies, at least until the opening of the violent hostilities against both Huguenots and Port-Royalists during the personal reign, and by then it was too late. Protestant "histories" came to be read solely by French Protestants, Englishmen, and Dutchmen; the "public" of literate Frenchmen who helped establish the literary reputations of authors and books ignored them.[5]

The literature of praise, contemporary history, and fictionalized memoirs and histories seemed to resemble each other more and more during the 1660s and 1670s. After having been a strong partisan of the princes and of Cardinal Retz, Saint-Réal turned to writing *Don Carlos* (1672), which Bayle called "une nouvelle historique ou roman." Very well received, this work, and the works of Antoine Varillas, Courtilz de Sandras, and the political testaments of Richelieu and Colbert, all reflect a generation's lack of interest in historiographical controversies and interest in careful, lucid accounts of events and persons.[6]

Don Carlos, a courtly history about real events and people, was intended to edify the reader through the examples of depravity and/or virtue that it presented. Yet the fictional elements in the work and the genre it represented seemed in no way to interfere with these purposes, which, in a classicistic culture, had been conventionally defined as iden-

4. Lucien Goldman, *The Hidden God: A Study of Tragic Vision in the "Pensées" of Pascal and the "Tragedies" of Racine*, trans. Philip Thody (New York, 1964), part. 2.

5. Bossuet's very well-received *Histoire des variations des églises protestantes* (Paris, 1688), like Maimbourg's *Histoire du Calvinisme* (Paris, 1682), consolidated the Gallican perspective and filled the void left by the ill-received or long-silent Huguenot historians who attracted little public attention after Agrippa d'Aubigné's *Histoire universelle*, published between 1616 and 1620.

6. Gustave Dulong, *L'Abbé de Saint-Réal* (Paris, 1921), p. 165.

tical to those of history. Popular as much for its bold literary style as for the macabre subject of Phillip II's alleged murder of his son by poison, the fictional elements, like the speeches in the histories written by the ancients, were seen as neither ahistorical nor anachronistic, but merely as support for powerful, "true" events of past human experiences that stimulated the readers' emotions.[7] Almost any "liberty" could be taken by a writer of history in the seventeenth century, as long as his style was agreeable and his work helped transport readers back into remote times. But political partisanship inspired either by such conflicts as the Day of the Dupes or by international rivalries did not generally stimulate new critical perspectives or impede the creation of a flawless, historicized image of the king. In fact, quite the opposite might have been the case owing to the necessity of proving one's loyalty as a Frenchman and one's fidelity to one's king before attacking policies that were ostensibly the consequence of bad advice from evil councillors. Ministerial government had had the long-run effect of removing the king from history and of increasingly linking his actions with France and with the divine.

Early Career

While elusive and enigmatic at points, Paul Pellisson-Fontanier's career and historical writing reveal how the social, religious, and to a certain extent intellectual foundations for a historian's independence and detachment vis-à-vis his king could be rejected in favor of dependence on Louis and willingness to write his history. With more or less intensity, and reflecting differences in social or religious background, the careers of many other writers of the age of classicism follow the same path toward Versailles taken by Pellisson. Pellisson possessed all save one of the available social and religious foundations for independence if not hostility to the King: high aristocratic birth. He had been raised a Huguenot in one of the leading learned robe families of Castres, which at the time served as a Protestant legal capital because Henry IV had seated a *chambre de l'édit* in the town. As a court especially created for Protestant litigants who believed they could not obtain justice from the other royal courts owing to the predominance of Catholic judges,

7. Dulong observed that in all the accounts of the Don Carlos affair by seventeenth-century French historians, a cleavage exists between those entirely favorable to Philip and those completely unfavorable to him. Dulong suggests how the *dévot* and anti-*dévot* parties and their corresponding views of Spain remained attractive subjects to both historians and the public (*ibid.*, pp. 122 f.).

the *chambre de l'édit* was a source of pride for robe Protestants and continued to attract the more strongly Protestant sons of the robe to a court where they were assured numerical superiority. Pellisson's father had been instrumental in establishing the court in which he subsequently served after his legal training at the University of Toulouse, a faculty that had counted Bodin and Cujas among its members in the sixteenth century.

The legal humanists' approach to history seems to have held little attraction for young Pellisson. Instead, he learned how to "ride and study law."[8] Despite his passion for reading novels and writing verse, he "always came back to *my* Cicero and *my* Terence, which I found much more sensible."[9] Received into the houses of some of the great parlementaire families of Toulouse and a friend of Pierre de Fermat, he remained fixed in the study of the classics, like many other Frenchmen who eventually would migrate to Paris. As an early adolescent student, his four favorite books were Cicero's *Eight Orations*, Sirmond's *Coup d'Etat*, Balzac's *Lettres*, and Queen Marguerite of Navarre's *Mémoires*, a list suggesting that Pellisson had already become preoccupied with the movement to infuse classical form and thought into works written in French. He described how he had read Marguerite's *Mémoires* twice in one night from one end to the other, after which he began "not only to cease scorning the French language but even to love it passionately and to study it with care, and to believe even as I do today [1652] that with genius, time, and work, it could be rendered capable of everything."[10] Pellisson's emotional commitment to French in no way implied a rejection of Greek or Latin. Quite the contrary. The men of letters of his generation answered the appeals of Estienne, Pasquier, and the humanist movement in general to reform French by holding up the works of the ancients, particularly Latin grammar and rhetoric, as models for the reform. Joining that movement rather than settling back in scholastic theology or neo-Bartolist jurisprudence[11] or philological studies of early French law signified

8. François L. Marcou, *Etude sur la vie et les oeuvres de Pellisson* (Paris, 1859), p. 10.

9. *Ibid.*, p. 9.

10. *Relation contenant l'histoire de l'Académie française*, subsequently expanded by Pierre-Joseph Thorellier d'Olivet and republished as *L'histoire de l'Académie française*, ed. Charles L. Livet (Paris, 1858), *passim*; and Marcou, p. 13.

11. He announced in a speech to the Academy in 1652: "J'ai toûjours regardé l'art de bien écrire, comme la fin et le dernier but de tous mes travaux (*Discours, harangues et autres pièces d'éloquence de Messieurs de l'Académie françoise* [Amsterdam, 1699], p. 7).

adherence to the general heritage of sixteenth-century humanism, of which classicism was the fulfillment.

At nineteen Pellisson published his first book, a French "paraphrase" of the first book of Justinian's *Institutes*.[12] The question of just how the ancient Romans interpreted the *Institutes* is implicit in the text, in a manner similar to Pasquier's approach in the translation of the same work that he prepared for his children. The principal interest for both translators lies elsewhere, however, in subtly deriving from the text moral and political truths that will edify readers. That Pellisson dared publish such a familiar Latin text in French is testimony to both his abilities and his courage at a young age. His chief concern was whether French was capable of conveying the meanings and nuances of so famous a Latin text. Could he inspire admiration for a French rendition of a text that had so long been reputed entirely admirable in Latin? Although the book went through only two editions,[13] it won Pellisson the respect of both younger and older men of letters. Chapelain later remembered it with favor when he wrote his assessment of Pellisson in the "Liste des gens de lettres" prepared for Colbert in 1662.[14]

There is a story that Pellisson abandoned his career in the court of Castres because the scars left by smallpox prompted the other judges to laugh at his ugliness every time he spoke.[15] There seems to be no way of discovering whether the story is true, but it is clear that by the time Pellisson had completed his studies in Toulouse, he was already aware that Paris was the center of literary activity. Castres may not have seemed very exciting after Toulouse, provincial though that city was; yet it is clear that after Pellisson had definitively abandoned the south for Paris, he eagerly sought news about current legal and literary happenings there and in no way abandoned his family or those friends who had stayed behind.[16]

Pellisson's reception as a young man of letters from the provinces into a relatively open and ebullient literary society occurred through the protection of his fellow Protestant, Conrart.[17] As one of the principal founders of the French Academy and a sought-after *saloniste*,

12. Published anonymously by Sommaville and Courbé, 1645.

13. The second was published by the Compagnie des libraires of Paris in 1664.

14. Denis-François Camusat, ed., *Mélanges littéraires tirés des lettres de M. Jean Chapelain de l'Académie françoise* (Paris, 1749), p. 249.

15. R. Peter, "Pellisson," A. Pauphilet et al., *Dictionnaire des lettres françaises, XVIIᵉ siècle* (Paris, 1954), p. 793.

16. See particularly his correspondence with Doneville in Marcou, pp. 439–485.

17. René Kerviler, *Valentin Conrart* (Paris, 1881), pp. 174 ff.

Conrart not only put Pellisson in touch with every literary and scholar-ly group in Paris, but also made stylistic criticisms of his poems and essays. By early 1651, Pellisson had written a friend in Toulouse that Furetière was his "intimate" friend and that an ode he had written was being read by his "masters" in poetry, Conrart, Gombault, and Chapelain.[18]

In Conrart's milieu, and certainly as a result of Conrart's contacts, Pellisson had an opportunity to become familiar with the heritage of learning and the vestiges of late-sixteenth-century religious and polit-ical controversy. For example, although Conrart admired Charron's *Sagesse*, he admitted that it was dangerous for young readers.[19] In 1646, Conrart eagerly cooperated in an effort to publish a life of Fra Paolo Sarpi[20] and a new edition of his great history; and he could still become excited over the historiographical controversies regarding Joan of Arc. After noting that du Haillan and Lipsius had written about her from the perspective of "declared enemies," Conrart serenely deferred to Pasquier's refutation of the assertion that Joan had been a "débauchée" and continued: "Quant à moy, Monsieur [Rivet], je ne la voudrais pas faire passer pour une sainte, ni jurer que sa vocation a esté miraculeuse; mais je trouve bien sa valeur, sa conduite es ses actions admirables. Comme bon François, je revère sa mémoire."[21]

Other elements of the sixteenth-century historiographical and ideo-logical perspectives might also be mentioned, but these examples suf-fice to demonstrate that in Paris Pellisson could have built upon his robe and Huguenot heritage had he chosen to do so.

As a founder of the Academy, a critic, and a writer, Conrart held the esteem of both the writers and the men of power of his generation (he was born in 1603); in addition, he possessed the gift of being able to cultivate intimate friendships with persons much younger than he. In a letter of September 1650, Conrart had referred to Pellisson as one of his "intimate friends."[22] Pellisson was infatuated with the long hours of conversation, the reading of Conrart's Italian books,[23] and above all a milieu in which literature and politics were combined.

18. Letters to Doneville, December 1650 and January 1651 (Marcou, pp. 456 and 459). During this same period, Pellisson mentioned that he was sending Furetière's *Mercure burlesque* to Fermat, another indication that he had in no way rejected those who had impressed and perhaps helped him most in Toulouse (p. 460).

19. Kerviler, p. 300.

20. *Ibid.*, pp. 316–319.

21. February 1647, *ibid.*, p. 341.

22. *Ibid.*, p. 555.

23. January 1651, *ibid.*, p. 460.

His letters to a friend back home record his growth as a man of letters; they are models of literary style in themselves, an eloquent *badinage* worthy of a place of honor in the humanistic epistolary tradition. At one point, in an anecdote about Pasquier, who apparently criticized a judge for filling his speeches with Latin and Greek citations, one of the leading *érudits* of the sixteenth century is made to speak on behalf of eloquence and concentration of thought, and against pedantry.[24] At another, Pellisson remarked that the subject matter of the great literary works of the ancients actually was very meager, and he held up the *Iliad* and the *Aeneid* as examples. This ideal of a great literary work written with almost nothing as a "fondement" appealed to the men of Pellisson's generation, and it went hand in hand with a revulsion against controversies and attention to minute details.

Pellisson had also been reading political works, the *Journal de Richelieu* and Saint-Evremond's *Apologie de Beaufort*; but in almost every instance his comments about these works are stylistic. About the *Journal* he observed: "J'ai pris plaisir à y voir les bagatelles des grands et du cabinet, qui ne sont quelquefois que celles des bourgeois et du vulgaire. J'y ai vu aussy avec plaisir, melé pourtant de quelque sorte d'indignation, combien il y avoit alors de personnes qui luy [Richelieu] vendaient le secret de leurs maîtres et de leurs amis."[25] From the early allusions to such works as Sirmond's *Coup d'Etat* and from these ambivalent remarks about court politics, it seems plausible to suggest that in adolescence Pellisson had been psychologically prepared for a career of loyal service to a minister or to his king.

The work that turned Pellisson from simply a promising writer to a well-established one was his *Relation contenant l'histoire de l'Académie Française*. Published anonymously in 1652, and ostensibly addressed to a relative in the south, it was an immediate success. Conrart had suggested the topic and furnished the personal details about the Academy's founding. The style, the mixture of praise and criticism, as well as the level of fact or detail included in the narrative, were certainly Pellisson's own. Members of the Academy were so impressed that they voted Pellisson the next vacant seat with a proviso that this anticipated election would not constitute a precedent.

The work is a *relation* in every sense of the term, rather than a history. Through its informal style, its use of the first person, and its inclusion of "banal" or personal details—all of which were considered unworthy of history but acceptable in a *relation*—it reveals what men of letters wanted to believe about themselves and their function in

24. May 1651, *ibid.*, p. 472.
25. July 1650, *ibid.*, p. 447.

society during the years after the Fronde. The older humanist tradition of simply praising the character and achievements of leading men of letters was inappropriate here, for most of these men were still living, and praising one would raise difficulties about the others. Thus, instead of following the pattern of lauding both men of power and men of letters or scholars—a tradition that dated from the reign of Francis I and the all-too-familiar *topoi* about that reign—Pellisson set out as eloquently as possible to narrate the founding of the Academy by implying that the early years had been a kind of golden age for those members still alive.[26] The account of these events in the history of *belles lettres*, Pellisson asserts, may be read with as much interest, utility, and profit as accounts of wars and affairs of state—a bold claim indeed for an age in which genres inherited from Antiquity still played an influential part in determining what was "worthy" of being recorded as history. Pellisson regrets that there are no histories about the men of letters writing in the days of Caesar Augustus and Maecenas. Thus he either ignores or does not bother to point out that in Antiquity the history of *belles lettres* did not exist as a genre at all.

Pellisson's skill as a historian is, however, most apparent on the delicate political questions concerning the Academy's foundation. What should be said about the "protector," Cardinal Richelieu? In the language of the seventeenth century, several expressions had developed that appeared to connote praise but actually signified neutrality. The two perhaps most frequently employed were "fameux" and "extraordinaire." Pellisson applied both to the Cardinal, thus ingeniously avoiding the issue of either praising or condemning Richelieu in the days when the Fronde had barely subsided.[27] On the ticklish question of whether the early members had wanted to accept the Cardinal's "protection" or had been obliged to do so, Pellisson states that this protection prompted fears because it might endanger the Academicians' positions with their "maîtres," the princely patrons. These patrons still had power: Jacques de Serizay, an early member, held an intendancy

26. *Relation* . . . , p. 9. It was a period in which "toute l'innocence et toute la liberté des premiers siècles, sans bruit et sans pompe, et sans autres lois que celles de l'amitié, ils goûtoient ensemble tout ce que la société des esprits et la vie raisonnable ont de plus doux et de plus charmant."

27. *Ibid.*, p. 14. The formal letters addressed to Richelieu by the nascent Academy are included in Pellisson's *Relation*. . . . They are an enfilade of *topoi* about how France had had a number of very courageous men whose value was unknown because of the weaknesses of the French language; but now that French was being pulled from among the other barbarous tongues, "tous nos voisins [le] parleroient bientôt, si nos conquêtes continuoient comme elles avoient commencée" (*ibid.*, p. 22).

in the Duke de la Rochefoucauld's household; Claude de Malleville was a secretary to Marshal Bassompierre, who had been imprisoned in the Bastille on the Cardinal's orders. If Pellisson's reporting is accurate, it is possible to infer that in the 1630s men of letters could scarcely conceive of independence from all "protectors." Their social position as they saw it was fundamentally one of dependence on the great. In other words, the notion that the intellectual, independent of his social origins, stood outside the political culture in order to criticize or support it had not yet developed in the *monde des lettrés*.[28]

More revealing, however, than the formal remarks is Pellisson's almost offhand observation that Richelieu loved the theater: "For everyone who felt as if he had some talent did not fail to work on the theater, because it was a way of approaching the *grands*."[29] In an age when outward serenity was de rigueur and published controversy scorned, this remark provides a clue to what must have been a broad and very sophisticated level of verbal discourse about the relationship between men of power and men of letters. This awareness of the influence that men of the pen and men of power exerted upon one another probably did not extend far beyond the Palais Cardinal, Conrart's rooms, and conversations among knots of Academicians leaving the Hôtel Séguier after a weekly meeting. But a glimpse into the higher level of political-cultural discourse makes us cautious about inferring that seventeenth-century men of letters lacked an awareness or a sensitivity about their place in society vis-à-vis men of power. Pellisson's remark is actually derisive if not contemptuous of his peers. He borders on the same tone when he observes that persons of "condition" had been elected to the Academy for no other reason than their social status and implies that from the beginning men like Conrart and Chapelain had drawn a distinction between the election of persons of "merit" and persons of "condition."[30]

28. Particularly illuminating on this question is Boisrobert's effort to lure Balzac into the Academy.

29. *Relation* . . . , p. 34. The sensitivity about noble status was joined with that passionate desire to present oneself to one's fellow Academicians in the best possible light. Pellisson cynically remarks concerning the discussions about privileges once the Academy's letters-patent had been prepared: "On eut ajouté aux autres privilèges, et en apparence facilement obtenu l'exemption des tailles: mais parce que tous les academiciens d'alors en étoient exempts ou par noblesse ou autrement, personne ne fut d'avis de la demander, de peur qu'il ne semblât en avoir besoin pour lui-même, et ils préférent un honneur asses imaginaire au solide et véritable intérêt de leurs successeurs."

30. *Ibid.*, p. 34.

If there was a rush from one genre to another as a consequence of changing fortunes or accidents of patronage, influence must also have been exerted on the precise definitions of the genres. Louis XIV and Colbert would be magnets that drew writers toward the genre of history, especially contemporary history, and toward the literature of praise. The balance had been leaning that way for much of the century. Pellisson may not only have been swept up by the King's designs to write history, he may also have been aware of that fact. Beyond this conjecture there is only enigma.

Pellisson defines history as a faithful report that must leave the moral judgments to the reader. At the point in his narrative where he offers this definition, he was still discussing the 1630s, that is, the period of the Academy's history before Richelieu's death. As Pellisson and Conrart together reviewed the older man's recollections, Conrart may have recalled the Richelieu-Chapelain exchange about whether moral judgments should be included in history. Though Pellisson came down firmly on Richelieu's side, Chapelain did not deign to renew an old controversy, despite the influence of Pellisson's book.[31] Questions of historical method had lost their attraction; almost any *obiter dicta* evoking the rules of the classical rhetoricians seemed acceptable. This failure to carry on a controversy is but one more example of how little the more formal questions of historical method had managed to break away from the general *topoi* about genre and style during the early-modern period.

In 1638, as Pellisson records it, the Academicians decided to draw up lists of the most celebrated writers of prose and poetry. The names themselves are not surprising, nor was their function as examples for the Academicians. Then, quite on his own, Pellisson added two names omitted by the Academy: Bodin and Pasquier. In this instance he seemed to be emphasizing one aspect of the heritage from the sixteenth century —legal humanism—that none of the Academicians had thought to include either explicitly or implicitly.[32]

In general, however, the *Relation* was delicately balanced between praise and the polite skirting of sensitive literary and political issues. The account of the quarrel over the *Cid* does not add to Richelieu's stature as a protector. At another point the Cardinal is held partly re-

31. Though Conrart and Chapelain were close friends, matters such as Conrart's role in the preparation of Pellisson's history may have piqued Chapelain. After all, Conrart must have known full well that Pellisson's definition of history as omitting moral judgments marked a point against Chapelain. The latter may have retaliated by failing to mention Pellisson's *Relation* about the Academy when he assessed Pellisson for Colbert.
32. *Relation*, p. 105.

sponsible for all the difficulties between the Academy and the Parlement of Paris. Had he not "pushed royal authority very high"?[33] The consequences could only be opposition from the Parlement, which viewed the Academy as but one more weapon against it in Richelieu's arsenal.[34] Pellisson is also harsh with the Parlement, for he recounts the two and a half years of delaying tactics adopted by the judges to prevent registering the Academy's letters-patent. In all of this Richelieu is depicted as effectively and quietly working to overcome the obstructionism of the judges. Pellisson ends the discussion, however, by quoting a humorous remark made by a judge (readers in 1657 had no difficulty substituting Scarron's name for the asterisks used to hide the judge's identity) who recalled that there was once an emperor who, having broken the power of the Roman Senate, consulted it on the question of what sauce might best accompany a large turbot he had received as a gift.[35] Thus the delicate balance essential to the success of a work published in 1653 is preserved. Indeed, the *Relation* reflected and epitomized the relationships between politics and protectors acceptable by the Academicians, who enjoyed the honor and wealth that men of power could bestow but who may also have implicitly regretted the golden age when liberty reigned supreme among friends.

With the exception of the great Corneille, the Academicians and their works are described soberly and without praise. Raised above all the others for having written the *Cid*, it was Corneille whom Pellisson selected as a hero and exemplar among his contemporaries. The tradition of praising men of letters so characteristic of humanist historical writing still exerted a dominant influence in determining how men of letters wanted to perceive themselves. By elevating Corneille exclusively, Pellisson avoided the touchy matter of having to praise all members of the Academy; and at the same time his decision probably reflected an implicit agreement among all Academicians over the illustrious achievements of the Norman dramatist.

Pellisson had implied that he possessed the necessary talent to assess the quality and probity of writers and their works. As the star of Nicolas Fouquet began to rise, it became evident that the talents of the one would be useful to the other. By 1657, Pellisson and his close friend, Madeleine de Scudéry, had become firmly established in Fou-

33. *Ibid.*, p. 41.

34. Urbain-Victor Châtelain, *Le Surintendant Nicolas Fouquet, protecteur des lettres, des arts et des sciences* (Paris, 1905), p. 144. Châtelain believes that the parlementaires were correct.

35. *Relation*, p. 46.

quet's household. *Le Remerciement du siècle à M. le surintendant Fouquet*, and *Le Remerciement à Mgr. le surintendant* demonstrated that Pellisson knew how to praise in both verse and prose. In addition, he had a sense of what Fouquet must do in order to become recognized as a great patron.[36] Fouquet set to work immediately, and by 1661 a flowering of literary creativity dedicated to the Superintendent had already appeared. Pellisson had been the "lieutenant" of the poets;[37] he had selected them and, in a sense, had set the standards for all whom Fouquet protected. For in the seventeenth century pensions alone did not stimulate the creative energies of writers. Rather, high standards, respect for one's critics, and an almost personal competition among writers contributed to regenerate old talents and train the young. Pellisson encouraged Corneille and Gombault to return to their verses;[38] and among the younger poets who were his friends he knew how to encourage those with the potential of La Fontaine and Molière. The esteem in which Pellisson was held by writers helped establish the critical boundaries of literature at Vaux-le-Vicomte, for try as he might, Fouquet could not do this himself.[39] Pellisson had assumed the role of intermediary between patron and writers that Boisrobert had earlier played under Richelieu, and he served as the model for the patronage system that Chapelain and Colbert subsequently put together almost immediately after Fouquet's arrest.

This literary culture of Vaux has merited attention here because, like the Academy, it placed no emphasis whatsoever upon the writing of history. Fouquet was not from an illustrious family that deserved research and discussion; his career in the Parlement had certainly not endeared him to those judges who still revered the "ancient constitution" and were devoted to legal humanism. Contemporary reasons motivating the writing of history were lacking. Fouquet, upon Pellisson's advice, had not sought to include the *doctes* or *érudits* in these literary circles, though some learned poets—Ménage is a good example—came into favor through their poetic talents. Johann Friedrich Gronovius, the

36. Châtelain, p. 120.

37. A contemporary poet wrote: "pour être passé en reveue / par notre lieutenant, le fameux Pellisson . . ." (*ibid.*, p. 121).

38. See Corneille's undated letter to Pellisson asking him to support his candidacy for a pension from Fouquet in *Oeuvres de Pierre Corneille*, ed. Charles Marty (Paris, 1862), vol. 10, p. 477.

39. An enigma, Fouquet nevertheless showed himself capable of extremely naive and potentially destructive behavior as a patron, for he insisted that La Fontaine write a poem of thanks every time his quarterly pension was paid (*ibid.*, p. 526).

philologist, had received pensions from Fouquet, but the latter seems to have been primarily interested in verse and light prose—genres that Jacques Dupuy had scorned as "feminine." Pellisson himself had long since turned away from the study of the law, and his interest in history seems to have waned from those days when he had insisted that Bodin and Pasquier be placed in the pantheon of great French writers.

The Essays from Prison

No sooner had Fouquet and Pellisson been arrested in September 1661 than Colbert began to organize an effort to encourage the writing of history, perhaps because this was one of the genres of *belles lettres* that had received so little attention under the aegis of Pellisson and Fouquet. This abrupt shift in patronage after 1661 from Fouquet to Colbert, and from poetry to history, sheds some light on the forces that may have been acting in literary circles to press history continually toward the panegyric. Colbert's respect for the utility of history (either for making treaties or for preparing propaganda) prevented the development of a lopsided emphasis in royal patronage. As we have already observed, the *érudits* would always receive royal support. Poets would never write the *érudits'* "sort" of history, hence the rise of panegyric.

The shifts from one protector to another never occurred without incident. La Fontaine, for example, never accepted royal favor after the disgrace of his former patron at the hands of the King and Colbert.[40] La Fontaine's intimate friend, Pellisson, would make eloquent appeals on behalf of Fouquet and himself from the Bastille, thus keeping alive the old *fidélités*. Former Frondeurs felt the hot blood that stimulated rebellion coursing within their veins as they rallied to Fouquet's cause. The most eloquent defender of the disgraced Superintendent was none other than Pellisson.[41]

The *Premier Discours*, addressed directly to Louis XIV, went through three printings and aroused a great deal of interest in both the writer-prisoner and his cause. Voltaire later praised it—and the other discourses

40. But as has often been remarked, this may have been as much out of hostility toward Chapelain and some of his friends, who now occupied positions of influence while Pellisson was in the Bastille, as out of loyalty to Fouquet or repugnance for Louis XIV.

41. Châtelain, p. 180, points out that Pellisson owed Fouquet large sums of money, especially since Pellisson had lacked the capital to purchase the various venal offices he held.

addressed to the public that followed it—as "something approaching Roman oratory . . . they are in the same genre as several of Cicero's orations," which he meant as a compliment.[42] The arguments from history that Pellisson made on Fouquet's behalf were in the best tradition of legal humanism, for the moral and political implications he raised went to the heart of what had happened to the French constitution in the past. Here precedents and *topoi* were stated eloquently, both to edify and to motivate political action.

After beginning with protestations of respect and veneration for Louis XIV, Pellisson charges that the commissioners appointed by the King to try Fouquet have no jurisdiction to do so. Does not Fouquet's status as a *gentilhomme* [sic] and high royal official (*procureur* of the Parlement) make it an injustice for him to be tried by anyone but the King through the constituted sovereign courts, and especially the Parlement of Paris? Moreover, in the letters-patent establishing the powers of *surintendants*, was there not a clause stating that they were responsible to the King alone, and to no other individual at court?[43] This distinction between "ordinary" and "extraordinary" justice, which Pellisson was quick to make, went right to the heart of ancient French constitutional conflicts. The Frondeurs had opposed the *commissaires*, those "judges" trumped up by the king to thwart the jurisdictional claims of parlements. Pellisson has not entirely forgotten his training in the law and in the court in Castres during the years when verses and tax contracts had been his principal concerns.

Then, after this close look at the letters-patent and *commissaires*, Pellisson moves on to trace the long history of the Monarchy's solemn oaths not to use extraordinary justice, beginning with the oath of Charles the Bald. On his coronation day did not Louis XIV swear to uphold the ordinary judicial procedures? Henry IV, the "Great," had never once used *commissaires*. As if history were not enough, Pellisson next implicitly threatens Louis XIV with a divine reprimand. Since he holds his power from God, the king may not be responsible before God if ordinary justice ends in a bad judgment; but if extraordinary justice is employed and a miscarriage of justice follows, is the king not all the more accountable before God for such a miscarriage? With a telling effect Pellisson inserts anecdotes—such as having the "voix du peuple" cry out to send Fouquet before his "natural" judges. Arguments of this sort had not been so broadly diffused since 1648–1649.

42. Voltaire, *Siècle de Louis XIV*, Chap. 32.

43. *Oeuvres choisies de Pellisson*, ed. N. L. M. Desessarts (Paris, 1805), vol. 1, pp. 133 ff.

When the former Frondeurs—whether princes, *curés*, or judges—heard once more the assumptions of the absolutist constitution called into question, they rallied to Fouquet's defense.[44]

No one could have been better prepared than Pellisson to discuss the intricacies of royal finances. In these discussions of money he generally relies on plain logic When considering the wealth that Fouquet has accumulated, for example, Pellisson challenges anyone to assume simultaneously both the Superintendent's property and debts, implying that the latter were greater than the former. But in all these discussions the shadow of Mazarin and his conduct as principal minister begins to loom over other considerations. Had not the King followed the illustrious and wise Cardinal's advice on all matters, and had not the latter come to rely very heavily on Fouquet during the turbulent years of the Fronde? The implication is clear: if Fouquet is guilty of peculation, so too was Mazarin. Had there not been secret personal gifts from the King to Fouquet? And had not Mazarin encouraged Fouquet to buy Belle-Ile, the property that now served as partial grounds for Colbert's attacks on Fouquet? [45]

But, even if Fouquet is guilty, royal clemency is required: for history, that "true, wise, and faithful councillor of great kings,"[46] indicates that Louis's royal predecessors who disgraced *surintendants* gained nothing. Pellisson implicitly threatens Louis with a popular revolt should he persist in following the same course.[47] What *gloire* have kings acquired by condemning so many *surintendants*? Henry IV knew how to pardon rather than to prevail over some subjects and bring about their destruction. During the Fronde, Fouquet's loyalty remained unquestioned, at a time when "la couronne [était] presque chancelante sur la tête de Vostre Majesté."[48]

Pellisson's final argument leaves history altogether by turning to the question of what should constitute the King's future *gloire*. None of his predecessors gained immortality by trying *surintendants*; the King may efface the memory of his predecessors only by spilling the blood of his enemies and sparing that of his subjects. Pellisson deliberately switches to the past definite tense in the conclusion, employing grammar to evoke changing temporal perspectives. The question has be-

44. Though favored by Fouquet, the Jesuits dropped his cause immediately, while the Jansenists—or at least some Jansenists—came to his defense. On the general history of the trial, see Jules Lair, *Nicolas Fouquet* (Paris, 1890), vol. 2, *passim*.
45. "Premier Discours," in *Oeuvres choisies*, vol. 1, p. 183.
46. *Ibid.*, p. 191.
47. *Ibid.*, p. 196.
48. *Ibid.*, p. 214.

come: which would contribute more to Louis's immortality, the trial of a *surintendant* or an act of clemency? By writing as if the King's immortality were already assured and as if the anticipated act of clemency had contributed to it, Pellisson makes his conclusion read like an epitaph for the Sun King written long after his death. The mastery of rhetoric and the "purification" of the French language had made it possible to write about the present as if it were a past event and to write about the past as a prescription for the future. It ultimately became possible to write as if the future had already occurred.[49] The preoccupation with immortality so characteristic of all the literature and history about Louis XIV accounts for the use of devices that offered a vision of the future as history.[50]

Knowledge of the past had been brought to bear very effectively on the general argument. The history of how resorting to "extralegal" justice had violated solemn royal oaths must have had a telling effect, as did the accounts of previous trials of *surintendants*, which had failed to eliminate peculation among officials. To members of social groups that still shared something of a "common-law mind," these and similar precedents might have been a convincing argument that Louis should release Fouquet. But in the seventeenth century this unreinforced sort of historical knowledge—both in political pamphlets and in histories— appeared insufficient to the larger reading public. The mere accumulation of more and more knowledge about the past had been devalued as pedantry once the rhetorical arts provided a variety of ways of evoking the past or drawing lessons from it—lessons that strictly speaking had little or no relation to actual events.

Pellisson's second and third discourses in Fouquet's defense were intended to sway public opinion rather than to convince Louis.[51] Perhaps

---

49. "Que l'histoire marque un jour dans ses monumens éternels: Louis XIV, véritablement donné de Dieu pour la restauration de la France, fut grand en guerre, grand en paix. . . . Il eut autant de bonté et de douceur, que de fermeté et de courage, et ne crut pas bien représenter en terre le pouvoir de Dieu s'il n'imitoit aussi sa clémence" (*ibid.*).

50. No claim is made that this was a new device. Quite the contrary. It was a logical development from the humanistic preoccupations of the sixteenth-century Pléiade.

51. Young Racine wrote to his friend Le Vasseur: "Mais à propos d'Académie, que le pauvre Pellisson est à plaindre, et que la Conciergerie est un méchant poste pour un bel esprit! Tous les beaux esprits du monde ne devraient-ils pas faire une solennelle députation au Roi pour demander sa grâce? Les Muses elles-mêmes devraient-elle pas se rendre visibles afin de solliciter pour lui? *Nec vos, Pierides, nec stirps Latonia, vestro docta sacerdoti turba tutistis opem!* Mais on voit peu de gens que la protection

as a consequence the proportion of argument based on history diminished. He gives detailed descriptions of the actual financial operations of the treasury and refutes the application of the principles of Roman law, which had been evoked by proponents of the Crown to justify the commissioners' legal powers to try Fouquet.

But, above all, the questions raised by Pellisson focus on Louis's character and the nature of kingship. Many of the conceits about princely conduct, which had appeared as early as Budé, are reiterated here to persuade the King to emulate the great men of Antiquity. After remarking that some friends had warned him that he might further endanger his life by writing these defenses, Pellisson was able to define his sovereign in such a way that his own life seemed to depend on royal generosity and respect for the rights of a subject who dared to speak up.[52] "C'est un beau nom que la chambre de justice, mais le temple de clémence, que les Romains élèvèrent à cette vertu triomphante en la personne de Jules César, est un plus grand et un plus beau nom encore."[53] All the conceits about the conquering hero, the just monarch, and the clement king are juxtaposed in a way that virtually compels Louis to pardon Fouquet because the lessons of history taught by the great rulers of Antiquity required it. A balance between justice and clemency is harder to achieve than the conquest of a city, but such an achievement would be as significant as military victory for Louis's *gloire*.

The discourses constituted an implicit critique of the young King's father, Louis XIII, known as "le Juste," and served as a warning that the balance should not be made to tip further toward "justice" by trying Fouquet and perhaps accepting his execution. Thus the psychological element that always lay at the heart of humanist history, and that writers of the seventeenth century in no way abandoned, constituted Pellisson's ultimate appeal to Louis XIV: he must not be like his father. The trials and executions of Chalais, the Marillac brothers, Montmorency-Bouteville, Cinq Mars, and de Thou, and the sufferings of a host of individuals still living who had survived years in prison or exile because of Louis XIII's "justice," testify to the imbalance between justice and clemency during the years preceding the Fronde. These el-

---

des Muses ait sauvés des mains de la justice. . . . Cela doit apprendre à M. l'Avocat que le solide n'est pas toujours le plus sûr, puisque M. Pellisson ne s'est perdu que pour l'avoir préféré au creux; et sans mentir, quoiqu'il fasse bien creux sur le Parnasse, on y est plus à son aise que dans la Conciergerie" (26 December 1661, *Oeuvres complètes*, ed. Raymond Picard [Paris, 1966], vol. 2, p. 411).

52. *Oeuvres choisies*, vol. 2, p. 7.
53. *Ibid.*, p. 163.

ements loomed large, though perhaps only on a subconscious level, in the minds of readers, perhaps even in the mind of Louis XIV. Pellisson's achievement was to evoke—without mentioning his name—a dreaded historical personage whom everyone seemed desirous of forgetting.[54]

In the decades after the Fronde there was an almost unconscious agreement, a near taboo, against discussing the unhappy times of the preceding reign. This phenomenon may indirectly clarify one of the most important functions of historical thinking during the seventeenth century; for in a political culture so preoccupied with *gloire* and immortality, the silence surrounding Louis XIII may reveal a desire of both public and academic opinion to relegate that unhappy king to oblivion. Not to be written about, or talked about, or "paralleled," to say nothing of the still more edifying function of being held up as a historical ideal of life, was a fate worse than death in the classicistic culture of the seventeenth century. Indeed, Louis XIV rarely referred to his own father.[55]

Through his *Discours* and subsequent letters of appeal directed to Louis XIV, Pellisson developed and refined both the images of the truly great prince that he wished to project and the crisp, eloquent style that would serve him when he undertook to write the history of Louis XIV. Finally released from the Bastille in January 1666 and presented at court by prominent dukes shortly afterward, Pellisson soon pulled himself together and began to attempt to attract the attention of the principal literary patron in the realm since Fouquet's arrest: Louis XIV himself.

Pellisson's debts were enormous. No judicial or administrative office would have enabled him to pay the sums owed to his creditors plus the enormous fine for peculation ordered by Colbert's *commissaires*. There was no way out from his financial burdens other than building on his reputation as a man of eloquence and probity, for certainly none of his aristocratic friends were in a position to grant him the pensions and offices he needed to recover his self-respect.

54. Tallemant des Réaux thought that Richelieu feared that the King would be known as Louis the Stutterer (*Historiettes*, ed. Antoine Adam [Paris, 1960], vol. 1, "Louis XIII").
55. Bibliothèque de l'Arsenal, mss. fr. 6081, fol. 62, records that in October 1664 the young Louis XIV asked Pierre Corneille to prepare a life of his father; but might this not have been Chapelain's and Colbert's suggestion rather than Louis's? Since the letter to Corneille was not a personal one (countersigned by Guénégaud), it may merely reflect Colbert's desire to have each writer undertake a specific task at the time he received his initial pension.

Abandoning, at least publicly, the by now sentenced Fouquet, and once again veering away from constitutional and fiscal subjects, Pellisson wrote whimsical, poetic, often enchanting accounts of parties and other events at court. The reading public seems to have bought anything and everything written about such ceremonies and colorful events at their young King's court. Writers enjoying the prestige of a large reading public were tempted to fulfill this public's dream about court life by describing Versailles almost as if it were in a fairy tale. Both French and foreign newspapers were filled with enthralling accounts of life at court. While still under Fouquet's protection, Pellisson had proved himself a master craftsman in the art of depicting such events. The accounts of court functions that he began to write in 1666 were in exactly the same modes as those he had once written for Fouquet. The emphasis on entertainment; the almost *précieux* language; the preoccupation with praising the patron and the physical beauty of gardens, buildings, and women; and the projection of ideals of *gloire* had been shifted from Fouquet to Louis XIV almost without missing a rhyme. Since historical writing as a genre was still intimately linked with other prose forms, notably battle narratives and discourses, it could also be shifted from one patron to another with no changes in style, purpose, or use of evidence.

It is anachronistic to refer to this literature—when its principal subject is the head of state—as propaganda. As a descriptive term, "propaganda" does not help to define the nature of either historical or other literary genres in the reign of Louis XIV; for in a sense *fidélités*—royal, aristocratic, and parlementaire—encompassed virtually all literary activity.[56] The preeminence of the royal patron after Fouquet's arrest tended, however, to make patron-writer ties overlap—a structural-social change in the political culture that was not of Louis's making.

Pellisson's abilities as a writer were recognized by the King, who began inviting him to attend the more intimate parties at court and accompany him on military campaigns. On one occasion the King turned to him on a point of grammar,[57] conveying his preoccupation with "purity of language." The ideal of the conquering hero who recorded his own history was being realized in the preparation of Louis's *Memoirs for the Instruction of the Dauphin*. But this project in no way ex-

56. Upon La Fontaine's election to the French Academy in 1684, he chose in his discourse to honor his patroness, Mme de la Sablière. The *discours* is devoid of political content: nowhere does the discussion of her *gloire* touch upon subjects that could be interpreted as opposition to the Crown (Charles-A. Walckenaer, *Histoire de la vie et les ouvrages de J. de La Fontaine* [Paris, 1821], p. iv).

57. *Lettres historiques* (Paris, 1729), vol. 1, p. 89.

cluded the possibility that the King's most talented subjects might also attempt to write his history. Did not the Academy exist in part as a group of great writers who would be available to record momentous events or actions?[58] Louis occasionally chose Pellisson from among the dozens of courtiers or military officers in attendance and shared some thought with him, sensing which actions and thoughts might immortalize him in history. To someone like Pellisson, who had always turned to the ancients for inspiration, Louis's self-conscious preoccupation with his personal immortality seemed the fulfillment of the heroic princely ideal of immortality. At last France seemed to possess a king who both honored men of letters and appeared eager to learn from history and to write it himself.

Pellisson would be the first historiographer royal since Bernard to follow in the king's footsteps at court and on his military campaigns.[59] Gone were the historiographer's claims to making the title a venal charge; for in a sense Pellisson had already become a courtier while in Fouquet's service. Later Racine would resemble Pellisson completely in his personal enjoyment of *les honneurs de la cour*. But changes and testings still had to occur before Pellisson could gain increased intimacy with the king. In the meantime he was mastering the art of writing battle narratives.

The panegyric on battles, be it prose or poetry, was in special favor among early-modern writers. Its origins lie in the mists of Antiquity; its renaissance had occurred at the time of the Franco-Italian wars of the late fifteenth century.[60] Malherbe's verses on the battle of Ivry served as a model for generations of poets, persisting as late as Voltaire, whose *Fontenoy* reveals that the genre was still very much alive in the mid-eighteenth century.

The prose narratives of battles had been refined by those great pioneers in propaganda, Richelieu and his journalist-editor, Renaudot.[61] The seventeenth-century reading public never seemed to find enough reading matter about battles, and Colbert and Louis were not ones to

58. The "Ninth Discourse," given by Gomberville before the French Academy on 7 May 1635; *Relation . . . ,* p. 75.

59. Périgny's status after March 1663 was *lecteur du roi*. Moreover, it appears that from the beginning his role had been defined as royal collaborator rather than as historiographer. By contrast, Pellisson had every intention of writing a general history of France from the time of his appointment immediately after Périgny's death in 1670 (Charles Dreyss, *Etude sur les "Mémoires de Louis XIV"* [Paris, 1859], p. li).

60. Joukovsky, pp. 430 ff.

61. Howard Solomon, *Public Welfare, Science, and Propaganda in Seventeenth-Century France* (Princeton, 1972), Chap. 5.

deprive the public of accounts of French victories. The themes—the ways of depicting danger, the conceits about the commander, the descriptions of courageous and heroic acts, and the sense that warfare was noble—had all become conventionalized during the sixteenth century. Accounts could not demean the enemy; combat had to be depicted as if it were a rational, dignified series of events.

Indeed, in 1639, Chapelain had advised the Marquis de Gesvres about how to prepare a narrative of his own military exploits.[62] Chapelain specified that the text be in the third person, even though the writer of the account is recording his own actions; that counsels about war and examples of courage be inserted directly into the narrative; and that the final significance of victory be described in such a way that the commander's *gloire* not be elevated over and above that of the others contributing to the victory. This last prescription is of particular interest, because it was frequently violated. When kings, princes, and other *grands* had participated in battles, they were always depicted as dominating the action and being more courageous than the other participants. Of course, Chapelain may have been implying that a hierarchy of *gloires* existed, a hierarchy paralleling that of rank. Since the Marquis de Gesvres was not a *grand*, it would therefore not be appropriate for him to attribute more *gloire* to himself than that due a man of his status.

The model battle narrative of Pellisson's time and literary circle— *L'histoire du siège de Dunquerque*—had been written by his close friend, Sarasin. Sober and panegyrical, extolling "us," the French, more than the commander, Condé, Sarasin's narrative, republished posthumously, had been praised by Pellisson.[63] It reflected the darkened mood of the year 1646, during a time when fiscal exhaustion was reaching a high point but had not yet led to civil war. The beacon light of victory might help reassure a demoralized Parisian reading public. Condé's *gloire* is described without diminishing the fortune bestowed on the French. Thus the account lacks that adulatory quality found in most battle narratives about Rocroy and in those subsequently written about Louis XIV's campaigns.

Moreover, Sarasin portrays the conduct of this siege as equal in heroism to the great sieges described by ancient historians, though he implies that it was difficult to ascertain just how great those earlier sieges

62. *Lettres de Jean Chapelain*, ed. Philippe Tamizey de Larroque (Paris, 1880–1883), vol. 1, p. 374. See also the note about a battle narrative that Chapelain himself wrote and addressed to Longueville (p. 741).

63. Pellisson's introduction to Sarasin's works is a fine illustration of how the phrases about *gloire*, immortality, and accomplishment could be applied to a man of letters (*Oeuvres choisies*, vol. 1, pp. 113 ff.).

were. The ancients serve as the standard of comparison, but Sarasin sounds an occasional note of skepticism about the truthfulness of the events described by panegyrical historians. Were not the historians of Antiquity in the habit of enhancing the actions of men of the past, he says, in order to diminish the significance of the heroic actions of the contemporaries about whom they were writing? [64] This argument has several implications. Seventeenth-century writers occasionally were able to perceive the political motivations of their predecessors in the ancient world, but they rarely stated their views about the double temporal modes that ancient historians employed. Praise of earlier events could thus be interpreted by Sarasin as an expression of discontent over present political events.[65] In this instance, however, Sarasin also wanted to imply that he had consciously rendered justice to the greatness of the men besieging Dunkirk by claiming that their valor equaled the military exploits of the ancients, who had benefited from historians' general exaggeration of heroic deeds.

By the time Pellisson accompanied Louis into Franche-Comté, the national crisis seemed resolved. But no decline in the cult of heroes had accompanied the newly established stability of the 1660s. Since the days when Corneille's *Cid* had moved the hearts of Parisian audiences,[66] writers had developed a very elaborate and coherent literature about the psychology and attributes of the heroic prince. In a eulogy of Condé, Charles de Saint-Evremond wrote: "[Curtius's] guerres d'Alexandre et les commentaires de César le touchent infiniment; le premier luy semble plus capable d'eslever l'esprit et d'inspirer la grandeur de l'âme. Il croit qu'on peut s'instruire mieux avec l'autre; l'un a plus de rapport avec son génie, l'autre gagne plus sa créance et son esprit."[67] Pierre Coste, Condé's biographer, asserted that Monsieur le Prince also liked to read Plutarch's life of Alexander. As long as writers believed they could attract the attention of leading aristocratic patrons by writing about Alexander or translating Quintus Curtius, Caesar, the *Historiae Augustae*, or any number of other works in which heroic attributes were discussed, they would continue to do so. Even after Saint-Evremond had lost Condé's favor, he remarked that the "*versions* by Vaugelas and d'Ablancourt made [Alexander and Caesar] heroes in

---

64. *Ibid.*, p. 115.

65. Thus the standard interpretation found in Voltaire's *Siècle de Louis XIV*, in which the philosophe's enthusiasm for Louis XIV's actions is seen as a covert criticism of the *fainéantisme* of Louis XV.

66. Paul Bénichou, *Les morales du grand siècle* (Paris, 1948), pp. 14 ff.

67. "Eloge de M. le Prince," *Oeuvres*, ed. René Ternois (Paris, 1962), vol. 1, p. 196.

all our conversations, with individuals becoming supporters of one or the other according to inclination or whim." [68]

Did men of letters in the mid-seventeenth century converse frequently about Alexander's and Caesar's attributes? The answer to this question seems to be in the affirmative. Such topics of conversation were ways of talking about the "science" of leadership; but Alexander and Caesar also were discussed with patrons or in salons attended by princely patrons. The attributes of each hero provided subjects on which men of letters could claim expertise before their patrons. The history of Alexander and Caesar provided a convenient political language during the decades when Louis XIII was not filling the unconscious needs for leadership felt by authors, nobles, and perhaps the French literate public in general.

The elaboration and refinement of the heroic cult from the days of the Corneillean heroes to those of Racine in the 1660s and 1670s had profound influences on the writing of history, as the princes went down to defeat in the Fronde and then were partially rehabilitated by Condé's and Turenne's victories during the early years of Louis XIV's personal reign. This flood of writings about heroic character had historical dimensions; indeed, it functioned as "history" in the political culture centered about Versailles. There is an astonishing amount of literature about Alexander the Great as Louis XIV, and Louis XIV as Alexander the Great.[69] This subject appealed to great and mediocre writers alike, while serving the political purpose of establishing a dialogue between writers and their patrons—including Louis—and the increasingly large reading and theatergoing public. In treatises on education, in plays, in histories, and even in the private correspondence between men of power and writers, the conceits about Louis XIV as Alexander became all-pervasive during the first decades of the reign.

The ancients had drawn distinctions between biography and history,[70] but these in no way demanded different approaches to the use of evidence. Biography should resemble a "portrait" that emphasized familiar, anecdotal, and psychological elements. The rhetoricians had defined history as of necessity including all of a king's battles and other worthy actions; in Hellenistic and Roman times history had been rendered ponderous and formal, if not constraining to writers wanting to emphasize character study. Of course, as in the days when Budé had

68. *Ibid.*, p. 197.

69. There is no study of the Alexander conceit that brings together the entire literary-artistic effort as still another manifestation of the "historical ideals of life" that Johan Huizinga defined in *Men and Ideas* (New York, 1959), pp. 77–96.

70. C. P. Jones, *Plutarch and Rome* (Oxford, 1971), pp. 70–73.

translated them into Latin, Plutarch's *Lives* continued to provide the primary historical evidence considered sufficient for the study of heroic leadership. Amyot's translation into French merely served to extend this fascination with the cult of heroes to an even wider reading public. The efforts of the writers in the Pléiade had been directed at forcing the hero to "s'incarner dans l'histoire,"[71] but the tendency to confuse contemporary and ancient attributes when preparing parallels that functioned as "historical ideals of life" gave this literature an atemporal quality. Montaigne's debate with himself about the various weaknesses and strengths of Alexander and Caesar had been couched so as to strengthen the inclination felt by readers of Plutarch—especially pedagogues—to develop "parallels" between the two men and to measure the actions of contemporaries by these standards.[72]

What has been said about Plutarch applies to his followers as well. "He expands a doctrine of historiography that preferred leniency to severity, patriotism to impartiality, optimism to pessimism. . . . Faced with a fault in his hero, the biographer should treat it as an artist treated a blemish."[73] Thus the fundamental need of early moderns to perceive perfection in individuals of the past placed Plutarch and Livy among the preferred authors because their writings satisfied a need for edification.[74] Writers were irresistibly tempted to imitate them when writing about Louis XIV, Condé, Longueville, Montausier, Turenne, and various other *grands*. Plutarch's resolution of the problem by frequently omitting discussion of the weaknesses or immoral actions of his heroes —with an implicit Platonic justification—had a strong appeal in human-

71. Joukovsky, p. 272.

72. Henry IV may have been boasting to his queen when he described his love of Plutarch, but there was certainly an element of truth in what he said: "Plutarque me sourit toujours d'une fresche nouveauté; l'aimer c'est m'aimer, car il a esté l'instituteur de mon bas age. Ma bonne mere, à qui je doibs tout et qui avoit une affection si grande de veiller à mes bons déportemens, et ne vouloit pas, ce disoit-elle, voir en sons fils un illustre ignorant, me mit ce livre entre les mains, encor que je ne feusse à peine plus un enfant de mamelle. Il m'a esté comme ma conscience, et m'a dicté à l'oreille beaucoup de bonnes honestetez, et maximes excellentes pour ma conduicte et pour le gouvernement des affaires" (3 September 1601, *Lettres missives de Henri IV*, ed. M. Berger de Xivrey et J. Guadet [Paris, 1843–1876], vol. 5, pp. 462 f.).

73. Jones, p. 88.

74. The statistical studies of ancient authors by Henri-Jean Martin bear out these preferences. For example, Tacitus and Thucydides were never as attractive as Livy and Plutarch to any social group (*Livre, pouvoirs et société au XVIIe siècle* [Geneva, 1969], vol. 1, *passim*, but especially pp. 502–512).

ist cultures throughout Europe. Learning was best achieved by comparing and balancing the good forces or virtues in an individual.[75] Thus the Plutarchian conceits about Alexander became a kind of historicized psychological labyrinth in which to explore the heroic personality, the characteristics of kingship, and the ideal prince incarnate as Louis XIV. The older critiques of individual *gloire* that had served as a basis for curbing princely claims to be morally above the law had lost their significance after the humiliation of the *grands* during the Fronde. Condé had made his peace with Louis XIV. By the same token, after 1660 the prince as a historical ideal of life, the personal kingship of Louis XIV, and France in its dynastic sense became unified in literature, history, and art. The unreserved acceptance of and enthusiasm for all of Louis's actions, including military conquest, resulted from a convergence of social and literary changes occurring in French political culture at the beginning of Louis XIV's reign.

The Plutarchian mode revealed an individual's character quintessentially through his sayings.[76] In the case of the conceits about Louis XIV, every attempt was made to include actual quotations based on remarks overheard by a member of his court or by a historiographer royal. Thus Pellisson's battle narratives, like those of many of his contemporaries, contained quotations and little incidents reflecting the King's character. Prodigies—stars, dreams, storms, flights of birds, and other omens associated with heroic behavior—also had their place in these narratives. In the descriptions of battles, interest concentrated on the heroic general; his subordinates were scarcely mentioned.

The *topoi* about heroic divinity found in Plutarch had been a disquieting element for many sixteenth-century writers. When linked to the prodigies—those violations of the natural order that supposedly fascinated Alexander himself—the meaning and significance of these *topoi* might have led to an examination of the divine favor if not the divinity bestowed upon French monarchs. Montaigne had scrupulously examined Alexander's beliefs and those of his contemporaries concerning this Greek hero's divinity and concluded that Alexander's greatness had derived solely from his human qualities. This skeptical tradition was represented in Saint-Evremond's *Sur Alexandre et César*, written at about the time both he and Pellisson were seeking Fouquet's

75. For the literary and psychological structures in portraits, see Leo Spitzer, "Saint-Simons Porträt Ludwigs XIV," *Romanisch Stil und Literaturstudien* (Marburg, 1931), vol. 2, pp. 1–47; and Jules Brody, "Structures de personnalité et vision du monde dans les *Mémoires* de Saint-Simon," *Cahiers Saint-Simon* (1976), pp. 13–32.

76. J. R. Hamilton, *Plutarch: Alexander; a Commentary* (Oxford, 1969), p. xxv.

patronage. Saint-Evremond maintains Montaigne's critical perspective. His close reading of Plutarch had led him to conclude that although Alexander "faisoit couler cette créance [in his divinity] parmy les Barbares pour en attirer la vénération,"[77] he was well aware that he was a mere man. But, in a manner reminiscent of Pasquier's shift from a discussion of the improbability of Joan of Arc's miraculous works to an acceptance of her as a national heroine, the writers in the Age of Louis XIV continued to evoke the Plutarchian *topoi* about Alexander's divinity in order to imply veneration for Louis XIV's divinity. The prodigies or omens added to most narratives of battles under Louis XIV support this conceit—but not those written by Pellisson. This indicates that the dominant Plutarchian mode of writing about the King influenced historical writing in the literary circle around Louis, but that it did not overwhelm that writing to the point where Colbert or the King encouraged the use of conceits about divinity.[78]

In his *Discours* Pellisson had learned to evoke the image of a dignified, majestic, and magnanimous king, yet he made no attempt to superimpose either Alexandrian conceits or the psychology of a conquering hero upon the life of Louis XIV. Pellisson's battle narratives clearly owe something to Plutarch and other ancients who wrote as if the commander were omniscient at a siege or battle,[79] but we cannot conclude from them that the seventeenth century identified values about *gloire* with what was thought to be the heroic personality of Alexander. The distinction is significant because it represents a continuous cleavage between the royal memoirs and the histories written on Louis's behalf.

The history of the circle that produced Louis's *Memoirs* and nu-

77. Saint-Evremond, *Oeuvres*, vol. 1, p. 223.
78. It is impossible to say whether Louis himself perceived a deeper and more cynical meaning in those Plutarchian texts that he either knew directly or read summarized in "parallels." For example, Saint-Evremond praises both Alexander and Caesar for their "love of literature" ("Parallèle . . . ," *ibid.*, vol. 1, p. 204). Alexander, he asserts, wanted to be more learned than others and wanted "to raise himself up above other men as much through [his knowledge of literature] as through arms." By contrast, Caesar "seems to have loved literature only for its utility." Since eloquence could save the lives of the prisoners after the Catiline conspiracy, the parallels about ancient heroes may have presented Louis with alternative views on how to project his actions and person before his subjects (*ibid.*, p. 206). A prince did not have to read Machiavelli to learn Machiavellian principles of ruling in an age when texts from Antiquity offered him a wide variety of perspectives on that art.
79. None was published in his lifetime. See especially the *Relation du siège de Dôle en 1668*, ed. L.-Augustin Vayssière (Dôle, 1873), *passim*.

merous other works deserves some attention, for Pellisson joined it in about 1667–1668 and continued to work at writing the King's history until replaced by Racine and Boileau in 1677. Louis, Colbert, Montausier, Charles Perrault, Périgny—and less directly Chapelain, François Charpentier, and Siri—were all engaged in related but separate historical projects. Recruitment seems mainly to have been carried out by Colbert, who also appears to have assigned the writers to different tasks. Charles Perrault describes how they all collaborated to "correct" the panegyrics submitted by those writers who had received a share of the hundred thousand *livres* that Colbert had allocated through Chapelain for literary patronage. In addition to preparing these works for publication, each man also worked on his own account of "les belles actions de Sa Majesté."[80]

Perrault records how he was selected for this intimate circle after having become known to Colbert through his already influential brother, Claude, and through Chapelain's recommendation. Before granting him an appointment, however, Colbert decided to test whether Charles Perrault could write prose as well as verse[81] by asking him to write a discourse on the acquisition of Dunkirk. This work apparently was well received. Having thus passed the test, Perrault was assigned the task of writing the King's words in a register—in effect recording *sententiae* that could later be inserted into a narrative history of the reign: "Il [Colbert] me faisoit aussi écrire des actions fort considérables de Sa Majesté, lesquelles étoient ou peu connues de tout le monde, ou dont les motifs et quelques circonstances n'étoient scues que de luy seul. Je me souviens qu'il me dicta toute l'affaire de M. Fouquet d'un bout à l'autre, que j'y retouchai trois ou quatre fois différentes et par son ordre avant que de la transcrire dans le registre."[82]

The collaborative effort continued apace. At times they worked on "ouvrages de commande," which suggests that, in addition to composing the phrases to be carved into the façades of royal buildings, the group may also have been preparing histories for propagandistic purposes.

Once again on Chapelain's recommendation, François Charpentier had been added to the group; but almost immediately afterward he apparently requested interviews with Colbert in an attempt to obtain

80. *Mémoires de ma vie*, ed. Paul Bonnefon (Paris, 1909), pp. 38–48. Perrault unfortunately does not discuss how Colbert arrived at the amount of one hundred thousand *livres* for this project. It may simply have been an arbitrary decision.

81. It seems that Cardinal Mazarin had admired Perrault's verses (*ibid.*, p. 36).

82. *Ibid.*, p. 40.

secret memorandums for writing history. When Colbert refused to cooperate, Charpentier left the intimate circle. This incident is difficult to interpret. Perrault sincerely regretted Charpentier's departure (because he was a good writer?), but Colbert seems to have wanted to establish a collective work pattern for the *petite académie*.[83] Charpentier's own motives may have been historiographical—that is, he may have believed that he had to know state secrets if he was to write the type of history he deemed appropriate for Louis XIV. A tradition that historiographers royal shared state secrets may have been invoked to support this request. Or else Charpentier may have requested these secret materials in order to increase his influence with Colbert. In a sense, intimacy was synonymous with influence in seventeenth-century courts. The incident provides some indirect but illuminating evidence about Colbert's conception of these historical projects, and especially about how he used the collaborative effort to develop an institutional arrangement that allowed him to control the amount of information made available to writers. In other words, the writers never knew more than Colbert and the King wanted them to know, and yet they collectively believed that they had access to Colbert and to Louis himself. The collaborative organization limited individual probing, yet—as became clear in the case of Pellisson's history of the campaign of 1668—it permitted either the King or Colbert to develop intimacy with one or another of the writers in this intimate circle for the purpose of preparing a special historical project.

Whatever Colbert accomplished in the arts and literature remains ingenious, subtle, and enigmatic. Did the primary impetus for taking history so seriously stem from him? In the circle around Louis—including Colbert, Louvois, Montausier, and Hugues de Lionne—Colbert appears to have been the only one obsessively preoccupied by history. For the others it always seemed an avocation; for Louis it was something to be written after a crisis in his health had raised the specter of another decade of Frondelike years.

After Charpentier's withdrawal from the group, Perrault noted: "Ce

83. This group, which Racine later joined and which Mabillon occasionally attended, was eventually chartered as the Académie des Inscriptions et Belles Lettres. Mabillon wrote Niçaise about the *petite académie*: "je crois que vous savez que l'on travaille aux devises des médailles que l'on doit faire sur les grandes actions du Roi. M. l'abbé Tallemant, M. Félibien, M. Charpentier, M. Rainssant, avec deux autres dont les noms ne me reviennent pas, sont chargés de ces devises. Ce n'est une petite occupation" (Raymond Picard, *Corpus Raciniarum* [Paris, 1956], p. 130). It is amusing to note how the dramatist, Racine, and the satirist, Boileau, were so unfamiliar to Mabillon that he could forget their names.

fut une grande perte pour la petite académie et un bonheur pour M. Pellisson, et particulièrement pour MM. Racine et Despréaux, qui ont été chargés d'écrire l'histoire du Roy par Madame de Montespan, qui regarde ce travail comme un amusement dont elle avoit besoin pour occuper le Roi."[84] This passage reveals the date at which Pellisson became a member of the intimate circle and in addition confirms a number of observations that would merely have the force of gossip had Perrault not believed them and been an eyewitness to the events. This observation shall be discussed later.

Like Perrault's, Pellisson's entrance into the group was preceded by a "test," but in this instance the request probably specified the preparation of a *projet* on how to write the King's history. After all, Pellisson had demonstrated to everyone's satisfaction that he was a master of French prose. The "Projet de l'histoire du roi Louis XIV" was addressed to Colbert, who evidently liked it, since Pellisson was invited to join the group. Pellisson's plan was to write about the "last war"— that is, the War of Devolution—not in the form of a journal, a relation, a eulogy, or a panegyric, but as a "grande histoire à la manière de Tite Live, Polybe, et des autres anciens."[85] The description of Europe in the introduction should serve to permit the "secret comparison" of Louis XIV with other sovereigns—the implication being that through these "parallels" the King's virtues will clearly predominate. Noting that this history is written for posterity, Pellisson states:

> Ces manières de portraits, ou caractères, quand ils sont bien touchés, qu'ils ne sont ni en trop grand nombre, ni tout d'une suite, mais dispersez et placez avec quelque art . . . produisent un effet admirable. C'est un des grands secrets pour rendre l'histoire animée, et pour empecher qu'elle languisse. . . . Entre tous ces caractères, celui de Sa Majesté doit éclater, il faut louer le Roi par tout, mais pour ainsi dire sans louanges: par un récit de tout ce qu'on lui a vû faire, dire et penser qui paroisse désinteressé; mais qui soit vif, piquant, et soutenu. . . . Pour en être mieux crû, il ne s'agit pas de lui donner là les epithètes et les éloges magnifiques qu'il mérite, il faut les arracher de la bouche du Lecteur par les choses mèmes. Plutarque, ni Quinte Curce n'ont point loué Alexandre d'autre sorte, et on l'a trouvé bien loué.[86]

84. Perrault, p. 42. Carl J. Ekberg, *The Failure of Louis XIV's Dutch War* (Chapel Hill, 1979), p. 44, touches on the ways Louis shared the details of warfare with Montespan.
85. *Lettres historiques*, vol. 3, pp. 421 ff.
86. *Ibid.*, p. 424.

It would be difficult to find a more succinct or accurate description of the purpose and results of the writing produced by the *petite académie*. Praising without seeming to praise, edifying soberly and quietly, suited Colbert's purposes—and apparently Louis's as well. The writing officially sponsored by Colbert and the Crown was more restrained than those panegyrical histories spawned by the Academicians, larded as they were with conceits linking Louis to Alexander. A remark about Louis's supposed irritation with those writers who had hailed him as a conquering hero long before he went to war indicates a significant cleavage between the official history and the academic genre of laudatory history as a rhetorical exercise. The specter of Plutarch lay at the heart of both, along with the reading public's apparently limitless appetite for images of heroic kingship.

Pellisson implied in his *projet* that he would accomplish other aims as well. He could—"not as a lawyer but as a historian"—refute in passing *Le bouclier d'Etat*, a work by "un habile homme [Lisola] et qui fait beaucoup de bruit chez les Etrangers."[87] Did Pellisson develop this more specific propagandist purpose? Whether or not this point appealed to Colbert is less important than the substantial evidence indicating that Colbert had already undertaken a campaign to counter the effects of Baron Franz de Lisola's work by having a treatise on the just claims of the Queen prepared and translated into the various European languages.[88] Writers, in this instance Pellisson, may have lagged behind such men as Richelieu and Colbert in perceiving what must be done to counter the propaganda efforts of France's enemies.

Perhaps a bit like Charpentier, Pellisson dared to press for intimacy. He asked for Louis's personal approval of the project, "qui ne peut presque se bien executer sans elle."[89] Did he know about Charpentier's attempt? And did he perceive that, through his assertion that the King must in some way participate in the project, he risked the disgrace that

87. *Ibid.*, p. 422. On Lisola see Alfred F. Pribram, *Franz Paul, Freiherr von Lisola, 1613–1674* (Leipzig, 1894).

88. The story of the effort to refute Lisola may be pieced together through Chapelain's correspondence. As early as 10 October 1667, he wrote Wagensill: "Pour nouvelles, on respond aux sophismes, déclamations, cavillations du baron de Lisola" (Chapelain, vol. 2, p. 532).

89. *Lettres historiques*, vol. 3, p. 424. The Monarchy developed regular procedures to govern access to secret materials. Pellisson never seems to have had access to the papers of the secretary of state for foreign affairs. Cf. the memorandum written by Joachim Le Grand (?) in 1710–1711, B.N., n.a. fr. 7487, fol. 398 v. I owe this reference to Professor Joseph Klaits of Oakland University.

had befallen Charpentier? The difference between the two men may have counted a great deal. Pellisson was already known to Louis, who had accepted his presence in the royal entourage during the Flemish campaign about which Pellisson now proposed to write.

The campaign of 1668 saw Pellisson in almost constant attendance upon the King. Evidently his *projet* had pleased; but Colbert and/or Louis had in effect decided that it would be better for Pellisson to spend his time recording what he heard and saw on the next campaign than in completing his *projet* of a history of the previous war. Pellisson's battle accounts are centered upon Louis's actions and thoughts; minor details about the military camp and royal gestures and remarks are combined in an almost pure Plutarchian style, to portray the King's character and deeds. The campaign of 1668, aimed at the conquest of Franche-Comté, is depicted as if it had been entirely conceived and executed by the King. And yet Louis decided against publication of the text.

Years after the events in question, Pellisson wrote his friend and collaborator, Boisot, Abbot of Saint-Victor in Besançon, that "ce que j'ay escrit de la première conqueste de la Franche-Comté n'a point esté imprimé ni donné à personne qu'au roi seul."[90] Had Louis disliked what Pellisson had written? Were this the case, he would not have appointed Pellisson to succeed Périgny as historiographer royal in 1670. It is more likely that Pellisson's narrative served to supplement Périgny and Louis's preparation of the King's own memoirs. After all, other narratives of the campaign were published; propaganda purposes had been satisfied without using Pellisson's text. The fact that the King *alone* had seen Pellisson's text provides still another glimpse into the ways in which collaborative efforts could lead to special short-term efforts, since apparently not even Colbert had received the material dealing with 1668. Louis developed exactly the same pattern in dealing with his ministers. He would share some matters with one and then with another, yet all the ministers shared a certain amount of general information on questions of policy. The *petite académie* functioned along the same principles as the Conseil d'en Haut—at once informal, exclusive, and secretive, yet free from terrible conflicts over responsibilities because Louis would allow no such conflicts to develop. From these arrangements the royal memoirs also developed.[91]

The members of the *petite académie*—joined by Périgny, Montausier,

90. 16 July 1686. Bibliothèque de Besançon, mss. fr. 602, fol. 59.

91. On the differences between this historical genre and the memorial genre, see Marc Fumaroli, "Les mémoires du XVIIe siècle: Au carrefour des genres en prose," *XVIIe Siècle* 94 (1971): 7-37.

and Louis XIV—accepted as a fact the premise that lessons may be learned from history. Therefore, the King's memoirs, if properly written, could serve the same function for the Dauphin that the works of Plutarch and other historians had served in Louis's early education and in French political culture. The cardinal principle had always been to teach through "good" *exempla*, rather than through "bad" ones. Thus it is not surprising to find that in his memoirs Louis does not linger over his weaknesses or errors of judgment.[92] Equally significant, the *Memoirs* are free of those obvious allusions to Alexander that had become characteristic of so much of the writing done outside the *petite académie*. Since Pellisson inherited the position of principal collaborator on the *Memoirs* after Périgny's death in 1670, it is worthwhile to glance briefly at the manner in which these memoirs were written and at their relationship to other works of official history sponsored by the Crown.

Louis's formal education in history occurred in two quite different stages;[93] in both he showed respect for the expertise of his teachers and apparently adopted many of the principles they attempted to teach him. In the first stage the King grasped the duties of Christian princes and learned something of the *gloire* of his predecessors. The Latin *sententiae* about Christian kingship that Louis, like many other schoolboys, struggled to copy or to transpose into his "own" Latin are an excellent example of humanist pedagogy at work. Learning a language was linked to familiarity with if not actual memorization of brief, pithy moral and religious precepts.[94] As was the case in Racine's education, such precepts about politics could function as the "lessons" of history. It is therefore interesting to note that Caesar's *Commentaries*, Hardouin de Péréfixe's *Histoire du règne de Henri IV*, written especially for Louis by his preceptor,[95] and Mézerai's *Histoire de France*, which was read to the King at bedtime "d'un ton de conte," may have provided Louis with a veritable humanist storehouse of principles and their "illustration" through the narration of "true events." Did the clamor about seeking to become the equal of Alexander, or to surpass him, reach the royal nursery in the Palais-Royal? There is little explicit evidence to suggest that Louis was brought up on an Alexandrine "his-

92. At this time the fundamental work on the *Memoirs* is Paul Sonnino, "The Dating and Authorship of Louis XIV's *Mémoires*," *French Historical Studies* 3 (1964): 303–337; and "Louis XIV's *Mémoires pour l'histoire de la Guerre de Hollande*," *French Historical Studies* 8 (1973): 27–50.

93. On the King's education see John B. Wolf, *Louis XIV* (New York, 1968).

94. Lacour-Gayet, pp. 74 f.

95. There seems no evidence whatever to support the contention that Mézerai wrote this work.

torical ideal of life." Rather more important was the emphasis on learning principles in the form of *sententiae* that could be related to history and to day-to-day decisions.

The second stage of Louis's education took place after he had assumed the powers of decision making upon Mazarin's death, and after an illness had raised the possibility that his own son might also be forced to live through a long and turbulent minority. Louis's preceptors had collaborated on his boyhood lessons and had instilled a confidence that proper grammar and a knowledge of history were marks of kingship. Therefore his decision to work with a collaborator in the preparation of his memoirs continued in his twenties and thirties the work habits that he had known as a boy. Like the young royal ministers, Périgny was about thirty-five at the time he began to help the King, possibly as early as 1663, when he became *lecteur du roi*.[96]

Louis's remarks about history included in the *Memoirs* reveal his purpose to raise the narrative of his actions and events during his reign to the level of a *politique*. Périgny's task lay in supplying appropriate *topoi* that could be learned and remembered along with those events.[97] This process of adjusting narratives and finding *topoi* to fit them resembled that employed by other historians who revered the ancients and sought to write like them. Périgny, and perhaps the King himself, may have had to search through Pierre Le Moyne's *Art de règner*, Machiavelli's *Discourses on Livy* and *Prince*, and other still-to-be-identified works in order to glean the *topoi* that logically could be derived from the narrative of royal decisions and actions.[98] This method of historical writing was, of course, humanist par excellence.[99] Had Louis possessed a book of *topoi* copied out as a child, research in Le Moyne or Machiavelli might have been unnecessary.[100] But Périgny seems to

96. For all the problems of dating, see Sonnino's articles cited above, and Dreyss, p. li.

97. Lacour-Gayet, p. 79. The first volume of Mézerai had just been published (1643) when Louis was five.

98. Sonnino, "The Dating and Authorship," p. 314.

99. It had been Cardinal Richelieu's, whose *Maximes d'etat et fragments politiques*, ed. Gabriel Hanotaux (Paris, 1880), is a commonplace book from which the Cardinal's memoirs and other works, perhaps, were written by his collaborators.

100. Charles Perrault remarks proudly that even as an adult he preserved the "extraits" made in his youth while reading Tertullian, de Serres's *Histoire de France*, Davila, Virgil, Horace, and Tacitus (Perrault, p. 21). Note how the editor has confused Tacitus's first name with that of the playwright Pierre Corneille.

Le Moyne's *De l'histoire* (Paris, 1670), is a contemporary treatise on how to write history. It provides the conventional definitions of *topoi* (Aris-

have been willing to undertake this task and to discuss the implications of these *topoi* and how they could be joined to the narrative, until Louis was satisfied with the results. The revisions continued. In a sense, the project was never completed, not even for any specific year, because it is possible that the King continued to revise earlier years in the light of subsequent events.

Various suspicions arise in the reader who is not captured by the eloquence of the *Memoirs* or who is not reading them for the purpose of learning how to govern France. For little is said about the actual conduct of policy, and the reasons given for going to war seem to have been reduced to a justification for decisions made on other grounds. Louis's memoirs run counter to the indecision and conflict over alternative policies, supported by divided councillors, that any historian of politics realizes must have been present as the young King made his decisions. Still more disturbing is the way the King took full credit for so many of the suggestions and decisions made by his ministers—Le Tellier, Colbert, and Louvois. Owing to his humanist education, Louis believed that if the Dauphin were taught principles of government supported by historical examples, there would be no need to narrate all the ups and downs of decision making. In the *Memoirs*, the *topoi* concerning making peace and war and choosing ministers and learning to work with them were judiciously selected by a man who feared his own death. Louis's interest in the *Memoirs* declined when the Dauphin reached adolescence. As he grew older and infirm, the King seems to have made no effort to assure the preservation of the "precious sheets of paper" nor to think of having them presented to the future Louis XV for his instruction.

But, like the study of so many collaboratively written texts,[101] the

---

totle's) and how they are to be inserted into a historical narrative. This work appeared in English translation in 1695. The introduction begins with an assurance that possessing or reading this book by a French Jesuit will "not make anyone Impeachable upon the Statute. . . . And there is nothing of our English Growth to be compared to it, so I do not think our soil or climate are capable of producing a commodity of the like goodness." See Phyllis Leffler, "L'Histoire Raisonné: A Study of French Historiography, 1660–1720," Ph.D. dissertation, The Ohio State University, 1971, Chap. 8.

101. It is remarkable that scholars have made no effort to compare the manner in which Richelieu's memoirs were prepared with that used for Louis's, and yet both efforts have attracted considerable scholarly attention. The "Rapports et notices" preceding Richelieu's *Mémoires*, Société de l'Histoire de France (Paris, 1907–1914), vols. 1–3, contain many fruitful analytical devices that might be applied to the problems about Louis's memoirs that scholars are still trying to solve.

scrutiny of Louis's memoirs leads into the wilderness of unverifiable speculation, unless the general purpose of the memoirs and their relationship to other works of the time are kept in mind. Louis would not have worked at writing his memoirs, his advice to the Dauphin, or even those letters about governing addressed to his grandson Philip V, the newly crowned Spanish king, had he not earnestly believed that history—in this instance his own personal experience—could serve as a guide to the conduct of affairs of state. As he attempted to record history for his son, Louis revealed how significant it had been to him. Hence we are not surprised to find that the *topos* exhorting the Dauphin to learn from history enjoys a prominent place in the *Memoirs*. A desire for brevity had caused the collaborators to prune away everything extraneous to the narrative and its related *topoi*. But the *topos* about the value of learning from history remained to serve as an introduction to the purpose of the *Memoirs* themselves. Pellisson summarized his conception of that purpose in a draft he either prepared or revised to cover the events for 1661: "Des princes qui ont écrit pour leurs enfants, les uns n'ont laissés que des préceptes sans histoire, ce qui est moins agréable; les autres que l'histoire sans préceptes, ce qui est moins utile: la perfection est peut-être à joindre les deux."[102] Such a truism was sustained by the authority of the ancients, Louis's preceptors, and perhaps the King's own experience. Instead of being perceived as banal, it evoked in Louis's milieu the same respect due a prayer that had been learned in childhood to be used as a spiritual guide throughout life.

Conversion and Appointment as Historiographer Royal

While Périgny lived, Pellisson may merely have been generally familiar with the *petite académie* and its labors; his text about the campaign of 1668 may have been considered by Louis and/or Périgny, only to be rejected for the *Memoirs*, without their author's knowledge. Pellisson may not have been sufficiently intimate with the King to permit him to begin work on the *Memoirs* until after 1 September 1670, the date of Périgny's death.[103] There was, however, one obstacle to Pellisson's ap-

102. *Mémoires de Louis XIV*, ed. Jean Longnon (Paris, 1923), p. 266, n. 80.
103. Some months before Périgny's death Pellisson had, however, been granted a pension and access to the royal chamber. Louis Nublé wrote to Gilles Ménage on 12 January 1670: "Jeudi dernier le Roy aiant donné à M. de Pellisson une fort longue et tres favorable audience, qu'il luy avoit fait

pointment as historiographer royal and collaborator on the *Memoirs*. Like d'Ablancourt, he was a Huguenot.

Ever since his years of enforced leisure in the Bastille, when he had read the Church fathers, especially on the Eucharist,[104] it had been rumored that Pellisson might convert to Catholicism. During the 1660s a conversion, especially that of an Academician and a defender of Fouquet, could only be a public act. Turenne's and the numerous Duras-Durfort conversions had been described in detail to the public and employed in tracts and sermons as examples exhorting the remaining Huguenots to follow their lead. Gradually the Protestant literate and political elite had been dissolving. Montausier, himself a former Huguenot, may have pressed Pellisson to convert at the time of Périgny's illness and death by suggesting that Pellisson might become a candidate for preceptor to the Dauphin, a position that surely would necessitate his conversion. For men of letters raised in the humanist tradition, no position was more honorable than preceptor—being the Aristotle of a young Alexander and attempting through instruction to raise him to be an ideal prince. Such a suggestion must have made Pellisson reel in speculation about the future. The question became not whether to convert, but how to do so in a seemly and pious fashion. Pellisson feared that the congruence of events—Périgny's death and his conversion—would cause people to challenge the sincerity of his formal conversion,[105] which took place just five weeks after Périgny's death. In the interval Bossuet had been named preceptor; Pellisson became historiographer and collaborator on the *Memoirs* after his abjuration and retreat for intense devotions at the Abbey of La Trappe.[106] The transformation of Pellisson, former provincial Protestant judge, into a Catholic court-

esperer deux jours auparavant, il lui, je ne dirai pas accorda, car son discours ne tendoit à rien moins qu'à cela, mais il luy donna de lui mesme et de la meilleure grace du monde, une pension de dis mille ecus sur ses menus plaisirs et les entrées de la chambre le soir et le matin: ce qui augmente ce present de plus de la moitié. M. de Pellisson ne croioit pas que la chose se dûst executer[?] si tost. Mais dès le jour mesme le Roy donna les ordres pour cela, et publia luy mesme la chose; dont il fut generalement loüé d'un chacun, de sorte que dès huit au matin [Scudéry received] un billet de la part de M. de Pellisson, par lequel il la prioit expressement entre autres choses de vous en faire part" (B.N., Rothschild Autograph Collection, XII, letter 962). I owe the discovery of this account of Pellisson's interview to Patricia M. Ranum.

104. *Les chimères de M. Jurieu* (Paris, 1689), p. 11.

105. Marcou, p. 274. See also F. Desmons, *L'Episcopat de Gilbert de Choiseul* (Tournai, 1907), p. 314.

106. Marcou, p. 275.

ier entrusted with recording the King's actions was now complete.
He never exerted great influence on the writing of the *Memoirs*, in
part because Louis gradually lost interest in them.[107] Because Pellisson
had won favor by accompanying the King on military campaigns and
writing about these events, he continued to go with Louis and prepared detailed accounts of what he saw and heard.[108] Mademoiselle de
Scudéry, his old friend and supporter while he was in the Bastille, received these reports in letter form; only a selection of this voluminous
correspondence survives in the *Lettres historiques* published in 1729.[109]
These reports are of interest because they permit us to note the differences between a historiographer's informal, confidential reports and his
finished histories. In a sense, they are structurally the complement of
the *Memoirs*, that is, events without *topoi*.[110] Through these differences
between the various drafts of a historical work, if anywhere, it is possible to perceive the effects of rhetoric and political and propagandistic
influences on the historical genre.

The *Lettres historiques* are relaxed in tone, familiar, and above all
impressionistic: they mention muddy roads, torrential rains, encounters
with peasants and townsmen, quarrels among courtiers, the humdrum
of camp life.The King is portrayed as a young man sure of himself and
to the very last detail aware of his responsibilities. Pellisson recorded
the details of Louis's daily conduct, rather than strategic and diplomatic
decisions. In fact, he had little choice. Louis never once took him aside

107. In 1671? See Sonnino, "The Dating and Authorship," p. 326.
108. He also applied his talent as a writer to preparing "manifestos" to
sway public opinion on such crucial issues as a European war. "Il y a sous
presse, pour sortir demain ou après, une déclaration du roi qui défend le
commerce avec les Hollandois et Pellisson travaille à un manifeste au sujet
de cette guerre, et l'on est dans l'impatience de vous attacquer, et l'on com-
mencera dans cet hiver" ("Avis secret de Paris, donné à Jean de Witt," 27
November 1671, *Correspondance du Grand Pensionnaire Jean de Witt*, ed.
François Combes [Paris, 1873], pp. 374 f.).
109. Pellisson refers to incidents that he had previously described, but
these incidents are not included among the selected letters, indicating that
his eighteenth-century editors were not particularly careful in making their
selection from the correspondence.
110. Pellisson revised his notes for some if not all parts of his history.
B.N., mss. fr. 23331, fols. 300 ff. is probably the manuscript that served for
his *Histoire de Louis XIV, depuis la mort du Cardinal Mazarin en 1661
jusqu'à la paix en 1678* (Paris, 1749), 3 vols. The differences between the
manuscript and the published work are editorial, such as, for page 58 (the
ms. has its own pagination) "Monsieur de Turenne" became "Vicomte de
Turenne" (vol. 1, p. 251).

during the Dutch War of 1672–1678 to explain his motives or discuss his worries. The fact that Pellisson regularly heard the King's news reports at the royal *coucher*, which was attended by the court, indicates the minor significance that Louis attached to Pellisson's efforts at writing history. Balanced against this, however, were the propensities of Louis, the Dutch, and perhaps the Imperials during the early years of this war to use newspapers as vehicles for discussions of peace terms. The parties stated their terms publicly; the *gazettes de Hollande* circulated through the French camps, accessible to literate troops.[111]

Louis also could be frank at his *coucher*; on occasion he expressed his worries and shared his thoughts about the war and the future with those in attendance. In several instances he gave summaries of the costs of the war and the sums he had spent on fortifications, certainly an innovation of his to counter war protests back in France. In other words, the public manner in which the royal campaigns were fought shifted the traditional advantage held by historians to the writers of *gazettes*. Pellisson refers so frequently to the *gazettes* that one senses he was trying to write down only those details that might not appear in them. He did not speculate about diplomatic negotiations, though he occasionally recorded rumors. Military operations are also murky, partly because Pellisson had little access to correspondence among the generals, but primarily because he seems not to have understood the general movements of these campaigns. Always very much a man of letters who has gone to war, Pellisson was incapable of seeing beyond individual acts and viewing the war at large.

For this reason he almost unconsciously records the rising tensions as the war dragged on. From the parades and lavish receptions in some Flemish towns, the scene shifts inexorably to crucial sieges and the conviction that everything depends on Turenne in the Rhineland.[112] Pellisson knew almost nothing about the eastern war, but he sensed

111. The "menteries" of the Dutch papers facilitated the mobilization of French opinion behind Louis. Pellisson records quite accidentally how this effect was evident at court while the King was on campaign (*Lettres historiques*, vol. 1, p. 226).

112. The sieges had already begun to assume the special character they would have for the wars of the 1680s and 1690s. For that of Valenciennes in March 1677, Pellisson also prepared an account that was more detailed than his letters to Scudéry (*ibid.*, vol. 3, p. 187). Perhaps this had been his practice all along, and if so the letters were merely to serve as anecdotal materials to help fill in details when he came to write the history. This same procedure was later followed by Racine: letters to Boileau, and his own accounts, which he did not trust to couriers.

Louis's preoccupation with it and the anxiety that accompanied lack of news. Then, on 29 July 1675, Pellisson learned "une des plus cruelles nouvelles du monde," the news that Turenne had been killed. The details that Pellisson records about this "malheur" center on the emotional responses of the leading participants, including Turenne's troops. Quietly, but as a master rhetorician, he notes that the same courier who informed the King of Turenne's death was bearing a letter from the Marshal. In that letter Turenne had written, "qu'il falloit périr ou battre les ennemis, et qu'il avoit envoyé à Brisach pour faire des prières publiques, et exposer le Saint Sacrement."[113] Then Pellisson reports the King's reactions: "Il n'est pas besoin de vous dire que le Roi, quoiqu'avec beaucoup de fermeté et de constance, en est et paroit extrememment touché. . . . Les regrets sont infinis. Chacun croit avoir perdu son ami."[114]

In the next letter, Pellisson reports still more news from the front, including the response of Turenne's soldiers, who said to one another, "Notre pauvre père est mort, mais il le faut venger."[115] Turenne's attachment to the infantry is recalled, and his reputation for leniency with pillaging troops is mentioned, though without the moral judgment that Pellisson usually makes on such matters. The story was circulating through the army that a few days prior to his death Turenne had come upon a band of soldiers who had stolen some cows from peasants and were trying to hide them. Turenne had asked, "Que faites-vous là?"—to which they had replied, "Nous cachons les vaches jusques à ce que le Vicomte [de Turenne] soit passé." In reply, Turenne reportedly said, "Il pourra passer bien tôt. Mais une autre fois je vous conseille de vous mieux cacher de peur d'être pendus."[116] If not an actual record of an incident from the popular culture, this is at least a perception of what men of Pellisson's status wanted to believe about the relations between the hero and his troops and their affection toward each other. Those troops who had lagged behind or had violated Turenne's orders may have been forced to develop anecdotes of this sort to relieve their sense of guilt after the seeming providential act that carried off their commander.

Yet Pellisson in no way consciously interprets Turenne's death as an omen of defeat; in fact, his only personal interest seems to have been in the spiritual status of the Marshal who, like Pellisson, was a

113. *Ibid.*, vol. 2, p. 380.
114. *Ibid.*, p. 381.
115. *Ibid.*, vol. 3, p. 387.
116. *Ibid.*, vol. 2, p. 388.

convert to Catholicism.[117] Why else would Pellisson have inquired about Turenne's spiritual state from one of the Marshal's friends in the Parlement? The precise account of engineer Paul's conversion a few hours before his death interests Pellisson in the same way, because he seeks edification from it.[118] Through this personal preoccupation, Pellisson also touches on the general theme of his history, namely, the restoration of Catholicism in the conquered Protestant cities.

Pellisson was, however, constrained to record only that material deemed worthy of inclusion in the historical genre: military operations, names of dead or wounded officers, and royal deeds of leadership, clemency, and justice. The Flemish towns—"very clean," with their incessant bellringing and receptions for Louis—are described only enough to provide a setting for a discussion of the King's reception in the former Spanish territories. Once back in Paris, Pellisson could transform his letters into history merely by adding *topoi* and pruning out those few personal remarks that his contemporaries would have deemed inappropriate in a royal history.

Pellisson could be cynical about some of the material he collected merely because it could not be omitted from a history. The prodigies, or omens, are a case in point: "Au reste, puisque les historiens les plus solides de l'antiquité tiennent registre des prodiges faux ou véritables, qui ont précédé les grand évènemens, vous [Scudéry] ne trouverez pas mauvais que je mette trois ou quatre choses extraordinaires dont on parle depuis peu."[119] Such omens were of little interest to Pellisson, yet he recorded that a nun in "odeur de sainteté" had prophesied two years earlier that masses would be said publicly in Utrecht; that the preceding year the "marche françoise" had been heard beneath the walls by the mystified populace of Nijmegen, although there was no one there to play it; and that a nocturnal *Te Deum* had been heard in the still-

---

117. *Ibid.*, p. 391. Pellisson seems to have wanted to believe that Turenne desired peace and was about to "se retirer à l'Institut" in order to lead a more religious life. That Louis had difficulty accepting his own and the court's morbid preoccupation with Turenne's death seems indicated by his recounting of his own brush with a cannon shot (*ibid.*, p. 391). This is probably less of a glimpse into Louis's psychology than into the primordial influence that heroic and providential acts had on individuals in the seventeenth century. In this instance, Louis responded as if he were a child trying to equal another child (who was receiving a great deal of attention because he had been hurt) by telling how he once had narrowly escaped injury.

118. *Ibid.*, vol. 1, p. 332.

119. *Ibid.*, p. 131.

Protestant church of Rheinberg, an omen indicating that Louis's armies would restore that church to Catholicism. Pellisson seems to have wanted to believe in such omens, yet he did not.[120] He may have perceived royal actions and Louis's statesmanship in much the same manner: they, too, were miraculous, but he could not really believe in miracles.

The war itself, as seen from the perspective of a man of letters, slowly changed from a delightful romp through the Spanish Netherlands to a grim duel in the Rhineland.[121] Pellisson recorded the changes as a subconscious response to the rising tensions around him. He wanted to depict war as it should be for a man of letters: heroic. Acts of cowardice, defeats, and desertions are not part of his history. He could admire "ces grands corps d'infanterie, et de cavalerie, marchant en si bon ordre, en bataillons et escadrons égaux, à distances égales sans rien entre deux, à peu-près comme les compartiments d'un parterre,"[122] but he could neither perceive clearly the reasons for which Louis was fighting nor sense the outcome of the struggle. True, he recorded public statements of terms, but he seems to have had no interest in negotiations or rumors about them.[123] When Louis permitted soldiers publicly to accuse their officers of corruption, Pellisson was there to record the exchange of words. He admired the soldiers' courage in speaking up and Louis's for not punishing a soldier who had falsely accused his officer.[124] With an unerring eye for his public, Pellisson preferred, however, to record acts of bravery. After remarking that the bravery of the French certainly equaled that recorded by the ancient Greek and Roman historians, he quoted a wounded soldier who said, "Ce n'est rien. Le régiment a fait son devoir."[125] The story of the soldier who, having extended his hand to help a marquis, only to have it shot through,

---

120. One instance where he seemed to want to believe an omen is the case of the metal hat that fell from the tomb of the House of Orange—the *Libertas Batava* (*ibid.*, p. 237).

121. The perspective of the literary as distinguished from that of the political historian or the historian of ideas is still very much alive in the discussion of writings about the Dutch War. See Nicole Ferrier, "Les écrivains français et la conquête de la Hollande en 1672," *XVIIᵉ Siècle* 92 (1971): 100–116, for an analysis of writers' attitudes toward war that is brought to parallel United States policy in Indochina, without a discussion of how conquest was an integral part of European political cultures during the seventeenth century.

122. *Lettres historiques*, vol. 1, p. 66.

123. *Ibid.*, p. 253.

124. *Ibid.*, p. 357.

125. *Ibid.*, p. 330.

simply extended the other hand, was included to please his readers. War was described as it should be by observers on the battlefield: "les nôtres,"[126] as Pellisson called the French troops, seemed destined to victory.

The image of Louis that Pellisson could create from the incidents he recorded rarely extends beyond the evidence supporting *topoi* about royal leadership. The King distributed money throughout the countryside. A "rather comely" peasant girl boldly asked him for enough money to get married, whereupon Louis obliged her by giving her four *pistolles*. Pellisson remarked, "Husbands are cheap in this country, because money is so scarce."[127] Louis's acts of justice—particularly of the exemplary sort, which usually involved the death sentence for pillaging or desertion[128]—as well as his acts of clemency[129] were recorded as deeds worthy of a monarch on campaign.

Occasionally some incidents were recorded that seemed to go beyond the range of exemplary justice. The act of extreme social deviance could be neither instructive nor edifying, and Pellisson implied as much about the case of the two "wretches" who were hanged after having been caught in a cabaret drinking from a chalice.[130] Did Pellisson perceive this incident as an act of Protestant defiance? It is doubtful, for throughout the *Lettres historiques* he remains eager to grasp at every wisp of evidence favorable to Catholicism and the French presence in the Low Countries. Thus he may have seen Protestant defiance as extreme social deviance, like that of an insane individual who steals a candlestick from a church.[131] No such deviant acts should be recorded in a history. The French of Pellisson's generation could envisage no lessons to be learned from what were defined as acts of madness.

Exactly the opposite were those incidents in which Louis showed himself a calculating, magnanimous, and self-confident statesman. Pellisson seemed to find just the right amount of pomp, exemplary justice, bad lodgings while on campaign, troop reviews, displays of bravery, consultations with generals, ceremonial banquets, masses, and private devotions to confirm his image of the ideal monarch incarnate in Louis XIV. Louis's display of self-confidence—or perhaps arrogance—elicited Pellisson's admiration. Upon accepting a letter from the estates given to him by the Dutch ambassador, the King added: "Qu'il la liroit si l'ambassadeur le vouloit, mais que cela n'estoit pas nécessaire, ses su-

126. A good example is *ibid.*, vol. 2, p. 85.
127. *Ibid.*, p. 21.
128. *Ibid.*, vol. 1, pp. 283 and 112.
129. *Ibid.*, p. 191; and for the condemned Swiss troops, vol. 2, p. 344.
130. *Ibid.*, vol. 1, p. 305.
131. See especially the letter from Zeist, *ibid.*, p. 210.

périeurs ayant pris tant de soin d'envoyer cette lettre en toutes les cours de l'Europe qu'il en couroit des copies, et qu'il en avoit une dans sa poche."[132] Pellisson always was proud when the King spoke well or demonstrated an ear for language. As if Louis were their pupil, men of letters were exhilarated by his mastery of the literary arts. On the other hand, Pellisson recorded without comment Louis's "touching" to heal through his thaumaturgical powers.[133] More important is the implicit belief that military campaigns go well when the king joins his armies in the field.

There are more intimate glimpses as well: "Nous l'avons vû ces jours passés à son petit coucher, en se joüant, le dos tourné à une grande carte géographique faite exprès, mettre le doigt sans y manquer jamais, sur tous les endroits de quelque conséquence qu'on lui pouvoit nommer."[134] The courtiers in attendance may have been careful to select those cities that they were virtually certain Louis could find. A courtier who stumped the King would have been mortified. Such schoolboy mental agility as giving speeches from memory seemed to inspire admiration among those who made it their business to observe men of power. In this Pellisson was no exception. Apart from these very infrequent anecdotes of a playful king, however, Louis's conduct and remarks were recorded only when they conformed to the *topoi* associated with a French king. Among these, the sacerdotal *topoi* were reduced to that single reference to Louis's touching already mentioned. His attendance at mass was frequently noted, as were his private devotions, but neither saintly nor miraculous qualities were stressed to characterize Louis's behavior. He was commended as a judge of men and morals; his caution and sobriety, rather than his passion for conquest of his impetuosity, were the principal attributes that Pellisson saw in his master. None of the Plutarchian attributes about divinity or those superhuman qualities credited to Alexander were observed in Louis or attributed to him.

While the war continued, Pellisson began to undertake new tasks for the Monarchy, first to defend royal rights related to such rich abbeys as Saint-Germain-des-Prés and then to administer the royal income not only of that abbey but of Cluny and Saint-Denis as well, in order to hasten the conversion of Protestants. He wrote legal briefs, letters to bishops, and refutations of Protestant attacks upon the King. Having become a proficient financial manager under Fouquet, Pellisson now used his abilities in a vast campaign to convert all Huguenots and reward them financially—that is, "compensate" them—for having done so.

132. *Ibid.*, p. 58.
133. *Ibid.*, vol. 3, p. 251.
134. *Ibid.*, vol. 1, p. 78.

In 1677—perhaps out of the Marquise de Montespan's pique, but more likely as a result of Pellisson's growing influence over Protestant affairs —two new historiographers royal were named: Racine and Boileau. The task of answering Pierre Jurieu's attacks on Louis, corresponding with Leibniz over projects for the union of the churches,[135] and preparing a weighty historical treatise on the Eucharist[136] were all undertaken by Pellisson on behalf of the Crown within the spirit of the functions of a historiographer royal.[137] Satires against him were soon published, as were outright attacks from enraged Protestants. Pope Innocent XI addressed to him a letter of congratulation on his work.

As was often the case with a converted Huguenot, Pellisson's death in 1693 led some contemporaries to speculate about the sincerity of his conversion, for it became known that no priest had been in attendance during his last moments.[138] Pellisson had spent the final decades of his life fervently working for the conversion of Huguenots, but this did not satisfy those who wanted to view his death without the sacrament of extreme unction as a return to Protestantism. Having inquired about the circumstances surrounding his uncle's death, one nephew, the famous historian of England, Paul de Rapin de Thoyras, reported quite simply that death had surprised Pellisson and caught him unaware, but not unprepared.[139]

135. Marcou, Chap. 10.

136. *Ibid.*, p. 377. His correspondence with Boisot (Bibliothèque de Besançon, mss. fr. 602) reveals the extent of his dependency upon Boisot in his refutations of Protestants, and in his letters to Leibniz. In April 1690 he completed a critique of Varillas's *Histoire de François I* (fol. 121).

137. Pellisson's later years as a publicist and financial administrator merit closer attention than Marcou has given them.

138. Marcou, p. 404.

139. "Lettre écrite de Paris à Salomon de Rapin-La Fare," *Bulletin de la Société de l'histoire du protestantisme français* 7 (1858): 27–30.

Chapter IX
Racine Learns to Be
a Historiographer

OUIS XIV's translation of Book I of Julius Caesar's *Commentaries on the Gallic War* was printed on the royal presses in the Louvre in 1651.[1] The King was thirteen years old. There is no way of knowing how much his tutors guided the pen held by their illustrious pupil.

With the exception of Georges Lacour-Gayet and John B. Wolf,[2] historians have not bothered to study Louis's education; yet the surviving manuscripts, curriculum, and educational methods employed could be studied in order to reveal the presuppositions and aims not only of his tutors but also of the French Monarchy in the mid-seventeenth century. Tutors were very carefully selected, and the courses of study were prepared to initiate the prince in the art of governing. Louis's Latin may have been only rudimentary; but the moral, religious, and political principles conveyed in and through the Latin he attempted to learn may have taken firmer root than the grammar and syntax.

Caesar would not have been chosen to encourage whatever pacifist inclinations the young King might personally have had. Although the *Commentaries* were not a sacred religious text, the adolescent Louis could not possibly have perceived them as containing errors or ideals that were open to question. There is no evidence to suggest that, as a model of conduct, Caesar's account was balanced by other sources indicating that commander's shortcomings. The *Commentaries* were still thought to be perfect history by the men of learning of Louis's generation, because they had been written by a participant—indeed, the principal actor—in the events narrated and were couched in eloquent language. Caesar combined all the virtues of a man of war and a man of letters.

Moreover, Caesar provided information about the early history of the young King's lands and about the ancestors of his subjects. It is

1. Georges Lacour-Gayet, *L'éducation politique de Louis XIV*, 2d ed., revised (Paris, 1923), pp. 75 f.

2. John B. Wolf, "The Formation of a King," *French Historical Studies* 1 (1958): 40 ff.

impossible to say just what Louis may have grasped about the desirability of men of virtue becoming conquerors, but nothing in the translation or its scholia implies criticism of Caesar as a conquering hero. And in relations among peoples and states, could Louis have failed to note that the mutual jealousies of the various Gallic tribes had permitted their enemies in Germany to gain a foothold on the Left Bank of the Rhine? The Gallic chiefs had appealed for Roman aid and received it, only to find themselves under the Roman thumb in the bargain.

When Louis later undertook the composition of his own memoirs, he may have been trying to fulfill the ideal of a man of letters and man of war that Caesar exemplified. None of his ancestors had attempted or in any way successfully sponsored the writing of their memoirs. Since this had been a source of complaint among men of letters for at least one hundred and fifty years, Louis may have decided to do something about it. The classicistic banality of Louis's education, and the fact that his biological father's career could not be used as a model of conduct, may shed light on why the Sun King's later behavior could attract so much attention among educated Europeans. Caesarian-Apollonian ideals of life were familiar coin throughout Europe. The fact that Caesar's family was ancient and of divine origin may have discouraged some young readers from attempting to emulate him, but Louis probably did not feel constrained by these qualities, since birth and religion permitted him to make similar claims.

When, in 1663, the *petite académie* that Colbert had assembled to work on the King's history was presented to Louis, the monarch told them: "Vous pouvez, Messieurs, juger de l'estime que je fais de vous, puisque je vous confie la chose du monde qui m'est la plus précieuse, qui est ma gloire. Je suis sûr que vous ferez des merveilles; je tâcherai de ma part de vous fournir de la matière qui mérite d'être mise en oeuvre par des gens aussi habiles que vous êtes."[3] This quotation reveals Louis's complete familiarity with the distinction between action and writings about action, a view of history that Budé had evoked to Francis I and that had become a favorite *topos* for writers. At an early age the Sun King had learned to compliment those who served him. In this instance he implied that the literary talents of this group were more than adequate to the task of writing the history of his reign, with the eloquence necessary to preserve his memory for all time.

In 1665 the dedicatory letter that Racine addressed to Louis about his play, *Alexandre le Grand*, ends in a peroration on the same *topos*:

3. Charles Perrault, *Mémoires de ma vie*, ed. Paul Bonnefon (Paris, 1909), p. 41.

VOTRE MAJESTE se couvrira Elle-même d'une gloire toute nouvelle; que nous La reverrons peut-être, à la tête d'une armée, achever la comparaison qu'on peut faire d'Elle et d'Alexandre, et ajouter le titre de conquérant à celui du plus sage roi de la terre. Ce sera alors que vos sujets devront consacrer toutes leurs veilles au récit de tant de grandes actions, et ne pas souffrir que V.M. ait lieu de se plaindre, comme Alexandre, qu'Elle n'a eu personne de son temps qui pût laisser à la postérité la mémoire de ses vertus. Je n'espère pas être assez heureux pour me distinguer par mes ouvrages; mais je sais bien que je me signalerai au moins par le zèle.[4]

The fact that as early as 1665 Racine was engaged in a public dialogue with Louis XIV over the writing of history is as significant as the topical structure of the dialogue itself. The King's speech—that is, the promise to attempt actions worthy of being recorded by such talented men of letters—and writer's response—in this case a vow to work hard in order to create prose equal in elegance to the greatness of the royal actions—form the two parts of the same public dialogue. Racine's shift from a discussion of the course of action to be taken by Louis's subjects to an evocation of his own "zeal" and literary works is a polite bid for attention, expressed as a compliment.

Men of letters, royal ministers, tutors, and Louis himself shared a common discourse about historical thought, the actions expected of a prince, and the services rendered by men of letters. The elements in this discourse would be refined and transformed time and time again into compliments that were at once the same and yet always carried within them specific allusions to political actions and writings. The elements in the larger discourse had narrowed since the days of Budé, as *topoi* about Christian kingship gave way before an expanding and enriching identification of French political culture with Antiquity.[5] But there is no need to demonstrate this constant evocation of Antiquity, since we are aware of the many editions of Plutarch, Curtius, Julius Caesar, Livy, and Tacitus published during the seventeenth century.[6] The *monde des lettrés*, rather than the kings, had classicized French political culture. Etchings of Louis XIV on his knees before an altar bearing a crucifix were intended only for the most popular consumption, when they were produced at all; instead, the images of the Sun King—like

4. "Au Roi," dedication to *Alexandre le Grand*, in *Oeuvres complètes de Jean Racine*, ed. René Picard (Paris, 1951), vol. 1, p. 194.

5. See above, p. 42.

6. Henri-Jean Martin, *Livre, pouvoirs, et société au XVIIe siècle* (Geneva, 1969), *passim*.

the histories of his reign—were classical. Louis never seems to have objected to being portrayed as a Roman emperor.

The writings of the ancients could, however, be made to refract a wide spectrum of ideological, psychological, and religious perspectives. In what ways had the Catholic Reformation in France diminished, muted, or shaded some of the more republican, stoical, and anticonquest thought of Antiquity? The practice of limiting the assignments for pupils in Jesuit schools to selected passages from ancient authors readily comes to mind. Racine's Jansenist teachers at Port-Royal were careful to excise scabrous passages from the works they gave their pupils, but otherwise they were committed to the principle of having their charges read complete works.

And what of the impact of divine-right absolutism? Of the decline and then repression of Protestants? The Fronde had rekindled arguments favoring a balanced constitution, a *chose publicque*; but the senatorial power of the parlementaires lost adherents before the rising enthusiasm for the princes among nobles and *peuple*. Then the disenchantment with the princes after 1651 shaped public opinion to accept increased royal authority.[7]

Obviously these general questions may only be answered by further extensive research on the education and beliefs of the literate elites. The study of the career of a single individual cannot answer them. Yet, if a Jansenist bourgeois who had many reasons for keeping his distance from Versailles nevertheless sought and gained patronage from the Sun King, it is reasonable to assume that men with lesser cause to remain aloof might already have totally identified with, or seen themselves expressed in, the monarchy of Versailles. The *monde des lettrés* had long since accepted royal patronage and service as the ideal toward which they strove. After the Fronde, old animosities were for a time submerged in the praise of the young monarch.

Early Education

The obscurity of Pellisson's early career does not permit us to discern what Antiquity had contributed to his education beyond an interest in Roman law. The sources on Racine's early education are much richer and enable us to see how, even after the Fronde, the ancients could still be held up as models in formal instruction, to pierce through the web

7. The standard works on the subject are P. R. Doolin, *The Fronde* (Cambridge, 1935); A. Lloyd Moote, *The Revolt of the Judges* (Princeton, 1971); and E. H. Kossman, *La Fronde* (Leiden, 1954).

of Catholic-Reformation and divine-right-absolutist thought. Plutarch and Tacitus were the principal historical sources that provided Racine with a critical perspective on the alterations occurring in the French Monarchy under Louis XIV and enabled him to be circumspect about the impact of princely power upon historical thought.

Racine was about sixteen when he read and annotated Plutarch's works.[8] He also read Tacitus's *Annals* and compiled a notebook of sentences, which he boldly entitled "Taciti Sententia Illustriores excerpta Anno 1656."[9] Perhaps he prepared this notebook of selected passages because no cheap Basel edition of Tacitus, like those of Plutarch and numerous other ancient authors, was available to him at Port-Royal. The Latin sentences were copied out in a clear hand; his marginal glosses are also chiefly in Latin. Those in French are in a lighter ink and perhaps in a more mature hand, suggesting that they are later additions by Racine or someone else. The reading and annotating of these ancient authors was supervised by the maîtres of Port-Royal. As in the case of Louis XIV's translation of Caesar, it is impossible to be certain that Racine grasped the nuances of the passages he copied out. But, unlike Louis, Racine had beyond doubt mastered Latin and Greek. Moreover, equal or perhaps more care was shown in his education than in the King's. The number of tutors per pupil in the Palais Cardinal and at Port-Royal was roughly the same, and their dedication to teaching was comparable.[10]

8. *Oeuvres complètes*, vol. 2, p. 1140.

9. B.N., mss. fr. 12888.

10. For Racine's education, see René Picard, *La carrière de Jean Racine* (Paris, 1961); and Louis Vaunois, "La jeunesse de Racine," *Cahiers Raciniens* 14 (1963): 30–55. For the relationships that bound Racine to his great teacher, Antoine Le Maître, the following letter, addressed to "le petit Racine," 21 March 1656, conveys a sense of mutual service and collaboration in the pursuit of learning. "Mon fils, je vous prie de m'envoyer au plus tôt l'Apologie des saints Pères [by Antoine Arnauld] qui est à moi, et qui est de la Iᵉ impression. Elle est reliée en veau marbré, in-4. J'ai reçu les cinq volumes de mes Conciles, que vous aviez fort bien empaquetés. Je vous remercie. Mandez-moi si tous mes livres sont au château [Vaumurier], bien arrangés sur des tablettes, et si tous mes onze volumes de saint Chrysostome y sont, et voyez-les de temps en temps pour les nettoyer. Il faudrait mettre de l'eau dans des écuelles de terre où ils sont, afin que les souris ne les rongent pas. Faites mes recommandations à Mme Racine [Marie Desmoulins, Racine's grandmother] et à votre bonne tante [Agnès de Sainte-Thècle], et suivez leurs conseils en tout. La jeunesse doit toujours se laisser conduire, et tâcher de ne point s'émanciper. Peut-être que Dieu nous fera revenir où vous êtes. Cependant il faut tâcher de profiter de cette persécution, et de faire qu'elle nous serve à nous détacher du monde, qui nous paraît si ennemi

Racine's glosses on Plutarch and, still more, his copying out and glossing of sentences from the *Annals* were but a beginning in sophistication and politics. These glosses were not thoughts in the usual sense of created products or original speculations. Instead, they reveal the degree of Racine's exposure to ancient thought that bears within it presuppositions about politics and that serves as a tool for analyzing the exercise of power, the meaning of virtue in Republican Rome, and the role of men of letters during the first century of the Principate. Racine used unabridged editions of Plutarch and Tacitus. In reading the ancients, his eye may have been sustained or directed by a certain reverence for the truths they contained, be they religious or secular, and an implicit contempt for the thought of his own day. Racine's library included almost no books in French, and in later years he frowned upon all but a few of the nonancient authors in whom his son was interested.[11] He remained an *Ancien* all his life and sought to perpetuate the tradition of respect for the ancients and adherence to their works as having greater authority than those of modern writers. Louis XIV's supervision of the Dauphin's education was almost identical with Racine's supervision of his son, even to the harsh discipline that left both Jean-Baptiste Racine and the Dauphin fearful and hesitant before the world in adulthood. The similarity of their aims in educating their children and their rigorous insistence upon the classics reveal the role played by these two fathers' recollections of their own educations, if not of particular elements of thought learned from a specific ancient author. Racine's mastery of the works of Antiquity would always earn him deference as a man of learning from courtiers and *doctes* alike. He was one of those who never "lost his Greek."[12]

Racine's glosses on Plutarch are often paraphrases but never quick summaries of the action. In the life of Romulus, however, beside Plutarch's observation that the senators informed the populace that Romulus had been removed by the gods and "after having been a

---

de la piété. Bonjour, mon cher fils. Aimez toujours votre papa comme il vous aime. Ecrivez-moi de temps en temps. Envoyez-moi aussi mon Tacite in-folio" (Vaunois, p. 39).

11. When Jean-Baptiste Racine was permitted to read in French, the father strongly recommended a translation of Herodotus, "qui est fort divertissant, et qui vous apprendrait la plus ancienne histoire qui soit parmi les hommes, apres l'Ecriture Sainte" (9 October 1692, *Oeuvres complètes*, vol. 2, p. 527).

12. In the heat of controversy over Perrault's "impertinent" theorizing about literature and the Moderns, Racine scornfully implied to Boileau that his antagonist lacked control of Greek: "M. Perrault ne peut-il pas avoir quelque ami grec qui lui fournisse des mémoires?" (1693; *ibid.*, p. 543).

beneficent king was going to become a propitious god for them," Racine wrote in the margin, "Saint Louis."[13] Then, in the life of Caius Marcius Coriolanus, where Plutarch describes how bribery and corruption had turned the city from a republic into a monarchy and how the populace feared electing an aristocrat (Coriolanus) who might take away their rights once he was office, Racine grasped the man's character in the sentence, "La solitude est la compagne de l'arrogance."[14]

No party or body of the electorate would have much to do with Coriolanus, whom they respected and almost venerated as a military hero, although they feared his power. As Racine read on and learned about Coriolanus's rejection by the populace and his abandoning Rome to join the enemy armies—which he had earlier defeated—in their attack upon the city, he wrote: "Monsieur le Prince." The parallel refers to the Grande Condé, victor over the Spanish at Rocroy, who became embroiled in the Fronde and, having alienated all but his most faithful clients, eventually went over to the Spaniards during the years when schoolboy Racine was reading Plutarch. Thus the parallels with ancients could include not only the departed Saint Louis but a contemporary, Condé. In the life of Alcibiades, just after Plutarch records Alcibiades' impeachment and narrates how he goes over to the Spartans' side to aid them against his compatriots, Racine again noted: "Monsieur le Prince."[15]

As he grew older, Racine became increasingly subtle when drawing parallels between ancient and modern behavior and between individual ancients and his contemporaries, but the fundamental mechanism of using parallels as a mode of historical analysis remained unchanged.

Still more significant, the study of the ancients brought Racine to the threshold of active participation in the political life of the realm. This marked an important step out of a life of solitude and inertness. Without wealth or social standing, the seventeen-year-old Racine could scarcely have believed that he would meet and converse with Condé. But, in a sense, Plutarch prepared him for that day. The study of history permitted the young man of inferior birth to live among the great, to observe their strengths and weaknesses—in short, to form his own character and to perceive the character of others.

Purely stylistic and grammatical questions appear infrequently in the glosses, indicating that the text was read primarily for moral instruction. For the life of Alexander the glosses include: "Contre ceux qui s'amusent à décrire des guerres et des combats par le menu—La nature

13. *Ibid.*, p. 934.
14. *Ibid.*, p. 936.
15. *Ibid.*, p. 937.

d'un homme se reconnaît plutôt dans une petite action que dans beaucoup d'autres grandes—Donner de bons précepteurs aux jeunes rois—Ne
point flatter les rebelles—Ne croire trop les calomnies—C'est une chose
plus digne d'un roi de surmonter ses passions que de vaincre ses ennemis . . .—C'est une chose digne de la grandeur d'un roi, de souffrir
qu'on parle mal de lui lorsqu'il fait bien . . .—Les rois ne doivent trop
s'éloigner du milieu de leur royaume."[16] A comparison between these
glosses and the integral text of the life reveals that Racine found nothing
to say about Plutarch's discussion of the difference between a biographer, which he claims to be, and a historian.[17] These more formal
questions of genre would interest Racine a great deal after his appointment as historiographer in 1677.

No parallels between the king reigning in 1656 and Alexander are
made, but taken as a whole the glosses on kingship from Plutarch are
the colors and brush strokes for a portrait of a great king. Similarly, at
this stage no parallels are drawn between men of letters in Antiquity
and Racine's contemporaries. No factual matters clutter the glosses;
Racine either was familiar with the details of Alexander's life from
other sources, or his masters at Port-Royal had instructed him not to
confuse actions themselves with the moral reflections that these might
inspire. Here the young man's notes reveal Jansenist pedagogy and also
provide evidence for the ever-present *coupure* between actions and
writing about those actions.[18] It was the fabric of moral principles, and
not the event or action, that Racine recorded in his notebook—thus
making the transposition from Louis XIV to Alexander as easy as that
from Coriolanus to Condé. The temporal direction, forward or backward, made no difference, and the specific event that inspired the reflection was of less importance than the reflection to which it gave rise.

For individuals living in times as remote as the seventeenth century,
we can only rarely discern the degree to which they could escape
from or repudiate pedagogical, moral, religious, and political principles
learned as schoolboys. But in Racine's case this reconstruction is possible. His own son, Jean-Baptiste, left for diplomatic service in Holland
before his education under Charles Rollin had been completed. Thus,
through the correspondence between father and son, we can note what
Racine considered essential in a young man's education. On virtually
every point he was anxious that his son learn exactly what he himself
had learned, and in the same ways. The father wanted the son to make

16. *Ibid.*, p. 941.
17. "Life of Alexander," *Plutarch's Lives*, ed. B. Perrin, Loeb Classical
Library (New York, 1919), vol. 7, p. 225.
18. See Lacour-Gayet, pp. 73 ff., for a discussion of Louis XIV's own
notebook of *sententiae*.

extraits of French history,[19] read Plutarch's *Lives*,[20] and, in his *versions* into French, exercise care to convey the exact meaning of the original Latin. The boy had to submit his exercises for scrutiny by his father, who unhesitatingly stressed the moral and political themes in the ancient works he had studied as a youth and still occasionally reread for pleasure.

At one point Racine was disappointed by his son's selection of one of Cicero's letters to Atticus, because the letter was simply factual. He recommended that Jean-Baptiste select another: "Il y en a tant de belles sur l'état où était alors la République, et sur les choses de conséquence qui se passaient à Rome. Vous ne lirez guère d'ouvrage qui soit plus utile pour former l'esprit et le jugement."[21] Thus, some thirty-five years after having completed just such exercises, Racine still believed in Port-Royal's methods of teaching and forming character.

The gleanings from Tacitus merit more attention than they can be given here, but even a cursory exploration will reveal that Racine's reading of the *Annals* provided him with a critical perspective or analytical dimension for the study of Louis XIV's character. In later life, what parallels may Racine have drawn between the effects of flattery and dissimulation upon historical thought—which Tacitus says occurred under Tiberius—and the effects of the Sun King's reign upon historical thought in France? Only those passages from the *Annals* that Racine copied out and glossed because they seemed particularly noteworthy will be used here to reconstruct information that the future historiographer may have recalled from his school days.

The relationship between literary creativity and political life is virtually Tacitus's first theme in the *Annals*. Talented writers had existed during Augustus's reign ("temporibusque Augusti dicendis non defuere decora ingenia").[22] But historical writing had then begun to suffer from political oppression under Tiberius, Gaius, Claudius, and Nero. During the reigns of each of these emperors, writers had grown fearful of telling the truth about Roman politics. Even after the ruler's death, hatreds were still too fresh to permit the writing of impartial and dispassionate accounts of these reigns. Racine glossed the sentence, "Adulatio ingenia deterit" (Flattery weakened their talents), and added, "Metus et odium historiae pestes" (Fear and hatred are the plagues of

19. *Oeuvres complètes*, vol. 2, p. 557.

20. *Ibid.*, p. 617.

21. 4 October 1692, *ibid.*, p. 524.

22. B.N., mss. fr. 12888, p. 3 (Tacitus, *Annals*, I.1). Else-Lilly Etter, *Tacitus in der Geistesgeschichte des 16. und 17. Jahrhunderts* (Basel, 1966), is the best introduction to the subject.

history).[23] The inferences he draws from the text sum up one of Tacitus's central themes in the *Annals*: the temptation to flatter may influence, indeed, almost determine how history is written, if the political regime tolerates or encourages such flattery. The powerful may also become angered by the truth about the past. The coupling of flattery and fear seems obvious: but nowhere in seventeenth-century French treatises on the art of writing history have I found such a coupling, either as an observation independently derived by an author or as a *topos*.

Tacitus held that Augustus had innovated when he applied the law of *majestas* to authors who had published allegedly scandalous libels. His successors undermined still further writers' freedom to praise or blame past actions. Roman public discourse became even more corrupted by Tiberius's dissimulation. For Tacitus, those senators and writers who fall over themselves to please and flatter the Emperor are as odious as the Emperor himself. Glory and virtue are undermined; these men come to love the enemies of virtue at a time when the only events that constitute history consist of cruel orders from the Emperor, treacherous friendships at the highest levels of government, and continual public accusations. Just as Tacitus places great emphasis upon the fate of Cremutius Cordus, so does Racine.

Publicly accused of excessively praising Brutus and Cassius in his writings, Cordus is threatened by Sejanus's clients with execution under the law of *majestas*. The speech that Tacitus gives to Cordus rings with phrases in defense of freedom of expression concerning the past. Racine copied the sentence "Verba mea, patres conscripti, arguuntur: adeo factorum innocens sum" (It is my words, o senators, that are being incriminated, for my actions are completely innocent).[24]

Then, in the speech that follows, Tacitus has Cremutius make historical arguments to prove to his accusers that under Augustus there had been greater freedom to write about the past. Had not Livy praised Pompey without losing Augustus' friendship? Had not Julius Caesar answered Cicero's praise for Cato only by a written oration, not an attempt to silence him?

No one replies to Cremutius in the *Annals*. Instead the Senate orders the aediles to burn his books. Tacitus insists that the accusation against Cremutius constituted a legal innovation. Since no member of the divine-imperial family had been slandered, the law of *majestas* did not apply. In his peroration, Cremutius asserts that posterity renders every-

23. *Ibid.*, p. 3 (I.i).
24. *Ibid.*, p. 71 (IV.xxxiv).

one the honor that is due him ("Suum cuique decus posteritas rependit") and adds that those who remember Cassius and Brutus will also remember and honor Cordus.

The Cremutius *exemplum* supports Tacitus's assertion that the freedom to write about the past had been stifled under Tiberius, and not before. Why had Julius and Augustus Caesar not censored historians? With the cynicism that his name evokes about politics, Tacitus remarks that one is permitted to laugh at those who in their madness believe they have the power to extinguish the memory of someone for future generations. Racine added a gloss in French: "Livres défendus."[25]

In addition to grasping Tacitus's arguments about the relationship between historical thought and politics, Racine also copied out many passages about the causes of shifts in the forms of government, that is, from a republic to a tyranny. He copied out several of the explicit remarks about forms of government in which Tacitus says that all nations are ruled by either the populace, the great, or a single individual. The state composed of just the right amount of each is easier to praise than to establish, and if it is established it does not endure: "Nam cunctas nationes et urbes populus aut primores aut singuli regunt: delecta ex iis et consociata rei publicae forma laudari facilius quam evenire, vel, si evenit, haud diuturna esse potest." (All nations and cities are governed by either the people, the great, or a single individual. A form of republic composed of these powers in proper proportion is easier to praise than to establish, and if it is established, it cannot last long.)[26] Racine did not gloss the sentence where Tacitus describes the conditions that undermined the republic, but he notes almost all the factors involved in its decline. Private good had come to be preferred over public utility, the populace was undisciplined, luxury was widespread, and the civil

25. *Ibid.*, p. 72 (IV.xxxv). The glosses in French seem to be in a lighter ink and perhaps a different hand. The difficulties in identifying Racine's handwriting at different periods are so great that they do not permit dating of a text on the basis of handwriting alone. But if Racine's Latin glosses were made while he was copying the sentences, might we not infer that the French glosses were added at a later date? No internal evidence has been found to confirm the notion that Racine reread and annotated his Tacitus in preparation for his duties as historiographer. That he kept all his notebooks and early library and treasured them is beyond a doubt. At this point the only evidence of Racine's second exposure to Tacitus is his review of his son's notebook. Yet the fact that the French glosses are in lighter ink brings us a step closer to the possible assertion that in later years Racine recalled Tacitus's analysis of the relationship between tyrannical government and stifled historical thought. Certainty, however, is impossible.

26. B.N., mss. fr. 12888, p. 70 (IV.xxxiii).

wars had led Roman citizens to abandon power to a single individual. It is neither a dictatorship nor a monarchy, "sed principis nomine constitutam rem publicam" (I.ix). Racine either overlooked Tacitus's distinction between a monarchy and Augustus's rule as *princeps*, or else he had been influenced by other texts and ideological considerations to disagree with it, for in the margin he wrote "monarchia necessitas"[27] opposite this passage where Tacitus categorized Augustan rule as a principate. The *excusata*, those reasons that brought about the exercise of power by one individual, are also copied out and summed up under the gloss "need to assure peace."

Tacitus's alternate explanation for Augustus's rise to power—namely, his lust for power and his ambition masked by filial respect—is also recorded by Racine. Tacitus points out that the peace brought by Augustus was a bloody one (I.ix), a repression. There is no evidence to suggest that Racine interpreted one explanation as more accurate than another, or that he perceived how they complemented each other to form a single interpretation of Augustus's rule.

Racine was fascinated by the bickering, quarreling, and murders among members of the imperial family. Almost every petty rivalry, every marriage that bred enmity, every act by a powerful, plotting, protective mother, and every instance of incest and prostitution is copied out. Tacitus had suggested that, unlike earlier historians whose subject matter had been war and other major events, he would reveal in his histories how the often neglected minor incident indicates momentous changes in the state. Thus, through the study of such allegedly insignificant events as feuding within the imperial family, Tacitus would demonstrate how the Roman Republic had changed from the rule of the few to the rule of one, a tyrant in the person of Tiberius (IV.xxxiii–xxxiv). The portrait of Tiberius consists of noting the tiny pique, the off-guard moment, the backing and filling, the insignificant remark or facial expression. The descent into tyranny had obliged Tacitus to write a history with no heroic actions, for he did not see the tyrant as capable of bold, courageous, and effective leadership in the Senate or on the battlefield. Along with such *exempla* as the trial of Cremutius, Racine copied out most of these apparently banal actions.

He grasped virtually all the elements of Tacitus's portrait of a tyrant. Had not Augustus's own inhumanity and lack of affection for the public good been most evident in the selection of Tiberius as his successor? Augustus had shown an all-consuming desire to enhance his own glory by choosing a weak and cruel successor, for the dismal reign of Tiberius would enhance the memory of his predecessor's rule. Augustus had

27. *Ibid.*, p. 6 (I.ix).

been unwilling to leave anything to the gods; he had appropriated for himself all the marks of veneration previously reserved for the deities (I.x). Still, he had not stifled discourse in the Republic, though his mere presence had changed its orientation from honesty and sincerity to flattery. Tiberius would complete the perversion of political language. The descent into the maelstrom of false accusations, military defeats, and family feuds is accelerated by the rising influence of the favorite, Sejanus, his ambitious wife, and their clients. The remedy for defeat on the battlefield lay in flattering Tiberius. A remark at table could be transformed into a weapon to bring about someone's disgrace. But Tiberius's own vagueness and insincerity were the worst of all. In writing to the Senate on behalf of his accused friend, Cotta, Tiberius began: "Quid scribam vobis, patres conscripti, aut quo modo scribam aut qui omnino non scribam hoc tempore, di me deaeque peius perdant quam perire me cotidie sentio, si scio." (If I know what to write to you at this time, o senators, or how to write it, or what not to write, may heaven plunge me into a more cruel ruin than I feel overtaking me every day!)[28] Tacitus added: "His crimes and wickedness had redounded to torment him," and he evoked Socrates on the minds of tyrants—if they could be opened they would reveal wounds, mutilations, and suffering brought on by cruelty, lust, and evil intentions. Racine noted in the margin: "Tyrannorum mentes."[29] Why did Racine not interpret these remarks as merely one more example of dissimulation and insincerity in Tiberius's public discourse? Because Tacitus interpreted the latter as more than mere dissimulation; it was a "cri de souffrance." The tyrant, that suffering figure who assumes responsibility for the evil actions of his friends and relatives in order that they may be free of guilt, is the political and psychological role that Racine grasps out of Tacitus. It is an integral part of the tyrannical form of government, since without Tiberius's perverse thoughts and actions, Sejanus could not climb higher over the bodies of those whom he had murdered. Racine records these sentences, adding "favory" as the gloss; but he makes no comment upon the relationship between favoritism and tyranny.[30]

If there are principles guiding Racine's selection of sentences from

28. Tacitus, VI.xii.

29. B.N., mss. fr. 12888, p. 85.

30. Sir John Eliot compared Buckingham to Sejanus in a speech delivered at the impeachment of the Duke, indicating that Racine's use of the word "favory" may be a standard parallel for seventeenth-century readers of the ancients. Cf. Mark H. Curtis, "The Alienated Intellectuals of Early Stuart England," *Past and Present* 23 (1962): 27; and Harold Hulme, *The Life of Sir John Eliot* (London, 1957), p. 143.

Tacitus, they were certainly moral and political, not grammatical or syntactical. An expanded rhetorical-political vision by Port-Royal may have been at work to bring together politics, psychology, and language. Louis-Isaac Le Maître de Saci, Claude Lancelot, and Jean Hamon did not drain the classical texts of their moral and political meaning.[31] Racine's education included a distinctly political, indeed almost ideological dimension, as a result of the manner in which history was studied at Port-Royal.

Port-Royal's use of Tacitus as a basis for the reconstruction of some of the central features of classical republican ideology was in itself probably quite conventional, for that ancient author's works had come to be associated with the reason of state believed to have first been recommended by Machiavelli. Racine did not interpret Tacitus as an apologist for reason of state. Quite the contrary. His use of Tacitus for the specific purpose of emphasizing tyranny's stifling effects upon historical thought and political discourse reveals that the *maîtres* of Port-Royal held an unconventional if not pioneering perception of the linkages between politics and discourse.

The career of Jean Racine lay ahead of him. In many respects, until the last decade of his life, his fulfillment as playwright and historiographer appeared an abandonment if not a repudiation of the principles learned at Port-Royal. Familiarity with the thought of Antiquity never receded from Racine's mind, however, and he seems not to have questioned the desirability for young men to grow in wisdom through reading Plutarch and Tacitus.

When Racine began the public dialogue with Louis XIV in the letter accompanying *Alexandre le Grand*, it was an act born of self-assurance and a willingness to encounter the great. His education had given him a knowledge of character and a familiarity with the sort of discourse a man of letters might hold with his prince. And, by the late 1660s, Louis XIV had spent years reading and hearing men of letters express their eagerness to record his great actions in eloquent prose; he felt it was now time to do something worth writing about.

Racine's First Dialogues with the Sun King

Racine's debut as a writer came in 1659, with a sonnet in praise of Cardinal Mazarin. The next year Louis XIV's marriage provided an

31. See Louis Marin, *La critique du discours: Sur la "logique de Port Royal" et les "Pensées" de Pascal* (Paris, 1975), pp. 205 ff.

event worthy of celebration; like many other poets Racine wrote about it. His cousin, Nicolas Vitart, took this ode, *La nymphe de la Seine*,[32] to Chapelain, and that arbiter of taste liked it but made some suggestions for improvement. Vitart also gave a copy to Charles Perrault, Colbert's assistant. When asked by Colbert in 1663 to prepare a list of writers whom he thought worthy of royal patronage, Chapelain did not forget Racine. Perrault may have concurred. As a result, Racine received annual royal pensions as a poet long before he became historiographer.

During the years of increasing success in the theater, Racine pursued even higher connections at court and in the Church. He had intimate friends in the theatrical world and knew a number of writers; but there is little indication that he identified with men of letters as a group. In the letter of 1665 to Louis XIV that accompanied *Alexandre*, Racine had remarked that all the King's "subjects," not merely men of letters, would have to turn their talents to writing in praise of his actions. This suggests that Racine did not share some of the narrower, more comfortable elements of the group identity that had developed during the sixteenth century. As the son of Port-Royal abandoned Jansenist teachings and even criticized them publicly, he reached across social boundaries as a courtier with a special talent for writing verses, not as a man of letters seeking to insinuate himself at court.[33] In making friends with great noblemen, ministers, and the clergy, Racine proved himself to be an exemplary courtier and *dévot*.

By the mid-1670s he was sending drafts of his plays to the influential Jesuit, Father Dominique Bouhours, to ask for stylistic criticism and also to find out if there were faults "d'une autre nature."[34] Through Bouhours, Racine's plays were being passed on to Father René Rapin, another leading man of letters in the Jesuit order. Rapin also was on sufficiently familiar terms with Racine to be able to criticize the young man's plays. This closeness between Racine and such influential Jesuits may have facilitated his rise both in the theater and at court. As a very talented "son" of the Church who was returning to the fold despite his Jansenist upbringing, Racine may have received special attentions and favors from clerics committed to converting or winning back those who had erred in the past. The behavior patterns linking majority and minority religious groups resemble those of ethnic groups on their

32. For every aspect of Racine's career, the indispensable work is Picard, pp. 39 ff. Picard sheds light on virtually every aspect of late-seventeenth-century society through his minute analyses of the financial arrangements within the Racine family.
33. *Ibid.*, p. 374.
34. 1676? *Oeuvres complètes*, vol. 2, p. 462.

frontiers, that is, where the conversion and assimilation of individuals is most active.

Racine perceived the differences in outlook among the Jesuits at Versailles; he tended to associate the persecution of Port-Royal with the king's confessor, Father François de La Chaise, but perhaps not with Bouhours and Rapin.[35] Had the Jesuits sought to bar Racine from favor at court, they probably could have done so, for he had neither the social status nor the powerful protectors necessary to overcome a Jesuit *cordon pieux*, had one been developed. More than likely this talented young man who had publicly repudiated Port-Royal and who gave every appearance of great piety and learning actually found his career at Versailles facilitated by those who acted as his unofficial censors and protectors.

The connections with the Duke de Chevreuse, a Port-Royal school-mate in 1656, and with the Colberts moved from formality and respect to fidelity, protection, and intimacy. These patrons and friends signed Racine's marriage contract and stood as godparents for his children. It should come as no surprise that the first-born son of the Racines received the Christian names Jean-Baptiste, to honor his father's protector, Colbert. Thus, with one exception—the satirist Boileau—when Racine refers to "nos amis" in his correspondence with his most intimate relatives, he is referring to his protectors at Versailles.

Sometime between his success with *Alexandre* in 1665–1666 and 1669—or perhaps 1672—Racine became an intimate friend and literary associate of Boileau. The origins of the friendship are obscure, but the pair began to appear together in the circle around Madame de Montespan, and their names became increasingly linked at court. As a satirist who had aroused the ire of nobles, clerics, and above all, other men of letters, Boileau also stood outside the typical identity of the *gens de lettres*. He had a number of learned and witty friends, but he belonged to no special coterie and had not hesitated to ridicule Chapelain's poetry.

The circle formed by Montespan is shrouded in mystery.[36] So is that of her sister, Madame de Thianges. The archivist–historical novelist, the Abbé de Saint-Réal, may have been a go-between for Montespan, much as Chapelain was for Colbert after 1663. That is, other writers would see him, discuss their works with him or ask him to read them, and hope for Montespan's protection. Saint-Réal was on good terms

---

35. See below, p. 324. This is not meant to suggest, of course, that Racine thus became free of criticism by the Jesuits. Such was not the case. See the debates over *Esther* and *Athalie* in Picard, pp. 393–433.

36. *Ibid.*, p. 195.

with Antoine Varillas, the historian-archivist who worked in the royal library to produce fictional-historical works specifically designed to shape public opinion in favor of French foreign policy. The direct links between royal policy and such works as Saint-Réal's *Dom Carlos*, and the quarrels over pensions for their authors, suggest that these writings emanated from an as yet virtually unstudied team of propagandists that had its origins in the circles of Gabriel Naudé and Antoine Aubery under Cardinal Mazarin.[37] The *Dom Carlos* denigrated the Hapsburgs by depicting tyrannical ministries, inquisitions, and conspiracies in the court of Philip II of Spain and, of course, evoking the mysterious death of Carlos. It seems impossible to learn how familiar Racine became with this milieu of propagandists through his acquaintance with Saint-Réal. The anonymity of many of their works and the absence of correspondence have thus far prevented scholars from reconstructing this milieu. Since Joseph Klaits's model study of the interconnections between propaganda, literature, and public opinion in a similar milieu under Colbert de Torcy a few decades later, the significant questions for studying similar milieus have been posed.[38] It should now be only a matter of time before other scholars explore the habitués of the royal library, whom Racine certainly knew during the 1670s and 1680s. Yet he never seems to have turned to these writers for advice about carrying out his tasks as historiographer.

Intelligent, well-read, and perhaps eager to draw attention from her adultery by relying upon men of letters to support her against calumny, Montespan commissioned literary-artistic creations in praise of her royal lover. In the grand tradition of feminine aristocratic patronage, Montespan would discuss literary and historical subjects with writers and the King. She may have shared just that quality of respect for unpedantic learning that pervaded the young royal household—Queen Maria Theresa being the exception—and was evidenced in Colbert especially, in Louvois, and in Louis himself. The planning and execution of plays, operas, and fêtes would continue for years with Racine in attendance.

With Colbert's direct intervention on the King's behalf, Racine was elected to the French Academy in 1673.[39] The majority of the Academicians had probably opposed his candidacy on the grounds of his Jan-

37. Gustave Dulong, *L'Abbé de Saint-Réal* (Paris, 1921), 2 vols., is a brilliant exploration of the relationships between historical thought and fiction in the seventeenth century. For *Dom Carlos*, see vol. 1, pp. 115–165. The subject had long since become a traditional one for mobilizing anti-Spanish sentiment.

38. *Printed Propaganda under Louis XIV* (Princeton, 1976).

39. Picard, pp. 210 ff.

senist heritage and his rather brutal triumph over rival playwrights in the competition for public acclaim. But after the death of Pierre Séguier, the old protector of the Academy, Louis himself became protector; and Colbert, through his creature, Charles Perrault, indicated that the Crown would henceforth have a stronger voice in the operations of the Academy and in the elections to replace deceased "immortals." Forming part of the vanguard of the royal intrusion into the affairs of the Academy, Racine's *Discours de réception* was the first to be given during a public session. As an Academician Racine dutifully voted in favor of the candidates proposed by Colbert and his party. After the minister's death in 1683, divisions developed, as did more independence of action against the influence of Perrault, whose campaign on behalf of the Moderns prompted rebuttals from Boileau and Racine. Racine was confronted by the possibilities of further humiliation from aristocratic cabals supporting other playwrights, a quasi-retirement to the Academy, or promotion at court.

The timing of his and Boileau's appointments as *historiographes royaux* in 1677 remains mysterious. On the one hand it resembles Pellisson's appointment, though instead of abjuring Protestantism Racine had publicly abandoned the theater. And, as in Pellisson's case, historiographers had already been appointed. Indeed, in 1677, Pellisson was still a historiographer and was still expected to be working on the history of the reign. Like many other appointments at court, those of Racine and Boileau cannot be explained by any bureaucratic or meritocratic model. Had Montespan and her circle become sufficiently engaged on Racine's side of the quarrel over *Phèdre* to want to see her poets triumph one way or another? For Racine the appointment as historiographer marked the recovery of the steps up the path of ascendancy that had been lost in the quarrel over *Phèdre*. We cannot discern the relationships between *cour* and *ville*, aristocracy and "bourgeois" ministries, aristocratic mistresses, and policies of aristocratic absolutism, because, unlike Namierite England, Versailles and Paris had no Newcastle to keep accounts of expenditures in the battles over literary patronage. Yet it is clear that Racine and Boileau were appointed historiographers royal at the instigation of Montespan and Colbert.[40]

Raymond Picard refers to the year 1677 as the apogee of the cult of Louis XIV. Poets, historians, artists, and artisans attempted to surpass themselves in a litany of praise that would assure Louis of true *gloire*. Discourse in the Academy had long since become panegyric. The theater, the opera, religious music, sermons, gardens, and fireworks

40. *Ibid.*, p. 279. Paul Sonnino, "Jean Racine and the *Eloge Historique de Louis XIV*," *Canadian Journal of History* 8 (1973): 185.

employed a typical Renaissance discourse to raise the Sun King to the stature of a divine hero.[41] Contemporary observers, notably in Holland, held Louis personally accountable for this outburst of royalist occultism. Montespan, Colbert, and perhaps Louis, may have attempted to curb this royalist enthusiasm by appointing additional historiographers.

After beginning his personal discourse with Louis in *Alexandre le Grand*, Racine had restricted his allusions to the King's great actions to an occasional remark in prologues and academic speeches. No praise for Louis can be inferred from the great tragedies of the 1660s and 1670s.[42] Moreover, in his dramas Racine did not evolve to a more facile perception of antique politics and morality in order to make these accord with his own times. In comparing Nicole Pradon's play dealing with the same theme as *Phèdre*, a contemporary remarked that Racine continued to write according to the "goût" and customs of Antiquity. Modern scholars, notably R. C. Knight, are quick to point out the discrepancies between Racine's drama and the plays of Euripides and other ancient Greek dramatists; but instead of measuring Racine's historicity against some "true" perception of ancient Greek drama—if in fact the latter exists—it is more important to stress the rather uncompromising historicity of Racine's works in comparison with those of his contemporaries in the French theater. When the quarrel between the Ancients and the Moderns became overt, thanks to Perrault's manifesto on behalf of the Moderns, Racine and Bolieau remained firmly on the side of Antiquity. Their position implied that neither would join his fellow men of letters to assert that the King had surpassed Alexander the Great or Julius Caesar. And what could be a better guarantor against excessive praise than the appointment of the leading satirist of the age as historiographer royal? There is some evidence that, in the years immediately following their appointment, the King personally sought to curb Racine's and Boileau's tendency to praise him.

If Racine's manner of praising Louis seemed promising enough to win his appointment as historiographer to Montespan and Louis, what did Boileau's career and writing represent? His frequent reiteration of the themes of sincerity and independence confirms the impression that both Boileau and Racine were appointed in order to mute hyperbole and restore simplicity to the writing of history.

41. See Ernst Kantorowicz, "Oriens Augusti—Lever du Roi," *Dumbarton Oaks Papers* 17 (1963): 119–177. For a discussion of opposition to Louis's politics see Klaus Malettke, *Opposition und Konspiration unter Ludwig XIV* (Göttingen, 1976), *passim*. See also Robert Isherwood, *Music in the Service of the King* (Ithaca, 1973), *passim*; and Anthony Blunt, *Art and Architecture in France, 1500–1700* (Baltimore, 1953), Chap. 7.

42. Picard, p. 278.

Boileau's First Dialogues
with the Sun King

Just as Racine's dialogue with Louis had begun with a letter accompanying a copy of *Alexandre le Grand* in 1663, so Boileau's began with a *discours au roi* in 1665. Posing as endowed with meager talent—certainly not enough to praise Louis XIV—Boileau scorns other men of letters:

> Qui, dans ce champs d'honneur, où le gain les amène,
> Osent chanter ton nom sans force et sans haleine;
> Et qui vont tous les jours, d'une importune voix,
> T'ennuyer du récit de tes propres exploits.[43]

There is no suggestion that Boileau considered himself adequate to the duties of historiographer. And as for praising the King in verse, Boileau evokes Horace:

> Pour chanter un Auguste, il faut être un Virgile:
> Et j'approuve les soins du monarque guerrier
> Qui ne pouvait souffrir qu'un artisan grossier
> Entreprît de tracer, d'une main criminelle,
> Un portrait réservé pour le pinceau d'Apelle.[44]

The playful use of *topoi* that were being piously evoked by other poets evidently pleased Louis. In the *avis au lecteur* added by Boileau when publishing the *Epître I, au Roi* (1669) he explains that the Grand Condé had objected to including the fable of the oyster in a work addressed to the King. The story of the judge who eats an oyster rather than attempt to render justice to the one who ought really to have received it has little if any political overtones. Condé may have objected to the fable as an inadequate way of ending the *Epître*. But the fact that Condé remained so influential an arbiter of literary taste in the 1660s reveals that authors still had to reckon with far more than Louis, Colbert, and Chapelain in their bids for patronage. As Boileau put it in his usual blunt way: "Je n'ai pas cru, pour une vingtaine de vers, devoir me brouiller avec le premier capitaine de notre siècle."[45] Having publicly heeded the prince's advice, Boileau included the fable of the oyster in a later work, perhaps to demonstrate his independence from Condé.

43. *Oeuvres de Boileau*, ed. Charles-Antoine Gidel (Paris, 1870), vol. 1, p. 33.
44. *Ibid.*, p. 36.
45. *Ibid.*, vol. 2, p. 141.

In *Epître I*, Boileau also praises peace and its benefits for society. Having never praised war and conquest, he could not be accused of inconsistency. While not demeaning conquest as an aim for princes, Boileau simply stresses the economic, fiscal, judicial, and social benefits of peace and harmony:

> Mais, quelques vains lauriers que promette la guerre,
> On peut être héros sans ravager la terre.[46]

Boileau evokes Emperor Titus, who gave the Romans peace and prosperity. The entire *Epître* has a Colbertian resonance, for it implies that the *gloire* earned through administration and justice is equal to that won by conquest.[47] Then, in almost interrogatory discourse, Boileau addresses Louis directly:

> Toutefois, si quelqu'un de mes foibles écrits
> Des ans injurieux peut éviter l'outrage,
> Peut-être pour ta gloire aura-t-il son usage;
> Et comme tes exploits, étonnant les lecteurs,
> Seront à peine crus sur la foi des auteurs,
> Si quelque esprit malin les veut traiter de fables,
> On dira quelque jour, pour les rendre croyables:
> Boileau, qui, dans ses vers pleins de sincérité,
> Jadis à tout son siècle a dit la vérité,
> Qui mit à tout blâmer son étude et sa gloire,
> A pourtant de ce roi parlé comme l'histoire.[48]

That favorite *topos* of practitioners of the *ars historica*—that their work contains the truth—appears here in verse alongside the satirist's claim to be sincere and unflattering. In all his subsequent works Boileau weaves in this theme whenever he addresses public issues. In a sense, these lines addressed to Louis XIV invite the King to invite Boileau to write history.

In the autobiographical *Epître V*, after describing his father's legal career and how he himself had been destined for the law by his family, Boileau narrates his decision to become a poet:

> Dès lors à la richesse il fallut renoncer;
> Ne pouvant l'acquérir, j'appris à m'en passer;

---

46. *Ibid.*, p. 148. Charles-Augustin Sainte-Beuve, in his edition of Boileau, *Oeuvres* (Paris, 1858), p. 127, remarks that these verses were inspired by "une âme vraiment citoyenne."

47. See Orest Ranum, *Paris in the Age of Absolutism* (New York, 1968), pp. 259 ff.

48. *Oeuvres de Boileau*, vol. 2, pp. 153 f.

Et surtout redoutant la basse servitude,
La libre vérité fut toute mon étude . . .
Mais du plus grand des rois la bonté sans limite,
Toujours prête à courir au-devant du mérite,
Crut voir dans ma franchise un mérite inconnu,
Et d'abord de ses dons enfla mon revenu.[49]

In praising and actually evoking patronage without attributing inspiration from the patron as well, Boileau asserts his independence. And he
could expect to pay dearly for his repeated scorn of Chapelain and
other Academicians. Montausier—tutor to the Grand Dauphin, intimate of Louis, and patron of Chapelain—had accused Boileau of "lacking in respect." Louis nevertheless granted the satirist a pension.

In the more explicitly historical *Epître IV*, celebrating the *passage
du Rhin*, Boileau carries on the venerable tradition of mentioning the
courageous actions of numerous officers long after it had become the
habit among poets to praise Louis XIV alone for successful military
actions. The King is praised, but not at the expense of others; *gloire*
is a quality not attributable to princes alone. Even in this work Boileau
could not refrain from humor, asserting that it is impossible to be lyrical
in verse when place names such as Doësbourg, Zutphen, Wageninghen,
Harderwick, and Knotzembourg have to be rhymed.[50]

Boileau read aloud before Louis in 1674 and was given a pension on
7 February of that year. On 28 March the privilege for the reedition of
his works was renewed. Chapelain had died in the interval, on 22 February 1674.[51] Perhaps as much out of respect for the old poet as for his
influence, Louis and his councillors waited for death to remove the
possibility of any further ill feelings between the author of the *Pucelle*
and the satirist. As royal recognition and favor increased, Boileau maintained his views. *Epître VIII* (1675) is more conventionally full of
praise at a time when the Dutch War was going badly. Yet he reiterates
about the satirist, "Nous sommes un peu nés pour être mécontents,"
and reminds his readers that his royal pension will discredit what he says
about Louis:

Il me semble, grand roi, dans mes nouveaux écrits,
Que mon encens payé n'est plus de même prix.

49. *Ibid.*, pp. 192 f.
50. "Des villes que tu prends les noms durs et barbares
N'offrent de toutes parts que syllabes bizarres,
Et, l'oreille effrayée, il faut depuis l'Issel,
Pour trouver un beau mot, courir jusqu'au Tessel."
(*ibid.*, pp. 169 f.)
51. Jules Brody, *Boileau and Longinus* (Geneva, 1958), p. 32.

> J'ai peur que l'univers qui sait ma récompense,
> N'impute mes transports à ma reconnoissance,
> Et que par tes présents mon vers discredité
> N'ait moins de poids pour toi dans la postérité.[52]

Over and over again Boileau explored the theme of remuneration and its effects upon the writer's credibility. Indeed, even if the writer knew he was telling the truth, the public would not believe him because he had accepted money from the person about whom he was writing. After his appointment as historiographer, Boileau evoked Louis in only a few lines, notably in the *Ode sur las prise de Namur* (1693).

Thus it was as an independent writer with enemies in the Academy and elsewhere that Boileau was appointed historiographer in 1677. What did Louis anticipate from the appointment? As always, the King remains inscrutable. Evidence from memoirs and other unreliable sources suggests that he admired Boileau's verses and enjoyed his frank good humor. Louis always expressed pleasure at seeing Boileau at court, but the poet avoided Versailles as much as possible.

More revealing of Racine's development as a historian and of the impact of the office upon him and Boileau is the latter's first speech before the French Academy. In the correspondence there is so much evidence of the complete cooperation between Racine and Boileau on every aspect of their tasks as historiographers and in their dealings with the court that it is safe to conclude that Racine wholly approved the contents of Boileau's *Discours de remerciement* (1683).

Having by then been historiographer for six years, Boileau speaks as if he must explain or justify his appointment. After the compliments for Richelieu, Séguier, and his predecessor in the Academy, Boileau observes that the Academy has "égard ni au rang ni à la dignité; que la politesse, le savoir, la connaissance des belles-lettres ouvrent chez vous l'entrée aux honnêtes gens."[53] Then, as if to reiterate his point, he remarks that the Academy does not hesitate to "replace a first-ranking magistrate, a most eminent minister," with someone who has no "title other than the one merit has given him on Parnassus." After inquiring what possibly could have brought about his election, he observes that it may have resulted from the "goodness" of Louis XIV, who "has desired that I work with one of your most illustrious writers [Racine] to collect into a body the infinite number of his immortal actions."[54] The notion of a historical work as a *corps*, or body of actions, seems to preclude any role for the writer other than that of accumulator.

52. *Oeuvres de Boileau*, vol. 2, p. 225.
53. *Ibid.*, vol. 3, p. 255.
54. *Ibid.*, p. 256.

Boileau makes no claims for his eloquence. Quite the contrary. He asserts that since many other writers are more capable than he of doing justice to these actions by recording them in a beautiful style and magnificent words, it is rather that Louis XIV "n'a pas trouvé mauvais qu'au milieu de tant d'écrivains célèbres . . . un homme sans fard, et accusé plutôt de trop de sincérité que de flatterie, contribuât de son travail et de ses conseils à bien mettre en jour, et dans toute la naïveté du style le plus simple, la vérité de ses actions, qui étant si peu vraisemblables d'elles-mêmes, ont bien plus besoin d'être fidèlement écrites que fortement exprimées."[55] Such a *discours* served as more than a manifesto on behalf of plain prose; it implicitly reproached other writers for depending upon hyperbole rather than upon true eloquence. Were not Louis's actions sufficiently illustrious in themselves?

At another point in the *Discours* Boileau mentions Thucydides, Xenophon, and Tacitus—obviously with praise. There is no reference to Herodotus, Livy, Sallust, or Suetonius, perhaps indicating that he had selected those ancient historians who had avoided the language of praise when writing history. The compliment for his collaborator, Racine, also indicates Boileau's willingness to play a subordinate role in writing the King's history.

Nor had the appointments gone uncriticized. Other men of letters were envious, and there was a flood of anonymous verses stressing the poor qualifications of the two poets for writing history. Criticism from Madame de Sévigné was at once explicit and ideological. Her cousin, Roger de Bussy-Rabutin, had long hoped to be appointed historiographer.[56] His hunger for titles reminds us that men of letters from old noble families could be just as deliberate in their search for a place at Versailles as their bourgeois and robe counterparts. Sévigné approached friends in high places on Bussy's behalf; anyone with influence appears to have been enlisted, and for thirteen years various attempts were made to have Bussy appointed. The reasons he and his supporters gave in favor of his appointment shed some light on the fate of the civic identity that Bodin and others had enunciated in the mid-sixteenth century.

Their argument ran that since Bussy-Rabutin was from an old noble family, he naturally would be better able to write military history than anyone with bourgeois origins. The du Bellay *exemplum* so brilliantly elucidated in Bodin's *Methodus* had become part of a defensive ideology of the privileged nobility.[57] In 1679, Bussy addressed Louis XIV

55. *Ibid.*, pp. 257 f.
56. The standard work on Bussy is still Emile Gérard-Gailly, *Bussy-Rabutin, sa vie, ses oeuvres, et ses amis* (Paris, 1909).
57. See above, p. 85.

indirectly through one of the secretaries of state, saying: "Ce qui donnera encore beaucoup de créance à ce que j'écrirai de vous, Sire, ce sera de voir que je ne suis pas payé pour en parler."[58] This remark should not be interpreted to mean that Bussy was not interested in receiving a pension. Quite the contrary. It was just that a man of noble birth who received a pension would not be seen as having been corrupted by that pension into distorting the truth about the past. Bussy's supplication fell on deaf ears. He asserted that he would write the history of the reign anyway and did in fact do so. In 1691 he finally was offered a pension and accepted it. In form and ideological slant Bussy's history of Louis XIV resembles those of many other writers of the age. Neither Racine nor Boileau took the trouble to defend himself against Bussy or any of the other envious writers who attacked them.

Racine Learns to Write History

Once his appointment had become official, Racine spent the next few years of his life accompanying the King on military campaigns and at court and in learning how to write history. The reading he undertook has the character of a program. It was a personal choice, but it also reveals an Ancient's assumptions or attitudes toward historical thought. He was a mature writer with a well-established reputation. In seeking to switch from verse to prose, and from works of the imagination to ones of truth, Racine conscientiously learned his new trade by what he considered the best possible method. His son Louis summarized his father's studies: "Mon père, pour se mettre ses devoirs devant les yeux, fit une espèce d'extrait du traité de Lucien sur la manière d'écrire l'histoire. Il remarqua dans cet excellent traité des traits qui avoient rapport à la circonstance dans laquelle il se trouvait, et il les rassembla dans l'écrit qui se trouvera à la suite de ses lettres. Il fit ensuite des extraits de Mézerai, et de Vittorio Siri, et se mit à lire les mémoires, lettres, instructions et autres pièces de cette nature dont le Roi avoit ordonné qu'on lui donnât la communication."[59] Since most if not all of Racine's notes have been preserved, it is possible to reconstruct his thought about history as a genre and to discern what he considered the dangers in writing about the past, dangers prompted by the climates of opinion in France during the late 1670s.

As an Ancient, it never occurred to Racine that he might have something to learn from the sixteenth-century writers on historical method.

58. Picard, p. 319.
59. "Mémoires sur la vie et les ouvrages de Jean Racine," *Oeuvres complètes*, vol. 1, p. 69.

Indeed, all his researches may be classified into two groups. The first was methodological and involved only works from Antiquity, and the second was contemporary history, for which he read Mézerai, Jean de La Barde, and Siri.[60] Racine may have been typical of his day in neglecting his own national school of historical thought. Indeed, allusions to Bodin's *Methodus* or citations from Pasquier and La Popelinière are virtually nonexistent among both the learned and the eloquent groups during the later seventeenth century. Bayle, who might be expected to show familiarity with sixteenth-century historical method, ignores most of it and is caustic toward Pasquier for ideological reasons.[61] And if Perrault may be taken as the leading spokesman for the Moderns, his praise for the achievements of French men of learning does not include recognition of a new historical method surpassing that of the ancients. Yet in the roots of the *ars historica* tradition Racine consolidated his commitment to write history without flattery.

In Racine's copy of the Lehmann edition of Lucian—published in Paris in 1615 and now preserved in the Toulouse library—only the short treatise on the writing of history is annotated.[62] Although these annotations reveal a wide interest in questions about historical method, at virtually every point where Lucian mentions the distinctions between panegyric and history and how a historian ought not to flatter, Racine not only marks the passage but translates the Greek into French. These commonplaces about historical thought may seem banal, but for Racine they were endowed with the authority of Antiquity: "Le panégyrique et l'histoire sont éloignés comme le ciel l'est de la terre. . . . L'utilité est le principal but de l'histoire; le plaisir la suit comme la beauté suit la santé. . . . Le lecteur est rigoureux comme un changeur qui examine la bonne et la mauvaise monnaie. . . . Alexandre jeta dans la rivière le livre d'un historien flatteur. . . . Il faut qu'un historien soit lui-même capable d'agir . . . ; [et] qu'il ait été dans un camp. . . . Que l'historien ne soit d'aucun parti. . . . L'architecte du Phare songeait à l'avenir, et non pas à son siècle."[63]

It is clear that Racine liked the anecdote about how the historian should imitate the architect of the lighthouse at Pharos—who put the name of the king who had hired him in plaster on his building but under the plaster placed his own name carved in stone—because he not

60. Similarly, his religious reading, with few exceptions, ranged from the Church fathers to contemporary writers.

61. *Dictionnaire historique et critique* (Rotterdam, 1697), especially the discussion about Pasquier's errors in research on the life of Abelard, vol. 1, pp. 23–27.

62. Cf. *Oeuvres complètes*, vol. 2, p. 1045.

63. *Ibid.*, pp. 201–203.

only annotated the passage but translated it in the *extraits*.[64] The architect knew that in time the plaster bearing the king's name would be washed away, revealing his own name "eternally" graven in stone. The other passages completely translated reveal a steady preoccupation with the distinctions between panegyric, poetry, and history and with the historian's need to be independent.

And, in a vein reminiscent of Bodin's criticism of Paschal for having denigrated the capacities of Francis I's Hapsburg enemies, Racine translated Lucian's observation that "Il y a des historiens qui croient faire grand plaisir à un prince, en ravalant le mérite de ses ennemis. Achille serait moins grand, s'il n'avait défait que Thersite, au lieu d'Hector."[65] At another point Racine remarked: "Surtout [the historian] doit être libre, n'espérant ni ne craignant rien, inaccessible aux présents et aux récompenses; appelant *figue*, une figue, etc.; ne faisant grâce à personne, et ne respectant rien par la mauvaise honte; juge équitable et indifférent, sans pays, sans maître, et sans dépendance."[66] Concerning proper style, Racine includes Lucian's warnings against the use of a "style si magnifique et si guindé" and his emphasis on the value of more familiar usage.

In addition to Lucian, Racine annotated and translated passages from *On Thucydides* by Dionysius of Halicarnassus. Here it becomes apparent that Racine had been reading Thucydides as well, for at several points he expresses his disagreement with Dionysius. For example, where Dionysius expresses his preference for agreeable subjects, Racine remarks: "Fausse critique; comme si les malheurs n'étaient pas aussi agréables à lire que les bons succès."[67] On another passage he remarks: "Paroles qui sentent le rhéteur,"[68] perhaps indicating his awareness of Dionysius's function in classical literary culture.[69]

The annotations in recently published histories and the fragments of Racine's narrative that have survived include no comments on method. He did not even bother to make stylistic criticisms of Jean de La Barde's *De Rebus Gallicis historiarum libri decem*; he was reading only for specific facts such as the dates of battles, promotions, disgraces, deaths, and defeats and for anecdotes about the character of principal personages. The sequence of diplomatic negotiations also interested him,

64. *Ibid.*, p. 199.

65. *Ibid.*, p. 197.

66. *Ibid.*, p. 199.

67. *Ibid.*, p. 204. See Cargill Sprietsma, "Du Racine inédit à Columbia Université," *La Renaissance de l'art français et des industries de luxe* 7 (1924): 401–6.

68. *Ibid.*, p. 206.

69. William Kendrick Pritchett, *Dionysius of Halicarnassus: On Thucydides* (Berkeley, 1975), pp. xxii ff.

though it is clear that he had great respect for Vittorio Siri's *Memoria Reconditi* on this subject. In addition, Racine seems to have particularly enjoyed discovering the sources on which these other historians had relied. He clearly cultivated his ability to recognize sequences of events that had been lifted from some pamphlet, gazette, or work of history, a clue as to how pre-nineteenth-century historians perceived criticism of sources. Racine always seems to be searching for the earliest and most complete sources; he does not have the modern, indeed post-Rankean aim to reconstruct sequences of events entirely from such record sources as diplomatic dispatches. To him sources for modern history may have resembled one individual narrating to another the relationship between occurrences. As long as participants were living, speech may have carried greater authority as a source than written documents. On several occasions Racine notes what he had heard—for example, the comments of an Englishman about the Norman Conquest, the total sum of bullion in England, and the trained bands. It is as if an authority speaking to him on these subjects would be more veracious than anything he might discern from reading histories of England. Though Racine certainly was a voracious reader and a prolific writer, the particular modes of conveying truths through speech still constituted an element in his general notion of history.

He questions his sources as he reads them, almost as if he were holding a conversation with the writer. The annotations reveal that he by no means accepted as true all that he read or heard. Instead, his research was a dynamic procedure of questioning and answering.

De La Barde's *De Rebus Gallicis* was read after Siri's *Memoria*, with the greater credence given to the latter as a source. Siri—who was still alive—had been on familiar terms with members of Mazarin's entourage and very possibly held the respect of such actors in the Fronde as Le Tellier and Colbert.[70] These features would have attracted Racine to his works. Siri's narrative is fuller than de La Barde's and is imbued with the *politique* sense of interpreting events that Chapelain had so admired in the Italians. Indeed, by comparison with de La Barde's rather stilted narrative, Siri casts French history in a European perspective and the study of human nature in an analytical framework of fortune and circumstances rather than typologies of virtue and evil. As a simple *commis* to Chavigny while the latter was secretary of state for foreign affairs, de La Barde had been faithful, but plodding.[71] The weaknesses in his history stemmed from his modest intellectual capacities rather than from his respect for the canons of the *ars historica*. But Siri, not

70. See above, p. 158.
71. See my *Richelieu and the Councillors of Louis XIII* (Oxford, 1963).

unlike Davila, often tended to emphasize personal pique and rivalry to explain major political events. Plots and intrigues carried him ever deeper into an analysis of the Fronde as it would any Tacitean, and it is clear that Racine followed his text with interest. Since Siri's works were among the most wide-ranging and authoritative written by a contemporary of Mazarin, and de La Barde ranks among the best sources to complement him, Racine was reading the best available narrative sources for the early history of the reign of Louis XIV.

Racine carefully summarizes Siri's account of how the Parlement found that the Crown had violated its privileges in 1648. The conduct of the princes as recounted by Siri interested him less. The parlementaire outlook on the civil war may have been less familiar to him than that of the *grands*, who, after all, had appeared fictionally in the theater since the 1630s, whereas the judges, with their concern for precedents and duty, had been used for satire. When de La Barde observes that the parlementaires opposed the Crown's fiscal innovations because they personally had lent money to the *traitants* for high interest and therefore did not wish to lift a finger against fiscal abuses, Racine notes these views without comment.[72] In general, he did not consider de La Barde's narrative of the Fronde as solid as Priolo's *Histoire des dernières guerres civiles*.

Siri's ability to extrapolate from a single incident to a general analysis at once true, timely, and timeless obviously attracted Racine. Some of these observations have slightly more ideological implications than the usual sort of "judgments" found in de La Barde. For example, in describing the Merovingian mayors of the palace, Siri observes that they "font bien voir que les Français sont toujours prêts à subir le joug de quiconque ose leur commander, pourvu qu'il ait en sa main la disposition des grâces."[73] The links between national character, corruption, favor seeking—in short, the willingness to exchange independence for money—forged by Siri are reminiscent of the historical thought of his sixteenth-century compatriots. Again it is Siri who observes that "Les Français, si hardis et si prêts à exposer leur vie dans les batailles, tremblent à l'aspect d'un homme de justice; et que les rois n'ont jamais mieux fait que d'établir ainsi entre eux et les grands un juge qui, sans qu'ils s'en mêlassent, pût châtier les grands et protéger les petits."[74] Though Racine found these sentences of sufficient interest to copy

72. *Oeuvres complètes*, vol. 2, p. 296. Siri's views on the French constitution nonetheless are firmly *thèse royaliste*.

73. *Ibid.*, p. 305.

74. *Ibid.*

them in his notebooks, he never included such sentences in his own historical narratives.

With the exception of the *Abrégé de l'histoire de Port-Royal*, his historical works are admittedly scanty; but they are nonetheless sufficent for one to infer that Racine either rejected the Tacitean or sixteenth-century civic-humanist preoccupation with discerning historical changes in forms of government, or that he thought the effort unproductive. He knew Siri's view that all rights in the French Monarchy had originally emanated from the Crown but that under the later Merovingian kings revolts had occurred and transformed "gouvernements" into seigneuries, rights of vassalage, and inferior justices—in short, a loss of royal power. That their successors, the Carolingians, and more particularly the Capetians, had bit by bit subjugated these "states" and lands is also noted. For Racine, and indeed for historians of the seventeenth century, the great alterations in governments may have appeared to be over, very remote in time. And yet the spectacle of the Fronde lay before them. The litany of French kings, not the discernment of changes in forms of government, remained the fabric of history despite what the Parlement of Paris or Condé and the other princes had attempted to stand for.

On religious issues, Racine either misunderstood Siri's views or disagreed with him. Perhaps a former Jansenist was unable to perceive the Erastian views of an Italian in French service. Siri manipulated charges of irreligiosity to conform to national ideological objectives. For example, Racine copied out from Siri that the Dutch "n'ont aucune religion, et ne connaissent de dieu que leur intérêt. Leurs propres écrivains confessent que dans le Japon, où l'on punit des plus cruels supplices tout ce qu'on y trouve de chrétiens, il suffit de se dire Hollandais pour être en sûreté."[75] Siri probably had no hope of convincing any but the most naive of his readers or anti-Dutch French and Italian readers mobilized by the bitter warfare between France and the United Provinces during the 1670s. It seems impossible to determine whether or not Racine believed this charge. He had had very little contact with the world outside Port-Royal and the theater.

Religious questions that were cast around the personal beliefs of an individual caused Racine to react differently. For example, Siri accuses Paolo Sarpi of having been a Lutheran and attempts to accumulate proof of this charge. Racine carries on a dialogue with himself over the evidence presented by Siri and finally concludes: "Tout cela, ce me semble, ne prouve pas grand'chose contre. F. Polo. Il faudrait avoir rapporté

75. *Ibid.*, p. 314.

quelques-unes des ces lettres pour juger si elles étaient hérétiques. Un homme peut écrire à des huguenots sans être huguenot lui-même."[76] Siri had pulled together the most suspect bits of evidence about Sarpi's alleged heresy. He had relied upon a virtual "red-scare" device to make his readers conclude that Sarpi was a heretic because he had corresponded with Huguenots.[77] Did Siri in fact know better? Perhaps. He was a very subtle propagandist, and his works reveal a complete familiarity with all the devices writers had developed to shape reading opinion. That Racine took Siri's views on Sarpi so seriously suggests his naiveté about the bigger world of pamphlet literature and propaganda.

There is nothing in Racine's career that indicates familiarity with the international discourse about nations and religions. Nor does he ask himself how Siri's Italian readers might have responded to an attack on Sarpi in the later seventeenth century. Indeed, Racine's view of the matter is one-dimensional; a charge of heresy has been made, and the evidence presented contains innuendos. The ever-correct Racine ends up wondering about Siri's own faith: "Siri aurait mieux fait, ou de bien prouver la chose, ou ne pas noircir légèrement la mémoire d'un homme, qui vaut infiniment mieux que lui, et qui peut-être avait plus de religion que Siri même. Je ne sais si ce n'est pas même faire quelque tort à la religion de dire qu'un homme si généralement estimé des hommes n'a point eu de religion. Les impies peuvent abuser de cet exemple."[78] The lesson Racine draws is heavy and difficult to interpret. Had Sarpi's writings or his religious faith won Racine's respect? Racine's dialogue with himself over Sarpi suggests that he bore within himself a profound—though perhaps naive—commitment to writing the truth about the past.

The Fragments of History

The surviving fragments of historical narrative seem almost ready for insertion into a general history of the reign. Subjects as disparate as Portugal's successful drive to exclude the Dutch from Brazil, the family background of Orangist-republican conflicts in the United Provinces, Johan de Witt's republican family heritage, and the history of how the royal domains alienated for Catherine de Médicis were returned

76. *Ibid.*, p. 326.

77. The literary history of slander and innuendo is still to be written. That there was a structure to slanderous writing becomes immediately apparent after reading the pamphlet literature of the early-modern period. For some suggestions, see John H. M. Salmon, "French Satire in the Late Sixteenth Century," *Sixteenth-Century Journal* 5 (1975): 57–88.

78. *Oeuvres complètes*, vol. 2, p. 326.

to the Crown shed little light on the overall plan of Racine's history of the reign. Boileau and he were pulling together *matières* for the 1660s, year by year, which suggests that the projected history was to resemble the King's *Memoirs*. But if such was the case, it is difficult to see how these bits of narrative could have been integrated into that structure. Was Racine's canvas more vast? The manuscript that he and Boileau were preparing was inherited by their successor as historiographer, Jean-Henri Valincourt, and was destroyed by fire. The fragments were written to be included in a larger narrative to show how events in Brazil and the United Provinces influenced those occurring in France. These fragments of narrative also confirm the contention that Racine sought to avoid praise and be as serene and dispassionate as possible.

Finally, the notes taken from Mézerai and others attest to Racine's desire to be absolutely accurate about the events he was describing. He already had several narratives of events on which to build his own, so he searched for discreet facts that would illuminate the King's character and accomplishments. There are occasional allusions to diplomatic affairs and the causes of war, but these subjects pale alongside the military campaigns.

Racine attempted to capture how French subjects reacted to their king, even if those reactions appeared absurd. Upon learning that the King would visit Vitry, the populace disinterred a governor who had sided with the League during the sixteenth century, perhaps with the thought that the King might be offended by the presence of the man's tomb.[79] Just outside Guise, an old woman asked where the King was and, having had him pointed out, said, "Je vous ai déjà vu une fois, et vous êtes bien changé."[80] Racine notes that the peasants along the frontier are "zealous," presumably for the French, while those in Cateau-Cambrésis are "ferocious," perhaps indicating their pro-Spanish sympathies. When Louis took poor lodgings, drank bad wine, or became too exhausted from riding even to make the effort to go to bed, Racine notes these facts. Had his history been completed and published, some of these details might have been included in just the same way ancient historians had included such remarks about rulers and generals on campaign. Racine probably noted them because the *topoi* in the ancient histories had established the legitimacy of incorporating such facts into historical narratives.

Unlike ancient historians, however, Racine accumulated a considerable amount of statistical information. For example, he included the

79. *Ibid.*, p. 265.
80. *Ibid.*, p. 266. Picard has attempted to organize the "notes et fragments" into some order. Such an effort is pointless.

310 @ Artisans of Glory

total sum collected annually for the *tailles* for 1658, 1678, 1679, 1680, 1681, and 1685.[81] Except for the year 1685, which shows an increase, these years reveal *tailles* remaining almost steady at about thirty-five million *livres*. Did Racine omit years that were much higher, thus enabling him to give a series suggesting stability? He notes that expenditures for buildings (principally Versailles) amounted to sixteen million *livres* in 1685 and also records figures for the *don gratuit* of the clergy, the number of parishes in France (thirty-six thousand), and the size of the armies. There is a Colbertian quality to Racine's statistical notes, because they almost invariably permit some comparison over time. Would he have included them in his history? We can infer an affirmative answer, because these statistics are included among the same notes as the "bons mots du Roi" and other prime material.

On more specifically political matters, Racine includes rumors about ministerial conflicts and infers that Turenne was ambitious and had hoped for a position in the intimate circle of advisers around Louis.[82] He also includes the story about Colbert's deathbed expressions of bitterness and disenchantment with royal service. In many instances Racine prefaces these anecdotes with the phrase "on prétend que," but he appears to have accepted others as fact, for example, Cardinal Richelieu's "traits de folie."[83]

Yet at no point did he attempt to draw conclusions from the anecdotes he recorded. On occasion he would include a sentence with ideological and administrative implications—for example, "Celui qui a les finances peut toujours tromper quand il veut. On a beau tenir les registres."[84] Certainly not a profound observation by any means, but it indicates familiarity with some of the traditional complaints about the regime.

In addition to the "bon mots du Roi," the single most revealing anecdote about Louis as a statesman is the account of how, during the siege of Cambrai in 1693, a certain Du Metz advised the King to attack part of the fortress. Vauban had advised the King against it, saying, "Vous perdrez peut-être à cette attaque tel homme qui vaut mieux que la place."[85] Nevertheless, Louis decided in favor of the attack; and although the objective was accomplished momentarily, the defenders of the fortress counterattacked and killed over four hundred soldiers and

81. *Ibid.*, p. 276.
82. *Ibid.*, p. 287.
83. *Ibid.*, p. 289.
84. *Ibid.*
85. *Ibid.*, p. 278.

forty officers. Two days later Vauban retook the place that had been lost so dearly, losing only three men. And Racine added that Louis admitted his blunder to Vauban: "Le Roi lui promit qu'une autre fois il le laisserait faire."

There are observations that Racine found personally interesting and that he almost certainly would not have included in his history. For example, he narrates the story of the items found in Mézerai's lodgings after the old historiographer's death and lists the contents of his will. Racine refers to Mézerai's actions as "sottises," but he nevertheless takes the trouble to quote exactly the note found in a sack containing a thousand francs, in coin: "C'est ici le dernier argent que j'ai reçu du Roi; aussi, depuis ce temps-là n'ai-je jamais dit de bien de lui."[86] Yet Racine does not give his own views on Mézerai's anger toward his royal patron.

Nor does he record every remark that Louis made to him personally. On one occasion, however, he does so. Racine had just read before the King the *discours* he gave before the Academy in 1685. He records the event in this way: "Que je lui eus récité mon discours, il me dit devant tout le monde: Je vous louerais davantage, si vous ne me louiez pas tant."[87] The compliments on the *Discours* did not erase the memory of Louis's polite but firm remark about praise. Did the King really object to extravagant praise? The tissue of allusions to historical events that Racine wove as he wrote his *Discours* conveys the impression of a Louis exercising control over both European and French history. The course of events is under his control; indeed, the events themselves are described as "miracles." Racine's evocation of historical events to demonstrate Louis's power in the world is Homeric; and lest someone like Bossuet think his praise blasphemous, Racine took care to make his parallel specifically to Jupiter. An illusion of supreme power over human affairs is created by selecting just those key events that reflected Louis's influence, and the highest praise is reserved for making peace: "on n'est pas moins frappé de la grandeur et de la promptitude avec laquelle se fait la paix, que de la rapidité avec laquelle se font les conquêtes."[88] Prior to Louis XIV, only Jupiter had had such a large sphere of action in the lives of nations and kings.

Since the *Discours* had begun with the eulogy of the late Pierre Corneille, in form it resembles the attempt to synthesize letters and statesmanship that Seyssel and Budé had enunciated almost two centuries earlier. Indeed, Corneille's tragedies are paralleled not with those

86. *Ibid.*, p. 282.
87. *Ibid.*, p. 281.
88. *Ibid.*, p. 350.

of the Roman tragedians—because, says Racine, the Romans themselves recognized that none of their writers had excelled in this genre—but with the Athenians: "an Aeschylus, a Sophocles, and a Euripides."

Unlike Budé, who had linked literary creativity (eloquence) to patronage, Racine asserts that Corneille was a "personnage véritablement né pour la gloire de son pays." Corneille had, of course, received "bienfaits" from Louis and was thanking the King as death ended his ability to speak, but it was the "pays," not the patron, that remained Corneille's source of support. And as if to settle an old account on the subject of what functions bestowed greatness, Racine adds: "La Postérité, qui se plaît, qui s'instruit dans les ouvrages qu'ils lui ont laissés, ne fait point de difficulté de les égaler à tout ce qu'il y a de plus considérable parmi les hommes, fait marcher de pair l'excellent poète et le grand capitaine. Le même siècle qui se glorifie aujourd'hui d'avoir produit Auguste, ne se glorifie guère moins d'avoir produit Horace et Virgile. . . . La France se souviendra avec plaisir, que sous le règne du plus grand de ses rois a fleuri le plus célèbre de ses poètes."[89] In the place of the usual rememberer—time, eternity—Racine had put France, a not insignificant parallel in itself.

Regardless of whether Louis really objected to the parallel with Jupiter, his historiographer royal had proved himself a master in the genre of the panegyric. The *Discours* was very well received at the Academy. And why not? The Academicians had celebrated the works and conduct of the most illustrious members of the "république des lettres"[90] —Racine uses that term—and in doing so each may have felt a bit more self-confident and serene about his own creative efforts. The bold assertion that a poet could march at the side of a general consecrated the poet's efforts.

Although we shall never know what Racine's history of Louis's reign might ultimately have contained, it is possible to infer from his approach to learning the historian's craft that his work would have conformed to the canons of the *ars historica*. Certainly he would not have confused the use of historical evidence in panegyric with its use in history. For the latter, one really had to know what had happened, as he wrote Boileau from Luxemburg: "Je vois bien que la vérité qu'on nous demande tant est bien plus difficile à trouver qu'à écrire."[91] This correspondence provides ample evidence of Racine's sincere effort to learn exactly what had occurred and confirms the impression that the

89. *Ibid.*, p. 346.
90. In the "Discours prononcé à l'Académie française à la réception de l'Abbé Colbert," *ibid.*, p. 341, he uses "gens de lettres" as well.
91. 24 May 1687, *ibid.*, p. 477.

questions he asked and the subjects he planned to narrate conform to the canons of the *ars historica*. In Luxemburg during the campaign of 1687, he went to see Vauban, who provided an engineer to take the historiographer through the fortifications. He witnessed military reviews, sieges, and war councils and recorded the actual words of officers, King, and common soldiers. But always, there is the comparison with Antiquity:

> Le Roi fit hier [20 May 1692] la revue de son armée et celle de M. de Luxembourg. C'était assurément le plus grand spectacle qu'on ait vu depuis plusieurs siècles. Je ne me souviens point que les Romains en aient vu un tel; car leurs armées n'ont guère passé, ce me semble, quarante ou tout au plus cinquante mille hommes, et il y avait hier six vingt mille hommes, ensemble sur quatre lignes. . . . Je commençai à onze heures du matin à marcher. J'allai toujours au grand pas de mon cheval, et je ne finis qu'à huit heures du soir. Enfin, on était deux heures à aller du bout d'une ligne à l'autre.[92]

Racine's copious notes have not survived, but from his letters it appears that his battle narratives would have read like Xenophon, Caesar, and Plutarch. After the siege of Mons in 1690, Racine informed Boileau that he had "retenu cinq ou six actions ou paroles de simples grenadiers, dignes d'avoir place dans l'histoire."[93] There is ample evidence throughout all the surviving material to confirm the impression that action, word, and event were all perceived as pieces of a puzzle out of which a narrative might be written and that they constituted *belles matières* for history because ancient historians had considered them to be so. Still, Racine never had doubts about including something on the grounds that the ancients could not have known about it. He could be stunned by the horrifying conditions of war and by individual acts in battle. At the encampment before Namur in 1692 a soldier had placed a gabion, that is, a wicker basket filled with earth and used in fortifications, in the same spot three successive times, only to have it demolished each time by cannon fire. The soldier stopped, whereupon his officer ordered him to put a fourth gabion in the same spot. The soldier replied, "J'irai, mais j'y serai tué"; and in fact on the fourth attempt one of his arms was shattered by a cannon ball. Walking back, he said to the officer, "Je l'avais bien dit." Racine had not been an eyewitness to the incident.

92. *Ibid.*, pp. 507 f.

93. And to inform Boileau of where he was: "Je voyais toute l'attaque fort à mon aise, d'un peu loin à la vérité, mais j'avais de fort bonnes lunettes" (*ibid.*, p. 499).

He specifically explains that he had heard it recounted to the King; but he accepted it as true, and one senses him shudder as he narrates it to Boileau.[94]

This exploration of the surviving evidence from Racine's attempt to learn how to write history reveals a tone of sincerity and earnestness about his craft. Highly intelligent, well-read, and, I believe, genuinely committed to the ideal of writing only the truth about the past, Racine held the *ars historica* in such total respect that his historical prose has a highly stylized quality that later centuries could only read as propaganda.

Charles Bernard had not been subtle in his attempts to develop a conceit about Louis XIII as a saintly king; he had included *mots bas* and events that from the perspective of the *ars historica* were unworthy of memory. Yet his record of what he saw and heard may have struck his contemporaries as more revealing of actual happenings during Louis XIII's military campaigns than the surviving fragments from Racine's pen about the campaigns of Louis XIV. The aims of each historiographer had been the same—to edify readers and assure the *gloire* of French kings. But Racine's respect for Antiquity inevitably constrained his perspective of the events, motives, and causes to be included in history. As a result, had his history survived, it might well have produced the same disquieting effect upon readers that Bernini's bust of Louis XIV still creates for those who see it. On one level there is authentic portraiture; the nose, chin, and forehead especially are those of the King. On another level the conceit of Alexander the Great is so explicit as to render ahistorical the authenticity of the sculptured portrait. The *topoi* about actions in battle and the phrases about conquest, bad lodgings, courage, immortality, and *gloire* employed by Racine would have created a literary complement to Bernini's marble bust.

To be sure, there are also ideological resonances in Racine's historical thought that arouse criticism from readers who find distasteful the celebration of French military victories and the praise of her kings as the quintessence of the French identity. It is easy to charge that these resonances are untrue. In the heat of battle Racine wrote his wife, "Il faut espérer que Dieu continuera de se déclarer pour nous."[95] As a Frenchman and subject of his king, Racine is engaged in the outcome of the war. Indeed, whenever the providential theme is echoed, it recalls Louis XIV's own prayers for victory and hopes for divine support. On just these points, where Racine is perhaps most accurately representing the thought and behavior of both Louis and the French elites who sup-

94. *Ibid.*, p. 513.
95. *Ibid.*, p. 506.

ported him, readers in later centuries grow incredulous. For they are unfamiliar with or reluctant to believe in the truth of a divine-right monarchy that collapsed in the eighteenth century. Thus, both respect for the *ars historica*—indeed, a kind of fundamentalism about ancient rhetorical principles in writing history—and the ideological framework that upheld French political culture in the early-modern era combine to arouse charges of propaganda and naiveté from modern readers of Racine. Propaganda his history is, but only in the sense that it conformed to the dominant beliefs and aspirations of the political culture of which he was a part. By standing for the principle of recording only the truth, Racine and Boileau sincerely hoped to curb the excessive praise that writers were heaping on the Sun King. Their results, with all the constraints imposed by the *ars historica*, would have been no more and no less propagandistic than histories written by others whose political cultures sustained ideological perspectives on the past.

Seventeenth-century men of letters had the greatest possible difficulty in describing and interpreting their preferences for Italian historians. They usually stressed stylistic qualities; occasional remarks appear about the balanced narrative of Guicciardini. But until the eighteenth century vague concepts such as *politique* were all that was available in France to describe what would later be defined as ideological perspectives in historical thought. Of course, numerous French writers were commissioned by the Crown to write propaganda, as Joseph Klaits has shown. The self-conscious creation of negative images of enemies and positive images of the French, historicized and thematically linked to military campaigns and diplomatic negotiations, played their part in Louis XIV's efforts to humble Europe. Every state participated in these pamphlet wars; and though this consciously written propaganda shares with Racine's notes common assumptions about the Monarchy and the war, their purposes were not the same. Deciding how to further the *gloire* of Louis XIV, and preserve it, was Racine's duty as historiographer; and he sought to accomplish these aims by writing a prose narrative about the King that would be read as far into the future as the works of those ancient historians whom he so admired.

Racine's reverence for those principles of writing inherited from Antiquity had led to brilliant results in the theater. He had every reason to believe that the same would be true for history; and perhaps he could even be certain of success, for he had merely to record true events. But perhaps he felt freer to violate the literary canons of Antiquity in drama, since, after all, plays were only fiction. When a story writer is asked to write history, his talent may be constrained; the truth of "events" may inhibit the writer of fiction. Racine's reverence for the historians of Antiquity and the awesome responsibility of assuring Louis's *gloire* inhibited him greatly. He surely must have been familiar with the *topos* about the need for political and military experience if one was to write history—hardly a reassuring thought for him. But failure is not the end of Racine's story, for late in life he turned to writing a history of Port-Royal, a subject that engaged him more deeply than Louis's *gloire* and for which there was no antique model.

The Jansenist Historian of Port-Royal

As crop failures, wars, and advancing age lay heavier on Louis XIV and Versailles in the 1690s, Racine turned to writing a history of Port-Royal. Contacts with the King may have remained as frequent as in the past, while Racine climbed to ever higher lodgings and *entrées* at court; but they may also have become increasingly formal and less stimulating for the poet. Reading aloud before the King portions of the history that he and Boileau were writing brought enhanced prestige,[96] but the occasional phrases about life at court in Racine's correspondence express boredom. He continued to perform his functions, but instead of doing so from an eagerness to gain increased intimacy with Louis, he kept going by a sense of duty.

Through Madame de Maintenon, Louis's doctor, Félix, and Colbert de Seignelay, the historiographer enjoyed immediate access to everyone at the highest levels of government, but bureaucratic and courtly routine and the silences engendered by fear of offending someone in high places created a mood of anxiety at Versailles. Racine does not say so emphatically, but he implies that he could discuss only certain subjects with Louis, others with Maintenon, and probably still others with Colbert de Seignelay and Colbert de Torcy.[97] *Fêtes* occurred frequently despite economies brought about by the war effort—creating a momentary and artificial mood of gaiety and relaxation, after which everyone returned to conversation about the King's health, the weather, food, and literature. Racine does not discuss why life at court was the way it was, but his preoccupation with what would later be called psychology and social psychology may have permitted him to discern the way in which power, family, and clientage affect discourse and behavior in general. Where Racine pressed further to learn the inner workings of

96. "Le Roi se porte toujours de mieux en mieux. Il s'est fait lire, dans ses dernières après-diners l'histoire que font MM. Racine et Despréaux et en paraît fort content" (*Journal de Dangeau*, ed. M. Feuillet de Conches [Paris, 1854], vol. 1, p. 312, 20 March 1687).

97. He discussed Jansenist affairs with Torcy. See his letter to his son dated 19 September 1698, *Oeuvres complètes*, vol. 2, p. 633.

ministerial government and royal family life, did he not find the reality he had already depicted on the stage?

Madame de Maintenon had requested a religious play for Saint-Cyr. *Esther* was given in 1689. Another request led to the writing of *Athalie*, performed before Louis in 1691 by the girls of Saint-Cyr. Jean Orcibal has shown how both works not only allude to contemporary diplomatic and religious policies but in a sense exhort and pray Louis to take courses of action more favorable to peace and a kind of religious pluralism within the Gallican Church.[98] Racine's active political life may have found its ultimate expression in these plays, rather than in the histories he was commissioned to write.[99] Opposition to royal policies, especially those associated with Louvois and Father La Chaise, were frequently expressed in sermons; paralleling events affecting Old Testament monarchs and their realms, fables, parables, and classical history with events involving the Bourbon family posed no problems for Racine and his contemporaries. *Esther* and *Athalie* are history written in verse.[100] Writing profoundly religious and political plays seems not to have required a fundamental shift in thought for Racine; the demarcations between the religious and the secular, apart from their everyday meanings, presented little difficulty for him, no more than shifting from verse to prose, and back again.

Racine again accompanied the King and his armies to the northern frontier in 1691. His letters reveal a repugnance for everything about war. To Boileau he would recount anecdotes that might have escaped the authors of *gazettes*.[101] He gave up trying to observe the campaign more fully or more accurately than the gazetteers and was left with no function to perform in camp. His real preoccupations lay elsewhere. Though fathering a child almost every other year during this period of his life,[102] and though anxious to accumulate money and offices, Racine nevertheless began to take small but significant risks on behalf of Port-Royal.

Having spent his entire life in intimacy with clerics and having sought in vain a benefice for himself as a young man, Racine later received the revenues attached to the office of prior of Saint-Pétronille

98. *La genèse d'Esther et d'Athalie* (Paris, 1950), *passim*.

99. *Ibid.*, p. 25.

100. Here Racine's sense of history resembles Bossuet's, whose *Discourse on Universal History* he not only owned but annotated (*ibid.*, p. 96).

101. *Oeuvres complètes*, vol. 2, p. 515.

102. A pre-Malthusian birth rate: Jean-Baptiste, 11 November 1678; Marie-Catherine, 17 May 1680; Anne, ?, 1682; Elizabeth, 2 August 1684; Françoise, 29 November 1686; Madeleine, 18 March 1688; Louis, 2 November 1692.

318 🕸 Artisans of Glory

of Epinay, to which he was named in 1667. He probably could not remember when controversy had not divided Jansenists and Jesuits. As
an adolescent, in his *Ad Christum*, he had prayed for the Savior's protection of Port-Royal;[103] at twenty-eight he slandered Mère Angélique
by including an unedifying incident from her life in his *Lettre à l'auteur
des hérésies imaginaires*;[104] now, in his fifties, he turned to assuring the
survival of the religious community that he had known as a child and
that was now governed by his aunt. Racine had lashed out at Mère
Angélique because Jansenist-Jesuit rivalry had been allowed to pervert
Christian charity.[105] Blinded by controversy, Jansenists at the time—
and for centuries afterward—viewed Racine's attack as unpardonable,
but they ignored the fact that it had been made in the name of the
absolute standards of devotion and charity that Racine had learned as
a child at Port-Royal.[106] Thus, instead of perceiving Racine's career as
one of rebellion against Port-Royal, followed by his "conversion" back
to it in later life, it seems appropriate to stress a consistent respect for
its principles of devotion and charity. On an intellectual level, of course,
to stress the consistency in Racine's career is to suggest that he maintained an almost inflexible belief in the need to tell the truth that he had
learned as a child at Port-Royal.

The community had suffered slanderous attacks for years, and its
principal response to these had been an attempt to inform the constituted authorities—the archbishop of Paris and the king—of the truth.
If there is a distinction to be made between Port-Royal and Jansenism
—and it is perhaps only a nuance, but an important nuance—it is that
Port-Royal's response to calumny and persecution was prayer and the
pursuit of truth, whereas the response of the Jansenists, notably Antoine Arnauld, was theological and moral rejoinders. The Port-Royal
that Racine idealized and would defend was the Port-Royal of devotion
and truth, not of clerical squabbles.

Racine was very devout during the final years of his life, spending
hours a day in prayer, but he does not seem to have thought he could

103. Picard, p. 39.
104. *Oeuvres complètes*, vol. 2, p. 22.
105. Racine charged that Mère Angélique had ordered the withdrawal of
wine and good bread that had already been served to two Capuchins who
had sought hospitality, upon hearing a rumor that they were anti-Jansenist.
Then, after learning that the rumor was false and that they were actually
pro-Jansenist, she allegedly not only returned the superior food but actually
provided even more tasty nourishment (*ibid.*).
106. Though he does not deal with Racine specifically, Louis Marin
points to the way Racine may have understood truth as something borne
within systems of signs, rather than merely as a rhetorical *topos*.

expiate his sins by writing a history of Port-Royal. His religious expressions certainly extended to writing, but the welfare of his soul lay in prayer and contemplation. Nor does the *Abrégé* read like a work by someone who is researching and writing history in order to understand for himself what has happened, in this case to Port-Royal. Quite the contrary. It reads as one more attempt to communicate the truth to a world dominated by untruth. It is partisan, even ideological in the sense that it resembles the models of ideological conflict with which Western historiography is most familiar—Puritans and Anglicans, Jacobins and royalists, Communists and capitalists—and which have been historicized in a similar way as conflicts over the truth.

Through conversations with Maintenon and other *dévots* at court, Racine could glimpse Louis's impossible task of keeping peace within the Gallican Church.[107] Individual prelates pursued policies and scrambled for preferments, exacerbating the tensions and jealousies between regulars and seculars, between regulars and regulars, and between seculars and seculars. Quiet but powerful campaigns through the King's confessor, almoner, chaplain, and other members of his *conseil de conscience* were mounted to enlist the King's support for some specific course of action or promotion thought to be detrimental by others mounting similar campaigns. Racine was a master observer of ecclesiastical politics during a period of crisis in the Gallican Church. Conflicts were provoked as much, if not more, by the Church's great expansion and probably unexpected success through reform as by the more personal ambitions of individual prelates. Whichever way he turned in his *galerie des glaces*, Louis must have seen a prelate who was in fundamental disagreement if not open conflict with another prelate only a few feet away from him. And all these prelates were seeking Louis's support.

The nuns of Port-Royal and the leading Jansenist spokesmen had already suffered numerous defeats; but exemplary, pious leadership and the belief that eventually the truth would be known sustained them. Testimonials were published and legal proceedings begun, and attempts to record exactly what was said or done became the heart of Port-Royal itself. As early as 1652 a general appeal to write memoirs, testimonials, and histories went out to all the nuns of the abbey. The result was a record of truth and of providential acts; so, when Racine undertook to write a history of Port-Royal, he was merely taking up the

107. There is no complete discussion of this topic, but Aimé-Georges Martimort, *Le gallicanisme de Bossuet* (Paris, 1953); P. Blet, *Les assemblées du clergé sous Louis XIV* (Rome, 1972); and H. G. Judge, "Louis XIV and the Church," John Rule, ed., *Louis XIV and the Craft of Kingship* (Cleveland, 1969), pp. 240–264, are helpful. See also Appendix A of Orcibal for a brilliant note on Maintenon and Racine.

task that had been occupying other members of the community for decades.[108]

The nuns—and probably Racine—had from the beginning believed that if the truth were known to persons in authority, the persecutions would cease.[109] In 1695, with the arrival of Antoine de Noailles on the archiepiscopal throne of Paris, a prelate had at last been appointed who would be willing to listen and who might question what the Jesuits were saying about Port-Royal. Racine requested and received an interview with Noailles barely ten days after the Archbishop's nomination; his bull of provision had not yet arrived from Rome. When Racine spoke to Noailles as a virtual ambassador on behalf of Port-Royal, he received an encouraging response.

Writing the truth about Port-Royal may thus have appealed to Racine, as a son of the community and as a historiographer no longer intellectually engaged in the effort to immortalize Louis. There may have been more immediate reasons, still to be discovered. Perhaps his aunt wanted her nephew's judgment on the whole history of Port-Royal.[110] It is clear that Racine did not turn to the history of the abbey in order to find or to clarify his own religious beliefs or attain immortality; he was devout, and his salvation would be assured by piety—perhaps special *oraisons* and acts of charity—but not by the writing of history. The *Abrégé* is a partisan work, constructed with great skill to convince some perhaps mythical public as judge; it is not an essay of historical introspection. It reads like one more attempt to communicate the truth to a world in the clutches of untruth.

Debates over the truth about what happened produce historical thought that cannot be definitively refuted by any amount of further research and analysis. As the first historian of Port-Royal, Racine wrote a partisan history that may easily be shown to be in error on specific

108. Racine did not complete the *Abrégé*. Part 1 was published for the first time at Cologne in 1742, and Part 2 at Paris in 1767.

109. The manner in which Noailles received Racine suggests that the *Abrégé de l'histoire de Port-Royal* would have been neither a necessary nor a particularly desirable instrument for improving the Archbishop's view of the abbey. Racine shows himself a skillful diplomat with Noailles, not exceeding the instructions given to him by his aunt. The remarks in the *Abrégé* about the Jesuits and Retz, the coadjutor, would have been most diplomatic and ineffective in establishing a new foundation for relations between Port-Royal and the archbishop. If Racine wrote the *Abrégé* for a specific purpose, that purpose remains hidden.

110. Or the nephew wished to prove to his aunt his worthiness to serve as "ambassador" for Port-Royal in the forthcoming negotiations with Noailles?

incidents or acts, but whose general thesis and analysis cannot be refuted. Partisan and searching for a balanced account of the truth, Racine's *Abrégé* is also unforgiving in its criticism of the nuns of Port-Royal. But, like his criticism of Mère Angélique in the *Lettre à l'auteur des hérésies imaginaires*, these few negative remarks are all the more devastating because they appear in an otherwise favorable account.

The *Abrégé* begins with a description of the founding of Port-Royal. Racine's purpose is to convince the reader that the community enjoyed episcopal, aristocratic, and royal protection from its beginnings in the thirteenth century. The sense of time is almost immemorial when Racine evokes the donations on which the nuns had lived for almost five centuries. One of the larger donations was confirmed by Saint Louis, who for this reason came to be thought of as one of the abbey's founders. Pope Honorius III also helped establish the community on a sound footing, and it was he who in 1223 granted the nuns the right to admit laymen for spiritual retreats within the abbey.[111] When the *solitaires* lived at Port-Royal in the mid-seventeenth century, they were exercising that right. It is clear that Racine not only understood the arguments based on the origins of institutions but also recognized their effectiveness. That Port-Royal had enjoyed such illustrious protection for so many centuries constituted a warning to anyone, Louis XIV included, who might violate its privileges in the future. Throughout the *Abrégé* Racine emphasizes the violation of rights sanctified by time.

The great spiritual examples set by the Arnaulds and their divine support are stressed by Racine, but the hagiographical mode of biography, with which he must have been familiar, is avoided. His respect for the Arnaulds as reformers remains a central theme of the work, but one senses throughout the *Abrégé* that Racine believed Port-Royal's significance to be greater and more extensive than what might typically be associated with the saintly life of one individual or a small group of devout, even saintly individuals. His is the history of a community reformed by Providence acting through the Arnaulds and others. He stresses, in addition to the exemplary character of the reformist leaders, their strict respect for all constituted authority, the support they received from other reformers and the leading men of the time, and their religious orthodoxy. No change is made, no shift of emphasis occurs within the community without first seeking the approval of the general of the Cistercians—as long as the abbey was under his jurisdiction—or, in later years, the archbishop of Paris and the pope. Racine's purpose is to make those in authority who overturned the actions of

111. *Oeuvres complètes*, vol. 2, p. 37.

their predecessors appear inconsistent with the spirit and conduct of their office—a constitutionalist argument not unlike those frequently used by the Parlement of Paris.

When two nuns at Maubuisson, another house reformed by the Arnauld sisters,[112] began certain rites differing from those habitually practiced, these rites were immediately recognized as derived from the teachings of Molina and learned from the "Illuminés," a condemned sect from Roye.[113] Through recounting this incident, Racine establishes the fact that the nuns in charge of Port-Royal not only were sufficiently informed to be able to distinguish orthodox from heretical religious devotions but also had the authority to eliminate unorthodox practices within the community. Who, in succeeding decades, could dare accuse Mère Angélique of heresy, when from the beginning she and the community had made it clear to reformers and opponents of reform that Port-Royal would remain strictly orthodox?

To consolidate this picture of an exemplary monastic community Racine emphasizes the spiritual friendship and support for Port-Royal given by Saint Francis of Sales and Saint Jeanne de Chantal. Surely they would have suggested changes from the beginning had they thought them necessary; but no suggestions had come. In addition, various great nobles and Queen Marie de Médicis herself had lent Port-Royal their support, causing money to flow in and permitting a period of rapid growth both in buildings and in numbers, in Paris and at Port-Royal-des-Champs.[114] This public recognition and support becomes a theme throughout the *Abrégé*; Racine, the playwright, seems to have believed that the public's common sense could be counted on as something of a judge on earth. Over and over again he stresses the conformity between Port-Royal and public approval. The slanderous attacks on the abbey sponsored by the Jesuits—who, through their influence in the government, Racine asserts, succeeded in having their works published with royal *privilèges*, though the Jansenists could not—nevertheless failed to convince the public about the evildoing at Port-Royal.

112. Racine observed that not all the nuns of Maubuisson were moved to accept the reforms instituted by Mère Angélique (*ibid.*, p. 42).

113. *Ibid.*, p. 43.

114. Racine's preoccupation with the financial history of Port-Royal suggests that he believed that devotion and strict adherence to the rules governing the admission of novices ought eventually to lead to increased donations; money, the public, and Providence are therefore implicitly linked in his mind. Marie de Médicis did not give money, a negative fact that Racine explains away by observing that her protection was a greater benefit than the nuns had ever hoped to enjoy (*ibid.*, p. 44).

In its response to the miracle of the Holy Thorn,[115] the *Provincial Letters*, and the charity and medical care provided by the abbey, the public remained sympathetic to the community. In the *Abrégé* Providence and the public clearly share a common purpose. And yet this public was not a *chose publicque* in the sense Pasquier had used the term in the 1560s; it had no formal capacity for action.

In his discussion of how Saint-Cryan's and Antoine Arnauld's careers became intertwined with Port-Royal, Racine begins by stressing personal and familial factors in a Tacitean manner. Narrating how they came to quarrel with bishops, Richelieu, Mazarin, and others having authority over the abbey, he describes tiny personal piques and great doctrinal issues as if they were of equal weight in determining loyalties and divisions during the ensuing struggle. After initially respecting Saint-Cyran, Racine turned against him when Saint-Cyran refused a bishopric and then disagreed with Richelieu over the nature of grace and whether Gaston d'Orléans's marriage could be annulled without violating canon law. As for Arnauld, Racine emphasizes his family's and his own personal obedience to and defense of royal authority.[116]

Those who became the enemies of Saint-Cryan, Arnauld, and Port-Royal were, Racine finds, tainted by mental illness and weaknesses of character. Sébastien Zamet, bishop of Langres, is described as having an "esprit fort faible" and an "esprit malade."[117] When Péréfixe, archbishop of Paris, came to Port-Royal to exhort the nuns to sign the *formulaire*, he flew into a rage and swore at the nuns, using "beaucoup de paroles très basses et très peu convenables à la dignité d'un archevêque." He finally became so enraged that his nose began to bleed.[118] The implication is that such a person was mentally unfit to be an archbishop. For Racine, none of Port-Royal's defenders—including Saint-Cyran, whom Henry Bremond interprets as a psychopath[119]—seemed to have suffered from mental disorders.

Above the individual rivalries and quirks there prevailed those more powerful loyalties to *party* and *corps* that provide Racine's principal explanations for the persecution of Port-Royal. The *Abrégé* is the history of a battle between good and evil at this level, the Jesuits being

115. "La foule croissait de jour en jour à Port-Royal, et Dieu même semblait prendre plaisir à autoriser la dévotion des peuples par la quantité de nouveaux miracles qui se firent en cette église" (*ibid.*, p. 86).

116. *Ibid.*, p. 91.

117. *Ibid.*, p. 49.

118. *Ibid.*, p. 139.

119. Henri Bremond, *Histoire littéraire du sentiment religieux en France* (Paris, 1925), vol. 4, pp. 36 ff.

on the side of evil through their excessive loyalty to their order. Racine's partisanship against the Jesuits is so pervasive that he overlooks the attempts by more moderate Jesuits to restrain all parties in the battle; yet he seems to have genuinely sought to understand why they behaved as they did. The four principal reasons derive from the *esprit de parti*. Here Racine's history is analytical and as remote from the *ars historica* as any of history written in his generation.

For one thing, the Jesuits read only the works of other Jesuits; they close themselves off from the larger discourse within Christendom.[120] And without investigating for themselves, Jesuits hear that Port-Royal is an "abominable place" and then state this to the schoolboys whom they teach. For Racine the solidarity of a *corps* is a vice shared by most "gens de communauté," but it is stronger among the Jesuits than anywhere else: "Cet honneur est un espèce d'idole, à qui ils se croient permis de sacrifier tout, justice, raison, vérité."[121] The Jesuit casuists have gone so far as to assert that a monk may in good conscience slander or even kill someone whom he finds to be attacking the Society.[122] Like Blaise Pascal before him, Racine took pleasure in describing the contradictions into which the Jesuits became enmeshed as a result of the "faux honneur" of defending every act and pronouncement made by a fellow Jesuit, especially those violating the "constitutions fondamentales" of the Society.

In addition to the personal rivalries and exaggerated corporate solidarity that motivated the Jesuits, a "pique de gens de lettres" exacerbated the tensions. The Jesuits had become accustomed to holding the first rank among French authors, but during the quarrel with the Jansenists they found themselves incapable of publishing a work that won public acclaim. In the meantime, Jansenist-inspired works were being very well received. Racine adds: "En effet, il est assez surprenant que depuis le commencement de ces disputes, il ne soit sorti de chez eux aucun ouvrage digne de la réputation que leur Compagnie s'était acquise, comme si Dieu, pour me servir des termes de l'Ecriture, leur avait tout à coup ôté leurs prophètes."[123] He proceeds to describe the Jesuits' attempt to denigrate the Jansenists' success by inferring that the style of writing based on "politesse" was contrary to Christian truths. Father François Annat, royal confessor and a leading Jesuit in the disputes with Arnauld, fancied himself a talented writer; yet try after try, his works failed to win public acclaim. Was Racine serious when he im-

120. *Oeuvres complètes*, vol. 2, p. 65.
121. *Ibid.*
122. *Ibid.*
123. *Ibid.*

plied that the absence of Jesuit works held in public esteem was a providential act or a sign in favor of the Jansenists? There are allusions to
Providence that relate directly to the claims that Port-Royal was a divinely supported religious community—the miracle of the Holy Thorn
clearly being absolutely true for Racine. But in the case of allusions to
Providence's role in rivalries among authors for public recognition, the
effect is more self-consciously contentious. Racine adds example after
example of evildoing by the Jesuits. He evokes them as a monolithic
party that has a long memory and never forgives those who have attacked them[124] and that defends and promotes those of their number,
regardless of the mediocrity of their works.[125] Clearly they are not
"enfants de paix."[126] After all these examples, it is not surprising to
find a record of providential signs of disapproval. Racine gains the
maximum possible rhetorical effect by mentioning these signs—for example, the fact that no book by a Jesuit can earn public acclaim—but
he is always careful to suggest that these portents may be only coincidental. When discussing moral and devotional behavior, however, Racine does not hesitate. The Jesuits will have to answer before God for
what they have done.[127]

In the Jesuit-Jansenist rivalry over education, Racine tells how the
Jesuits became anxious when a few "personnes de qualité" turned to
Arnauld and the others associated with Port-Royal for the education
of their sons, even though the Jesuits held the preponderance in educating the elite. The works written especially for educating the young
by Nicole, Lancelot, and Arnauld are briefly mentioned, and the names
of some illustrious pupils are given (Racine does not include his own
name) to support the contention that the *petites écoles* were successful
despite the attacks made upon them. Then Racine adds: "Cette instruction de la jeunesse fut, comme j'ai dit, une des principales raisons
qui animèrent les jésuites à la destruction de Port-Royal; et ils crurent
devoir tenter toutes sortes de moyens pour y parvenir."[128] Since there
are virtually no other repetitions in the *Abrégé*, this double emphasis
upon the rivalry in education assumes special significance in Racine's
effort to explain why the Jesuits opposed not only Arnauld, Nicole,
and others, but Port-Royal itself.

On the controversies over doctrine and morals, Racine keeps an eye
on the specific points in dispute, but the focus of his narrative remains

124. *Ibid.*, p. 59.
125. *Ibid.*, p. 63.
126. *Ibid.*, p. 70.
127. *Ibid.*, p. 63.
128. *Ibid.*, p. 66.

the machinations of the Jesuits against Arnauld and the Augustinian teachings on grace. As a Jansenist, Racine does not seem troubled by the consequences of the dispute for the faithful. He knew what his own faith rested upon and had no fear of being a heretic.

Racine's analysis shows the Jesuits as favoring "innovations" and thus not tolerating a revived Sorbonne with Augustinianism as a principal focus in teaching theology to the young. Like the Ancients that they were, viewing Antiquity as culturally superior, the Jansenists favored the restoration of forgotten or corrupted teachings of the early Church. But, beneath the formal disputes, the controversies were fired by the "espèce de guerre" between the Jesuits and the University.[129] Then, during the attacks and counterattacks, the Jesuits appealed for support from the Crown and the pope to condemn what were alleged to be Jansenist teachings (the Five Propositions). Through an academic putsch they arranged to have the faculty of the Sorbonne condemn a number of propositions put forth by Arnauld. Racine seems dumbfounded by the violation of the faculty statutes[130] and cites learned doctors who opposed these violations. Like learning, piety is always on the side of the defenders of Port-Royal. A great Jesuit victory seemed at hand when Arnauld was condemned by the members of the only prestigious group that could support him. Were not the two archenemies of the Jesuits—the Sorbonne and the Jansenists—defeated in a single blow? Racine does not cite a Jesuit to affirm this conclusion, but points to their success in having the schools at Port-Royal closed immediately by royal order and the *solitaires* of Port-Royal-des-Champs dispersed.[131] He moves from motives to actions; he is not interested in discerning the conscious expression of aims, hopes, and failures—either for the Jesuits or for Port-Royal.

The fact that the Jesuits had been able to mobilize royal officials against Port-Royal is implied throughout the analysis of the controversy. Racine uses the pronoun *ils, ils, ils* for the Jesuits like a hammer against the whole French ecclesiastical and legal structure until these edifices are compromised and destroyed. After his account of the victory over Arnauld and the Sorbonne in February 1656, Racine deftly begins to describe Port-Royal as a divinely supported victim that had been condemned to death. Had not Saint-Cyran earlier been imprisoned by Richelieu through a "procédure fort irrégulière"?[132] Faculty statutes had been violated; the Jesuits had gained control of the procedures

129. *Ibid.*, p. 59.
130. *Ibid.*, pp. 79 f.
131. *Ibid.*, p. 81.
132. *Ibid.*, p. 52.

through which the Crown either authorized or censored books, and an abbess from outside Port-Royal was imposed on the community in complete violation of a royal charter granting the abbey the right to elect its own abbess.[133] Pope Urban VIII had also given his approval to these irregular procedures. But the ultimate violation of procedures and customs came at the instigation of the archbishop of Paris, Hardouin de Péréfixe, "au fond très bon homme, fort ami de la paix,"[134] supported by the *lieutenant civil* and his troops.

Recently installed and eager to end controversies within his diocese, Péréfixe quietly sponsored the preparation of a statement (*formulaire*) that it was hoped each member in the clergy could sign without feeling that he was jeopardizing his faith and his chance for salvation. Racine conveys the impression that everyone realized this was a face-saving device to end the apparent challenge to episcopal authority being made by the nuns at Port-Royal. Péréfixe went to the abbey and requested that the nuns come before the grill so that he might speak to them. This initial visit went well. The Archbishop promised that the nuns would have a month to reflect upon their decision and that they would be advised by two "savants ecclésiastiques" whom he would appoint and ask to reside at Port-Royal for that period.[135]

The statement cleverly separated *droit et fait* and remained vague on other critical issues. Racine observes that in signing it the nuns would merely have been recognizing the respect for and submission to archiepiscopal authority that they had offered many times in the past. But the nuns refused to sign. Why should they sign a statement when their actions and thoughts were in no way heretical or hostile to authority? In recounting the incident, Racine clearly loses patience with those whom he calls the "défenseurs de la grâce"—the Jansenists.

And the Archbishop exploded into a rage. Arriving at Port-Royal with troops to storm the abbey, Péréfixe decided to impose his authority on the community by force. In describing the tragic moment that followed, Racine attains impartiality. A well-intentioned prelate destroys his reputation by conducting himself in an undignified manner; the community of Port-Royal was dispersed for a matter not involving the faith; and the deaths of all the major participants were hastened by the violence of their actions.[136]

The nuns had only one defense. They carefully took testimony of

133. *Ibid.*, pp. 44 and 137.
134. *Ibid.*, p. 132.
135. *Ibid.*, p. 135.
136. The account of the incident occasioned much rewriting by Racine and modifications by Boileau; it was still unfinished at the time of Racine's death.

every act by the troops and all the "injures les plus basses" uttered by Péréfixe, in order to bring a case of *appel comme d'abus* before the Parlement of Paris. Though critical of the nuns for not signing the statement, Racine nonetheless believes that justice was on their side: "Et le crime pour lequel il [Péréfixe] les traitait si rudement, était de n'avoir point la créance humaine que des propositions étaient dans un livre [*De la fréquente communion*] qu'elles n'avaient point lu, qu'elles n'étaient pas capables de lire, et qu'il [Péréfixe] n'avait vraisemblablement jamais lu lui-même."[137] When the Parlement received the nuns' appeal for justice, the Archbishop used his influence at court to have the case evoked before the royal council and quashed. The Jesuit, Annat, says Racine, goaded Péréfixe ceaselessly to rid his diocese of Jansenists and Port-Royal.

Throughout his narrative Racine evokes the power of the Jesuits. They had influence everywhere, acted in concert with an obsessive fanatical unity of purpose, and willingly violated customs in order to overcome their enemies. And their maximum influence was exerted upon—and through—Mazarin, Anne of Austria, and Louis XIV. How could the King have learned the truth about Port-Royal when he was surrounded by Jesuits? "On sait que Sa Majesté a toujours un jésuite pour confesseur,"[138] and during the years of violent dispute this confessor was none other than Annat. Wherever the King went, clerics found themselves obliged to speak against Port-Royal from deference to Annat. Bishops harangued Louis against the Jansenists, while the pope exhorted him to exterminate them. Louis also heard that Jansenism was linked to revolt against his authority. "Quel moyen donc que la vérité pût parvenir aux oreilles du Roi?"[139] For a writer usually so preoccupied with finding the psychological foundations for human action, Racine draws a final portrait of Louis XIV that seems inadequate. The King simply failed to reach out beyond the web of untruths surrounding him, in order to discover the truth about Port-Royal. In this critical instance Racine depicts Louis entirely within the sphere of human action. Had the King perceived the truth and stopped the persecutions, Racine would not have written the *Abrégé*. There is no expression of disappointment with Louis; he is a mere human and therefore unable to alter the outcome of a duel that has assumed cosmic dimensions.

137. *Oeuvres complètes*, vol. 2, p. 138.
138. *Ibid.*, p. 106.
139. *Ibid.*, p. 107. This analysis of Louis XIV would seem to have been inappropriate for presentation to Noailles, or for that matter to anyone else in public life during the 1690s. It could, however, have been useful for the then abbess of Port-Royal, Mère Agnès de Sainte-Thècle, Racine's aunt.

It should come as no surprise that Racine shows Louis as failing to perceive the truth about the abbey. There were other instances in history when saintly individuals had been persecuted in the name of kings otherwise known for their piety. The depiction of Louis therefore confirms and recapitulates Racine's tragic analysis of the triumph of untruth over custom, common sense, and royal justice. In this great conflict God alone, not someone of human proportions, could sustain truth. In a world where belief in Providence still prevailed, the inflated images of Alexander the Great and the Bourbon kings paled when compared to divinely inspired power to act. God so acted, Racine believed, on behalf of Port-Royal through the miracle of the Holy Thorn.

Racine is casual in his use of sources throughout the *Abrégé*—except in his narrative of this miracle. Though he almost never takes the trouble to quote personages independent of the Jansenist perspective, in recounting the miracle he scrupulously reports names, dates, physical condition, and medical examinations that support his belief that a miracle did in fact take place.

Just after the Sorbonne had condemned some of Arnauld's propositions as heretical (February 1656), at a time when Port-Royal's fate appeared to be sealed, a terrible fistula in the tear duct of a little girl in residence at the abbey was miraculously healed as a sign from God. Racine names the physicians who had examined the child before the cure and cites their public testimony about the healing, much as one would present evidence in a court of law. Anne of Austria sent the royal surgeon, Dr. Félix, once, if not twice, to examine the now healthy eye. Racine notes that the little girl, now a grown woman, was still alive at the time he was writing the *Abrégé*.

The community's initial response was to keep what had happened quiet, but Racine says, "God did not want [the miracle] to remain hidden,"[140] for crowds began to come to Port-Royal in order to "y adorer et pour y baiser la sainte épine."[141] The public knew the significance of what had occurred.

The miracle upset the Jesuits. Annat hastily wrote a book in which he accepted that a miracle had in fact taken place and then, by "un grand nombre de raisonnements, tous plus extravagants les uns que les autres," attempted to prove that it occurred at Port-Royal in order to demonstrate that Christ had died for all mankind, including those infected by heresy. Racine declined to refute this argument; it was absurd. In the long run the miracle offered consolation to the nuns and their supporters, but it did not alter the train of events.

140. *Ibid.*, p. 84.
141. *Ibid.*, p. 85.

Racine does not seem in the least troubled by the fact that the miracle occurred at the very time when defeat and persecution were intensifying. From our post-Enlightenment perspective, just such a congruence of events augments our suspicion that a miracle had been fabricated. Racine's partisanship had infused his history with a cosmic dimension, and his religious beliefs had become so aroused that he became convinced that God had acted at the very moment when the possibility for right and truth to prevail had been extinguished. In the war between truth and untruth, the history of Port-Royal, as Racine recounts it, is reminiscent of the narrative of the Crucifixion.

The *Abrégé* was incomplete when Racine died. He could never have finished it, for his mode of analysis encompassed the entire life, death, and resurrection of Port-Royal. The last act of persecution occurred after his death, when the buildings of Port-Royal-des-Champs in the Chevreuse valley were dismantled and the bodies in the cemetery, including his own, were disinterred by royal order in 1710.

This outcome is foreshadowed by Racine's narrative. Like a tragedy for which there can be only one end—death—the *Abrégé* sought to convey the truth of Port-Royal to future generations. In historical thought Racine perpetuated a partisan quarrel from beyond the grave —a different sort of battle from the ones customarily immortalized by historiographers, but one in which the fury of clerical partisanship could teach all readers about the fragility of even the most divinely constituted authorities—papal, episcopal, and royal. And the *Abrégé* reveals what was structurally conceivable beyond the monarchical and Gallican paradigms during the late seventeenth century, the same paradigms that had circumscribed the historical thought of the *doctes* and *éloquans* of the sixteenth century—namely, the partisan providential drama of good and evil, of truth versus untruth. In Racine's prose the more explicit aims or methods of the *ars historica* are either subsumed or cast aside. The reconciliation of *esprit de parti* and truth is left to the reader; the categories and techniques adopted from the ancient orator only imperfectly describe what is happening in the text. In the end the *ars historica* seems to have little to do with trends in partisan historical thought.

The style of the *Abrégé* is informal and discursive. After wandering into summaries of theological and political squabbles, Racine remarks, "Mais pour reprendre le fil de mon discours,"[142] and at another time comments, "Mais pour reprendre le fil de notre narration."[143] As if

142. *Ibid.*, p. 73.
143. *Ibid.*, p. 93.

writing to be read aloud, Racine at one point remarks: "Je parlerai ailleurs de ces accusations de cabale, et j'en ferai voir plus à fond tout le ridicule."[144] The discursive qualities of the text are enhanced by his use of popular phrases and metaphors. Speaking in a relaxed tone, he refers to the medical services of the convent as "une espèce d'infirmerie,"[145] and at another time mentions "cette espèce de guerre."[146] To convince his readers (listeners) of what the Jesuits are doing, he remarks that in order to have *De la fréquente communion* condemned in Rome, they "remuèrent toute sorte de machines."[147] One of the ecclesiastics sent to Port-Royal to rid the community of Jansenist tendencies was himself so anti-Jansenist that "ses cheveux se hérissaient au seul nom de Port-Royal."[148] When Péréfixe flew into a rage before the grill at Port-Royal, his behavior was so undignified that he resembled "une petite femmelette."[149] Though not attacking Richelieu directly for having Saint-Cyran imprisoned, Racine quotes a joke at the Cardinal's expense. Jean de Werth, himself in prison, expressed bemusement at French ways of doing things, for he had observed a bishop at a ballet eagerly seeking the audience's approval and reflected that what surprised him the most in France was "d'y voir les saints en prison, et les évêques à la comédie."[150] Such statements all violate the rules that had been elaborated upon the belief that Antiquity was the only certain guide to the writing of history.

The often quoted remark about the *Abrégé*—that Racine had learned his rhetoric and then forgot it for the *Abrégé*—may be true. Racine's temerity in being so informal in this, the most noble of genres, surprises us. And yet there are reasons for doubting that he wrote the *Abrégé* as a history, as he would have defined the genre. Recall that it is an *abrégé*. Recall also his use of the verb *parler*, his use of the first person, and his frequent stress upon the word *discours*.

Though partisanship had freed Racine from the *ars historica*, it is not so certain that it freed him completely from the tyranny of genres. To be an Ancient was to accept an almost unimaginable degree of authority from the past over every creative effort. Be that as it may, the *ars historica* was momentarily abandoned in his effort to help the truth prevail. Yet it was as history that the *Abrégé* functioned, indeed

144. *Ibid.*, p. 74.
145. *Ibid.*, p. 58.
146. *Ibid.*, p. 59.
147. *Ibid.*, p. 61.
148. *Ibid.*, p. 109.
149. *Ibid.*, p. 139.
150. *Ibid.*, p. 52.

functions like any other writing about the past; it celebrates the actions of the dead and teaches the young.

Racine had returned to Port-Royal one last time to join the ranks of those who perceived that the battle was lost and were now merely preoccupied with assuring that future generations would know what had truly happened. They succeeded very well, since the historiography about Port-Royal has proven one of the richest, if not the most monumental of early-modern French historical thought.

Glancing Backward
and Forward

T is time to look over our shoulders and take stock of what we have seen. The journey has seemed long because we found no signposts to point out the new from the old, or the influential from the significant, as we crossed a century of French historical thought. It is sobering to discover how difficult it is for both writers and readers of history to travel without these signposts. No preconception focused our gaze one way or the other along the journey. We were not deliberately searching for origins, revivals, innovations, or continuities.

From the panoramic perspective that we now have, all those writers at work on the same subject while pursuing the same pensions and honors are a pitiful sight to behold. Their lives seem to have been excessively confining and their works scarcely worth the attention we gave them. So entrapped in the labyrinths of royal service as a result of the powerful myths about honor and immortality that they themselves had raised into a cult, these writers repudiated the sources of individual vitality in their lives and conformed to the styles of life and thought necessary if they were to hold royal office as men of letters. Though all received bits of income from other sources and possible alternative employment, they nonetheless pursued the career of royal service. Such powerfully individualizing traditions as Protestantism, libertinism, and Jansenism were either abandoned or so subsumed in their histories that it is possible to say that the monolithic quality that French political culture assumed under Louis XIV rested on the most fundamental social and psychological determinants at work in the age. No single king, no matter how powerful, could have brought about these shifts of allegiances and interests. Like the historiographers, Louis XIV was the product of these shifts, rather than the perpetrator of them. The *gloire* associated with writing about the kings of France was an enormously powerful acculturating force, and the results in books of history seem devoid of humane and individualizing qualities. To depend on the king or in some way to belong to him remained a powerful bond affecting writers' lives and thought throughout the seventeenth century.

Did the dependencies of writers never break down? Their history is certainly one of *longue durée*. To see beyond the massive elaboration of the Budean model it would be necessary to explore the thought of the philosophes about the relationships between writers and men of power. For example, in d'Alembert's *Essai sur la société des gens de lettres* (1754)[1] the psychological reasons for dependency upon aristocratic patrons are eludicated with new incisiveness. It is "amour-propre" that leads writers to seek approval from great nobles. The latter, obviously, are ignorant or in most instances too limited to assess the quality of a creative act, and the writers know this. Approval by an aristocratic patron allows the writer to believe his creative act is entirely his own,[2] while still accumulating the praise and rewards from the patron. For d'Alembert (the perpetual secretary of the Academy, Mézerai's old post), who can better assess the quality of a writing than its author?[3]

This insight was part of the general scrutiny of the individual as creator carried out by the philosophes—laying the foundation for a still deeper personalization and interiorization of the creative act far beyond that self-consciously perceived by monastic or humanist writers. D'Alembert dedicated his essay to a friend, Etienne de Canaye, a fellow writer who had helped him with his own writing: "Recevez, mon cher ami, ce fruit de nos conversations philosophiques, qui vous appartient comme à moi. Je ne puis mieux l'adresser qu'à vous, dont l'exemple prouve si bien qu'on peut vivre heureux sans les Grands."[4] The message of the *Essai* and of the Enlightenment is to tighten the bonds within the *monde des lettrés*.[5] Among the different "classes" of writers may be found respect and qualified critics. Neither the public at large nor the *érudits* may effectively fulfill these functions, for in one way or another writers pursue recognition ("renommée"), and recognition may be given only by those qualified to appreciate the significance of a creative act.[6] The *érudits* are a "nation jusqu'ici assez peu connue, peu

1. Published in the *Mélanges de littérature, d'histoire et de philosophie* (Amsterdam, 1773), vol. 1, pp. 321–412. On the title page we find, "Sine irà et studio, quorum causas procul habeo," from Tacitus, *Annals*, Book 1, Chapter 1. Tacitus makes this comment after having stated that he is offering the history of the principate of Tiberius to the reader. One is reminded of Bodin's emphasis on writing history without *perturbationes*.

2. In a magnificent bit of prose d'Alembert remarks that the "grands n'ont même pas le triste honneur d'être injuste avec connoissance." (*Mélanges*, vol. 1, p. 342).

3. *Ibid.*, p. 334.

4. *Ibid.*, p. 323.

5. *Ibid.*, p. 344.

6. "La renommée, espèce de spectre composé de bouches et d'oreilles

nombreuse, peu commerçante, et qui certainement n'en est pas blâm-able. Plusieurs ne sont encore que du seizième siècle, et ont le bonheur de ne pas connoître le nôtre."[7] One senses that, while the boundaries of learning and eloquence were certainly changing, a certain distance still separated them.

But being liberated from seeking recognition by noble patrons was only one aspect of the question. The more specific ideological and financial aspects of dependency were the others. Inspired by Tacitus, d'Alembert explored the relationship between tyrants and men of let-ters. Do not tyrants and writers join to hide the truth from *les peuples*?[8] However, a king who knows how to be king will chase the courtier-writers away in order that the truth may be known, a thought rem-iniscent of Pasquier's observations on the same subject.

Louis XV was not mentioned, nor were any of his ministers or censors, but d'Alembert observes that the despotic Richelieu had un-derstood that the democratic form of government was the only possible one for a "republic" of writers because liberty is its very life.[9] The *Essai* was written during a period when volume 3 of the *Encyclopédie* was being censored, yet one is struck by the absence of any allusion to the King as an individual.[10] The lifelessness of the Monarchy appears in passage after passage as d'Alembert laments the decay of language, the prevalence of luxury, and the overpowering influence of the great nobles.

And as for taking pensions, d'Alembert seeks to find ways in which money may be given without creating ties of dependency. Though providing some examples of monetary gifts without strings attached, he concludes that relative poverty is the only sure guaranty of liberty for the writer, and his *exemplum* is Diogenes' reply to the conqueror of Asia. This time the venerable *topos* serves to defend "liberté, vérité, et pauvreté,"[11] the slogan that writers ought always to remember. Many

---

sans yeux, une fausse balance dans une main, et une trompette discordante dans l'autre, fait entrer pêle-mêle dans le temple une partie des voyageurs, là tous les états sont confondus" (*ibid.*, p. 364).

7. *Ibid.*, p. 354.

8. *Ibid.*, p. 373.

9. *Ibid.*, p. 403. D'Alembert probably was relying on Pellisson's history of the Academy for his information. It stressed the fact that the Cardinal accepted the suspension of social rank in the membership.

10. Nevertheless he declined to publish Voltaire's article "Historio-graphe" in the *Encyclopédie*. It would only appear in 1765 in the *Nou-veaux mélanges*. François Fossier, "La charge d'historiographe du XVIe au XIXe siècle," *Revue Historique* 258 (1977): 75.

11. *Mélanges*, vol. 1, p. 399.

of the elements of the classical republican ideal of citizenship are evoked by d'Alembert for the republic of letters, but his thought extends beyond a mere restatement of antique ideals.[12] It is as if he were preparing a utopian republic of letters with its own hierarchy of classes based on merit, yet with a democratic form of government. He saw no reason for singling out writers of history from other writers or from mathematicians and scientists in his quest to understand the effects of dependencies. It is significant, however, that he scarcely stresses the performance of service for the state. His seventeenth-century forebears in the Academy would have been surprised at this omission, and Colbert perhaps would have been shocked, for under Louis XIV public discourse invariably stressed the element of service.

In reality, however, the services performed by writers scarcely seem vital to the life of the state. Under Richelieu and Louis XIV writers had no influence on decisions about peace and war, taxes, or justice.

Beneath the day-to-day level of policy, however, writers influenced the shaping and reshaping of the conceptions of the prince and the state that pervaded the whole political culture. Their influence rested on the primordial belief that the dead kings and their accomplishments had to be recalled, celebrated, and learned by the young. In performing the function of remembering the dead, writers complemented the work of those artisans who worked in paint, stone, gold, bronze, and wood. The emotions of love, fear, and respect inspired by the kings of the past in no way diminished in the seventeenth century.

Describing the same old kings, and yet creating ever-changing historical portraits of them, kept the writers forever adjusting their language. From being primarily Christian rulers with divine power to heal, monarchs came to be portrayed almost entirely as ancient kings and conquering heroes. French writers carried out this enormous shift from medieval to Renaissance kingship, just as others had done before them (an important example being the brief reign of Cola di Rienzo) and were simultaneously doing in other political cultures. The evolution in the historical ideals of French kingship became particularly significant as a result of the child Louis XIV's malleability in the hands of his tutors. The hopes of writers were at last fulfilled, for this French Alexander confirmed the "historical ideals of life" refined over and over again by writers.

12. D'Alembert anticipates some of the thesis of Paul Bénichou, *Le Sacre de l'écrivain* (Paris, 1973), when he asserts that: "Le rôle des Gens de Lettres est après celui des Gens d'Eglise le plus difficile à jouer dans le monde; l'un de ces deux états marche continuellement entre l'hypocrisie et le scandale; l'autre entre l'orgueil et la bassesse" (*Mélanges*, vol. 1, p. 382).

Only greater maturity, knowledge of men, and political experience would free Louis from the explicit Alexandrine synthesis that surrounded him as a boy, though he never completely abandoned it. And beneath the Alexander image Louis found himself as a mature king even more deeply bound by the ancestral history that had been offered to him by writers. The 1680s brought the first but not the last occasion when alternatives between peace and war seemed to pit the interests of his house against his own personal hope for a life after death as a Christian. If the early decades of the personal reign had been ones of pursuing *gloire* in an Alexandrine mode, the later decades were dominated by a stubborn defense of French rights as Louis perceived them in his family history. The eloquent historiographers had had their golden age; they were followed by the learned, who provided the historical underpinnings for such policies as the "réunions" and the acceptance of Charles II's will. The inflated claims by the men of letters may not have seemed so inflated during the long reign of Louis XIV, for they restated French family history in ways that obliged the monarch to carry out policies he could never empirically examine. There was literally no language or conception of kingship or of the state beyond those webs of myths and facts spun by writers, webs that bound the prince to the pursuit of *gloire*.

And by elevating princes to divinity and immortality in prose, the men of letters hoped to enhance their own *gloire*. The glittering honors, titles, gold, and *entrées* they acquired were amalgamated with copper and lead. In a society that still bestowed high status by blood, no writer became a prince, a duke, or a marquis; indeed, none succeeded in becoming a bona fide *gentilhomme*. No historiographer bore a title that he could claim by right of an ancestor's death on a field of battle; all their honors derived from the king's power to bestow identities upon others by offices. In the great chain of hierarchies within the state, the historiographers fell below the middle range of household servants. The more civic identities as *seigneurs* possessed of judicial rights or as officers administering royal justice or taxes were all above them.

We know little about Sorel's later years. It seems that only Mézerai jumped completely off the ladder of family promotion and accumulation of wealth to be passed on to the next generation. The rest scrambled for good marriages, titles, lands, and *rentes* for their children or nephews, conscious of what their families had bequeathed to them and of the importance of enhancing the patrimony for the succeeding generation. On a microcosmic scale they did what great princes and Louis XIV were doing—carrying out the lessons of their family histories.

Poor devils, these men of letters, we say; and because of the ideological elements and the mediocrity of their works, we prepare to drop them from our own genealogy of historians. Yet, just as we are about to forget them for all time, we remember that the genealogy of historians, like any family history, ought to include the failures and the mediocre generations. To exclude them now would be to deny their tiny claims to immortality and would also be a sign of insecurity or inordinate ambition on our part. Acceptance of their more humble and mediocre ancestors is a mark of self-confidence rarely found among literate elites in the *Ancien Régime*. And it is also possible to learn from essentially negative and unedifying *exempla*. After all, the lessons about the duties of kingship that Louis may have learned from his ancestors, the *rois fainéants*, could have been as influential upon his education as the historicized conquering hero. On the genealogical tree of historians, Bernard, Sorel, Mézerai, Pellisson, and Racine are thus painted in with simple letters in little, unadorned boxes among the crested and gilt names of those with heroic status: Bruni, Guicciardini, Pasquier, du Tillet, de Thou, Sarpi, Selden, and Cotton.

One of the reasons for our hesitation to include the mediocre among the illustrious is, of course, the dramatic extension of the criterion of merit in the patronage of writing history. The state turned patronage over to the writers themselves, and merit rather than charm, good conversation, good looks, and blood eventually prevailed when allocating funds. Chapelain's list of writers by merit and Colbert's pensions signaled a revolution in the forms of patronage and started the movement that would make the quality and productivity of research and prose the dominant criteria for support. The revolution did not occur overnight; no change so fundamental does. Writers as far back as Gaguin stress the quality of a work as criterion for support, and, long after the 1660s, princes continued to distribute pensions to writers simply because they liked the individual. Still, the synthesis of merit criteria and the bureaucracy created by Chapelain and Colbert shifted the *monde des lettrés* out of the royal household and into the marketplace. Another major development also pushed them toward the market.

The printing press and the consequent increase in the size of the reading public created a market for histories that influenced the way writers would present the litany of French kings. The market always favors eloquence; it either ignores or sneers at erudition.[13] Early-mod-

13. Here the classical *topoi* about the relationship between eloquence and liberty fall short of describing just how literacy, rather than verbal discourse and printing for a mass market, affect historical thought. See Jean Starobinski, "Eloquence et liberté," *Revue suisse d'histoire* 26 (1976): 549–559.

ern French readers wanted to learn about their kings and queens and about battles, conquests, pious acts, and family squabbles with about the same superficiality and structure of thought as that inculcated into Louis XIV by his tutors. The *érudits* could never satisfy this market. Why did seventeenth-century writers give the public what it wanted?

Taking their cue from humanist forebears, seventeenth-century writers attempted to edify their readers, to render them more respectful of the dead, and to instill in them moral and political values. Sales of history books were high, much higher than any other secular prose subject, and seventeenth-century writers generally accepted writing to please the public. Mézerai, to Chapelain's disgust, included impolite phrases and meaningless remarks about how it thundered when momentous events occurred in the life of the Monarchy. The reading public bought the abridged Mézerai, and after him there continued a dynasty of writers of history who sought to please the public. Chapelain, too, has his heirs, who publish harsh reviews of popular histories in learned journals. In general, however, *gloire* and the market as approbation became entangled in writers' minds, and along with them, praise of the monarch.

Giving Louis XIV the credit for inspiring the muses became the indispensable response to bureaucratized patronage. The Sun King himself, however, never quite adopted the outlook of his new bureaucracy. The merit system had thrown up Perrot d'Ablancourt's name for the coveted post of writing the royal history, but Louis declined to appoint a Huguenot. Efforts persisted to make the merit system function completely without prejudice or consideration of any factor other than talent, but these efforts were already in evidence when Chapelain tested Colbert and Louis, knowing well that Perrot might be rejected for religious reasons but recommending him nonetheless. Other signs of Louis's unwillingness to give up the old ways were his effort to continue some sort of personal discourse with writers and his unfailing renewal of some pensions regardless of the particular writer's productivity.

The monarchical form of government had about it a tendency to confuse the initiatives and actions of the prince and those of his servants. When writers looked into the mirrors of Versailles they sometimes saw the King. Louis was forever being told that, whatever he did, his act resembled an act accomplished by one of his predecessors or by a prince in Antiquity. When he looked in the mirrors he may only have seen Alexander or Augustus.

From our journey through French political culture in the seventeenth century we have learned that the state was a cunning leviathan. We thought we saw individual writers and their writings, but from a distance they all suddenly appear to resemble one another. They wrote in the same way about the same dead. And poor Louis, like his historiographers, struggled to write about the past, his own past, by adjusting the evidence in order to place his accomplishments in a more favorable light for posterity. Seventeenth-century men feared the judgment of future generations perhaps almost as much as they feared the Last Judgment.

As the leviathan recites the litany of its ancestors we perceive the familiar images of kings and writers engraved over the creature's entire body. The book it holds is a history, at once a bit different from all previously written histories, yet containing the same structure and content. Unless the leviathan recites this history, it will die; unless it learns this history, it believes it can accomplish nothing; unless it keeps writing and rewriting this history, it will be dismembered before our very eyes.

Index

Abelard, Peter, 138, 303n
Ablancourt, Nicolas Perrot d', 144n, 146, 191–93, 255, 269, 339
Abrégés, 146
Absolutism, 45, 234, 248, 281, 282
Academies, 41, 146, 163; French Academy, 30, 52, 118, 146, 152–53, 157–59, 164, 176, 181, 191, 196, 198, 202–4, 209, 217, 222–25, 229–30, 237n, 238–39, 240–44, 250n, 252n, 253, 294–95, 300, 311–12, 334, 336; *petite académie* (Académie des inscriptions et belles lettres), 261–64, 268, 279
Achilles, 89, 304
Aeschylus, 312
Africa, North, 89
Ahmed I, 216
Aiguillon, Marie de Vignerod d', 193n
Albigensians, 8
Alciato, Andrea, 85, 178
Alcibiades, 284
Alcuin, 54
Alembert, Jean d', 334–36
Alexander the Great, 17–19, 21, 42, 43, 46, 47, 79, 81, 89, 93, 114–15, 133, 255–59, 262, 265, 269, 276, 279–80, 284–85, 296, 303, 314, 329, 336–37, 339
Aligre, Pierre, 106
Alphonso of Spain, 89n
Alps, 218
Amelot family, 106
Ammirato, Scipione, 181
Amsterdam, 221
Amyot, Jacques, 85, 257
Ancients and Moderns, quarrel of, 21, 29, 66, 146, 163n, 283, 295, 296, 302–3, 326
Anglicans, 319
Anglophobia, 220
Annat, François, 324, 328–29
Anne of Austria, 122, 157, 177n, 208, 209, 212n, 213n, 234, 328, 329
Antiquity, 3, 11, 14, 18, 21, 28, 29,

32, 42–44, 46, 56, 62, 66, 68, 85, 95, 110, 117, 127–28, 132, 145, 155, 173, 175–76, 178–80, 187, 196, 250, 253, 255, 259n, 280–81, 283, 285, 291, 296, 303, 313–15, 326, 331, 339
Apollo, 154
Apollonius, 87
Appel comme d'abus, 328
Ariès, Philippe, 5
Aristotle, 31n, 42, 43, 48, 80, 86, 143, 269
Armagnac, Cardinal d', 71, 164
Arms, coats of, 4, 205
Arnauld, Angélique, 318, 321–22
Arnauld, Antoine, 282n, 318, 322–29
Arnauld family, 321–22
Ars historica, 3, 14, 17–21, 25, 46, 78, 90, 95, 119, 132, 146, 172n, 178, 180–81, 298, 303, 312–15, 324, 330, 331
Artisan, 22, 133
Artus, Thomas, 212
Asia Minor, 89
Asserac, Jean-Emmanuel de Rieux d', 201
Astrology, 127–28, 211, 233, 258
Atheism, 201
Athenodorus, 42
Athens, 80
Atticus, 286
Aubery, Antoine, 294
Aubespine de Châteauneuf family, 106
Aubigné, Agrippa d', 140n, 325n
Aumale, Charles d', 212
Aumont family, 106
Auvry, Claude, 167, 226–27
Avenel, M., 112

Bacon, Francis, 143, 144
Baluze, Etienne, 9, 25, 56
Balzac, Jean-Louis Guez de, 39, 152–57, 168, 187, 237, 242n
Baron, Hans, 21
Bartolism, 237
Basel, 282

Du Cange, Charles, 25
Du Chastel, Pierre, 37, 38, 40, 70–71, 153
Duchesne, André, 54, 145, 205n
Duchesne, François, 56
Duchesne family, 9, 25, 53, 118, 151
Du Haillan, Bernard de Girard, 54, 58–59, 70, 96–102, 133, 140, 239
Du Metz, 310
Du Moulin, Charles, 54, 85
Dunkirk, 254–55, 260
Dunois, Jean d'Orléans, 152
Dupleix, Scipion, 54, 55, 102, 143
Duprat, Antoine, 164
Dupuy, Jacques, 148, 159, 160–62, 216n, 246
Dupuy, Pierre, 162, 216n
Dupuy family, 9, 25, 53, 118, 151, 202, 215n, 217
Duras-Durfort family, 269
Dutch, 24, 235, 270n, 271, 307, 308
Du Tillet, Jean, 32, 55, 115, 338
Du Vair, Guillaume, 98, 164
Du Verdier, Antoine, 39, 54

Einhard, 7, 65, 87, 132
Elizabzeth I, 182
Eloquans, 29, 31–34, 44, 50–51, 54, 56, 100, 110, 115, 116, 330
Eloquence, 27, 32–33, 39, 43, 48, 50, 96, 135, 173, 184, 240, 251, 279, 301, 312, 335, 339n
Estienne, Henri II, 35, 237
Eudes, Charles, 198
Eudes, Jean, 198–99
Eudes family, 197–98. *See also* Mézerai
Eulogy, 14, 73
Euripides, 296, 312
Eusebius, 87
Evans, Wilfred H., 200
Exemplum, 5, 29–41, 44, 46, 47, 83, 168, 265, 288, 289, 335, 338

Fancan, François de, 168
Fauchet, Claude de, 35, 54
Faucheur, cabaret-keeper, 231
Febvre, Lucien, 5
Félibien, André, 261n
Félix, Dr. (Charles-François Tassy), 316, 329

Fénelon, François de Salignac de la Mothe-, 134
Ferdinand of Spain, 87, 89n
Fermat, Pierre de, 237, 239n
Fidèles, 10, 76
Fidélités, 12, 23, 33, 101, 110, 161, 188, 192, 246, 252, 293
Flanders, 165, 201n, 219, 271, 273
Flattery, 78, 80, 86, 94n, 146, 186n, 231, 287, 290, 303
Florence, 24, 180
Foreign policy, French, 215–22, 294
Fornovo, 89
Fouquet, Nicolas, 25, 148, 157, 160, 162, 165, 189, 191, 244–52, 253, 258, 260, 269, 276
Fouquet family, 106
Franche-Comté, 196, 255, 264
Francis I, 25, 30–32, 34–38, 42–46, 48, 70, 79, 82, 127, 170, 171, 172, 179, 215, 241, 279, 304
Francis II, 127
Francus, 64
Franks, 52, 54, 137, 221, 234
Froissart, Jean, 83, 86, 132
Fronde, 145, 147, 157–59, 161, 163, 164, 165, 168, 175, 176, 193, 200n, 209–10, 212, 225, 227, 231, 234, 241, 247, 248, 251, 258, 281, 284, 305–7
Furetière, Antoine, 69n, 190, 239

Gages, 97, 101, 147, 194. *See also* Pensions; Remuneration
Gaguin, Robert, 12, 44n, 65–66, 91, 132, 338
Galileo, Galilei, 128
Galland, Pierre, 37, 38
Gallicanism, 141, 183, 216, 234n, 330
Garcia, Alonso, 26n
Gaston d'Orléans, 150, 165n, 201n, 225, 323
Gaul, 35, 54, 218, 221
Gaulle, Charles de, 21
Gazettes, 271, 305, 317; *Gazette de France*, 52. *See also* Newspapers
Genres, 243, 246, 252, 263, 264n, 270, 273, 302, 312; mirror-of-princes, 42, 45, 48, 67n, 78, 80, 108, 109, 134, 143, 233n; historical, 234. *See also* Battle narratives

Germans, 8, 18, 186
Germany, 47
Gestes, 3–5, 7, 8, 13, 66, 70, 88
Gesvres, Louis Potier de, 254
Gevartius, Johannes Casparus, 195
Ghent, 55
Gibbon, Edward, 208n
Gifts, 160, 194, 196. *See also* Pensions; Remuneration
Gilles, Nicolas, 54, 132
Girard family, 96
Globe Theater, 13
Gloire, 3, 10, 17n, 35n, 40, 46, 47, 49, 51, 66, 116, 118, 122, 132, 133, 142, 157, 162, 170, 173, 174, 175, 189–90, 192, 193, 228, 248, 251, 252, 254, 258, 259, 265, 287, 295, 298, 299, 314, 315–16, 333, 337, 339
Godefroy, Denys, 54, 55–57
Godefroy, Denys II, 227n
Godefroy, Léon, 187n, 190, 194
Godefroy, Théodore, 51, 70, 102, 141
Godefroy family, 9, 25, 53, 118
Gombauld, Jean Ogier de, 162, 239, 154
Gomberville, Marin Le Roy de, 253n
Goubert, Pierre, 21
Government, forms of, 23, 93, 288, 307, 335, 336; mixed, 61
Grain shortage, 211
Grands, 38, 49, 66, 78, 104–5, 118n, 125, 127, 145, 150, 153, 161, 164, 167, 191, 227, 234, 240, 242, 254, 257, 284, 306, 322, 334, 335
Graziani, Girolamo, 195
Greece, 170
Greek, 234, 237, 240, 282, 283, 303
Gregory of Tours, 137
Gregory VII, Pope, 8
Grève, Place de la, 231n
Gronovius, Johann Friedrich, 245
Grotius, Hugo, 186, 201, 202, 205–6
Guenée, Bernard, 65
Guénégaud family, 106
Guicciardini, Francesco, 89, 181, 186, 315, 338
Guillemot, Matthieu II, 206, 208n, 212–14
Guise, 309

Guise, Henry of, 211
Guise family, 152, 164

Hack writing, 72, 102
Halles, 202n, 223
Hamon, Jean, 291
Hannibal, 79
Hapsburg, house of, 215, 294, 304
Harderwick, 299
Haults faits, 3, 6, 8, 11, 12, 17, 67, 77–78
Hauser, Henri, 83
Hay du Chastelet, Paul, 157
Hector, 304
Heinsius, Daniel, 197n
Heinsius, Nicolas, 148, 160, 187n, 195
Henry II, 72–73, 87, 88, 92, 127, 219n
Henry III, 34, 90, 91, 92, 97, 102, 124, 125–26, 211
Henry IV, 90, 94, 99, 100, 101, 105, 124, 127, 133, 135n, 188, 200, 207, 209, 213n, 236, 247, 248, 257n
Hero, cult of, 256
Herodotus, 283n, 301
Herouval, Antoine d', 56
Hesnault, Jean, 162
Historiographe de France, 22, 63, 68, 105, 133, 144, 152, 194, 208
Historiographe du roi, 22, 63, 68, 133, 145–46, 157, 158, 227
Historiographers royal, 119, 134, 138, 142, 145, 170, 190, 198, 225, 261, 264, 269, 276, 285, 291–92, 295, 296, 300, 301, 309, 312, 314, 320, 333, 337, 340; functions of, 13–14, 64, 71–96, 118, 125, 218, 277, 297; general definition, 22–27; erudite and eloquent, 53–57, 215n; officers and courtiers, 57–70; relations with patrons, 71–96; Pasquier on, 75–82; Bodin on, 84; La Popelinière on, 90–96; as a civic duty, 93, 94; pensions, 99, 158; *gages*, 101; list of (1572–1621), 102; Sorel on, 103; Richelieu, 106n; as a projector, 108; qualifications for appointment, 110; on military campaigns, 114–21, 253; as a *charge*, 131; must be Catholic, 191–92; and censorship, 228